Instructor's Set

ADMINISTRATIVE PROCEDURES IN THE ELECTRONIC OFFICE

Rosanne Bryce Sanders, Ed.D.

College of Business
Eastern Illinois University
Charleston, Illinois

PRENTICE HALL Englewood Cliffs, New Jersey 07632

Library of Congress Cataloging-in-Publication Data

Sanders, Rosanne Bryce (date)
Administrative procedures in the electronic office/Rosanne Bryce Sanders.
p. cm.
Includes index.
ISBN 0-13-019472-7
1. Office practice—Automation. 2. Business—Data processing. 3. Electronic office machines. I. Title.
HF5548.S25 1991 90-39024
651.7—dc20 CIP

Editorial/production supervision
and interior design: **Eleanor Ode Walter**
Cover design: **Bruce Kenselaar**
Manufacturing buyer: **Ed O'Dougherty**
Prepress buyer: **Ilene Levy**

Printed in the United States of America

10 9 8 7 6 5 4 3 2 1

ISBN 0-13-019472-7

Prentice-Hall International (UK) Limited, *London*
Prentice-Hall of Australia Pty. Limited, *Sydney*
Prentice-Hall Canada, Inc., *Toronto*
Prentice-Hall Hispanoamericana, S.A., *Mexico*
Prentice-Hall of India Private Limited, *New Delhi*
Prentice-Hall of Japan, Inc., *Tokyo*
Simon & Schuster Asia Pte. Ltd., *Singapore*
Editora Prentice-Hall do Brasil, Ltda., *Rio de Janeiro*

Contents

Preface

The role of the administrative assistant has expanded dramatically since the traditional office of the 1960s began its shift to electronics. Once known solely as *secretaries,* whatever the level and nature of their responsibilities, the secretaries of the 1960s came into their own as administrative assistants in the electronic office of the 1990s.

The title accurately reflects the role of persons who work in close conjunction with superiors in carrying out a myriad of administrative functions. Although the title varies somewhat across organizations, from executive assistant to administrative secretary or assistant, this text addresses all such persons as administrative assistants. Regardless of title, however, the same level of professionalism and expertise is implied.

Hopefully, all readers, whatever their titles, will find herein information that will enhance and promote their administrative careers in business. Such was the author's intent in writing the text.

The author wishes to thank the following reviewers of the manuscript:

Beverly Amoroso, Kirkwood Community College
Doris A. Edwards, National Education Center
Marian Tancy Finkbiner, Lincoln Trail College
Sheryl Gasaway, St. Philip's College
Arlene P. Hantjis, Bucks County Community College
Linda Kavanaugh, Robert Morris College
Michael Maki, Katherine Gibbs School
Nancy C. Wilson, University of Kentucky

A special word of appreciation is extended to the many organizations whose generous contributions of photographs and illustrations have enhanced the content matter of this text. A courtesy line identifies each of these organizations, with their contributed materials, throughout the text.

A special acknowledgement is due also to the contributors of chapter-opening photographs, whose names, together with corresponding chapter numbers, are listed below:

CHAPTER	*COURTESY OF*
1	Steelcase, Inc.
2	Apple Computer, Inc.
3	IBM Corporation
4	IBM Corporation
5	NBI Corporation
6	U.S. Postal Service
7	Panel Concepts, L.P., division of Standard Pacific, L.P.
8	TAB Products Company
9	Jeter Systems Corp.
10	KARDEX Systems, Inc.
11	IBM Corporation
12	AT&T Skynet Satellite Services
13	3M Corporation
14	Amtrak
15	Manpower, Inc.
16	Mellon Bank, Pittsburgh, PA.
17	Ad sponsored by Florida PSI chapter; picture by author
18	Eastern Illinois University Charleston, Illinois

UNIT I

THE ADMINISTRATIVE ASSISTANT IN THE ELECTRONIC OFFICE

The administrative assistant of the 1990s demonstrates a remarkable ability to adapt to the electronic technology impacting so powerfully on business operations. Assuming more complex responsibilities, the role of an administrative aide expands as new technologies are integrated into long-standing traditional procedures.

1
Role of the Administrative Assistant in a Changing Environment

INTRODUCTION

The administrative assistant of the 1990s enjoys a unique distinction as one who blends the traditional procedures of the pre-electronic office with the technological innovations of the 1990s. The electronic "intrusion" into a smoothly functioning office is welcomed not only because it represents progress, but because the electronic procedures have reduced the monotony of repetitive work, providing time for more challenging pursuits.

The role of administrative assistant has been expanded to include major responsibilities related to supervision, management, and decision-making. Consequently, as a result of electronics, the role has become more diversified, more challenging, and more rewarding.

Terms and acronyms in this chapter include:

ergonomics	masking systems
facsimile	electronic mail
CBMS	task lighting
work stations	landscaped office

ROLE OF THE ADMINISTRATIVE ASSISTANT

The administrative assistant plays a key role in helping the organization achieve a smooth transition from the manual processes of the immediate past to today's electronic procedures. Careful blending of conventional with electronic procedures merges both into an efficient support system for an employer. The company benefits in two ways: (1) state-of-the-art electronics are applied to those functions where speed and accuracy are critical, and (2) time-tested procedures which cannot be computerized are carried out with the administrative assistant's usual skill and efficiency.

Together, electronic and conventional procedures meld into an effective information system where productivity and employee morale are accorded equal emphasis.

Management Perceptions of Administrative Assistants

Administrative assistants and executive secretaries are coming into their own in many offices, accepting major managerial responsibilities delegated to them by their superiors. In some instances, the executives rely on the insights of their administrative assistants when weighing the alternatives of important decisions. Nor is it uncommon for management to encourage their administrative assistants to attend seminars on time management, assertiveness training, supervision, and similar topics, underwriting all costs for them to do so.

These and similar evidences of special accord attest to management's increased respect for their capable assistants. Growing numbers acknowledge that their own success is due in large measure to the able assistance and loyal support of their administrative assistants. Granting their assistants more authority and responsibility is one way of acknowledging their contributions to the company.

Self-Perceptions of Administrative Assistants

The self-image of administrative assistants is enhanced by their employers' recognition and trust. Taking pride in their work and in the contributions made to the company, they are motivated to stretch their professional talents and seek career advancement through professional growth. The following are typical of the avenues taken to pursue that goal:

- evening courses at local colleges or universities, often with the goal of an academic degree as the ultimate objective
- membership in professional organizations dedicated to special professional interests
- leadership roles in professional organizations
- special workshops and seminars designed to build self-confidence and/or "people" skills
- certification as professionals in special fields of interest such as data processing specialist, paralegal aide, certified professional secretary, and so on

Figure 1-1 Curved panels, an open staircase, a fully windowed wall, and potted plants add style to this functional work station. *Courtesy of Steelcase, Inc.*

According to their own descriptions, administrative assistants during the course of a typical workday or period of time will

compose memos, letters, and reports, not only for their principals' signatures, but on their own initiative and for their own signatures

participate in mutual goal setting with their principals on a regular basis

have a voice in determining ways to increase efficiency and productivity in the office

attend seminars, workshops, and other forms of continuing education

work toward achieving higher-education degrees when feasible

The Impact of Office Automation

Although electronic systems have imposed fundamental changes in the way information is processed, administrative assistants have adjusted well to the changes imposed on them. In most instances, their work has become more interesting, more challenging, and less tedious, thanks to the shift to electronic processes.

For instance, the shift from typewriters to word processors has brought about dramatic improvements in the way keyboarding errors are corrected, documents are altered, and multiple copies are made. The tedium of endless retyping to correct errors or to rearrange paragraphs is in the past. So is the inconvenience of dealing with carbon packs and carbon-smudged fingers.

Administrative assistants appreciate the help offered by computer systems and plan for the installation of a full complement of electronic equipment at their work stations. The fully integrated electronic office reduces the boredom of repetitive keyboarding, adds variety and interest to the work, provides time for more challenging and more responsible activities, enables administrative assistants to contribute substantive input to executive-level sessions, and increases productivity.

The Electronic Office: Components and Applications

The extent of electronic equipment in the office varies widely from one business to another, with company requirements and management attitudes accounting for most of the variance. The following electronic applications, however, are the ones most commonly used in the typical business office.

1. Electronic mail, in any of several forms
2. Advanced telecommunication networks
3. Electronic filing and image processing
4. Word processing and desktop publishing
5. Teleconferencing to supplant or enhance face-to-face meetings
6. Local area networks (LANs) cabling the components together into a total communication system

Each of these components is summarized briefly in this chapter, providing a cursory view of the office environment in which the administrative assistant operates. An in-depth exploration of each component is reserved for later chapters.

Electronic Mail One of the most widely used components of the electronic office, *electronic mail* is a generic term which encompasses at least five popular formats:

TWX and Telex, networks which span the globe, used primarily for brief messages and internal mail, that is, between the main office and branches.

Facsimile machines, a type of long-distance photocopying of documents and images. Merged with computers, FAX machines transmit images directly from the computer screen.

CBMS (computer-based message systems), transmitting and receiving messages from screen to screen of the users' computers.

Communicating word processors, which enable word processors to act as message transceivers as well as text editors.

Voice mail which stores and forwards messages via telephone lines.

Advanced Telecommunication Networks Advanced PBX technology gives users access to more and better telephone service without operator intervention or assistance. Upgraded with microprocessor units, the networks accept digital data as well as voice communications.

Electronic Filing and Image Processing Electronic filing can be described as the electronic alternative to the paper storage of records. It takes many forms, including:

Database management systems which store records magnetically on disks or tape. Once stored, records can be called up on command, altered, deleted, rearranged, or reproduced in hard copy by the user.

Micrographics, the process of storing and preserving records on film, then retrieving them electronically if a computer-assisted retrieval (CAR) system is in place.

Image processing which uses laser beams to scan documents and transfer the images to optical disks. The enormous storage capacity of the disks makes them especially attractive for library archives and encyclopedic storage.

Word Processing and Desktop Publishing Word processing remains the cornerstone of office automation as it is known today. With the addition of desktop publishing features, word processing programs prepare camera-ready copy for publication, including graphic images, columnar type, and various sizes and styles of type fonts.

Figure 1-2 Many administrative assistants enjoy the luxury of designer work settings. In this office, function and style are combined through a blend of traditional architecture with modular furnishings. *Courtesy of Steelcase, Inc.*

Teleconferencing Teleconferencing uses audio and video technology transmitted via telephone lines to conduct meetings electronically. It offers multiple advantages to users: Travel costs are reduced or eliminated and participation is extended to a broader spectrum of employees. Levels of sophistication extend from audio alone to full-motion video conferences.

Local Area Networks Local area networks are the means by which the electronic components of an office, or groups of offices, are linked into one fully integrated communication system. Not only can all units linked to the LAN communicate with each other, they can also share resources. For example, a powerful laser printer can be accessed by all units on the LAN, thus eliminating duplicate purchases of expensive equipment. Software programs can be shared in the same way. The span of the network is limited geographically to one building or group of buildings within close proximity to one another, as in a campus setting.

THE OFFICE ENVIRONMENT

Practical issues must be addressed by administrative assistants who work in the conventional/electronic office, attempting to blend the "old" and the "new" procedures into an efficient information system. Some of the more pressing issues are office layout, work station design, furniture selection, and ergonomic issues. In order to deal with these matters in a knowledgeable and practical way, the current chapter reviews some of the options in each category.

OFFICE LAYOUT

Changes in office layout reflect trends in public taste and furnishings as well as the internal restructuring of organizations. The latest trends in office furnishings can be viewed in the headquarters of large corporations where the image of success is perceived as vital. Conscious of their visibility, these companies have their public offices refurbished by professional designers periodically in order to display affluence and leadership in their fields.

Less visible organizations see office design from a different perspective. With them, changes in office layout become necessary when internal shifts in the company's organizational structure, or radical changes in office procedures, have taken place.

Currently, the predominant styles in office design are the landscaped office, often referred to as the open office, and modified versions of the open plan. All versions have their loyal proponents, from the totally open style of the original landscaped plan to the rectilinear grid plan still preferred by many companies.

Although the unyielding grid plan of earlier years has been largely replaced by more openness, many offices still opt for a modified form of the grid pattern as most suitable to their needs.

The Rectilinear Grid Plan

Prior to the early 1960s, office furniture in the typical business office was arranged in a strictly rectilinear layout. Workers' stations were aligned in rows and columns, each desk placed precisely behind those in front of it, or next to the ones beside it, in a straight row or column. No variance from the pattern was tolerated; the geometric pattern was not to be distorted by "out-of-line" mavericks jutting out into the measured aisles.

No screens or enclosures provided privacy for workers in the highly visible "outer" office. Managers and executives, however, were screened from the others by floor-to-ceiling walls. Their private offices were a symbol of status as well as a haven for privacy.

Although the pattern was very formal, supporters claimed that the neatly defined rows and columns projected an image of stability to the public. They also believed that the style promoted better utilization of floor space, better communication lines among workers, and easier supervision of workers.

Although the grid pattern as originally conceived still prevails in some quarters, its application is usually modified, its lines softened by color-enhanced panels and planters which afford some privacy to workers.

Certain facets of the grid pattern show signs of revitalization, however. Private offices, for example, are enjoying a resurgence in popularity. In many instances, the private office is a necessity; in most, it represents a level of achievement, a status which managers are not willing to forego.

The modified grid of the 1990s retains the privacy of a *few* executive offices, combined with low-paneled work stations (still in rectilinear patterns) for workers in the outer office—a functional, yet eye-pleasing, compromise between its former rigidity and contemporary openness.

The Landscaped Office

The landscaped office originated in Germany where it was developed as the "Burolandschaft" in the early 1960s. In the Burolandschaft, private offices were opened up by removing the walls. Communications were facilitated by employee groups working in close proximity to each other. In sharp contrast to the rigidity of the grid pattern, the Burolandschaft was characterized by an open, free-form pattern of work stations, with aisles curving freely among task groups.

Considered revolutionary at the time of its introduction, the landscaped design expressed in visible form the concept that the information needs of workers are at least as important as the status privileges of management.

Imported into the United States, the Burolandschaft became the landscaped office, the ideal layout for new, contemporary offices. It was characterized by:

employee work spaces identified by low screens or partitions, rather than walls

no private offices

acoustics, lighting, heating, and air-conditioning units centrally controlled, with individual controls provided as needed at work stations

planters of various heights, used to add aesthetic appeal

visual effects created by color, with screens of various hues identifying task groups and adding warmth to the setting.

Since its importation to the United States, the landscaped office has undergone compromises and refinements. Although openness still prevails, certain status indicators, such as private offices for senior executives, are often accommodated.

Visual Privacy in the Open Office Panel enclosures which surround the work stations in the landscaped or open office are, of course, the principal means of providing visual privacy for workers, with the panel heights determining how much privacy each worker enjoys. Panel heights also correspond to the workers' primary job functions and the amount of privacy their positions require.

Designers agree that providing employees with privacy, both visual and auditory, through the acoustical treatment of wall panels, "white noise," carpets, drapes, and equipment enclosures is a sensible alternative to expansive work stations requiring undue amounts of expensive floor space.

Figure 1-3 Glass-divider panels provide acoustical privacy with visual convenience. *Courtesy of Steelcase, Inc.*

Figure 1-4 Work stations featuring low-paneled enclosures utilize floor space efficiently while providing workers with spatial privacy. Planters and soft hued screens add to the decor. *Courtesy of Panel Concepts, L.P.*

Panels for Storage Tall panels serve a dual purpose. In addition to the greater sense of privacy they afford, they also provide generous vertical storage areas for each worker's supplies. The vertical space of the panels can be used for bookshelves, paper storage, a telephone index, files, disk storage, and miscellaneous items. They also provide workers with a space for personalizing their surroundings with pictures, plants, or personal mementos.

WORK STATION DESIGN

Good office design begins with an understanding of the types of work performed by employees, individually and collectively, within an organization. The space, furniture, and equipment needed to do each job efficiently determine to a large

Figure 1-5 Divider panels grouped around the "cluster-core" accommodate from three to six work stations. Panel heights determine the degree of privacy accorded each station. *Courtesy of Hamilton Sorter Co.*

extent which design is the most feasible. Accordingly, the employee's work station is the appropriate starting point for designing the "ideal" office layout.

Tailored to each individual's needs, the work station houses all the components necessary to carry out workers' assigned tasks. A typical fully equipped station will include the following hardware, software, and supplies:

a computer system with all the necessary peripherals, usually including a printer

the software needed by the individual worker, which may include word processing, desktop publishing, database files, spreadsheets, and communications software

telecommunications equipment

modems for communicating with distant computers via telephone lines

storage and shelf space

supplies (stationery, printer paper, pens, notebooks, blank disks, file folders, note pads, reference materials, and so on)

Specialized equipment is included for employees who require it; for example, a dictation/transcription unit for a stenographer or secretary, and an electronic calculator for an accountant. Of equal importance is a work environment which promotes the employee's physical and psychological well-being. Ergonomics is the science that seeks to achieve this objective.

Ergonomics and Work Station Design

Ergonomics is directed toward achieving harmony and balance between workers and their environment. Simply stated, ergonomics may be defined as the scientific shaping of the work environment to the employee. Psychology and physiology play an important part in ergonomic design.

Ergonomics was not widely known in the United States until World War II. The complex machinery used during the war and later in the aerospace program caused user problems, creating the need for a science that blended engineering and the human sciences; hence, the birth of "human-factors" engineering, a science closely related to ergonomics.

In business, the problems associated with human/computer interaction surfaced in the early 1970s when OSHA (Occupational Safety and Health Administration) began to hear complaints of eye strain and back problems from users of video display terminals (VDTs) and personal computers.

Urged by OSHA's reports of visual and postural problems associated with using computer terminals, suppliers of office equipment and furnishings responded positively. Ergonomically designed environments, including adjustable desks and chairs, nonglare VDTs, task lighting systems, and aesthetically pleasing colors became the watchword of office furniture vendors.

Industry has grown more supportive of the concept as workers in ergonomically designed work settings have shown substantial increases in productivity. Studies indicate that a well-designed work area can increase the productivity of clerical workers at least ten percent.

Where indifference toward the concept does exist, state legislatures are forcing businesses to reassess their attitudes. Approximately half of the states have passed bills regulating the use of video display equipment. Some impose stiff fines of up to $1,000 per day per worker for companies which ignore work-station regulations.

Designers incorporate the following objectives into their work-station designs:

1. Sufficient, well-planned spaces for storage
2. Reasonable amounts of work surface area for noncomputer activities
3. Effective lighting: ambient and task lighting
4. Moderate sound levels
5. Sufficient privacy and freedom to personalize one's station

Storage and Work-Surface Areas

Work-surface areas diminish as equipment and supplies increase. Desktop computers and peripherals, including keyboards, monitors, auxiliary disk drives, printers, and perhaps a modem for telephone hookup to outside computer users, now crowd spaces once reserved for a typewriter, telephone, and supplies.

Fortunately, the situation has inspired designers to create innovative designer solutions for reducing clutter and providing more desktop surface area. In particular, creative uses of vertical as well as horizontal spaces have resulted in cost-effective means for utilizing space.

Interchangeable storage and shelf modules provide flexibility in arrange-

Figure 1-6 A work station can be expanded or diminished in size with modular units.
Courtesy of Steelcase, Inc.

ment; stations designed to accommodate a variety of task assignments are divided into zones to bring more frequent activities within easy reach. Clustered work stations are particularly well suited to the zoning concept.

Zoning Areas

Zones 1, 2, and 3 divide the work areas according to the frequency of use, with Zone 1 the area where activity is most frequent. Zone 1, the primary zone, includes that part of the work surface which can be comfortably reached with the outstretched arm while seated. Within Zone 1, high-frequency activities such as telephone answering are carried out. The telephone is therefore placed within comfortable reach of the user.

Zone 2, the secondary zone, can be reached by the occupant's turning or rolling the chair slightly. In Zone 2, less frequent tasks, such as hard-copy printing of computer printouts, are performed.

Zone 3 areas can be reached only by leaving one's chair. For example, a conference area, with table and chairs for conferees and visitors, is a typical Zone 3. Unless one's rank and function warrant a Zone 3, none is included in the basic work chart. Only Zones 1 and 2 are included as standard work-station units.

Lighting Within the Work Station

Three sources of light should be controlled within the work station and the general office if employees are to derive maximum benefit from this important component of a healthy work setting. The first is natural sunlight from windows, atriums, or skylights; second, ambient light in the form of overhead fixtures; third, task-lighting fixtures designed for worker placement as desired on individual tasks.

Natural Lighting Natural sunlight, if properly directed over the left shoulder, provides the most healthful and convenient lighting for workers whose desks are placed near windows. Left-handed employees enjoy the same shadow-free effect if the sun's rays are directed over their right shoulders. When the sun is utilized as a major source of light in the office, horizontal or vertical blinds can be employed to direct its rays properly throughout the day. Atriums or skylights are occasionally utilized as light sources in contemporary offices.

Ambient Lighting Overhead or ambient fixtures provide light closely resembling daylight in terms of efficiency and "color." When designed for glare-free illumination, such lighting is ideal for a healthful office setting. Computer operators in particular benefit from these glare-free fixtures.

If improperly directed, however, overhead lights may cause severe glare and shadow problems. One solution is the shadow-free effect of fluorescent fixtures arranged in an overall grid at the ceiling level; glass panels placed beneath the fluorescent tubes diffuse the light evenly over the entire area, eliminating dark spots and shadows. Such ambience ranks as a fair substitute for natural daylight. It is widely used in large offices.

Task Lighting Task lighting is probably the most efficient and least expensive of manufactured lighting options. Depending on the design chosen, a task-lighting fixture may provide either direct or indirect lighting to the work area. Fixtures may be mounted on the top of storage components or on structural panels surrounding each work station. Lighting at each work station can also be individualized to fit the personal preferences of the employees. When integrated with furniture modules chosen to meet the employee's job specifications, task lighting provides optimum employee comfort.

A Lighting "Mix" Since the appropriate mix of natural light, ambient, and task lighting reflects positively on employees' health and well-being, their productivity on the job is likely to improve when lighting is designed to fit the employees' needs. Hence, it is important to coordinate all three in order to achieve a healthy environment.

Acoustics and Sound Control

Acoustics and sound control are major considerations in the design of work stations. Although office workers find it difficult, if not impossible, to concentrate in a noisy work setting, many architects fail to provide an acoustically suitable work environment. The most bothersome office noises reportedly come from two sources: jangling telephones and loud talking, with the latter reputed to be the more irritating.

Electronic devices also contribute to unacceptable noise levels. Although thermal printers are relatively quiet, the more common dot-matrix and letter-quality impact printers have noise levels as high as 70 decibels, an unacceptable level in an office environment. (European laws mandate printer levels of no more than 55 to 60 decibels at the operator's position.)

When each work station in an open office has one printer in operation, the compounded decibel level drifts above, around, and against the untreated surfaces of enclosure panels, irritating workers, sometimes to the level of stress. If external street noises are also present, the decibel count can become physically damaging to the ears.

Sound Suppressors

If office noise cannot be completely eradicated, its impact can be offset somewhat by sound suppressors or mufflers. Panel enclosures, for instance, can absorb as much as 50 percent of the noise generated around work stations. Panels of 6 feet or more in height muffle sounds exceptionally well if they are made of

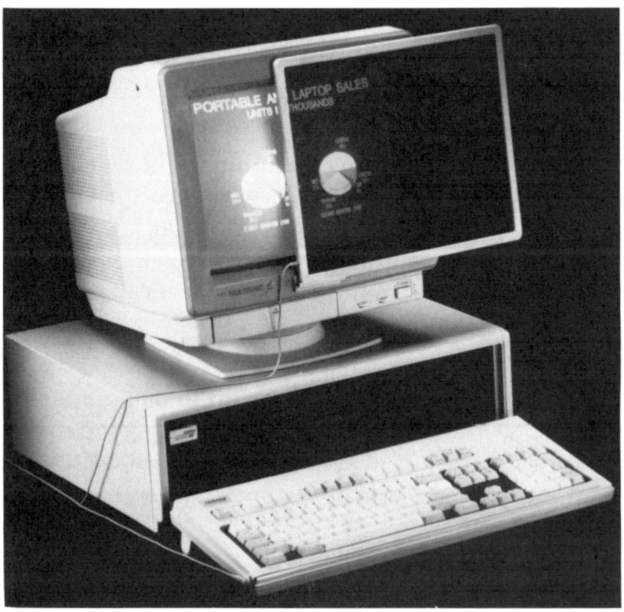

Figure 1-7 Filters for visual display terminals reduce the discomfort of glare for frequent computer users. *Courtesy of ACCO, International.*

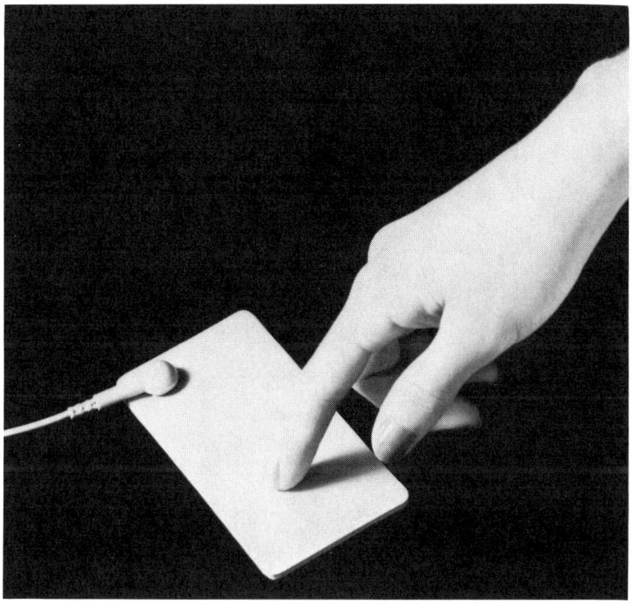

Figure 1-8 Static control devices protect users and equipment. The mouse pad defuses electrical shock. *Courtesy of ACCO, International.*

sound-absorbing materials. Carpeted floors, acoustically tiled ceilings, and windows draped with soft fabrics contribute to lowered decibel levels, too.

Masking systems, sometimes referred to as "white noise," gently mask all moderate noises. For example, the mask makes conversations unintelligible to disinterested listeners within hearing range. Designed to protect privacy, the electronically produced masking systems produce a sound similar to that of a central air conditioner in operation. Speakers are placed at ceiling level so as to distribute the sound evenly.

To reduce printer noise, acoustical enclosures are a handy remedy. A printer enclosure reduces the noise level by 20 to 25 decibels. Some covers are made of particle board and lined with foam, with an acrylic shield in front for visibility. Plastic covers are an inexpensive alternative to particle-board covers, but their sound absorption is less, too.

Laser printers eliminate the source of most printer noise—namely, the impact of a printhead striking a platen or paper. As these printers continue to increase their share of the market, one of the most common sources of office noise will be eliminated.

FURNITURE SELECTION

At one time, a business desk supplied with a telephone, an appointment calendar, an in/out correspondence basket, and a note pad served adequately the needs of the administrative assistant and most managerial personnel. If correspondence volume was substantial, a dictation unit on the manager's desk and the companion

Figure 1-9 Expansive windows combine with track lighting to provide visual comfort for workers. Carpets, upholstered chairs, and plants absorb unwanted sounds. *Courtesy of Apple Computer, Inc.*

transcription unit on the secretary's desk completed the desktop inventory for each manager/secretarial team. A typewriter was usually stored on a pull-out shelf of the secretary's desk, or on a stand adjacent to the desk.

Today, the administrative assistant is likely to have on or near the desk a personal computer, a printer, a telephone and modem to communicate electronically with distant computer users, a collection of specific software packages, a library of data-filled disks organized for ready accessibility, and blank disks for additional data storage.

High-tech installations necessitate significant modifications in work-station furniture and design. Work-surface areas must be expanded to accommodate additional electronic equipment and supplies; chairs must provide more back support for users who spend long hours before VDTs; storage capacity must be increased; and ergonomic demands for more healthful and pleasant surroundings must be factored into work-station design. In response to users' requests for more practical designs, manufacturers offer furniture designs which meet all these criteria. They call it "computer-support" furniture.

Computer-support Furniture

Designed to support computers and their array of peripherals, computer-support furniture describes furniture built specifically to complement the jobs of computer users.

Flexible enough to allow a variety of configurations, computer-support furniture is built to satisfy virtually all users' needs and preferences. Manufacturers produce two basic types: systems-support and free-standing furniture.

Systems-support furniture integrates furniture modules which can be mixed and matched to meet individual needs of the work-station occupants. For example, a keyboard platform or drawer, a stand for the computer display, a printer stand, a file drawer or cabinet, and open or closed shelves for storage of supplies can be arranged in limitless ways, since all modules are interchangeable.

Systems-support furniture also integrates the necessary power cords and electrical outlets, discretely tracking the cords along the enclosure panels. The panels are enhanced with sound-absorbing materials so that the entire work station provides both visual and auditory privacy when needed.

Free-standing computer-support furniture features the traditional stand-alone desk, modified to accommodate computer users' needs.

Enhanced with wiring for the electronic equipment, the free-standing desks are made more spacious through add-on units. For example, pedestal drawers which attach to the underside of the work surface, storage cabinets mounted on casters and rolled underneath the work surface, and free-standing file cabinets placed adjacent to the desk, add the functionality needed for computer support.

The added storage and work space may also be arranged vertically, attached to the enclosure panels above and around the desk. The end result is to

Figure 1-10 Systems-support furniture allows for interchanging of furniture modules to support individual users' needs. *Courtesy of Steelcase, Inc.*

make free-standing furniture almost as versatile as systems-support furniture, but with the added advantage of fitting more readily into tight corners and small offices.

Many designers choose free-standing furniture because it can be easily integrated into existing environments and matched to the furniture in use. In the view of many, it fits the image of the traditional business office. Combined with color-coordinated enclosure panels, it provides a cost-effective alternative to systems-support furniture.

Clustered Groups

Both free-standing and systems-support furniture may be grouped into clusters of two, three, or more stations to a group, with screens or storage cabinets marking the boundaries of each cluster. The cluster, or core, arrangement is a simple space-saving concept which arranges panels and work surfaces around a core, creating a central housing for all power cords and communications cables. The primary advantage of clustered work stations is economy in floor-space usage. An additional advantage is the ease with which materials can be shared among work-station users.

Color-coordinated, sound-absorbent screens and tack boards help complete the ideal working environment for both systems-support and free-standing furniture—one that is aesthetically pleasing, yet ergonomically sound.

Chairs

Specialists in ergonomic furnishings claim that well-designed chairs are a key factor in improving productivity. One cites a study which demonstrated an improved productivity of 20 to 30 percent when newly designed chairs, focused on physiological needs, replaced older ones.

Appropriate height is one of the most fundamental requirements of seating comfort. Chairs that are too high or too low cause workers to tire quickly, thus reducing productivity. If chairs are not custom-built for specific users, they must incorporate height-adjustment devices which can accommodate tall and short users equally well.

Users suggest that the adjustment device be readily accessible and easy to operate. An adjustment range of 3 to 5 vertical inches usually suffices. If at the maximum height the users' feet do not rest comfortably on the floor, a footrest provides the necessary elevation for comfort.

A chair with a "waterfall," or downward-sculpted front edge improves circulation in the legs and reduces worker fatigue during prolonged keyboarding sessions. Padded upholstery also reduces fatigue.

Since seated persons change positions, on average, every six minutes, the chair should also respond to posture changes. Good lumbar support for bodily twists and turns can be provided by padded back rests and contoured, slightly concave, seats. Sturdy casters on five-spoke pedestals also allow for freedom of movement and relative safety.

Good chair upholstery adds comfort and aesthetic appeal. Natural wool or cotton fibers are ideal upholstery fabrics. Natural fibers blended with synthetic fabrics, or high-quality soft vinyl and leathers, are satisfactory alternatives.

In summary, chairs which are most likely to contribute to the worker's energy and productivity levels incorporate these features:

1. Padded back rests with lower-back support
2. Seats with rounded front edge and adjustable seat heights
3. Padded and contoured, slightly concave seats
4. Sturdy casters on five-spoke pedestals

The wide assortment of ergonomically designed chairs available to buyers demonstrates the conscientious efforts of vendors to respond to users' health concerns. Handsome adjustable chairs and furniture modules dominate the office furniture market.

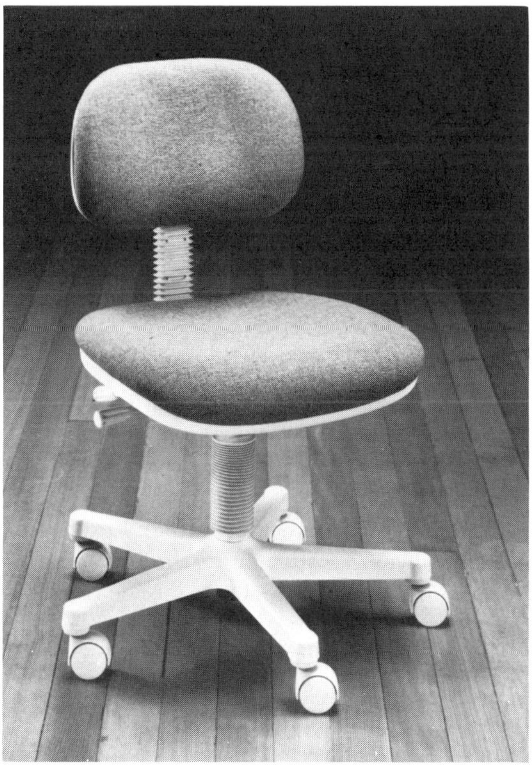

Figure 1-11 Ergonomic chair features a five-spoke platform, adjustable height device, and a downward-sculpted seat. *Courtesy of ACCO, International.*

ERGONOMICS AND PRODUCTIVITY

Recent studies indicate that significant improvements in worker productivity can be achieved through ergonomic improvements in office furniture and environments. For example, a five-year study conducted by Humantech, Inc. on the relationship between ergonomic office environments and productivity produced remarkable results.[1]

> A group of 123 office workers was selected to investigate the impact of ergonomic furniture on productivity. For eight months, workers kept diaries of the time they spent on various tasks.
>
> The absentee rate and the percentage of time that workers used their computers was monitored; the number of errors per document, and the average mean time to complete various clerical functions was analyzed. Managers, too, completed time diaries and evaluation sheets, rating their own effectiveness and that of their employees.
>
> Managers and workers then participated in a selection of new furniture and layout designs according to their own tastes. All the furniture from the selection group had been rated as ergonomically sound. The users were allowed to choose, not only the furniture and office accessories, but also the furniture finishes to be applied when the customized designs were built.
>
> Six months after the new furniture was installed and the layout designs implemented, these changes in employee behavior were noted:
>
> The productivity improvement was significant
>
> Absenteeism fell from 4 percent to minus 1 percent
>
> Error rates fell from 25 to 11 percent
>
> Computer usage increased from 60 to 86 percent (translating into an increase in active work time of more than 40 percent).
>
> More than 70 percent of the managers felt that their effectiveness had improved "very much," and 90 percent rated the productivity of their employees as "much improved."

The Norwegian State Institute in Oslo, Norway studied the incidence of back discomfort among its office workers. After improvements in work-station layout and seating, back-related absenteeism was reduced by 50 percent, turnover was down from 40 to 5 percent, and 40 percent of employees on disability leave returned to work.

The management personnel of a major automobile company used their computer equipment less than 12 percent of the day until after the introduction of ergonomic computer tables and improved chairs, at which time usage rate went up four times.

The performance of State Farm clerical workers improved as much as 15 percent with ergonomically acceptable work stations and seating.[2]

[1]M. Franz Schneider, "Why Ergonomics Can No Longer Be Ignored," *Office Administration and Automation* (July 1985), 26–30.

[2]Ibid, 27.

Most benefits from human-factor engineering create win/win situations for vendors and buyers of equipment and furnishings. In summary, the benefits translate into:

reduced training time at computer stations
reduced errors at data entry and retrieval
reduced turnaround time on computer tasks
improved worker morale, resulting in reduced absenteeism

SUMMARY

The role of the administrative assistant has been enhanced in recent years, due in part to the evolution of electronics in the business office. However, the electronic evolution has produced an altered style of operation for the staff; electronic software programs have replaced conventional procedures, and microcomputers have become pivotal equipment in the office.

Furniture selection has become critical as the need for fitting cumbersome equipment to inadequate work space is recognized as a major issue. Ergonomic issues are paramount as the administrative assistant and others choose work-station desks, chairs, and paneled enclosures. Concern for acoustics, sound control, and the privacy needs of employees have also become major considerations.

The role of the administrative assistant is much broader than it was "before electronics." Increased responsibilities, however, have brought greater job satisfaction and made the work more rewarding than ever before.

QUESTIONS FOR REVIEW

1. List six components of the electronic office commonly found in business offices.
2. Electronic mail can take many forms. Name each of the five forms described in this chapter.
3. Three methods of electronic filing are described in this chapter. Briefly define each.
4. Work stations arranged in clusters, or cores, are one answer to the efficient use of space. Explain the concept.
5. Name some of the characteristics of ergonomically designed chairs.
6. How is the productivity of office personnel related to ergonomics?
7. What are the components of a typical, fully equipped work station for an administrative assistant?
8. Name four factors which should be considered in designing the ideal work station.
9. How have legislatures affected the attitudes of employers toward employees' health and well-being?
10. Three light sources should be controlled within the work area for optimum comfort and productivity of employees. Describe the three light sources.

QUESTIONS FOR DISCUSSION

1. Several remedies are suggested for reducing or suppressing distracting noises in the office. In a large corporation employing hundreds of office workers and housing many pieces of electric and electronic equipment, which of the suggested sound suppressors do you consider most practical? Explain your answer.
2. Office personnel frequently voice their frustrations at having too little privacy; they complain that their stations afford them neither visual nor acoustical privacy. Discuss your perceptions of this problem; that is, are their complaints based on the need for personal "space" of their own; or, rather, on their concern for working without interruption and distraction; or a little of both?

   If you were in a position to act on this situation in your own company, what would you do? Clarify your position—positive or negative.

   Assuming that you act in favor of your employees, what would be the basis for your decision to acquiesce to their requests?
3. Most persons agree that a healthful and attractive work setting has a positive impact on workers' morale. Expound on this point of view and discuss the relative truth of this position with respect to:
   a. the landscaped office
   b. the role of color, especially the decorator "touch" in a color-coordinated design

SUGGESTED ACTIVITIES

1. Collect periodicals with pictures of office interiors, particularly those with designer features. Exchange the periodicals with your classmates, discussing those offices which appeal to you most. If the school offers audio-visual services for student/faculty use, have slides made so that everyone can enjoy viewing your selections projected on a large screen.
2. Conduct an informal survey among students in your city to determine how many are planning careers as administrative assistants. For comparison purposes, survey high school, junior college, and college students separately, noting the differences, if any. Solicit in the survey their attitudes toward these careers as doors to higher-level positions or lucrative salary opportunities.
3. Visit a local business office and note its attention (or lack thereof) to ergonomic design in its selection of furnishings, its provision for acoustical and visual privacy in work stations, and its use of sound-absorption materials to reduce noise.
4. Write to Professional Secretaries International, 10502 Northwest Ambassador Drive, Kansas City, MO 64195-0404.

   Ask for information on the CPS (Certified Professional Secretary) examination, including the fee schedule and application forms. Ask for the latest issue of *Capstone*, published yearly by PSI, briefly summarizing pertinent facts about the examination, including sample questions of the examination.

   Share it with all class members; discuss taking the examination as a student before graduation.

REFERENCES

General

GOLDFIELD, RANDY, "Aiming OA Towards the Top," *Modern Office Technology* (February 1985), 55–68.

PARKER, REGINALD, "Task Migration in the Executive Suite," *The Secretary* (January 1985), 17–18.

Furnishings, Space Management

GRAHAM, MARSHALL A., CMC, "Employee Needs are Primary in Effective Space Allocation," *Office Systems '85* (November 1985), 92–94.

KLEINSCHROD, WALTER A., "Office Landscaping—Planning for Tomorrow," *Administrative Management* (December 1985), 25-28.

MINICUCCI, RICK, "Office Furniture that Stands on Its Own," *Today's Office* (March 1987), 20–24.

STEINBRECHER, DAVID, "Computer-support Furniture: Fitting Form to Function," *Today's Office* (June 1987), 18–25.

WAKIN, EDWARD, "Facility Management: Making the Right Moves," *Today's Office* (December 1984), 29–34.

Ergonomics

BETTS, KELLYN S., "Reflecting on the Glaring Problem," *Modern Office Technology* (October 1985), 136 -140.

FERNBERG, PATRICIA M., "Designing the Workplace for the Knowledge Worker," *Modern Office Technology* (September 1985), 73–82.

HEALEY, MARTIN, "What is a Workstation?" *Datamation* (January 15, 1985), 55–57.

KROLL, JOHN, "Good Lighting Brings Open Offices Out of the Dark," *The Office* (March 1986), 72–78.

POVOTSKY, BORIS, Ph. D., "Ergonomic Work Stations," *Office Systems '86* (August 1986), 42–44.

Productivity

FERNBERG, PATRICIA M., "Modular Furniture is Your Link with Productivity," *Modern Office Technology* (August 1988), 41–46.

ROURKE, RICHARD, "Less Noise Means More Productivity," *Administrative Management* (November 1985), 42–49.

SCHNEIDER, M. FRANZ, "Why Ergonomics Can no Longer Be Ignored," *Office Administration & Automation* (July 1985), 26–30.

WALTER, STEPHANINE KYSER, "Ergonomics in the Office Environment Is a Matter of Dollars & Common Sense," *Office Systems '85* (September 1985), 75–79.

2
Equipment and Supplies for the Electronic Office

INTRODUCTION

Administrative assistants can be proud of smooth-functioning offices which process assigned tasks with speed and efficiency. All energies should be directed in pursuit of that goal with attempts to motivate their staffs to do the same. At least three factors relate to their achieving this objective:

1. Cooperative and talented personnel
2. A healthful work environment, conducive to high employee morale and productivity
3. State-of-the-art equipment and a well-stocked inventory of supplies

Chapter 1 explores the facets of a healthy work environment. Chapter 15 addresses the most important element—personnel. The current chapter reviews state-of-the-art equipment and the supplies needed to complement the equipment.

Terms in the chapter include:

CPUs	ETs
RAM storage	single-strike ribbons
printwheels	electronic fonts

ELECTRONIC OFFICE EQUIPMENT

The types of equipment found in business organizations vary from one office to another. A thorough list would include these popular pieces:

Word processors (PC based or stand-alones)
Electronic filing equipment of various types
Telephones and other telecommunications devices
Dictation/transcription units
Microcomputers
Printers
Electronic typewriters

Except for the last three listed, the equipment for each function is described in the chapters relating to their special functions; for example, Chapter 5 explores word processors and printers; Chapter 10, electronic filing equipment; and Chapter 12, telephone and telecommunication devices.

The current chapter reviews microcomputers, electronic typewriters, and printers insofar as they impact on the duties of the administrative assistant. Although printers are reviewed again in Chapter 5, a cursory review in this chapter reflects the important function of the printer and its multifaceted applications in the office—from spreadsheets, to desktop publishing, to database reports.

Microcomputers

The administrative assistant's tool "par excellence," the microcomputer, is a standard component in the electronic office. Its multiple applications make it the first-choice purchase of buyers when a business decides to "go electronic" with their business procedures.

Measured in terms of primary storage capacity, and exclusive of laptop computers which vary widely in storage capacity, microcomputers are the smallest system in the computer hierarchy. The range from smallest to largest usually includes four levels:

1. microcomputers
2. minicomputers
3. mainframes
4. supercomputers

Microcomputer systems have all the functional components of the larger computer systems; that is, they are organized to perform functions involving the primary storage area and the central processing unit (CPU). *The primary storage* area (or main memory) handles several functions:

1. Data are fed into the input storage section of primary storage where they remain until processing begins.

2. The working storage holds the data while being processed and the intermediate results of the data in process.
3. The program storage area contains the processing instructions.
4. The output area contains the final results of the processed data until released to a printer or a secondary storage medium, such as a magnetic disk.

No fixed boundaries designate where these processes take place; they vary from one application to another. Neither does any processing occur in primary storage; this is left to the central processing unit (CPU) of the computer.

The Central Processing Unit The central processing unit (CPU) is housed in an integrated circuit, or *chip,* called a microprocessor. The microprocessor contains the circuits which perform the arithmetic-logic (ALU) functions and control the functions of the computer. Together, the two components, the ALU and the control units, make up the central processing unit of the microcomputer.

All mathematical calculations and comparisons are done in the ALU. Comparisons such as that needed to list a set of names in alphabetical or numerical order are performed by the ALU. Data that need computational or comparative processing are fed to the ALU in sequential order via an input device such as

Figure 2-1 Floor-standing PC, 135 Mb hard drive with 4 Mb RAM. Model M380/XP5. *Courtesy of Olivetti USA.*

a keyboard. When processing in the ALU is completed, the data are sent back to primary storage for later exit to the output area.

The control section of the CPU oversees the entire processing operation, directing the commands from input to primary storage, then back and forth between primary storage and the ALU until processing is completed. Finally, in response to the command to store, print, or display the output, the data go to a disk or printer, usually after being displayed on the screen. Display screens and printers are the most used output devices.

Disk Drives The disk drives of a computer, even hard disks, are actually peripheral to the computer, not an integral part of it. They can therefore be discussed (and purchased) as separate units, and additional disk drives added to a microcomputer after its installation, for extra secondary storage. Disk drives of microcomputers may house the 5-1/4-inch floppy diskettes once so universally used, or the smaller 3-1/2-inch rigid disks, or a hard disk, sometimes called a fixed disk, or a Winchester.

Of the three, the hard disk has the greatest capacity, ranging from 10 megabytes up to 80, 100, and greater megabytes (Mb) of secondary storage. In contrast, the storage capacity of floppy diskettes has grown from an initial standard of 240 kilobytes to approximately 1.2 megabytes.

One megabyte is said to equal the storage of 250 single-spaced 3-1/2 by 11-inch pages, if each page contains approximately 4,000 characters. The change in format from single-density to double-density, double-sided (DD/DS) diskettes accounts for most of the increased capacity in the floppies.

Figure 2-2 This computer's small "footprint" requires minimum desk space and can be mounted on its base or its side. The mouse interface simplifes the use of most desktop publishing systems. *Courtesy of Apple Computer, Inc.*

The 3-1/2-inch rigid disks have greater tolerance for environmental hazards than the floppy diskettes, and their storage capacity is greater. These factors plus their handy "shirt-pocket" size make them appealing as a replacement for the 5-1/4-inch floppy diskettes. Hence, their popularity when users upgrade their systems or add additional drives to them.

Storage Patterns on Magnetic Disks Magnetic disks store data on invisible concentric circles called tracks. Beginning at the outer edge of the disk, the tracks are numbered sequentially. Each track is divided into pie-shaped sectors, usually eight to a disk.

The combination of track and sector divisions enables the read/write head of the disk drive to access a stored program randomly, rather than sequentially. That is, the search does not involve a sequential reading of every stored program on the disk until the requested file is found.

Random or direct access to stored files is quicker than sequential access; therefore, magnetic disks, which are normally DASDs (direct-access storage devices) make ideal auxiliary storage devices.

Microcomputer Monitors (Screens) Computer screens are too often taken for granted by the purchaser of a desktop computer. However, the administrative assistant who must choose monitors for the staff's computers must know how to evaluate their special features.

Two basic types are available: flat-panel screens and CRTs (cathode ray tubes). Laptop computers commonly use flat-panel models which economize on space and weight. CRTs, on the other hand, are the universal standard for desktop computers.

Two important factors must be considered when selecting the correct monitor: color and resolution. A color monitor is important for displaying vivid graphics and impressive presentations. Some color monitors display as many as 256 colors. A recent introduction offers 24-bit color, providing enough color combinations for the most intricate shading and blending. An expensive model, it is used when very realistic and lifelike presentations are needed.

Monochrome monitors display a single color on a contrasting background. They are appropriate for word processing, spreadsheets, and database files. Formerly the standard for these applications, monochromes are losing ground to color monitors as users incorporate desktop publishing and graphics software into their word processing and database applications.

Resolution is determined by the number of pixels displayed on the screen; the more pixels, the higher the resolution. (Pixels are rectangular shapes made up of invisible horizontal and vertical lines on the screen.) Some of the main standards for resolution include:

EGA (Extended Graphics Array) with 640 × 350 resolution
VGA (Video Graphics Array) featuring 640 × 480 resolution
8514A, with a resolution of 1,024 × 768.

Figure 2-3 The IBM Application System 400 (AS/400) is a combined hardware and software system which provides businesses with electronic mail, document storage and retrieval, calendars, database access and business graphics utilities. *Courtesy of IBM Corporation.*

Since low-resolution screens can cause severe eye strain, employees who spend many hours before their computer screens should have high-resolution monitors.

Selection of a Microcomputer The wide range of prices and features of microcomputers makes it difficult for the administrative assistant to select, or help an employer select, microcomputers for the office. In evaluating which systems best fit the company's needs, the following factors should be considered.

RAM (random-access memory) capacity. Integrated software packages, such as spreadsheet and database combinations, require substantial amounts of RAM storage. Desktop publishing and graphics require even more. The administrative assistant must consider what software is to be used, now or in the foreseeable future, and buy a microcomputer with enough RAM storage to accommodate applications planned for the near future.

Monitor characteristics. As explained before, selection of a color or a monochrome monitor, and of high-resolution or the less expensive low-resolution monitors, is determined in large part by the usage required. In any case, it must be remembered that high-resolution screens are easier on the eyes and therefore more acceptable ergonomically than low-resolution screens.

Vendor support for service and training. This factor may be critical when new computer systems are introduced to the staff, or when the business is located far from the vendor's place of business.

Figure 2-4 The user-friendly interface of InfoWindow's touchscreen display virtually eliminates the intimidation factor of computers. No keyboarding skill is necessary for viewers to select an option or answer a question. *Courtesy of IBM Corporation.*

The company's special needs. Each business has system requirements uniquely its own. These must be reviewed with the vendors vying for the company's computer contract, and the choice made on the basis of which computer best meets these needs.

Price. A negotiated best price should be resolved only after the other criteria are met. If the other criteria are ignored, price will make little or no difference.

Electronic Typewriters

Forerunners of the electronic typewriters so widely used today, *electric* typewriters, when introduced, were a major improvement over the manual typewriters they replaced. The power of electricity supplied a uniform force to all keystrokes and offered savings in energy and frustration formerly unknown to typists.

Electronic typewriters (ETs), on the other hand, offered even more. Enhanced by integrated circuitry on microchips, electronic typewriters brought "intelligence" and "memory" akin to that provided by word processors to the typist's station. Combining the ease and familiarity of the electric typewriter with limited memory and some of the functional processes of the word processor, the electronic typewriter has far outperformed its predecessor, the electric typewriter.

Introduced in 1978, electronic typewriters have been improved each year through additional electronic features, either built into the units or offered as add-ons by the manufacturers. As of 1991, more than 100 ET models are available, ranging in price from under $300 to over $3,000, depending upon the additional features, accessories, and software included.

Figure 2-5 Two vintage typewriters from IBM Corporation, the "Electromatic" typewriter of 1935, and the "Model A Executive," 1948. *Courtesy of IBM Corporation.*

Electronic Typewriters: Basic Features In addition to basic typewriter features such as centering, underlining, hyphenation, paragraph indention, decimal tabulation, and columnar layout, basic ETs now include

- search and replace
- block deletion and insertion
- superscript/subscript
- text editing
- right-margin justification
- buffer storage
- form fill-ins
- automatic correction
- mail merge
- automatic paper insertion
- boldface type

In addition to standard features, high-end models offer a wide range of options which may include:

- spelling checks
- address files
- dictionaries
- calendars
- liquid-crystal displays
- message pads
- 80,000-character disk drives for document memory
- note pads
- 12-inch screen displays
- calculators

Figure 2-6 The Wheelwriter 70 Series II typewriter with monitor is menu driven, with word processing functions similar to those of the IBM Personal Typing System in the background. The typewriters can exchange documents saved to their 3-½-inch diskette drives. *Courtesy of IBM Corporation.*

The electronic typewriter models which most closely resemble word processors are the screen-based electronic typewriters, known simply as SBETs.

Screen-based Electronic Typewriters (SBETs) Screen-based electronic typewriters (SBETs) are the ET manufacturers' latest response to word processor competitors. Claiming higher reliability, better software, and more affordable prices than word processors, ET vendors point out two saleable features of the SBETs: their dazzling tehnological and software improvements, and their price drop of over 100 percent since their introduction. (Originally priced at $5,500, comparable units now sell for $2,000 or less.)[1]

The makers' claims are not without merit. One firm's MS-DOS-based unit offers a 10-megabyte clock speed and 768 kilobytes of random access memory; another offers a 20-megabyte hard-disk drive.

One manufacturer has built the word processing program into the machine so that users need not load software at all. The same maker offers other software options on cards to be placed in expansion slots inside the typewriter,

[1]Eileen McCooey, "Features Abound on SBETs," *Today's Office* (May 1989), 56.

just as in microcomputers. In keeping with the microcomputer industry, most of the ET makers are also moving toward 3-1/2-inch rigid disk drives.

Choosing an Electronic Typewriter With the wide variety of capabilities and applications available, choosing the best model of electronic typewriter can be difficult. In making a selection, the administrative assistant should consider what applications the unit is intended to perform most frequently. For example, a limited memory of about 1,000 characters (one to two pages) may be sufficient for sales offices, while a legal office may require an internal memory of at least 150,000 characters.

Memory is important not only for storing text, but for providing various functions which ease the burden of producing letter-perfect copy. For example, *automatic correction* recalls typed characters from memory when the user wants to make a correction. The user returns to the end of a word or sentence that needs correction, presses the appropriate keys, and the entire word or line is erased automatically.

Phrase memory stores frequently used phrases, such as the opening and closing lines of a letter, to be recalled on command. *Format memory* stores page

Figure 2-7 The ZY-1000S screen-based electronic typewriter, equipped with dual 5-¼ inch disk drives, an 80-character × 25-line screen, and 320 kilobytes of internal memory, functions as a computer and word processor, as well as a typewriter. *Courtesy of Sharp Electronics.*

formats—margins, tabs, page length, and so on—available at the press of a single key. The user can switch from one format to another as needed. *Form memory* stores repetitive phrases and parts of letters to be used in form-letter composition. Internal memory is, of course, readily enhanced by a disk drive. The combination of internal and external memory makes a unit's storage capacity almost limitless.

The Future for ETs Just as the manual typewriter yielded its place of prominence to its electric counterpart in the 1960s, and the electric typewriter to the electronic unit in the 1980s, some observers predict that the electronic typewriter will yield its place to the word processor during the 1990s.

As the decade of the 1990s begins, however, the sales of electronic typewriters show little sign of abatement. According to a study by Venture Development Corporation, annual sales are expected to stabilize at 1.3 to 1.4 million units through 1993, with the high-end models accounting for more than 62 percent of the sales.[2]

Printers

As the standard companion piece for word processors, printers are discussed in detail in Chapter 5. Like microcomputers, however, printers have multiple print applications, only one of which is word processing. Spreadsheets, database reports, graphics, and other applications depend universally on printer output. Each software application has its specific print requirements which, ultimately, determine which type of printer is best suited to its purposes and output.

Printers are classified as impact or nonimpact printers, depending on the type of technology involved in making the print impressions on the paper.

Impact Printers Impact printers make alphabetic, numeric, linear, and other impressions on paper by the typist's striking an inked ribbon against a paper held securely against a hard surface. The inked ribbon leaves the impression of the letter or symbol struck by the user. Daisywheel and dot-matrix printers comprise the two most popular types of impact printers.

Daisywheels, so-called because of their daisy-shaped printheads, produce fully formed characters. Therefore, they are usually rated as superior printers for word processing applications.

Dot-matrix printers print letters, numbers, symbols, and graphics from a printhead made up of wire pins arranged in a matrix, or grid. The higher the number of pins, the more precise the character that is formed from the pattern of dots.

NLQ print (near letter-quality) mimics the output of word processors with *almost* as fully formed characters as those of word processors. Nine-pin matrices

[2]William M. Cowan, "ETs Keep Pace with Times to Meet User Requirements," *Office Systems '89* (July 1989), 64–70.

Figure 2-8 A 24-wire matrix with eight embedded fonts, IBM's Quickwriter features a sound hood to deaden noise during print operation. *Courtesy of IBM Corporation.*

were once the standard, but higher-resolution 24-pin printheads have all but replaced them.

Nonimpact Printers Laser, ink-jet, and thermal-transfer printers comprise the most used nonimpact printer types. *Laser printers* are the "Cadillac" of the trade, producing higher-quality print at faster speeds than any other reasonably priced printer. Laser beams "shoot" the digitally coded bits of data through glass fibers to a rotating mirror, causing the mirror to scan a printing drum; the laser beam

Figure 2-9 The Apple LaserWriter II family of laser printers handles a range of activities from general office applications to desktop publishing and volume printing. *Courtesy of Apple Computer, Inc.*

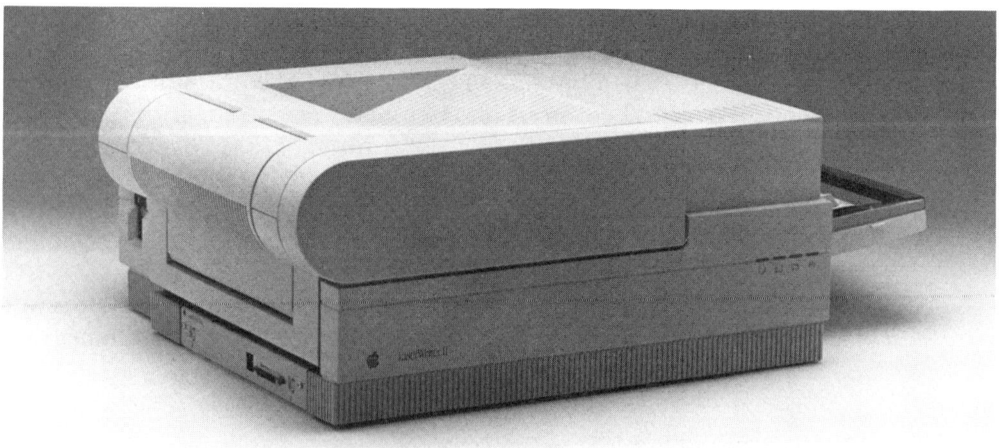

then strikes the drum and transfers the image from the drum to the page, where it is fused by heat and pressure.

Laser-print quality is outstanding. In addition, its quiet operation and high speed earn it high marks by users. Although it produces images with a pattern of dots, its dot pattern is very dense, with 90,000 dots to an inch. The output is comparable to typeset text and its graphics to professionally produced copy.

Ink-jet printers squirt ink droplets to the page to produce an image. The process is a quiet and well-developed technology which lends itself to color printing as well as black and white images.

Thermal printers use heat to produce an image. They are much like dot-matrix printers except that the wires are electronically heated. Thermal printer ribbons are coated with a waxy ink that softens when heated. When the ribbon is pressed against the paper, the softened ink adheres, forming the final printed image. Like ink-jet printers, they are quiet and can produce in color.

Except for the daisywheel, all of these printers handle graphics as well as text. The quality of both text and graphics in the dot-matrix, ink-jet, and thermal units depends on the number of jets or wires in the printhead.

Selecting a Printer The administrative assistant must assess the needs of printer users before selecting a printer for purchase. If needs vary, more than one type of printer may be needed to fill all requirements. Obviously, if graphics are a major application, one of the graphics producers must be chosen. If fully formed characters are important for executive-level correspondence, a daisywheel or a laser printer is appropriate.

Figure 2-10 Computer-support accessories deaden printer noise, reduce glare, and enhance the decor of the work station. *Courtesy of TAB Products Company.*

For speed, the laser excels all others. It is also an excellent choice for desktop publishing applications. Although the laser printer probably requires the greatest dollar investment, prices appear to be plummeting and by the mid-1990s may be competitive with other models.

SUPPLIES FOR THE WORK STATION

The steadily mounting budget for expendable office supplies demands constant diligence on the part of the administrative assistant. To remain within the limitations of a restricted budget and still keep the staff supplied with quality work materials, effective control procedures must be established for the selection, purchase, and distribution of office supplies. To this end, personal responsibility must be assumed for these activities:

1. selection of materials which are the most cost effective for the equipment and applications of each work station.
2. adoption of economy measures in the purchase of supplies.
3. establishment of inventory control procedures, including monitoring the issuance of supplies to office personnel.

Four items dominate in the supply side of electronic office equipment: ribbons for printers and electronic typewriters, printwheels and fonts, paper, and magnetic media.

Ribbons

Ribbons are a major determinant of the print quality of output from both typewriters and computer printers. They are available in three basic types: fabric, single-strike film, and multistrike film.

Film Ribbons Known for their high-print quality, film ribbons are generally preferred for daisywheel printers. Made of carbon-coated mylar or polyethylene, they come in two varieties: single-strike film and multistrike film.

Multistrike ribbons, relying on a heavy concentration of ink to fill in character elements, accept keyboard strikes at virtually the same spot several times before advancing. Moving forward only a fraction of a character width with each strike, film ribbons provide higher character capacity and lower cost per ribbon than single-strike ribbons.

Single-strike ribbons advance a whole character width with each strike, thus providing the sharpest, crispest print quality available. Because of their lower character capacity and resultant higher cost, most firms reserve single-strike ribbons for high-priority documents, such as executive letters and memos, and sales or public correspondence in which appearance is almost as important as the message itself.

Fabric Ribbons Fabric ribbons are normally one to two dollars cheaper than film ribbons but have disadvantages which offset the price advantage. Saturated with ink, fabric ribbons often cause a buildup of ink on the printwheel; they also tend to splay characters, leaving nonuniform deposits of ink on characters.

Most fabric ribbons are made of nylon, which is less expensive yet more durable than cotton or silk. Nylon fabric ribbon is therefore widely used in dot-matrix and high-speed line printers.

Correctable Film Ribbons Correctable film ribbons allow for error lift-off corrections by the operator. When first introduced, correctable film ribbons had just one print path. Now, however, correctable ribbons with two or three vertical print paths are available from several manufacturers. By giving the user two to three times more characters per ribbon, the multiple-path ribbons provide a considerable cost saving. A correctable thermal ribbon, designated for use with some portable units, corrects and adds color to thermal-typewriter or laptop-computer output.

Cartridges Most printer ribbons are sold in self-contained cartridges. Fabric ribbon cartridges usually contain about six feet of inked ribbon wrapped in an endless loop that circulates in front of the typing element continuously. When the print impression dims, the cartridge is removed and replaced by a new one.

Fabric cartridges that automatically reink the ribbon are also available. They use a device—usually a sponge or a roller—to apply ink to the ribbon as it circulates, thus increasing the life of the ribbon cartridge several times. Problems related to the reinking process, however, have been experienced by some users. Poor transfer of ink, leaking, and ink clogging are some of the problems that need to be addressed by manufacturers before the reinking technology is perfected.

Quality and Cost The administrative assistant will discover that determining the quality of a ribbon is a difficult task. However, quality is the most important criteria in choosing ribbons for the printers and typewriters in the office. Usually, a systems-matched ribbon—one that the printer or typewriter manufacturer sells for use with its own products—will deliver a high-quality image with little or no operational problems.

In determining cost, the administrative assistant must remember that the true measure of a ribbon's cost is its cost per character, not per ribbon. The extended life of high-capacity ribbons may, in fact, make them less expensive than short-lived "bargain" ribbons with limited character capacity.

Unsatisfactory printouts, too, are a less obvious but very real cost factor to consider. Skimping on ribbons meant for expensive printers and electronic typewriters may be a costly error, since, in the final analysis, the output of electronic equipment is no better than the supplies that support it.

Printwheels

Printwheels are another determinant of document quality. Regardless of the quality of the typewriters or printers being used, the choice of an inappropriate printwheel can nullify the good impression otherwise projected by a writer's message. In order to choose the most suitable printwheel for each usage, the administrative assistant must be familiar with the choices available. Printwheels are offered in three basic types: metal, monoplastic, and dual plastic.

Metal printwheels are the most expensive of the three. However, they offer the longest life of the three types, ranging from 25 million to 35 million characters per wheel.

Monoplastic printwheels, constructed of a mineral-filled plastic reinforced with polyester, are the lowest in price of the three wheel types. Their lifespan is relatively short, however, ranging from 7 million to 10 million characters. The print quality, too, gradually flattens and broadens the characters.

Dual-plastic printwheels are constructed of very hard thermoset plastic characters bonded to the spokes of the wheels. Their print quality is excellent and their lifespan, 10 to 20 million characters. In price they range slightly higher than monoplastic wheels.

For two reasons, *cartridge-loaded printwheels* are now replacing original wheel styles. They are easier to load than the original printwheels and they protect the printwheel from damage.

Printer Fonts

An adequate supply of type styles (Roman, Gothic, Prestige elite, and so on) must be available so that all printing applications can be served appropriately. For example, executive correspondence, spreadsheet entries, news releases, and financial reports require different font styles to give them the appropriate professional "look." Resident fonts built into the printer, or font-character sets that can be readily inserted by the operator, are necessary for this purpose.

Electronic fonts—memory chips which house the standard characters found on most elements or printwheels—are a relatively new development. One microchip may house the standard characters found on most elements or printwheels, plus foreign language and special character sets, as well. To achieve the same variety of characters as those seen in one electronic font-character set, as many as 20 different elements or printwheels may be necessary.

Paper

Paper products for computers include labels, envelopes, file cards and postcards, invoice and statement forms, multipurpose checks and forms, and carbonless multipart forms. The bulk of paper usage, however, is in multipurpose printout paper for printers and letter-quality bond for word processing applications.

Paper for use with computer printers can be broadly classified into two types: *continuous-fold tractor-fed paper;* and *cut-sheet single-feed paper,* fed manually or by sheet feeder. Although the growing popularity of laser printers has led to an increased demand for cut-sheet paper, the demand for continuous tractor-fed paper remains equally strong.

Multipurpose Standard Printer Paper The varieties of printer and word processing papers available from office supply stores are too numerous to detail here. Basically, however, tractor-fed printer paper is sold in cartons of approximately 1,500 to 3,000 perforated sheets per carton.

Sheet sizes are standard letter size (8-1/2 × 11) or legal size (8-1/2 × 14) and may be all white or have a 1/2-inch green bar imprint on the surface. Multipart sets with carbon interleaves or carbonless finishes are also available. To accommodate larger printers, the paper is available in 132-column width as well as the standard 80-column size.

Letter-quality Bond Paper For business stationery, high-quality bond paper in 20 lb. weight is desirable. For distinctive appearance and durability, high rag content (50 percent or more) is also recommended. The company logo, along with the rag content in the paper is often displayed in a watermark impressed on business stationery.

Copier and Fax Paper Either sulfite or fiber paper may be used for most copiers. The manufacturers' directives on correct paper usage, however, will determine what type of paper to choose for maintenance-free operation. Thermal copiers and some facsimile machines require specially treated thermal-sensitive paper for copying and/or transmitting images.

Magnetic Media Storage Devices

The types of disks, tapes, and other magnetic media kept on hand in the office depend on the types of computer systems in use.

Soft-sector "floppy" disks in the 5-1/4-inch size are usually purchased in the DS/DD style; that is, in double-sided, double-density formats, ranging from 360 kilobytes (low density) up to 1.2 megabytes (high density) storage capacity. The smaller *rigid disks of 3-1/2-inch* diameter are also available in high-density or low-density formats.

Magnetic tapes are also used as storage media, especially for mainframe computers. With the increased usage of hard disks, magnetic tapes are becoming increasingly popular as backup media for the hard disk data.

Optical Disks Another option for the storage of electronic data, optical disks are currently impractical for general office usage because they are not readily erasable. However, optical disks hold great promise for the future, and the administrative assistant must keep abreast of developments in this technology. (See Chapter 10.)

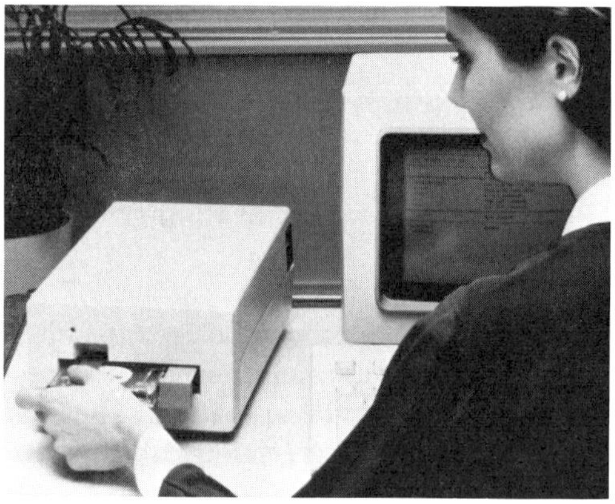

Figure 2-11 Three types of secondary storage for computer users: 3-½-inch diskettes and 5-¼-inch diskettes to store files created on personal computers, and a streaming tape drive to back up fixed disks. *Courtesy of IBM Corporation.*

BUDGETING FOR SUPPLIES

The office supplies budget is a substantial component of operations overhead. Well-defined policies of purchase and control of inventory, therefore, are absolutely essential to the cost-conscious firm. The administrative assistant, or a person working directly under his or her supervision, is frequently assigned this responsibility.

Purchase Economies

Buying in bulk quantities in order to receive volume discounts is a tempting lure to buyers of consumable items. However, while bulk purchasing does offer substantial savings, some drawbacks need to be considered.

For example, the shelf life of items—such as floppy disks and printed forms is relatively short; therefore, they should not be stocked in quantities to last beyond six months to a year. Also, shelf space for inventory items may be too limited to store great quantities, especially of bulky items. The trade-off between discounts received and storage space sacrificed may yield less to the buyer than first "meets the eye."

Sometimes, a special arrangement is made with the vendors whereby they deliver to the buyer, at prearranged times, portions of a volume order, rather than the entire order. This arrangement provides the best of both worlds for the purchaser—volume discounts for bulk purchases, plus "free" temporary storage space at the vendor's warehouse.

Better organization and economies of purchase may also be realized through adoption of these buying procedures:

1. Have one person do all the ordering; have others in the office make their requests through him or her.
2. Shop the "mailings"; mail order catalogs run frequent sales on special items.
3. Do comparative pricing on large items; consider service and convenience of local vendors, however, in purchase decisions.
4. Order in standard packs—10 pads to a box, 12 gross to a case, and so on.
5. When placing an order, have all available information at hand, such as account number, catalog numbers, colors, and weight.
6. To speed up delivery, order rush items by telephone, telex, or fax; the time saved may be as much as three days. Or request next-day delivery from the postal service or UPS.

Inventory Control

To insure inventory control these procedures are recommended:

1. Have a central location for the supplies inventory. Issue keys only to the person in charge.
2. Develop an internal requisition form for users to present in requesting items from the supplies inventory. Have frequently requested items preprinted on the form so that a check-off system may be used.
3. Maintain an updated count of each inventoried item so that reordering may be done as needed.
4. Keep a copy of order forms to check the merchandise received.

Electronic communication channels between suppliers and purchasers are gaining in popularity. Electronic ordering takes the place of the traditional procedures of manually counting and ordering supplies. The need for well-ordered monitoring, however, remains paramount to good inventory control.

SUMMARY

The administrative assistant is aware that the two principal components of a smooth-functioning office are a healthful work environment and efficient, cooperative personnel. However, it is important to realize that one other component is almost as crucial—adequate equipment and supplies.

Without good equipment and a ready stock of supplies, the personnel working in the healthful environment are powerless to "make things happen" in the office. Accordingly, the administrative assistant must be familiar with current equipment designs and keep a ready stock of supplies on hand. Since microcomputers, printers, and electronic typewriters are universal tools in today's offices, it is imperative that the administrative assistant understand these three pieces of equipment particularly well.

In terms of supplies, a broad-spectrum inventory is needed for both electronic and manual applications. Four items in inventory dominate the supply side of electronic office equipment. They include (1) paper, especially tractor paper, (2) ribbons for printers and electronic typewriters, (3) printwheels and type fonts, and (4) magnetic media.

Challenged to monitor the supplies budget, the administrative assistant practices certain economies in purchasing and establishes inventory control procedures as well. Through careful monitoring of the purchase and issuance of supplies, the company may save thousands of dollars annually.

QUESTIONS FOR REVIEW

1. What should a person consider when purchasing a computer?
2. List some of the features of electronic typewriters.
3. List the most popular styles of impact and nonimpact printers.
4. What is the average lifespan of a metal printwheel?
5. How do electronic fonts broaden one's choices in font selection?
6. What weight bond paper is recommended for business stationery?
7. With reference to 5-1/4-inch and 3-1/2-inch disks, what appears to be the trend for the future?
8. Describe specific suggestions for maintaining control of the supplies inventory.
9. What is meant by RAM memory?
10. What is the function of the arithmetic-logic unit in the microcomputer?

QUESTIONS FOR DISCUSSION

1. In an economy move, the authorities of your company have proposed certain "cost-saving" measures, some of which relate to the purchase and distribution of office supplies. As the administrative assistant, give your reaction to each of the following proposed measures.
   a. All paper purchased for computer printers (except for the laser printers) will be the least expensive sulfite paper available.
   b. Monoplastic printwheels will replace metal and dual-plastic printwheels as the latter wear out.
   c. Fabric ribbons will replace film ribbons.
   d. Floppy disks (5-1/2-inch size) will be bought in one- to two-year quantities in order to get volume discounts.
   e. Budget for supplies will be cut 20 percent "across the board."

f. An "honor" system will replace the requisitioning of supplies from inventory. The inventory control clerk will be reassigned to clerical duties, thus saving a "one-half" position.

2. The executives of a large construction firm are considering the purchase of electronic equipment to replace the aging electric typewriters the company has had for the past several years. Give your reaction to the following proposals:
   a. Purchase general-purpose microcomputers and the software needed for word processing. Buy no typewriters at all, since the microcomputers will suffice for all keyboarding tasks.
   b. Purchase electronic typewriters having all the sophisticated add-ons of high-end units. Since these typewriters can "word process" almost as well as micros and word processing software, no microcomputers will be purchased.
   c. Purchase microcomputers and word processing software, supplemented by electronic typewriters for form fill-ins, envelopes, and brief notes.

SUGGESTED ACTIVITIES

1. Consider yourself a potential purchaser of an electronic typewriter. Before buying, you want to gather enough information to make an informed decision.

   You enlist the aid of your fellow students; they agree to help by forming groups of four or five each to explore pictorial and printed information on electronic typewriters. To do this, they agree to carry out the following activities:
   a. Visit office supply stores to review catalogs and vendor brochures; they plan to share the materials with other class members if the store manager agrees to loan the materials.
   b. Research computer periodicals from the school library for articles and pictures which can be photocopied.
   c. Interview teachers and businesspersons who teach or use electronic typewriters regularly.
   d. List and compare the features of various brands of electronic typewriters, including price.

   When all the materials are gathered, one person leads a discussion which summarizes the features of each machine, concluding with a vote on which machine is the best "buy" for your purposes.
2. Following the preceding basic procedure, consider yourself the potential purchaser of a:
   a. microcomputer
   b. printer

   Decide in each case which is the best "buy" for your company.

REFERENCES

ANDERSON, CAROL, "For Most Applications, Supplies are Essential," *Office Systems '88* (January 1988), 37–38.

ANTONOFF, MICHAEL, "Living with a Laptop," *Personal Computing* (February 1989), 94–100.

BRINDZA, STEPHEN, "Watching Your Budget," *Modern Office Technology* (August 1987), 62–66.

BURNACZ, JOANNE G., "Eyeing PC Monitors," *Today's Office* (July 1989), 8–13.

CAMARRO, KEN, "Sizing up Screen-based Electronic Typewriters," *Today's Office* (May 1989), 54–57.

COWAN, WILLIAM M., "ETs Keep Pace with Times to Meet User Requirements," *Office Systems '89* (July 1989), 64–70.

FERNBERG, PATRICIA M., "Understanding the Product," *Modern Office Technology* (March 1989), 48–50.

FULVIO, JOSEPH, "Laser Printers are on the Beam," *Office Systems '89* (June 1987), 42–47.

HART, ROGER, "Computer Printers," *Office Systems '89* (October 1989), 47–51.

"How to Choose a Computer Printer," *St. Louis Business Journal* (January 1988), 20.

JENKINS, TOM, "Laser Printers, An Inside Look," *Office Systems '88* (May 1988), 78–80.

KMETZ, KEITH R., "Increase Your Impact with Serial Matrix Printers," *Todays' Office* (September 1988), 31–34.

MCCOOEY, EILEEN, "Features Abound on ETs," *Today's Office* (May 1989), 56.

MORTENSEN, ERIK, "Personal Computers: Tools Par Excellence," *The Office* (August 1988), 12–30.

SCHALLAN, JOE, "Laser Printers: Too Many Vendors Drive Prices Down," *Electronic Business* (April 15, 1988), 104–106.

TANZER, JOSHUA, "Backing Up: A Few Steps Toward Safer Data," *Administrative Management* (March 1988), 27–31.

Case Problem 1 Unit I *"Humanware" Needed*

The impact of office automation on federal government offices in Washington, DC is substantial. Millions of dollars are spent on hardware and software, thousands of microcomputers are placed on professionals' desks, and electronic networks are used to communicate between and among departments as well as with the White House itself.

According to one of the directors at the Center for Communications and Administrative Management in the Office of Personnel Management, the technology can be a very effective tool in the hands of competent managers who understand how to manage the "humanware" along with the software and hardware.

1. What does the term *humanware* mean to you?
2. What should be the attitude of managers toward staff members who "grew up" with the typewriters and manual procedures which many consider "old hat" today and who hesitate to adopt the new technology? How can managers ease the fears of these employees?
3. What educational avenues are open to businesses for training their employees in computer skills?

Case Problem 2 Unit I *"Thou Shalt Not Pirate Software"*

Except for certain applications, the copying of software programs is a violation of U.S. copyright law as amended on December 12, 1980, dealing with "limitations on exclusive rights: computer programs." The exceptions to the law involve copying which is essential for running of the program, and copying for archival purposes. (Public domain software is not affected by the law; it belongs to everyone.)

To protect their financial interests in their marketed software packages, many companies have resorted to "copy protection," a form of software or hardware deterrents to users' unauthorized copying of their software application programs.

However, this method of protection has so annoyed many users, particularly large corporate users, that the "big" software developers are relenting on their copy-protection schemes and depending instead on the honesty of their customers, trusting them *not* to cheat by illegally copying their software.

As the problem of software piracy mounts, developers are torn between the demands of their customers for more user-friendly access to their programs, and the developers' need to protect their software from pirates. No simple solutions have as yet been found to solve this dilemma.

1. Do you believe that the illegal copying of software is a common practice on your campus? in your city? If so, what can be done to alleviate the problem?
2. Do you recognize a similarity between this form of "stealing" and the stealing of another person's creative writing, or artistic endeavors?

Case Problem 3 Unit I *"Do-It-Yourself" Ergonomics*

Tight budgets and expensive furnishings prohibit many companies from making the kinds of improvements they would like to make in their office settings. For example, ergonomically designed furniture and special lighting may be beyond the means of businesses at the "cutting edge" of profitability.

As a cost-effective alternative, one state implemented a "do it-yourself" ergonomic approach to show users how to improve their work environment on their own. Thirteen state coordinators administered the program, teaching computer users how to combat health problems such as irritated eyes, blurred vision, and muscle strain.

In week-long courses, users were taught eye-relaxation exercises, controlled eye movements, and methods of relieving muscle tension in the back, arms, and legs. Workers were also encouraged to take hourly breaks of 30 seconds to three minutes for relaxation exercises.

They were shown how to reduce glare on their screens by repositioning their equipment or shielding overhead lights. Training was also given in short-term memory skills so that workers could recall blocks of text after a brief glance at their computer screens. The memory skills enabled them to increase their speed and accuracy while reducing the eye strain caused by constant focus on the screen. After the program was installed, productivity increased and morale improved.

1. Is this "do-it-yourself" approach to worker health and comfort appropriate? Should workers be asked to assist in providing for their own health and comfort?
2. Would you recommend that similar programs be installed in other offices? Explain.
3. Does such a program relieve the state agencies of any further responsibility in providing ergonomically designed work spaces and equipment?

Case Problem 4 Unit I *Do's and Don'ts of Automation*

One successful method of introducing automation into the office is through pilot automation projects. Called "trial balloons" by backers, pilot projects which deal with automation introduce users to electronic office procedures without committing them to a permanently installed system. That is, pilot projects allow users to try out a system before buying it.

Not all pilot projects are successful, however. For example, the employees of Marnie Edwards Manufacturing Company were surprised to hear that a pilot project for automating accounts was due to be installed in the accounting department within the next few weeks.

Most of the accounting staff were unaware that the revolutionary change was to take place until the leased computers arrived on the scene one Friday afternoon. They had not been consulted on the selection of either the software or the hardware to be used in the project. These decisions had been made by the board of directors, in consultation with company executives.

When installed, the vendor briefly introduced the hardware and software to the accounting staff, leaving instruction manuals for each. Users were encouraged to give the system their "best shot."

Two months later, the company abandoned the project. Company executives were disappointed that computerization neither sped procedures nor generated a marked improvement in account collections. Operators were frustrated by their inability to handle competently either the hardware or the software. All agreed that the company should return to its former manual procedures and abandon automation as nonfeasible.

1. What do you see as the cause for the failure of this pilot project? Was the project doomed from the start? Explain your answer.
2. How would *you* have handled this pilot project to assure a fairer appraisal of its worth? What advice would you give executives should they try automation again in the future?

UNIT

II

COMMUNICATIONS MANAGEMENT: MANUAL AND ELECTRONIC

Written communications progress through a three-phase cycle in business—from origination by the dictator to a dictation unit (or to a secretary) to final distribution to the intended receivers.

Identified as input, processing/output, and distribution, each phase exacts detailed attention. Dictation of the letter or memo requires knowledge and practice in the composition of documents which are clear, concise, and accurate in content, written with attention to rules of grammar and syntax. Keyboarding demands exactness in editing the written document, copying it for the files, and obtaining signatures. The distribution phase requires a knowledge of the options for mailing documents, shipping them by courier, or sending them electronically over telephone wires, and retaining disked or printed copies for file.

3
Business Letters, Memos, Reports

INTRODUCTION

Letters, interoffice memos, and business reports constitute the bulk of written communications regularly processed in the business office. To be effective in communicating with customers and clients, administrative assistants must continually sharpen their writing skills.

Sample documents presented in this chapter, together with guidelines for composing similar documents, are designed to help writers develop respectable writing skills. The guidelines presented are not meant to alter the communicator's writing style; that is, the individuality of the writer as expressed in writing, but they do suggest some "do's and don'ts" for successful writing which have proven themselves over the years.

The letters included represent a sampling of the types most frequently composed and read in the business environment. Broader and more thorough coverage of these and other types of business correspondence is left to texts devoted solely to business communications.

Terms in this chapter include:

doublespeak
business clichés
formal reports
open punctuation

COMPOSING BUSINESS LETTERS AND MEMOS

Effective communications, both written and oral, are vital to the success of a business. Business consultants consistently rank communication as one of the most important skills of business executives.

Communications which build goodwill by attracting (and keeping) customers provide businesses with a competitive edge. Companies with a good product and effective communicators succeed where their competitors, lacking one of these components, lose a proportionate share of the market.

Poorly written letters are costly, too. Each year the average cost of a business letter rises to a new high. Yet, studies show that many executive and managerial personnel, as well as administrative assistants, demonstrate weak writing skills.

Three common faults of writers are the use of dated business clichés, a lack of sensitivity to readers' points of view, and lack of clarity.

Business Jargon, Clichés

"In reply to your letter, we wish to advise" is typical of the clichés still accepted by many writers as standard openers for business letters. Such worn expressions bore readers and brand writers as "dated" in their writing styles. The following excerpts are typical examples of similarly "dated" expressions:

"Yours of the 31st received and contents noted"
"In re your order of the 15th"
"In reply to same"
"Enclosed please find"
"Trusting in your early reply, I remain"
"Thanking you in advance"

Lack of Reader Centeredness

Some writers unintentionally overuse ego-centered "I" and "our" in their business letters. Like business jargon, the "I" focus tends to bore, if not offend, readers. Although writers do not intentionally project an egotistical image, their lack of "reader centeredness" has the same effect.

A "you" and "your" focus, on the other hand, attracts the attention of readers and tends to draw a positive response from them.

Lack of Clarity

A writer's use of obscure terms and vague explanations may be unintentional or it may be a form of escapism. In the latter case, writers who want to avoid making commitments or taking responsibility for their actions employ ambiguous terms which imply something other than what the words actually say.

Ambiguity is the stock in trade of persons who deliberately deceive their readers. When readers misconstrue the meaning and intent of a message *implied* by the writer, the writer may feel excused from any obligation to perform as "promised," since in fact the message does not actually *say* what is implied.

Business writers who do not *intentionally* mislead their readers often net the same effect through their choice of ambiguous terms. Whatever the intent, this form of faulty communication has a name. It is called "doublespeak." Plain English is its antidote.

"Doublespeak" *Doublespeak* has been defined as language designed to hoodwink the reader into accepting a lie as truth. Public officials who say one thing and mean another use doublespeak. "Con" artists use doublespeak to prey on unsuspecting victims of their deceptions.

The U.S. Office of Consumer Affairs studied the language of federal agencies in Washington and found that doublespeak is preferred to plain English. The report said that the U.S. Office of Education uses unclear English 36 percent of the time; the Social Security Administration, 47 percent of the time.

Plain English *Plain English* is language that cannot be misunderstood by the average person. The language is forthright, without artifice of any kind, spoken in the idiom of the person of average educational background.

Some business organizations, in an attempt to bolster their employees' abilities to speak (and write) in plain English, have launched major campaigns to improve communications skills. For example, Ford Motor Company established a "Plain-English" subcommittee to revise its warranty information booklet and technical service bulletins.

A sample "before" and "after" excerpt from their warranty booklet demonstrates the success of their "plain-English" rewrites:

> *Old Version:*
>
> Repairs to correct perforation from corrosion of any body sheet metal panels are covered to 36 months from the warranty start date, regardless of mileage. (Repair of corrosion due to a defect, without perforation, is covered for 12 months or 12,000 miles, whichever occurs first.)[1]
>
> *New Version:*
>
> Here are details about your corrosion coverage.
>
> What is covered?
>
> > The body sheet metal panels of your car or light truck are covered against corrosion due to a defect.
>
> How long does corrosion coverage last?
>
> > The period of coverage depends on whether the corrosion causes holes. If the corrosion does not cause holes, the corrosion damage is covered for 12 months or 12,000 miles, whichever occurs first.
> >
> > If the corrosion does cause holes, the corrosion damage is covered for up to six years or 100,000 miles, whichever occurs first.

[1]"Ford Warranty Information," 1986 and 1987 Model Cars and Light Trucks, Ford Motor Company.

Figure 3-1 Administrative assistants may be assigned to handle many of the correspondence duties on their own initiative. *Courtesy of IBM Corporation.*

Other documents from the Parts and Service Division were also revised. Customers responded positively; they expressed appreciation especially of the company's avoidance of "legalese" in its explanation of warranty provisions. Ford designated the new Warranty Information Booklet the "star" of its campaign to rewrite the company's documents into plain English.

LETTER FORMATS AND PUNCTUATION STYLES

Three letter styles dominate in business communications today: the modified block style, the block style, and the AMS simplified style, designed by the Administrative Management Society in the 1950s.

In the block style, all lines including the date, closing lines, and paragraph openers begin at the left margin. This style is widely accepted for its contemporary appearance and its practical time-saving features.

The modified block style may or may not have indented paragraphs, but the closing lines are indented, usually to coincide with the date line. Less formal in appearance than the block style, it presents a balanced "picture-frame" format which appeals to many writers.

The AMS simplified letter is blocked to the left margin; it does not utilize the traditional greeting or complimentary closing lines. Instead, in place of "Gentlemen," the AMS style uses a subject line typed in all caps. In place of the complimentary closing, the signature and title (if given) is shown in all caps.

Interoffice Memos

Designed to save time and effort for both writer and reader, interoffice memos omit the inside address, salutation, and complimentary closings normally used with outgoing correspondence. Instead, headings identify: "Date," "To," "From," and "Subject." Samples of memos and letters, identified by type, follow.

Punctuation Styles

"Open" punctuation in business correspondence utilizes no mark of punctuation following the salutation or the closing. "Normal" or "mixed" punctuation includes a colon after the greeting and a comma following the complimentary closing. Both styles are illustrated in the following letters.

TYPES OF LETTERS/MEMOS

Business letters can be classified into one of the following three categories by the type of message each conveys:

Letters/memos which *inform*
Letters/memos which *attempt to influence or persuade*
Letters/memos which *convey a personal message for a special occasion*

The first two categories—informational and persuasive messages—comprise the bulk of business communications. Special-occasion letters, though less frequent in number, focus on an integral component of all communications—the human element.

Informational messages are the least difficult to write of the three types. Straightforward and factual, informational letters focus simply on the facts, presenting them with courtesy, clarity and completeness.

Persuasive messages require sensitivity to other persons' needs as well as a powerful mastery of words. Their objective is to convince, sell, influence, or in some way affect the reader positively so that he or she will act favorably toward the writer.

Special-occasion messages require a special "touch." Responding to associates' personal triumphs with notes of congratulation; or to their distress in times of sadness—these letters present a special challenge. Nevertheless, occasions which call for such letters are frequent enough to warrant expending the effort required to learn to write them well.

Letters that Inform

Letters which inform or seek information include most of the day-to-day correspondence processed in the office. Some of the most common letters of this type are:

1. Inquiries (requests) for material or information; responses to inquiries; acknowledgments
2. Orders for service or merchandise (when order forms are not available); corrections and adjustments on flawed orders, bills, or merchandise
3. Covering letters accompanying merchandise or printed materials

Inquiry Series The inquiry series consists of brief, direct letters providing or asking for basic information. Courtesy is projected through positive words of appreciation and cooperation. Typical letters of inquiry, response, and acknowledgment are shown on the following pages. Note the following features in the first letter of the series, a request for more information on the Collector's Library of Literary Masterpieces.

> The writer provides the reader with a complete reference on the source of her information regarding the Literary Masterpieces. The company can thus identify which of their published ads have been most effective in winning customer interest.
>
> Although the writer *hints* that the ad writer may have erred in failing to provide complete information in a recent advertisement, no annoyance or frustration is expressed.
>
> The closing requests a specific action by the reader, leaving no doubt as to the writer's request for verification or correction.

The manager responds to the inquiry promptly. Notice these features of her response (p. 62):

> The letter opens with a "thank you" for the inquiry, and an acknowledgment of oversight in failing to list all of the titles in the series.
>
> A flyer giving more details on the Masterpieces is enclosed to help Ms. Brandt reach an affirmative decision on ordering the Collector's Library.
>
> "You are correct, Ms. Brandt," in the second paragraph fulfills the writer's request for verification and adds a friendly tone of affirmation.
>
> The final paragraph encourages the potential customer to order the complete library.

Ms. Brandt is delighted with the information and sales literature the company has sent her about the Collector's Library. She sends an acknowledgment and order to the company (p. 63). Note her courtesy and her definitive subscription order.

Orders and Adjustments Letters are necessary for placing orders when order forms for goods or services are not available to would-be buyers. Like letters of inquiry, letters which place orders are normally brief, factual, and uncomplicated. Simple to master, the order letter includes the name of the item(s) ordered, the catalog number (if known), size if applicable, reference to an enclosed check or the number of the account to be charged, and the name and address of the purchaser.

August 24,1991

Treasures In Print Inc.
1000 White Oaks Road
Milwaukee, WI 53201

Gentlemen:

Your recent advertisement in the *Journal of English Poetry* offered the Collector's Library of Literary Masterpieces at a cost of $19.95 per volume.

The ad did not say how many volumes comprised the complete set, nor did it give a complete list of the titles and authors included. From the description and pictures provided in the ad, however, I feel certain that the Collector's Library of Literary Masterpieces is for me. I would appreciate your sending me a list of all the titles and authors included in the set.

I understand that if I order the series, I will be billed monthly with the receipt of each volume, and that I may discontinue the series at any time without further obligation.

Please verify or correct this information so that I may decide whether or not to subscribe to the series.

Thank you.

Sincerely,

Laura Brandt
2960 Golfing Green
Dallas, Texas 75234

sk

Letter Style: Block
Punctuation Style: Normal (Mixed)

TREASURES IN PRINT, INC.
1000 WHITE OAKS ROAD
MILWAUKEE, WI 53201

August 27, 1991

Ms. Laura Brandt
2960 Golfing Green
Dallas, TX 75234

Dear Ms. Brandt:

Thank you for your inquiry about the Collector's Library of Literary Masterpieces. Please forgive our oversight in failing to list all the titles included in the series. The enclosed flyer lists each of the 20 volumes by title and author and provides sample pages from these exquisitely bound masterpieces.

You are correct, Ms. Brandt; if you subscribe to the Collector's Library, you will be mailed one volume per month, together with an invoice and a return-addressed envelope for your convenience in remitting the $19.95 cost. You can also cancel your subscription at any time without further obligation.

We are certain that you will be delighted with the Collector's Library of Literary Masterpieces, Ms. Brandt. We look forward to receiving your order.

Thank you for your inquiry.

Sincerely,

TREASURES IN PRINT, INC.

Adele Michenor, Manager
Customer Service

lh

Enclosure

Letter Style: Modified Block
Punctuation Style: Normal

September 1, 1991

Treasures in Print, Inc.
1000 White Oaks Road
Milwaukee WI 53201

Gentlemen

The sales flyer on the Collector's Library of Literary Masterpieces arrived yesterday, providing all the information I requested in my letter of August 24.

Thank you for your immediate response.

Yes, I do look forward with delight to receiving each of the volumes in the Masterpiece series. Please enter my subscription and send me the first volume promptly. You may bill me monthly with each volume sent. The number of my credit card account is given below.

Thank you.

Sincerely

Laura Brandt
2960 Golfing Green
Dallas TX 75234

sk

VISA Credit Acct. No. XXXXXXXXXXXXXX
Expiration date: ------------------

Letter Style: Block
Punctuation Style: Open

Figure 3-2 Dictation and transcription is a team effort between the executive and the administrative assistant. *Courtesy of IBM Corporation.*

For the sake of clarity, an order letter is often written in tabular style; that is, the items ordered are enumerated under columnar headings similar to the format of an order form. For example, items ordered from a retail catalog might look like this:

CATALOG NUMBER	*QUANTITY*	*DESCRIPTION*	*UNIT COST*	*TOTAL PRICE*
R639-4688	2	AT&T Answering Machine	159.99	319.98
R639-5032	3	AT&T Cordless Telephone 4400	119.95	359.85
		Total price		$679.83

The order for these items is incorporated into the letter on p. 65.

Adjustment Letters In companies where orders are filled on a regular basis, adjustments are necessary from time to time. Sales personnel, shipping clerks, bookkeepers, and intermediaries in the distribution channels are all prone to error occasionally; sometimes, too, the merchandise is flawed or damaged in transit and must be replaced.

Frequently, the customer is at fault in ordering the wrong items (too big, too small, incompatible with existing equipment, and so on). Or the merchandise does not suit the customer's taste in color, price, or style—factors outside the scope of the seller's area of responsibility.

PARKERSBURG OFFICE SUPPLY
Washington Avenue
Parkersburg WV 26100

July 8, 1990

J. C. Penney Company, Inc.
Catalog Division
Milwaukee WI 53263-0370

Gentlemen

Please send the following items to the Personnel Department, Parkersburg Office Supply, at the address shown in our letterhead. You may charge the sale to Account No. L-3289-01.

CATALOG NUMBER	*QUANTITY*	*DESCRIPTION*	*UNIT COST*	*TOTAL PRICE*
R639-4688	2	AT&T Answering Machine	159.99	319.98
R639-5032	3	AT&T Cordless Telephone 4400	119.95	359.85
		Total price		$679.83

We will appreciate your shipping this order to us as soon as possible. Thank you.

Sincerely

Elaine Newcomb, Manager
Personnel Department

rs

Letter Style: Block
Punctuation Style: Open

Typically, the customer's satisfaction is given the highest priority in all circumstances. The seller realizes that disputing the claim will probably cost more in future sales than the cost of a refund. Consequently, requests for adjustment are usually resolved in the customer's favor.

A typical response to a customer's request for adjustment follows on p. 67. The customer had ordered typewriter ribbons for 30 electronic typewriters, but received ribbons for computer printers instead.

Parkersburg Office Supply immediately acknowledges its error in filling the order improperly; it then offers an adjustment which hopefully will retain the customer's good will while it corrects the inventory clerk's mistake.

Notice in the letter that Elliot Edwards immediately assures the customer that the requested ribbons are enroute to him. He then apologizes for the "mix-up" and accepts responsibility for the error. In closing, he expresses the hope that the "mixup" will in no way damage the good relations "we have enjoyed for years with your company."

Covering Letters A covering letter is one which accompanies other materials, typically assembled for mailing to customers or potential customers. The covering letter serves to verify for both the sender and the receiver the content of the accompanying materials and the date on which they were mailed. It may also include an explanation of the accompanying materials. For example, a covering letter may accompany a sales brochure mailed to potential customers; internally, a covering letter may summarize a business report compiled for company executives.

Like all business letters meant primarily to inform, covering letters aim primarily at completeness and courtesy. No complex issues are involved; no persuasive arguments are needed to win the reader's support. Therefore, the cover-

Figure 3-3 Laptop computers enable executives to stay "on top" of their correspondence while traveling. *Courtesy of IBM Corporation.*

PARKERSBURG OFFICE SUPPLY
Washington Avenue
Parkersburg WV 26100

September 5, 1991

Biltmore Builders, Inc.
Accounting Department
3045 Osage Road
Mattoon IL 61938

Gentlemen:

Thank you for your letter of September 2 requesting an adjustment on your order NO. R-1432.

The electronic typewriter ribbons that you ordered are on their way to you today.

We apologize for the error; it is entirely our fault. The 30 printer ribbons mistakenly sent to you had been misshelved with the typewriter ribbons in our supply warehouse. The inventory clerk, in his eagerness to provide immediate and efficient service, failed to notice the markings on the box which clearly identified the contents as printer, not typewriter, ribbons.

At your convenience, please ship the printer ribbons back to us C.O.D. We do not want you to incur any expense, even shipping charges, because of our error.

We hope that this "mixup" has in no way damaged the good relations we have enjoyed for years with your company. Your account is very important to us.

Sincerely,

Elliot Edwards
Administrative Assistant

ds

Letter Style: Block

ing letter is fairly "matter of fact," including all the necessary information, presented courteously and concisely.

A typical example is seen in the letter on p. 69, addressed to Dunlap Paper Products. Notice that Parkersburg Office Supply lists the shipped items by catalog number, description, quantity, and price.

It also itemizes the disks and supporting materials included with each software program, thus simplifying the task of checking and verifying receipt of the materials. The letter closes with a courteous "thank you" for the order received.

Letters that Persuade

Most business people try to build support for their company or product, however subtly, in all their communications. Through positive language and tone, they attempt to "sell" their company in all their letters, regardless of the express purpose of each communication. However, letters which are expressly designed to persuade a reader to a point of view commonly fall into one of these three categories:

1. sales letters for a vendor's product or service
2. collection letters which attempt to retrieve past-due payments from errant debtors
3. personal letters of application which attempt to "sell" an applicant's capabilities to a potential employer

The common strain running through all persuasive letters is their final objective—convincing the reader to take the action the writer suggests.

Over 75 percent of the letters in the persuasive-letter category are sales and collection letters. The letter on p. 70 is a typical sales letter. It attempts to

Figure 3-4 Microcassette tapes and "shirt-pocket" dictation units enable travelers to dictate their correspondence at any hour of the day or night. *Courtesy of Dictaphone Corporation.*

PARKERSBURG OFFICE SUPPLY
Washington Avenue
Parkersburg WV 26100

September 12, 1991

Dunlap Paper Products
5200 Eleventh Street
San Angelo TX 76900

Gentlemen:

In response to your Order No. S-2890 requesting computer software programs for your office, the following items are included in the package attached hereto.

ITEM NO.	*DESCRIPTION OF ITEM*	*QUANTITY ORDERED*	*PRICE PER UNIT*	*TOTAL PRICE*
90-0496	Advanced Data Accts Payable	1 pkg	$600.	$ 600.
90-0495	Advanced Data Accts Receivable	1 pkg	$600.	$ 600.
90-0497	Advanced Data General Ledger	1 pkg	$600.	$ 600.
90-0215	Accounting Partner Plus	1 pkg	$795.	$ 795.
		Total		$2,595.

Each of the packages contain two system disks, a complete reference manual, a tutorial, and a quick reference guide.

Please verify that all listed items have been received by you in good order. If any items are missing, please let us know so that we can ship them to you promptly.

Thank you for your order.

Sincerely,

Elliot Edwards
Administrative Assistant

ds

Letter Style: Block
Punctuation Style: Normal

KLEAR-AIR CORPORATION
P.O. Box 1000
Detroit MI 48233

October 10, 1991

Parkersburg Office Supply
Washington Avenue
Parkersburg WV 26100

Gentlemen:

Congratulations! Your company's plans for expansion, as announced in the Sunday Times, is cause for celebration. As you develop architectural plans for adding a new wing to your present facility, let Klear-Air Corporation demonstrate how to provide a climatized environment for the entire plant.

Klear-Air leads the industry in sales of climate-control units for both commerical and residential buildings. Its record for reliability and cost effectiveness has never been surpassed.

Our representative, Ken Warren, will be in your vicinity during the week of October 19–23. At that time, he would like to meet with your facility manager to discuss how best Klear-Air can serve your air-conditioning requirements. Since our plans are customized to fit our customers' needs, we are sure that we can design the ideal installation for Parkersburg Office Supply.

Ken will telephone you within the next day or two to set up an appointment. Meanwhile, we enclose for your perusal a brochure which details the many superior features of a Klear-Air unit. We think you will agree that Klear-Air pays benefits far exceeding its installation and operational costs.

Sincerely,

Jason Neimeyer, Manager

s

Letter Style: Block
Punctuation Style: Normal

convince readers of the advantages of central air conditioning in homes or offices, and of the superior quality of Klear-Air Conditioners.

Collection Letters Collection letters usually start with a simple reminder to the overdue debtor that his or her account is overdue. If the debtor does not respond within a reasonable length of time, the reminder is followed up by a polite inquiry, as the second stage of the collection series. At this stage, the customer is still given the "benefit of the doubt" concerning his or her intentions to pay.

If this second stage of the collection series brings no response, communications take on a tone of urgency and/or demand, depending on the debtor's credit history with the company. The following collection letter to Dunlap Paper Products, Inc. is in the third stage.

The letter on p. 72 from Parkersburg Office Supply to the overdue debtor, Dunlap Paper Products, illustrates a firm but conciliatory tone. Two reminder letters had preceded the December 14 letter; neither had drawn a response. Now Parkersburg Office Supply attempts to motivate the company to action by appealing to company pride in their long-standing reputation as a good credit risk.

Had the customer been a first-time buyer, the tone might have been less conciliatory. But, because Dunlap is an old customer, the writer employs the soft approach, appealing to the debtor's sense of fair play and honor.

FINAL LETTER IN COLLECTION SERIES The final letter in a collection series is seen in the letter from Eisor Corporation to the Taylor Advertising Agency, shown on page 73. After a long series of fruitless attempts to collect the overdue amount, Eisor Corporation finally threatens to turn the account over to a collection agency.

Note, however, that despite all the negative pressures bearing upon the situation, the writer still endeavors to retain the debtor's good will. The letter to Taylor Advertising Agency, the final one in a series of four, exhibits an acceptable balance between sternness and conciliation.

Applications for Employment Letters of application attempt to persuade a potential employer that an applicant is qualified for a position with his or her firm. The primary objective of the letter is to secure an interview with a company official and, subsequently, a job offer.

Application letters present unique problems. Without projecting egotistical images, applicants must convince employers that they are well qualified for challenging positions.

Basically, applicants must "sell" themselves, a difficult task for persons who are not used to trumpeting their own talents. They must present their qualifications candidly, without understating (or overstating) their professional competencies. Their letters should incorporate, at minimum, these five factors:

PARKERSBURG OFFICE SUPPLY
Washington Avenue
Parkersburg WV 26100

December 14, 1991

Dunlap Paper Products, Inc.
5200 Eleventh Street
San Angelo TX 76900

Gentlemen

Your account with us, totaling $2,595, is now two months overdue. We wrote to you on October 14, reminding you of the overdue amount. Having received no response, we wrote a second letter to you on November 10. Almost five weeks have passed since our second mailing to you; still you have not responded.

We are puzzled by your inaction.

For many years, your company, as one of our most valued customers, has enjoyed unlimited credit with our firm. Please do not let an unresolved debt mar your credit standing with us now. If you are unable to mail us your check for the entire amount, let us work with you in devising a mutually satisfactory payment plan.

Your immediate action will restore your company to its former position as one of our best credit customers. Please let us hear from you as quickly as possible.

Thank you.

Sincerely

Allen Jenson, CPA
Accounting Department

sd

Letter Style: Block
Punctuation Style: Open

EISOR CORPORATION
5000 Skelly Drive West
Tulsa OK 74101

October 7, 1991

Mr. Bradford Taylor
Taylor Advertising Agency
Belleville IL 62223

YOUR OVERDUE ACCOUNT WITH US

Your account balance of $945, Mr. Taylor, is now four months overdue. Your June 8 order for paper and printing supplies was shipped to you promptly on June 10 as you requested, together with our invoice for $945, due within 30 days.

To date, we have written you three letters reminding you of the past-due amount, but you have ignored our letters. If financial circumstances prevent your paying in full, Mr. Taylor, we ask that you write us today. We will endeavor to arrange a schedule of small monthly payments due over the next three or four months.

We want to be fair, Mr. Taylor. Help us to do that by upholding your part of the sales contract. Please send us your check or write us your plans for payment within the next seven days.

If we do not hear from you within that time, we will be forced to place your account in the hands of a collection agency.

ALLEN JENSON, CPA

jr

Letter Style: AMS Simplified

September 21, 1991

Ms Janice Ochs, Vice-President
Accounting and Finance
Eisor Corporation
5000 Skelly Drive West
Tulsa OK 74101

Dear Ms Ochs

Mr. Michael Brennan of Eisor Corporation's Accounting department has told me of an opening for an Administrative Assistant in your company which will materialize on June 1.

On May 15, I will be awarded a B.S. Degree in Administrative Information Systems from Eastern Illinois University. As you can see from my enclosed resume, the course work I have completed in achieving this degree, plus my internship at R J Donnelley Corporation and three summers of work experience in suburban Chicago offices should qualify me well for the position as Administrative Assistant with your company.

I have held offices in three student organizations, and am currently president of Collegiate Business Women, the largest student organization for women students on campus. These leadership roles have strengthened my ability to shoulder responsibilities and to promote harmonious relations, abilities which should serve Eisor Corporation well.

I would appreciate the opportunity to discuss with you in person my qualifications for a position at Eisor Corporation. May I have an interview with you, Ms Ochs? I can be reached by telephone most afternoons at (217) 345-6128.

Sincerely

Janice Stillgartner
1801 Eighteenth Street
Charleston IL 61920

Letter Style: Block
Punctuation Style: Open

1. Be addressed to a particular person by name, if possible; or by title, if the name is not known.
2. Enclose a personal resume summarizing the candidate's educational qualifications and work experience.
3. Focus on the most positive aspects of the resume, especially as related to the prospective position.
4. Stress what the applicant can contribute to the company.
5. Ask for an interview.

The letter on p. 74 addressed to the Eisor Corporation illustrates how one applicant incorporated these factors smoothly into her letter of application.

Special-Occasion Letters and Memos

A wide variety of business communications comprise the category of special-occasion messages. Two types illustrated in this unit are messages which offer congratulations to colleagues who have been promoted or honored in a special way and condolences to bereaved employees or their families. A common thread running through all such communications is warmth and concern for the reader.

Letter of Congratulations An example of good taste in a congratulatory letter is illustrated in the interoffice memo on p. 76. Don Houghout has just been promoted to the position of Manager of Personnel at Eisor Corporation. Because this is an internal communication, it is written on the company's standard interoffice memo form.

Letter of Condolence Condolence notes are particularly difficult to write. The greater the loss, the more helpless people feel in responding to a bereaved colleague's grief. Frequently, however, "saying it with flowers" is not enough; a note of condolence, however brief, is appropriate.

The note to Mary Lynn Jacobs (p. 77) on the occasion of her husband's death illustrates good taste in a brief but genuine note of sympathy.

EISOR CORPORATION

Date: October 28, 1991

To: Don Houghout
Manager, Personnel

From: Sarah Jane Billings
Vice-President, Marketing

Subject: Your promotion

Don, congratulations on your recent elevation to the managerial ranks! I know that you will fill the position of Manager of Personnel with your usual vigor and enthusiasm.

No one at Eisor has proven such effectiveness on the job and loyalty to Eisor as you have, Don. Your seventeen years of devoted and untiring service to the company have earned you the respect of all members of the board.

Your promotion is well deserved.

May you enjoy many more years with the Eisor "family."

SJB

Interoffice Memorandum

EISOR CORPORATION
5000 Skelly Drive West
Tulsa, OK 74101

December 10, 1991

Mrs. Mary Lynn Jacobs
1834 20 Street
Portland, OR 97208

Dear Mary Lynn:

Word of Harry's death just reached our office. Please accept our sincere condolences.

Since Harry's retirement from Eisor, we had been pleased to hear on repeated occasions of the lovely vacation trips the two of you had taken. We're glad that you were both able to enjoy the retirement relaxation he had so long anticipated.

We feel your loss with you, Mary Lynn. If there is any way we can assist you, now or in the future, please do get in touch with us.

Sincerely,

L. A. Sumter
President

pd

Condolence Note

INTERNATIONAL COMMUNICATIONS

In communicating with persons in foreign countries, Americans frequently fail to make themselves clearly understood. By using idiomatic expressions unfamiliar to their foreign communicators, Americans may jeopardize their business relationships with a large segment of potential customers.

For example, executives who are accustomed to the everyday expressions "touch base," "bottom line," "uptight," and "home free" are surprised when non-Americans misinterpret the meaning of these expressions.

Foreign businesspeople, even when totally fluent in "textbook" English, are not prepared to bridge the communications gap between themselves and Americans on the basis of American idioms. Neither do they understand American punctuation.

In order to avoid miscommunicating with customers in other countries, good communicators should follow these guidelines:

Completely avoid the use of slang expressions or idioms unless certain of the reader's familiarity with the terms being used.

Overpunctuate, if necessary, in order to be better understood.

Write numbers and dates in the style used in the country of the reader.

Keep a dictionary at hand, one written in the language of the reader.

If communicating with one or two foreign countries regularly, invest the time and energy necessary to learn their languages. The energy expended will be returned in the form of good will and, probably, more business.

CONTROLLING COSTS

The amount of time and energy invested in business correspondence makes communications a very costly facet of business operations. To hold down costs, business analysts suggest some streamlined communications procedures. Some of their most practical suggestions include these:

1. Keep letters and memos as brief as courtesy and the complexity of the message allow.
2. Insofar as possible, reserve a special time each day for dictation, preferably early in the day. Have all relevant information at hand.
3. Dictate correspondence in order of priority.
4. Use form letters for repetitive correspondence.
5. Let the secretary answer routine letters.
6. Adopt simple letter styles, such as the simplified letter or the block style.
7. Opt for use of the telephone rather than written communications when a written record is not necessary.
8. Respond informally to some correspondents by handwritten marginal notes, returning the original letter with its response on the same sheet. Photocopy the

letter and its marginal response for the file before returning. (Exercise caution in employing this shortcut method; some correspondents may be offended by the informality.)

BUSINESS REPORTS

Business reports make up a substantial portion of written communications in business. Ranking second only to business letters, reports are generally, but not always, meant for internal use. In fact, the interoffice memo is the most frequent format chosen for informal report writing.

Reports vary in length and complexity from a half-page interoffice memo to a formal multipage manuscript reporting the results of complex research. Research projects, usually focused on issues pertinent to the company's growth or direction, are presented to company decision makers in formal manuscript-style reports.

For example, a three-month exploration of a new product's market potential might culminate in a twenty-page formal report presenting the research team's findings to company executives.

Figure 3-5 Mag card equipment introduced by IBM in the 1970s enabled users to store correspondence on magnetic cards for later retrieval and reprint. Predating contemporary word processors, the equipment represented a giant step forward in electronic convenience at the time. *Courtesy of IBM Corporation.*

Frequently, major decisions hinge upon the content of a business report; hence, their importance to management.

Less momentous reports are part and parcel of daily communications. Exchanged regularly among office personnel, informal reports provide answers and insights on current issues. As in formal report writing, however, informal reports require more than a "bare bones" presentation of information on the issues; the writer's personal conclusions are expected as well.

Examples of informal report writing are illustrated in the following inter-office memos. Note the directness and the brevity of the memos, coupled with the warmth of friendly exchange among business colleagues.

Formal Report Writing

Formal business reports vary in writing style. Traditionally characterized by the impersonal mode of third-person expression, the current trend in formal report writing is toward greater personalization. A casual first-person writing style is rapidly becoming the norm rather than the exception for most formal business reports.

The traditional style, however, is nowhere near its demise; many research specialists believe that serious research deserves nothing less than strict formal reporting, with all the rigors demanded of formal analytical reports.

Formats vary as well. Depending on the length and complexity of the report, the following elements may be included in a formal business report.

Prefatory Section

1. *Title Page.* The title page includes the report title, the date, the name and professional title of the authors, and in the case of team research, the members of the research team.
2. *Letter of Transmittal.* The letter of transmittal written by the authors is addressed to the persons who either authorized the research or are most likely to be affected by its content. If meant for the public, this may be a "To whom it may concern" letter.
3. *Synopsis.* The synopsis provides an overview for the busy reader, summarizing the purpose, procedure, major findings or issues, and sometimes recommendations by the authors. It may be titled a Summary, Epitome, Abstract, Precis, or Synopsis.
4. *Contents.* The contents section lists major topics and subtopics of the report, each indexed by page number. Illustrations, tables, and charts are often listed separately. Pagination of contents is not generally provided for reports of less than ten pages in length.

Report Proper

1. *Introduction.* The introduction is treated as the first part of the report proper. This includes the purpose, scope, and method of procedure followed in pursuing the research. Nonresearch reports include purpose or rationale for the report, and the scope of the issues discussed therein.
2. *Major Topics.* This is the formal presentation of the facts, objectively stated. Each major topic is divided into subtopics so all facets affecting major issues can be

EISOR CORPORATION

Date: November 15, 1991

To: Bill Sanford
Purchasing Department

From: Jim Higgins
Facility Manager

Subject: Purchase of three printers for Personnel Dept.

Bill, following up on our request for the purchase of three printers for the Personnel Department, I am attaching vendor flyers on two models that fulfill the specifications Personnel outlined in its requisition. Features of the two printers are compared in my table below; hopefully, this will make your selection easier.

MODEL	*PRINT SPEED*	*PRINTHEAD*	*PAPER FEED*	*COST*
X-2200	200 cps in draft mode; 55 cps LQ	24-pin Dot Matrix	friction-feed & tractor-feed	$499
HQ-409	220 cps in draft mode; 39 cps LQ	24-pin Dot Matrix	friction-feed & tractor-feed	$539

The Model X-2200 also feeds paper from both front and rear. Immediate service on both models is promised by vendors; however, the Model X-2200 is serviced locally, while the HQ-409 must be serviced from Longtree, some 30 miles distant.

Both models are:
compatible with our computers
have good service records
have desirable front-panel controls
are acceptable to Personnel

The choice is yours, Bill. Just let us know when we can expect shipment. Personnel is ANXIOUS to have them! J.H.

Interoffice Memorandum

SYDE CORPORATION

Date: July 6, 1991

To: Joseph Murray
Publications

From: Bill Werden
Employee Relations

Subject: "IN-SYDE"—suggestions for improvement

Several suggestions have surfaced from our recent survey of employees relative to our company newsletter, "IN-SYDE." The questionnaire solicited suggestions from employees at all levels—from the executive branch to operatives in the shipping department. Their suggestions are summarized below.

1. Use more pictures of employees with their families at special events, such as weddings and graduations.
2. Initiate a column for employee contributions. Here employees could offer suggestions or comments, or even air their gripes on work-related issues. Something like "Comment Corner" would be an appropriate title.
3. Publish the newsletter more frequently. *All* the respondents said that a monthly issue was too infrequent, but there was no unanimity on how often it *should* be published. Most frequently suggested: semi-monthly.
4. Improve the image of the newsletter by incorporating fonts and graphics similar to professional typesetting. This could be done by purchasing one of the many desktop publishing software packages.

If you would like to review the survey returns yourself, Joe, I will be glad to share them with you. I've outlined here only the most frequently suggested ideas; others may be equally valid.

Overall, you are to be commended for producing such a widely read publication. The employees do appreciate it, and certainly they *do* read it!

BW

Interoffice Memorandum

treated in depth. Analyses of the facts, illustrated through diagrams, charts, and tables, are important components of the body of the report.

3. *Conclusions.* The author's interpretation of the facts presented in Part 2 result in his or her conclusions, presented in Part 3. To be valid, the conclusions drawn must be supported by the data presented.
4. *Recommendations.* A course of action is recommended by the author, based on the conclusions presented in Part 3.
5. *References.* Sometimes placed in the appendix section, the reference section lists both primary and secondary sources utilized by the author. For the readers' convenience, these are usually classified under subheadings, such as "Books," "Periodicals," and "Other" secondary sources. If only secondary sources are used, this section can be labeled a "Bibliography."
6. *Appendix.* The appendix contains material which is relevant to the topic but not essential to its presentation in the body of the report. For example, the questionnaire used in a marketing research project is placed in the appendix, as are lengthy excerpts from secondary sources utilized by the author in the report.

SUMMARY

Informational letters comprise the major portion of communications processed by businesses on a "day-in day-out" basis. To be effective, informational letters must present complete factual data with clarity and courtesy. Three letter types which are classified as informational are (1) letters of inquiry, or responses thereto, (2) orders for service or merchandise, plus communications related to orders, such as adjustments or corrections, and (3) covering letters mailed along with accompanying merchandise or printed materials.

Letters which attempt to persuade the readers to the writer's point of view may include sales letters, collection letters, and applications for employment.

Persuasive letters require above-average letter-writing skill if they are to achieve their desired results. Such skills can be acquired, however, through study and practice. Sales and collection letters predominate in this category.

Special-occasion letters include congratulatory messages and letters of condolence. Key components of personal messages are the writer's warmth and sincerity.

Business reports deserve special attention, also. Report writing encompasses an infinite number of topics from minor in-house problems to issues of national importance. Length and complexity of the written reports range from interoffice memos to multipage research documents. Format and writing styles vary accordingly.

QUESTIONS FOR REVIEW

1. Business letters can usually be classified into one of three categories. Identify the three categories and describe the kinds of letters which fall into each type.
2. Which of the three categories is most frequently seen in business communications? How do you account for this?

3. Which of the three types requires the greatest skill in composition? Explain your answer.
4. What is the purpose of listing items in tabular style in a letter when placing an order?
5. How do persuasive letters differ from letters which inform?
6. Do all collection letters fall into the persuasive category? Explain.
7. Name some special-occasion events in business which usually require written notes to the persons involved.
8. What types or styles of documents do report writers utilize in their report presentations?
9. Name the component parts of a typical formal report.

DISCUSSION QUESTIONS

1. Considering the importance of effective communications in business today, how much emphasis do you believe should be placed on management's developing high-level skills in composition? What avenues are available in your area for their pursuing this objective?
2. Keyboarding courses are offered at the college level for both management and support personnel. Should management-level personnel be expected to keyboard their own documents? Explain your position on this issue.
3. Regarding collection letters, how much distinction, if any, should be made between regular and "one-time" customers in a company's efforts to collect *long* overdue bills? How many reminders should precede legal action or threats of legal action?

SUGGESTED ACTIVITIES

1. Compose a collection letter to an overdue debtor who has already received three reminders from you of his overdue status. The amount owed is substantial enough to warrant your suing for payment, if necessary.

   Be courteous but firm; name the amount due; give the date that payment is expected; threaten legal action if you so choose; invite the customer to ignore the letter if payment has already been sent. Since this is a customer of long standing (though often remiss in paying his bills on time), leave the door open for future business if you want to continue to do business with him.
2. You will graduate from college next month. You understand that a position as administrative assistant will become available at that time in a firm in your city. You are well qualified for the position, and you are anxious to work for this particular business firm.

   Write a letter of application to the personnel director, including a résumé of your qualifications and stressing your academic strengths which relate to the job in question. List, too, all applicable work experience which enhance your employment potential. Give the date of your coming graduation; ask for an interview; tell when and where you can be reached by telephone for character references from former (or current) employers.
3. Write for a copy of the latest annual report of a major corporation (such as General Motors, AT&T, General Electric, and so on). Analyze the report in detail, noting

in particular the style of writing used, the use of graphic aids to enhance the report, the "puffery" employed to appeal to stockholders, and the depth and breadth of topics included in the report. (If your college library maintains a file of annual reports from major firms, you may be able to check out a copy there.)

Put your analysis in writing and share it with your classmates and instructor. Ask them to "grade" the report in terms of its appearance, writing style, clarity, and general appeal.

REFERENCES

BOGERT, JUDITH B. W. AND REBECCA B. WORLEY, *Managing Business Communications: An Applied Approach.* Englewood Cliffs, NJ: Prentice Hall, 1988.

CARR-RUFFINO, NORMA, "Report Writing—Giving Organizational Techniques Equal Time," *Business Education World* (Fall 1985), 9–10.

CARUSO, DENISE, "New Ways to Outline Your Ideas," *Personal Computing* (September 1986), 79–83.

DONALD, ROBERT B. and others, *Writing Clear Paragraphs,* 3rd ed. Englewood Cliffs, NJ: Prentice Hall, 1987.

FORD MOTOR COMPANY, "Ford Motor Company Converts Warranty into Plain English for Consumers" (typewritten news release).

HUTCHINSON, BETTY AND WARNER A., *Business Letters Made Simple.* Garden City, NY: Doubleday & Co. Inc., 1985.

MITCHELL, CYNTHIA F., "Firms Seek Cure for Dull Memos; Find Windy Writers Hard to Curb," *Wall Street Journal* (October 4, 1985), 21.

WAKIN, EDWARD, "The CEO as Consummate Communicator," *Today's Office* (May 1985), 51–54.

"What Goes with a Formal Communications Policy?" Editorial, *Personnel Management* (January 1981), 13.

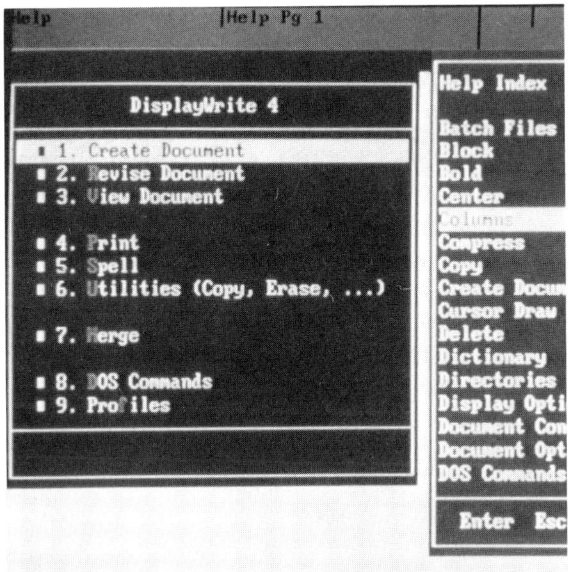

4 Dictation/Transcription Procedures and Equipment

INTRODUCTION

To compose and dictate letters to a secretary effectively, administrative assistants must perfect at least two skills; authoring quality letters for every occasion, and dictating them to a dictation machine or to a personal recorder.

Generally competent in their use of the basics of written communication—correct grammar, punctuation, and spelling—they must also learn to project a quality of caring for their readers.

In addition, administrative assistants often play a dual role: at times giving dictation to an assistant—at other times, taking dictation from a company executive. They must be familiar, therefore, with both facets of the letter-writing process—dictation and transcription. Fortunately, digital dictation systems and word processors make it possible for them to achieve new levels of efficiency, accuracy, and speed in both.

Terms introduced in this chapter include:

picocassettes
electronic dictation systems
desktop dictation units

GIVING AND TAKING DICTATION

Although the fact is well established that effective communication is a "must" in business, too little is said about good dictation and recording skills as elements contributing to that objective. Yet, good organization and excellence in the composition, recording, and transcription of documents are prime requisites for achieving quality business correspondence and reports.

The total process of producing written communications involves predictation procedures, applicable to both the dictator and the recorder; special procedures to follow in giving and/or recording the dictation; and finally, the means to effective transcription of recorded notes or tapes.

Predictation Procedures

Most correspondence is generated in response to incoming mail. The efficient administrative assistant develops a system for sorting the incoming mail and preparing it for written responses.

The following predictation suggestions are a compilation of the routines followed in many offices of medium-to-large size, but they can be adapted to fit offices of any size and type.

1. Open and scan each incoming letter or document.
2. Classify and sort the mail by type, level of importance, and need for a response.
3. Annotate the letters requiring a response, noting the action required.
4. Note what related correspondence, if any, should be retrieved from the files for reference in responding to the letter.

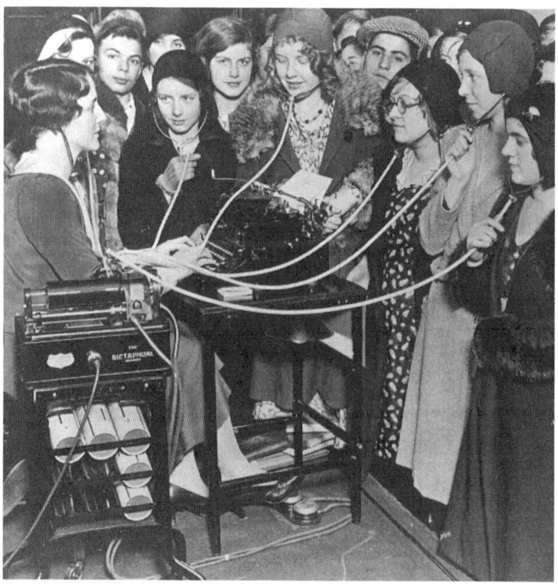

Figure 4-1 A demonstration of the *latest model* Dictaphone draws a crowd of interested ladies (and one gentleman) at a trade show of the 1920s. *Courtesy of Dictaphone Corporation.*

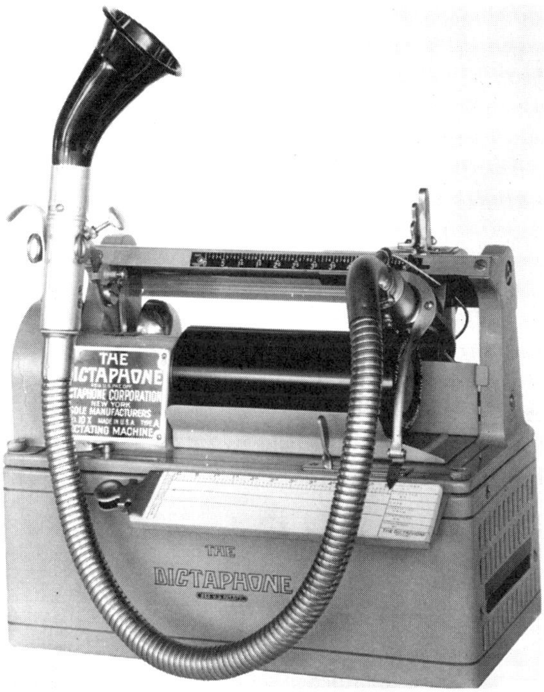

Figure 4-2 Wax cylinders remained the recording medium of this 1923 model and later models of the Dictaphone until after World War II. In the 1970s, wax cylinders were replaced with flexible plastic belts. *Courtesy of Dictaphone Corporation.*

5. Separate the letters requiring the executive's response from those requiring the administrative assistant's response.
6. Arrange both sets of correspondence in order of priority, with top-priority items on top.
7. Number the letters according to priority and attach to each letter any related correspondence retrieved from the files.
8. Prepare to dictate the correspondence, using the guidelines listed in the next section.

Giving Dictation

With reference to *giving* dictation, the duties of an administrative assistant vary from one company to another. In one firm, dictation may be done only rarely, if at all; in another, he or she may handle many of the responses for principals and dictate personal correspondence as well.

Although the time and skill committed to this responsibility vary widely, the career-oriented assistant will perfect these skills in anticipation of future, if not immediate, usage. The time-and-energy investment may be the key to career progression at some crucial point in the future. To that end, the following guidelines for before, during, and after dictation sessions may prove helpful.

Before Dictation Having observed the procedural steps outlined under predictation procedures, the administrative assistant may add the following procedures prior to the actual dictation of correspondence:

1. Visualize the reader; anticipate his or her reaction to the message being sent.
2. Briefly outline the key points to include in the message.
3. Give the secretary necessary instructions such as extra copies to be made or special mail services to be used.
4. If dictating to a machine, test the microphone and dictation units to see that they are functioning properly.
5. Identify oneself by name and title; tell what the message is—a letter, memo, or report.
6. If dictating person to person, see that the recorder has the necessary pens, pencils, and notebook ready for note taking.

During Dictation Some of the procedural steps for during and after dictation depend, in part, on whether the dictation is machine recorded or given "live," and whether the transcription is done on a word processor or a typewriter.

Although most of the following guidelines apply to all dictation procedures, regardless of the dictation or transcription mode, suggestions for each media are given when the procedures differ.

Dictation Guidelines

1. Speak distinctly, with good enunciation and voice control.
2. Use a moderate tone of voice.
3. Indicate pauses, periods, and question marks by voice inflection. Dictate paragraph separations.
4. Dictate special punctuation—dashes, exclamation points, semicolons.

Figure 4-3 This secretary utilizes the Executary Dictating Machine and the IBM Selectric typewriter to transcribe dictation in 1961. *Courtesy of IBM Corporation.*

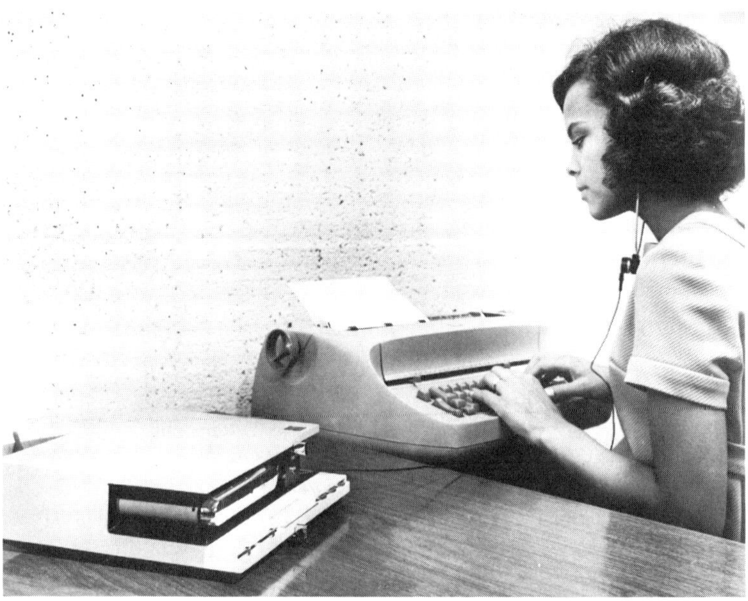

5. Adjust speed of dictation to the recorder's note-taking ability (if dictating person to person).
6. Avoid speed spurts, then long pauses.
7. Spell unusual words, terms, and proper names.
8. Encourage the recorder to ask for help if necessary to clarify instructions or the content of the dictated material (when given person to person).

After Dictation Important steps to follow after the dictation is completed:

1. Give special instructions on copy distribution. (If to be transcribed on a word processor, this can be done at the end of the letter; if typed with carbon copies, this instruction should precede the dictated letter.)
2. Replay the dictation (if recorded) or have it read back by the recorder. Listen for redundancies, awkward or stilted phraseology, offensive tone, or other faults in need of revision.
3. Give the recorder the material related to the dictated correspondence.
4. After the letters are transcribed, accept them from the transcriber for signing.
5. If additions, deletions, or corrections are necessary, ask that they be made by the transcriber. (Depending on the level of formality required, minor corrections may be made in pen by the dictator.)
6. Do a final proofreading.
7. If approved, sign the letters and give back to the secretary for mailout.
8. If revisions are necessary, give back to the secretary for rekeying.
9. Accept and sign for mailout after revisions are made as directed.

Figure 4-4 The Digital Express 7000 integrates dictation, voice mail and voice recognition in one system. Because it is digital, more than one person can access reports simultaneously. Users can request all information in the system on a specific subject, or all reports dictated by one individual. *Courtesy of Dictaphone Corporation.*

Taking Dictation

The ability to "take a letter" with speed and accuracy is still considered an essential skill of top-level secretaries. Long associated with the business office as *the* most important duty of a secretary, its prominence has waned but little with the advent of electronics.

Although sophisticated equipment and word processors have simplified the mechanics of taking and transcribing dictation, the fundamentals of doing so remain the same. Error-free copy is the result of careful attention to detail.

When the administrative assistant is *taking*, not giving, dictation, the following guidelines for before, during, and after the process may make the effort more successful.

Before Taking Dictation The administrative assistant or secretary who takes dictation regularly must be as well organized as the executive, ready to take notes from him or her at any time.

Speed in note taking, while an important component of the procedure, is not usually the primary consideration. Good organization, including preliminary planning and preparation, eliminate most of the stress associated with taking dictation.

To be prepared, the note taker must have at hand all the materials necessary to keep the procedure running smoothly. These include:

reference materials related to the correspondence being addressed
a calendar to verify dates
extra pens or pencils, including a red-ink pen for special instructions
paper clips to mark pages
a dictionary or spelling reference
notepaper for extraneous notes from the principal to "check airline schedules," "call Mr. Boyce to remind him of our appointment," and so on

The administrative assistant should also arrange for someone else to answer the telephone while he or she is recording, so that the dictation activity is not interrupted. If an important call is expected, the substitute should be instructed whether to interrupt the dictation session or not if the call comes through during the dictation session. Any other instructions for special situations should be clarified also before leaving the substitute with the telephone responsibility.

During the Recording of "Live" Dictation If the administrative assistant regularly takes dictation from more than one person, he or she may want to keep a separate notebook for each person. The dictator's name, together with the date of the first day's entries, should be written on the cover of each notebook.

The first page of each day's notes should also be dated. Placed at the bottom of the page, the date can be readily seen if a search for specific notes is initiated later.

During dictation, the recorder should not hesitate to ask the dictator to repeat any unfamiliar phrases or proper names. Nor is it improper to ask, occasionally, for the dictator to slow down if the dictation is too fast.

If the dictator interrupts the dictation to take a telephone call, the recorder can take the opportunity to read over the notes and make corrections.

After Taking Dictation Before transcribing handwritten notes or recorded dictation, the secretary should reread the notes or listen again to the recorded dictation.

If many items are to be transcribed they should be organized in the order of importance. "Rush" items should, of course, be done first, with the others following in priority order. A dictionary should be at hand for checking the spelling of unfamiliar words.

TRANSCRIPTION PROCEDURES

For consistently good results in transcribing from one's notes or from stored media, a systematic approach, similar to the following, will be helpful.

1. If transcribing on a typewriter, estimate as closely as possible the length of each dictated piece, so that it can be positioned properly on the stationery.
2. If interrupted during the transcription of penned notes, mark the notebook with a colored pencil so that the transcription can be resumed later without delay.
3. If interrupted while transcribing at a word processor, save the document before leaving the machine.
4. Proofread documents before removing them from the typewriter, or sending them to the printer from the word processor.
5. Draw a line through the notes that have been transcribed from pen-recorded dictation. File the hand-recorded notes for future reference.
6. Scan the printed documents once more before presenting them for signature. Place letters and other correspondence on the principal's desk for signature. Attach envelopes and enclosures

Proofreading

Since good proofreading skills are essential to error-free communications, the administrative assistant must develop a keen "eye" for errors by sharpening his or her proofreading abilities. The following steps usually insure error-free copy.

1. Let documents "rest" before proofreading.
2. Scan the copy first for glaring errors—typos, transpositions of letters (as in "teh" for "the"), and deletions.
3. Reread for mechanical errors—such as punctuation, word division, spelling, and grammar.
4. When an error is spotted, look for additional ones nearby. Errors, especially typos, tend to cluster.

5. At the second reading, check also for accuracy of names, addresses, dates, and other factual data.
6. List errors which are made repeatedly. Consider remedies for correcting the problem of repeated misspellings and keying errors.
7. Check calculations with a calculator.
8. If the correspondence is very important but is *not* confidential, read all or parts of it aloud, preferably to a listener interested in the message. Encourage the listener to critique for clarity.
9. Finally, read for content, taking special note of the tone of the message and its likely impact on the recipient. If either appear negative, rewrite the offending passages.

DICTATION/TRANSCRIPTION EQUIPMENT

Dictation equipment is most readily classified into three categories: central systems, desktop units, and portables. *Central systems* can be accessed by telephone-like handsets from the dictators' offices, or by standard telephones. Dictated material is stored in recorders kept in a centralized location until accessed for typing.

External, as well as internal, telephones can access the central recording system, making it possible for dictators to record after business hours or while away from the office.

Desktop units are a decentralized approach to dictation/transcription. They are widely used in small offices and in offices which are organized into small work groups. A desktop system about the size of a telephone may include a handheld microphone or, like the centralized system, a microphone which resembles a telephone handset.

The units may be configured as dictation-only devices, as transcription-only systems, or as combination dictation/transcription units.

A transcription-only system has a headset to review dictation and a foot pedal to control tape movement; the dictation-only unit has a microphone; and the combination units have all three accessories.

Functions included in desktop units include indexing to allow the user to mark the end of a document, automatic backspacing to review the last few words recorded, and a speed adjustment which allows transcribers to accelerate or decelerate the speed of recorded playbacks.

An increasingly popular feature of desktop units is VSC (variable speech compression) which speeds up the review of recorded material without distortion. This feature makes it simpler for both dictators and transcribers to review the most recent dictation without sacrificing clarity or time in the process.

Portable units represent the fastest growing segment of the dictation-equipment market. Their convenient size has led many people to adopt portables, not only for standard dictation purposes, but as note pads to jot down ideas and capture thoughts which memory might otherwise erase.

The battery-operated portables have a built in microphone. A leading vendor of dictation equipment has reduced the dimension of its portable units to

Proofreaders' marks are used to communicate changes or corrections to be made. You should learn both to type from copy that has been corrected with proofreaders' marks and to use these marks to edit copy.

Change	Proofreaders' Mark	Example
Insert	∧	You must ∧ (go) to the class.
Delete	ℓ	They went to ~~to~~ the movie.
Transpose	⌐‾‾‾‾⌐	It is largely due to . . .
Lower-case letter(s)	lc or /	He was taking Typewriting. or He was taking TYPEWRITING. (lc)
Capitalize	≡	Dan toured naples.
Omit space	⁀‿	Nancy came l ate.
Add space	#	We camehome late.
Move to left	⊏	⊏ I am tired.
Move to right	⊐	⊐ I know how to edit copy.
Single spacing	ss	Top management wanted to learn (ss) to keyboard for electronic mail.
Double spacing	ds	(ds) Communications is very important to management.
New paragraph	¶	¶ Proofreaders' marks facilitate making revisions.
Move as shown	○→	Some executives did not know how to (correctly) communicate corrections.
Ignore the correction	STET	Some of the ~~electronic~~ (STET) typewriters were outdated.
Spell out	sp	sp (N.J.)
Underscore	______	<u>The Reference Manual</u>

"shirt-pocket" size with its introduction of "picocassettes" as the recording medium.

Picocassettes, about one third the size of standard cassettes, measure just slightly longer than a paper clip and about one-eighth inch thick. Since the total dictation unit can be easily slipped into one's purse or shirt pocket, it is very popular with business travelers.

Two important features found on most portable units are speed control, which allows users to reduce the tape speed 50 percent in order to double its recording capacity, and pitch control, which corrects for uneven tape speeds and distorted voice tones.

Both portable and desktop units permit up to 60 minutes of distortion-free recording on magnetic-tape cassettes. Another feature common to both models is voice-activated recording (VOX) which turns the unit on automatically at the sound of the recorder's voice.

Combination Systems

Some companies combine desktop or central systems for in-office use with portables for off-site usage. One caution to observe when opting for a mix of units is to standardize the size of tape used, since all units must use the same size. The four available sizes of cassette tapes are

standard cassettes
minicassettes (about 2-1/2 inches wide)
microcassettes (about 2-1/4 inches wide)
picocassettes (about 1-1/2 inches wide)

Figure 4-5 Dictaphone's Digital Express System 3000 combines dictation and voice mail with the ability to select any message for hard copy transcription. *Courtesy of Dictaphone Corporation.*

Transcription Units

Most transcription units include foot pedal controls which enable the transcriber to control the tape without lifting one's hands from the keyboard. Cue tones on the tape alert the transcriber to special instructions; and fast-forward permits the transcriber to skip ahead to a high-priority document.

A special editing feature allows corrections to be put on a separate track on the cassette tape. When insertions are to be made, the tape automatically switches to the correction track for the insert, then back to the main track after the insertion is completed.

Electronic Dictation Systems

Electronic recording systems offer the most innovative development in dictation equipment. Designed for central recorders, electronic (or digital) systems eliminate the endless loop of magnetic tape commonly associated with centralized systems. In its place, digital technology converts analog voice input to digital data and *stores the data on a hard disk.*

Since tape handling is no longer required, the possibility of lost cassettes is eliminated, but, more importantly, users can integrate computers into their dictation systems, bringing a new level of computer-based electronic services into the system. For example:

Stored documents can be randomly accessed.

Multiple users can have simultaneous access to the system; that is, several people can work from the same memory disk, recording and transcribing at the same time. On a rush job, the work can be broken into segments and assigned to a number of transcribers.

Transcription can begin even while dictation is "coming in" to the system.

Authors can access the system by direct-wired handsets or by touch telephones.

Insertions or deletions can be done as easily as on a word processor.

Authorized users can listen to dictated messages before, during, or after transcription.

Access to the system can be restricted through privacy codes.

Systems tied in with the telephone network can record both sides of a phone conversation.

Work can be routed to specific departments or transcribers.

Systems with several recording tapes available can be coded for different usages; that is, letters, memos, reports, priority documents, and so on can be stored on different tapes. Recorders and transcribers access the desired tape by the proper code.

Top-of-the-line systems go directly from the recorder's voice to the computer screen, with no transcribers needed in the interim. From the recorder to

Figure 4-6 Administrative assistants of the 1990s utilize microcomputers and word processing software to transcribe documents quickly and efficiently.

the printer, the entire process is completed within minutes of the voice-dictated input. Hospitals are the primary users of this state-of-the-art equipment. For example, a radiologist can dictate a patient laboratory report, prefacing the report with the patient's ID; the transcriber can access the report at the transcription terminal by entering the patient's ID, then immediately print a copy of it for the physician. Vital information on a patient is thus supplied almost immediately.

Systems designed for multiple originators often include a supervisory monitor (usually a microcomputer) which tracks the flow of work in and out of the system. The monitor records productivity statistics, such as work recorded and transcribed, and how the transcription assignments have been distributed to the word processor operators. It also computes costs to be charged to the departments using the system.

Technology in this field is changing continually. Customized applications are made possible by the stored voice recording on hard disk integrated with the telephone and computer technology. Some vendors rightfully title their products "voice processors" rather than dictation units.

By whatever title, the newly digitized dictation systems can now be incorporated into electronic networks as bona fide components of the electronic office.

ADDRESS FORMAT FOR ENVELOPES

The U.S. Postal Service publishes a set of directives for users to follow in addressing envelopes. Developed for the automatic sorting of mail by optical character

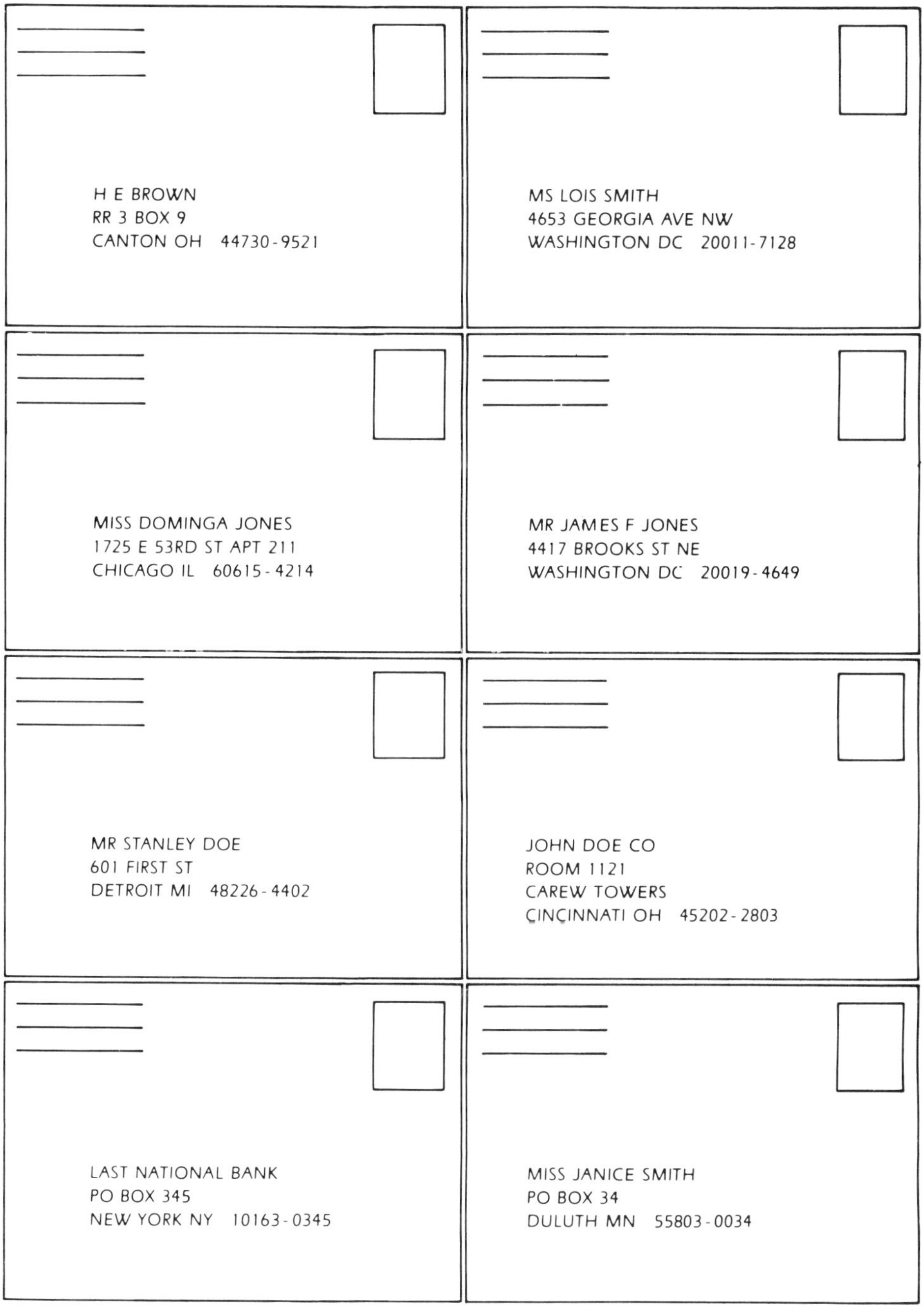

Figure 4-7 Proper address formats for civilian mail. *Courtesy of U.S. Postal Service.*

readers (OCRs), the address styles set forth by the Postal Service have these characteristics in common:

1. Only upper-case letters are used.
2. Lines are single spaced.
3. Attention lines are positioned in the address space, not in the lower left corner of the envelope.
4. Unnecessary punctuation, such as the comma between the city and state, and the periods after initials, are eliminated.
5. Nine-digit zip codes are used when known. (See Chapter 6 for more information on nine-digit zips and barcode sorting.)

Examples of envelopes addressed according to these directives are shown in Figure 4–7. A list of the two-letter state abbreviations follows.

State Abbreviations

Alabama (AL)
Alaska (AK)
Arizona (AZ)
Arkansas (AR)
California (CA)
Colorado (CO)
Connecticut (CT)
Delaware (DE)
District of Columbia (DC)
Florida (FL)
Georgia (GA)
Guam (GU)
Hawaii (HI)
Idaho (ID)
Illinois (IL)
Indiana (IN)
Iowa (IA)
Kansas (KS)
Kentucky (KY)
Louisiana (LA)
Maine (ME)
Maryland (MD)
Massachusetts (MA)
Michigan (MI)
Minnesota (MN)
Mississippi (MS)
Missouri (MO)
Montana (MT)
Nebraska (NE)
Nevada (NV)
New Hampshire (NH)
New Jersey (NJ)
New Mexico (NM)
New York (NY)
North Carolina (NC)
North Dakota (ND)
Ohio (OH)
Oklahoma (OK)
Oregon (OR)
Pennsylvania (PA)
Puerto Rico (PR)
Rhode Island (RI)
South Carolina (SC)
South Dakota (SD)
Tennessee (TN)
Texas (TX)
Utah (UT)
Vermont (VT)
Virginia (VA)
Washington (WA)
West Virginia (WV)
Wisconsin (WI)
Wyoming (WY)

SUMMARY

Since an administrative assistant may be involved in dictation from "either side of the desk," that is, as the originator or the recorder, techniques for doing both efficiently must be developed.

Only by establishing efficient routines for handling dictation, recording, and transcription duties can administrative assistants perfect their letter-writing skills. Suggestions for before, during, and after dictation/recording procedures can help them achieve this objective.

Proofreading techniques are important components of good writing techniques, too. The administrative assistant can incorporate those techniques which are most effective in discovering and eradicating elusive errors before the keyed correspondence is signed and mailed out.

With electronic systems, the dictation/transcription procedure can now be integrated into the total electronic office system, giving the administrative assistant all the computer-aided advantages such integration provides.

Although content is more important than style, the administrative assistant must understand the accepted styles for both business letters and envelopes. Letter styles were discussed in Chapter 3. Format for envelope addresses, as mandated by the U.S. Postal Service, are equally important.

Samples of envelopes addressed according to the postal directives, plus a list of the two-letter state abbreviations should be kept at hand for ready reference.

QUESTIONS FOR REVIEW

1. Give some of the suggestions listed for effective proofreading.
2. Describe how the administrative assistant may be involved in dictation from "both sides of the desk."
3. Describe the guidelines listed for the originator to follow
   a. *Before* giving dictation,
   b. *During* dictation,
   c. *After* giving dictation.
4. What materials should the recorder have at hand when taking dictation?
5. Dictation equipment is classified into three categories. Name the three categories.
6. What type of dictation equipment represents the fastest growing segment of the market? Explain its popularity.
7. Electronic (digital) dictation systems have many advantages. Name as many as you can.
8. How does the envelope-address format of the U.S. Postal Service differ from traditional forms of envelope address?

DISCUSSION QUESTIONS

1. In your opinion, are consultants and analysts right in placing so much stock in good letter-writing skills? Explain your position.
2. In your opinion, why are dictation skills so important? How can a dictator gain proficiency in the art of dictation?
3. Of the proofreading techniques listed in this chapter, which ones do you believe to be the most practical? Can you add others of your own? If so, describe how *you* would check for errors.

4. Shorthand is not so widely used as it was ten or fifteen years ago. Explain why, in your opinion, shorthand has lost its place of prominence in the office. Is its demise as a *primary* requisite for executive secretaries a regrettable situation? Explain your position.

SUGGESTED ACTIVITIES

1. Practice dictating a letter into a dictation machine. Listen to your recorded voice, noting the strengths and weaknesses of your message, your instructions to the secretary, and your delivery of the message.
2. Play the recording for the other students in the class. Have them take the dictation; then evaluate your performance as a dictator.
3. Arrange to visit the post office of a large city. Note how the envelopes are sorted by the OCR equipment. Discuss with the postal officials the importance of following the envelope-address formats suggested by the Postal Service and its relationship to sorting the mail.
4. Begin a collection of articles from local newspapers, noting errors in spelling, punctuation, and factual information. Write amended copy for each article corrected.

REFERENCES

COHEN, SHARON L., "Communication and Productivity," *Today's Office* (August 1984), 17–18.

GRAGG, ELLEN L., "Raise Output & Cut Costs with Dictation Equipment," *Office Systems '88* (October 1988), 68–71.

"Lanier Dictation," *Office Systems '89* (April 1989), 17. (No author given.)

SCHLACTENHAUFEN, JOHN, "Computerized Dictation" *Office Systems '88* (June 1988), 30–32.

5
Word Processing and Desktop Publishing

INTRODUCTION

Word processing is one of the most widely used applications of personal computers. Its popularity can be attributed to its primary function, text editing, which enables users to produce error-free documents, store them magnetically for later recall or revision, and print multiple copies on demand, all within a fraction of the time an electric typewriter would require for the same procedure.

Technological breakthroughs have enhanced word processing far beyond its entry-level state of the 1970s. A full-featured word processor incorporates a speller, a thesaurus, a style checker, a text outliner, graphics and word-count capability, and many of the functions originally attributed solely to desktop publishing systems.

Desktop publishing has come into its own, also. In-house publishing has advanced to a level rivaling that of commercial printing establishments.

The administrative assistant is faced with many options as he or she considers the company's software and hardware requirements for both word processing and desktop publishing applications.

Terms in this chapter include:

PC-based word processing	WYSIWYG
LQ; NLQ	DTP
image scanners	boilerplating
OCR scanners	word publishing

WORD PROCESSING: CORNERSTONE OF OFFICE AUTOMATION

Word processing is frequently credited with bringing computer technology into the mainstream of the business office. The user-friendly application of word processing to computer-based systems made it possible for clerks, stenographers, and secretaries to produce high-quality business documents quickly and accurately, with less effort than they had ever experienced prior to its introduction.

In time, personnel at all levels found word processors more indispensable than the typewriters which they replaced. The switch from typewriters to PC-based word processors became commonplace.

Word processors also bridged the gap between the computer professionals of the data processing department and the personal computer users of the "outer" office. Mutual respect for each other's professional competence grew.

To understand the phenomenal impact of the word processor on the electronic office, a review of the primitive equipment which predates current models offers some insights. Users and developers were motivated to keep trying; the need for something more than typewriters was there, if technology could only meet it.

Word Processing—Startup of a Phenomenon

Present-day word processors had their origin in the automatic typewriters introduced in the 1930s. The automatic typewriters could type form letters and contracts repetitively, using a punched paper roller mechanism similar to that found on player pianos. The paper mechanism was played and replayed until the paper media frayed and became unusable.

Figure 5-1 In 1964, IBM introduced the Magnetic Tape/Selectric Typewriter (MT/ST). Storing documents on erasable magnetic tape, the MT/ST represented a giant step forward in the evolution of text-editing equipment. *Courtesy of IBM Corporation.*

Enhanced by the addition of paper tape and electromechanical logic in the 1950s, automatic typewriters could do a limited amount of searching, selecting, and merging of text stored on the punched paper tape.

In 1964, IBM introduced the Magnetic Tape/Selectric Typewriter (MT/ST), which for the first time utilized a tape cartridge to store text. An evolutionary aspect of the MT/ST was that the magnetic tape could be erased and rerecorded. Primitive as the mechanism would seem today, the MT/ST represented a quantum leap forward in document processing.

In 1969, IBM first coined the term *word processor* when it replaced the MT/ST with the Magnetic Card Selectric Typewriter (MC/ST). The MC/ST, using a reusable magnetic card for storage, was popular from the start. In time, the MC/ST became the norm by which subsequent word processors were measured.

During the early 1970s, activity in the word processing market livened considerably. Wang introduced its first model in 1972, advancing rapidly to market leadership in the field. Vydek introduced word processing diskettes for the first time in 1973. Savin and Xerox entered the market in 1974. A. B. Dick, Lanier, and Digital Equipment made their entries in 1976. Lexitron, 3M, and a host of other manufacturers unveiled keyboard computer systems dedicated solely to word processing. The heated competition pushed prices downward, making word processors affordable for a broader range of users.

The predominance of *dedicated* word processors (equipment designed solely for processing and printing text) began to wane in the late 1970s, however, as word processing software for multifunctional computers lured buyers away from the single-purpose machines.

The variety of available software plus the flexibility of multipurpose computers made PC-based word processing a cost-effective option to the dedicated units. The dedicated word processor which had introduced computers to the "masses" now yielded its place of prominence to the desktop computer.

PC-based Word Processing

Personal computers as word processing platforms provided three immediate benefits:

1. A diversity of word processing programs available for the consumer's choice. The wide range of software packages allows users to choose programs that are well matched to the tasks at hand, at prices geared to fit almost every budget.
2. Ease in switching from one word processing program to another. The ability to change from one word processing program to another *on the same computer* not only lessens the trauma but speeds the learning cycle as well.
3. Cost effectiveness in using the versatile microcomputer for programs other than word processing. Users can utilize their spreadsheets, databases, and other useful programs without switching from their word processing hardware.

Many manufacturers who had produced dedicated units now switched to the manufacture of multipurpose hybrids in place of, or in addition to, the single-purpose machines.

Major manufacturers of both types defended their own machines: dedicated manufacturers emphasized the superiority of their units for processing text, while multipurpose makers stressed the versatility of theirs.

In contrast with the dedicated units, word processing software packages designed for PC-based units now incorporate all the features of the dedicated word processors; and, in addition, integrate text with graphics, communicate electronically with other units, and output typeset-quality documents on laser printers.

Word Processing Centers

During the 1970s, centers which housed multiple operators of word processing equipment handled virtually all the correspondence of an organization. Word processors were clustered in a special department, with operators working continually to transcribe the company's entire stock of business correspondence. One-on-one secretaries became the exception.

A supervisor coordinated all activities, assigning jobs to the word processing operators as the transcription orders "came in" and acting as liaison between the center and the users. Company executives took special pride in displaying for visitors their advanced communications department.

Today, word processing centers have all but disappeared from the business scene. PC-based word processors have replaced over 90 percent of the dedicated units formerly grouped into tightly supervised centers of 10 to 20 professional operators.

In their place, the PC-based units, designed primarily for single users, occupy offices over the entire plant, with immediate and convenient usage taking precedence over the professional services of the center's operators.

Nevertheless, word processing centers made their contribution to the current electronic environment. By glamorizing the contribution of word processing to fast, accurate communications, the word processing centers made people aware of the power of word processing. Businesses, impressed with what they saw, looked for ways to incorporate more word processing, then other software programs, into their business operations.

Today, certain types of businesses still employ a modified version of the word processing center for speedy, accurate communications. Large hospitals, for example, utilize one or two operators for 24-hour processing of their patient records. Paper-intensive industries, such as law and finance, employ distributed word processing clusters to process their heavy workloads.

But for general use, the word processing center as originally conceived is a thing of the past. Several factors contributed to its dissembling. The personal computer, now a permanent fixture atop every desk, made the keyboarding of one's documents easy and practical. Even executives opted to key their own documents. The many software programs on the market, designed to fit every communication need, gave word processing a broad appeal to all users, not just word processing "specialists." Individuals were motivated by the low-cost entry-level software to experiment with word processing on their own. Creative persons experimented with writing new manuscripts at their PCs. Access to classified information was more readily protected by restrictive codes and restricted physical access to the disks.

Full-featured Word Processors

Word processing software is rightfully credited with removing the drudgery from writing textual material, including the correction and revision of texts with a minimum of labor and frustration. Its primary function as a text editor has been so successful that word processing is the primary application of personal computer users.

According to one report, over 5 million word processing packages had been installed as of 1988, in contrast to 4 million spreadsheets and 2 million database packages.[1]

Despite its overall popularity and wide usage, however, many users do not utilize the many feature-laden functions of their word processing programs. Even the "under $100" packages have sophisticated features once reserved solely to the industry leaders.

To qualify as more than a *basic* word processor, full-featured word processing packages will include most of these functions:

Spelling checker
Thesaurus
Style checker
Automatic hyphenation
Split-screen editing
Search-and-replace capability
Word-count capability
Macros (recorded keystrokes to perform a function, such as printing a page, or printing an entire document)
Windows for viewing multiple files
WYSIWYG ("What you see is what you get"—Viewing on the screen what will be printed on paper)
Outliners (generating text outlines from user-specified headings, to produce a summary of what the document contains)
Automatic indexing (a database-type summary sheet which allows the user to provide information on a document when saving it, such as title, field categories, keywords, author, date, revisions, and comments)
Table of contents generation
Graphics importation from other files
Merger capability with spreadsheet and database files
Support for more than 100 printer drivers, including lasers, ink-jet, and thermal printers, as well as dot-matrix and daisywheels

[1]Rick Minicucci, "New WP Features Add Sizzle to Your Documents," *Today's Office* (March 1988), 25.

Easy change of typefaces or styles

File-conversion utilities to interact with other word processing programs

Mail merge, which can import database and spreadsheet information to merge with form letters

Desktop publishing functions

Basic Word Processing Programs

Basic programs are designed primarily as text editors, with simplicity and speed their principal attraction. Persons who use their word processors solely for letters, memos, and short documents have little use for the "bells and whistles" of the sophisticated programs. Rather, they look for programs that are easy to learn and simple to operate, with quick response time to editorial changes.

The more complex programs are not noted for their speedy response time; because of the complexity of their programs, full-featured word processing programs occupy most of the computer's RAM memory space, forcing user documents to the hard disk. Hence, the time delay in accepting and responding to editorial changes as the computer peruses the hard disk rather than RAM memory for the document.

Despite the primary attraction of simplicity and speed, however, newer "basic" packages include an impressive array of desktop publishing and other special features. One program, for example, provides WYSIWYG graphics; another has a built-in card file for database usage; and most offer mail-merge capabilities.

Selecting a Word Processor

Choosing the "right" word processor from the hundreds of models on the market is a difficult process, to say the least. To assure a wise choice, the ad-

Figure 5-2a Word processor, vintage 1976. Note the 8-inch diskette, the large console, and the paper-feed mechanism integrated with the unit. *Courtesy of IBM Corporation.*

Figure 5-2b Today's word processors are versatile desktop units which incorporate graphics, scanned images, and a variety of type fonts for professional quality output. *Courtesy of IBM Corporation.*

ministrative assistant should first clarify, in writing, what is expected from a word processor.

Four factors should be considered:

1. Which word processing features are absolutely essential for processing the company's documents?
2. Which special features would be beneficial?
3. What are the hardware requirements?
4. Who will be the primary users of the program?

Having identified and listed the major functions the word processor should perform, the administrative assistant can then cull from the list of word processors those which fail to provide these functions. From those remaining, a selection may be based on those which offer the latest technological advances, the most alluring special features, or the best price.

Checklist of Essential Word Processing Features

To safeguard against obsolesence, the prudent administrative assistant will put at the top of the checklist a requirement that the program be continually updated by the manufacturers. A live program is one which is updated regularly with current technological improvements and continually monitored for defects.

To determine which of the features are *essential*, samples of company documents can be gathered and ranked in priority order. The features—general or special—which would be valuable in producing these documents, can then be evaluated. For example, with documents in hand, these questions may be probed:

Would these documents have been improved with the use of a thesaurus?

Would ease in generating footnotes be a valuable addition?

Is a spelling checker a priority item?

Which formatting options are essential: columnar typing? subject-matter indexing? forms generation? automatic table of contents?

Is mail-merge a feature that would be used, even occasionally?

Would the addition of simple graphics add special appeal to company documents?

What desktop publishing features, if any, have special application to company documents?

Another major component is good documentation. A clear, easy-to-follow manual is essential if learning is to proceed smoothly without undue frustration on the part of the trainers or trainees.

Good revision handling is vital, also. Does it process document changes quickly and simply? Will the program "undo" the last command given it? Will it let the operator know that a disk is almost full? Can it be instructed to save keyboarded input automatically every 20, 30, or more minutes—to protect data in case of an equipment malfunction or power outage?

If frequent interaction of the word processing program with other software is anticipated, compatibility is essential. For example, if spreadsheet data are frequently incorporated into promotional letters, the convenience of importing the data directly without rekeying it mandates the use of conversion utilities that really "do the job." Likewise, if the equipment is to be linked with a local area network, compatibility with the network must be high on the list of priorities.

Special Features

Major word processing vendors work tirelessly to enhance their word processors with special features and improvements. Each release improves the previous version. The administrative assistant endeavors to keep pace with advances by replacing old versions with the new ones as they are released.

Some improvements target the basics of the program, such as increased speed of operation or additional printer drivers; others are designed to enhance *special* applications. For example, for offices which process a lot of preprinted forms, a package might include style sheets which precisely define the format specifications for headings, paragraphs, or even entire documents. Once set up, a single command activates all of the formatting codes. Where numbers are used extensively, decimal tabs and simple mathematical equations and columnar formats are available.

Boilerplating, the merging of one file into others, is made simpler by allowing users to create a library file of sections of text of any length, each one identified by a code name. After creating a table of contents to identify the sections, the user can mix and match either by section code or by paging through the boilerplate file.

For camera-ready reports, one program sets different margins for odd and even pages, leaving room for the binding at the side. For documents having numbered chapters and subsections, some programs provide a simple numbering system, along with automatic renumbering when sections are rearranged during editing.

Excellent graphics capabilities have been added to high-end word processing programs, including the integration of text and graphics, and the design of letterheads and company logos. Two-column (or more) text, tables, and a variety of type fonts give a professional look to documents.

With split-screen editing, a floating "magnifying glass" magnifies the document up to ten times, allowing the user to move around on the screen to cover any part of the document that needs to be enlarged. The area under the magnifier appears in the upper right-hand corner of the screen, magnified from two to ten times, as the user directs.

Seeing and retaining a record of changes is made possible with *redlining*. Redlining audits the trail of additions and deletions, automatically inserting boldface or strikeovers on deleted portions for the benefit of later readers.[2]

For network users, retrieval of files is made easier by using identifying data in the file rather than a file name. Conversion utilities which convert documents from one word processor to another are simplified through a "direct connect" from within the word processing program in use. Users are not required to exit the program to go through DOS and use the utility.

In exploring the word processing marketplace, the administrative assistant will no doubt learn of new features not previously considered. Adding some or all of these to the "shopping list " may generate an entirely new set of priority rankings. Tempting as it may be to purchase the most "featured" package on the market (and the most expensive), the administrative assistant is well advised to focus on the company's current needs, with reasonable allowances made for expanded usage in the future.

Hardware Requirements

The more features a word processor has, the higher its demands on the computer system running it. A full-featured word processor requires more RAM (random access memory) to accommodate its voluminous program than do the basic packages. A complex program may require the megabyte storage of a hard disk, or force users to resort to frequent floppy-swapping instead.

An elaborate program also requires a high-speed computer system to get acceptable response speed. Earlier, low-end systems were not designed to run long, complex programs at high speeds. Rather, their slow, awkward response tended to discourage users from attempting new software revisions on old machines, even when manufacturers assured them they would be successful in their attempts.

The operating system is a key component of software requirements. Programs are written for particular disk operating systems (DOS). Before selecting word processing software, the administrative assistant must make sure that the package chosen is compatible with the operating systems currently in use.

Printer compatibility is another major issue. Most printers handle all the *basic* features of word processors without hesitation, but the full range of formatting, proportional letter spacing, bold lettering, superscripting, and underlining may tax the capacity of some printers, especially the earlier models.

Fortunately, vendors are addressing the issue of compatibility between word processing software and printers. Wider support for all kinds of printers

[2]Robin Johnson, "Word Processing Software: Blazing New Trails," *Today's Office* (August 1989), 20.

is growing. However, the administrative assistant must not take compatibility for granted. One still needs to specify the computer system being configured with the printer, and what types of output are expected from it. Graphics, for example, are impossible on a daisywheel; a 24-pin dot-matrix printer handles most correspondence, and a laser printer is desirable for most desktop publishing applications.

Primary Users

Another vital consideration in choosing suitable word processing software is: Who will be its primary users? In a manager/secretary one-to-one relationship, the secretary will probably be the only regular user. If so, input from the secretary should be sought from the start, for practical as well as psychological reasons.

For example, typing speed and/or the degree of familiarity one has with dedicated word processors may make a difference. If one's previous experience has been with dedicated word processors, programs using function keys similar to those used on dedicated word processors will probably be preferred. A fast touch-typist with little or no word processing experience may prefer the type which uses control-key commands, easily reached from the home-key position.

Psychologically, secretaries who are *not* consulted about equipment or software purchased solely for their use will resent being ignored. Managers who ignore their input risk strong resistance to the newly installed equipment and software, however subtly it may be manifested.

Additional Guidelines

A word processor search *begins* with an investigation of the four major elements of word processing discussed previously: essential features, special features, hardware requirements, and the primary users of the equipment/software.

However, it does not end there. Many other factors deserve consideration as well. In a quest for the best word processing program, the investigator will find it worthwhile to probe the following issues:

How good is the program's documentation? Are the instructions presented in logical sequence, with terminology explained, and an index or reference guide included for quick reference?

Is vendor support readily available?

Does support include initial training for word processing operators?

Will future upgrades or enhancements be announced as they become available? Will they be supplied at no cost or at a nominal charge?

How does the software rank with other word processing software in terms of basic and special features, reviewers' comments, and price? (See comparison charts published regularly in current computer periodicals.)

What length documents are normally produced by company secretaries? Basic packages fit normal-length letters; documents of 50 pages or more call for a more complex package.

How much time can be devoted to learning a new package? Simpler packages, of course, have a shorter learning curve than the sophisticated packages.

Answers to these questions will help the administrative assistant and superiors decide whether a basic or an advanced package is best for the company's needs.

SCANNERS AND WORD PROCESSING

One study indicates that 75 to 80 percent of a word processing operator's time is devoted to keying text. Reducing the text-entry function by using a scanner can save that much time for more productive text editing.

Scanners have become a popular peripheral device for word processors, particularly since the advent of desktop publishing. The purpose of scanners is to transfer characters or images from one document to another document without rekeying the text or photocopying the image.

Two types of scanners exist: OCR scanners and image scanners. OCR scanners recognize textual characters on the source sheet and transfer them to the destination document. The user can then utilize the word processing software to manipulate the text as desired, just as if he or she had input the characters into the machine from the keyboard.

Image scanners capture an *image* of the document or graphic and store it in the computer *as an image*. Even though the image may be textual, it cannot be edited as text, since the characters are not coded for recognition by the computer.

Image scanners require much more RAM space than OCR scanners and they are less versatile. However, they are very useful for scanning line drawings, charts, and other illustrations used in desktop publishing applications.

A PC-based word processor plus an OCR scanner make a cost-effective combination for bringing typewritten documents into the mainstream of the electronic office. Working in conjunction with word processors, the scanners save

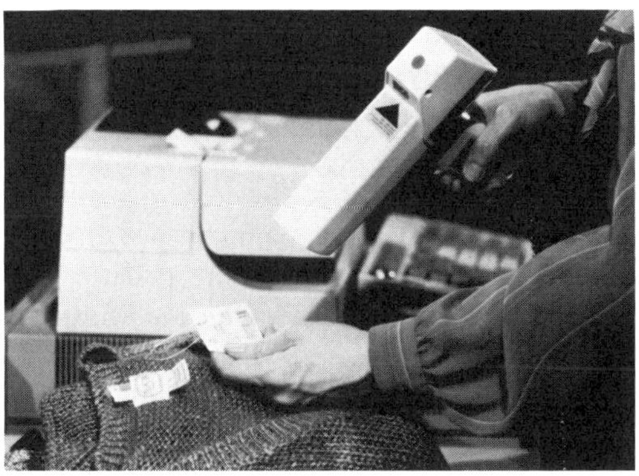

Figure 5-3a Scanners enter documents and data into computer storage by converting them to digital format. The 4680 handheld scanner reads the barcodes of items in a retail store. *Courtesy of IBM Corporation.*

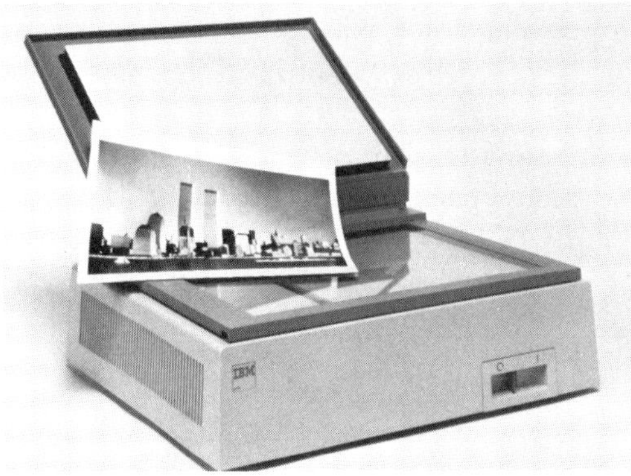

Figure 5-3b The 3119 image scanner translates any image, including pictures and handwriting, for storage in the computer. *Courtesy of IBM Corporation.*

hours of keyboarding input time by eliminating the process of rekeying incoming paper documents into the word processor.

The scanner is also valuable in dealing with incompatible computer systems. Even though two incompatible systems cannot communicate directly with each other, the operator can transfer a document from one system to the other by printing out a copy of the document, then submitting it to an OCR page reader for scanning, digitizing, and transferring it to the second word processor. Used for this purpose, scanning represents a considerable cost saving over conversion services offered by independent service companies. Three basic types of scanners are available.[3]

Handheld Scanners The least expensive, these are used primarily to add logos or artwork to documents. The quality of output from a handheld scanner depends on the skill of the user in maintaining steady control and consistent speed while scanning the image. Resolution is generally lower than that of other scanners.

Sheetfed Scanners These units scan one sheet at a time as inserted by the user. Automatic feeding mechanisms are available for these units, similar to those seen on copiers. Sheetfed scanners have some limitations, however; they do not allow for precise aligning of the document on the platen, nor can they scan pages in a book.

Flatbed Scanners These are the most versatile of all scanner types. Books, magazines, and single sheets of any size can be easily scanned by a flatbed scanner. They also allow for precise alignment of the image where the user wants to place it on a page.

Another important factor which distinguishes one scanner from another is its level of resolution. Like the computer screen, the scanner images documents into bits corresponding to the bit-imagery of the computer. The greater the number of dots per inch (dpi), the greater the resolution. The current industry standard is 300 dpi for commercial applications.

[3]Joanne G. Burnacz, "Expand Your Horizons with a Scanner," *Today's Office* (August 1989), 14.

Gray scale is a refinement of dot resolution; gray-scale scanners classify dots into scales of gray, from light to dark; the higher the levels of gray-scale resolution, the higher the output quality of the image. High-level gray scale requires tremendous amounts of storage, however, which may more than outweigh the advantages of the improved image.

Advantages of Scanner-equipped Offices

The purpose of scanners is twofold: to incorporate nontextual images into documents, and to save time and labor through reducing the keyboarding of textual material. Either factor in itself can cost-justify the purchase of a scanner, but the time-saving factor is the more significant of the two.

The number and types of applications made with the scanner, of course, determine how much keyboarding time is saved. Companies which retain legal, financial, or other important records over long periods of time use scanners to transfer records onto disks for magnetic storage.

Companies with limited storage capacity who save copies of all incoming correspondence can also utilize scanners to scan, index, and store copies of the correspondence on disks.

An added bonus of the scanner-equipped office is the efficient usage of personnel and equipment. With the assistance of a scanner, fewer personnel and fewer word processors are needed to produce the same amount of document output. During peak periods, typists plus scanners, rather than word processing operators alone, can keyboard the material and send it from typewriter to scanner to the word processor for editing, printing, and saving to magnetic disk.

Selection of a Scanner

Purchasers of image or OCR scanners may be intimidated by vendors' conflicting claims for their products. Getting their responses to a checklist of questions such as the following will demystify the process. The administrative assistant should consider the needs of his or her own company while seeking answers to these questions:

Will the OCR scanner read the fonts of our typewriters?

How many fonts are included in the initial cost and what is the cost of additional fonts?

What is the scanner's error rate and its rate of speed?

What are the hardware requirements?

What is the scanner's level of resolution?

For the company's usage, is an image scanner or an OCR scanner the most practical? Can the purchase of both be justified?

Of the three types (handheld, sheetfed, and flatbed scanners), which is the most practical for the company's purposes?

Obviously, some of these questions must be pondered by company users, not vendors, but vendors can offer considerable expertise to new purchasers of this equipment.

The Future for Scanners in Business

The future shows considerable promise for scanners in business. As more people become aware of their many advantages, the use of OCR scanners is growing. As desktop publishing continues to grow in popularity, the sale of image scanners continues its ascent as well. Remarkably, as technology continues to improve both types of units, the price of each is going down. The combination of improved technology and lower prices portends success for scanners as standard components of the electronic office for the immediate and distant future.

PRINTERS FOR PC-BASED WORD PROCESSORS

The fanciful kingdom of the paperless office, once touted as the wave of the future, has yet to materialize. In spite of the widespread usage of the computer, local area networks, and magnetic storage devices, the world of *totally* electronic communications has never come into being.

Rather, the avalanche of paper mounts, due in part to the ease with which hard copies of computer-generated documents can be created, and in part by the paranoia of cautious computer users who don't "trust" the permanency of electronic storage. Unless or until a reversal of attitude takes place, hard copy output remains a staple of the electronic office.

Accordingly, the printer marketplace continues to grow at a phenomenal pace, with specialized segments reaching out to every facet of the communications industry: high-speed lasers for excellent-quality printouts, rugged line printers for fast data processing tasks, thermal printers for quiet operation, ink-jet printers for beautiful print quality, and the ever faithful dot-matrix printers for cranking out everyday communications.

To better understand electronic printers and to choose the type(s) best suited to each company's word processing needs, the administrative assistant must sort out the various options available. Since no one printer is best for *all* office applications, the ones which come closest to filling the company's regular printing needs must be chosen. A logical first sort divides all units into one of two groups: impact and nonimpact printers.

Impact Printers

Impact printers imprint characters on paper by the impact of the keyed characters striking an inked ribbon which transfers the images to the paper. Impact printers currently dominate the market, although nonimpact units are gaining increasing acceptance. In the impact group, two types—dot-matrix and daisywheels—are the most common.

Daisywheel Printers Daisywheel printers print high-quality fully formed letters, numbers, and symbols. The printhead is made up of spokes extending from the center of a flat daisy-shaped disk, with the keyboard characters positioned at the end of each spoke.

When first introduced, daisywheel printers were considered essential for executive correspondence and legal documents. Their initially high price, however, put them beyond the reach of many users. Although prices have dropped dramatically, the daisywheel has lost many of its initial supporters to the more versatile (and less expensive) dot-matrix printer.

One of the major drawbacks of the daisywheel is its inability to print graphics. When the printer was first introduced, graphics was not an issue. With the new emphasis on the importation of graphics into letters and reports, however, the daisywheel's inability to print graphics became a major limitation. In speed, too, the daisywheel lost place to many of its competitors.

In spite of its limitations, however, this first of the "beautiful" printers, remains the preferred choice of many executives. Its fully formed characters set it apart from the dot-matrix printer groups, and its downward price spiral has made it more competitive in price than it was initially.

Dot-matrix Printers At its inception into the personal computer environment, the dot-matrix printer was welcomed as a low-cost, high-speed "workhorse," suitable for printing rough drafts, in-house communications, and limited outside correspondence. However, its low-quality output made it inappropriate for communicating with customers or clients.

Figure 5-4 Tandy LP 1000 laser printer has four resident fonts and production speed of six pages per minute. *Courtesy of Radio Shack, a division of Tandy Corporation.*

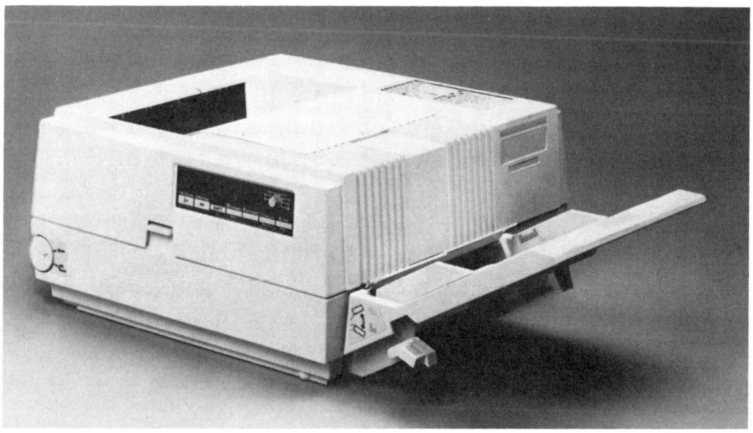

Later advancements in dot-matrix technology, however, brought the workhorse into the executive suite, in direct competition with more expensive contenders. The approximately 5 million dot-matrix printers sold annually attest to their current popularity.

The printhead of a dot-matrix is made up of wire pins arranged in a grid (or matrix) which when activated creates dots in the shape of the characters the keyboard operator strikes. The more pins in the matrix, the higher the resolution of the printed characters.

A nine-pin printer, for example, can print 240 dpi (dots per inch) while a 24-pin model can provide as high as 360 dpi. In terms of speed, the dot-matrix can print 10-pitch characters as high as 300 cps (characters per second) in draft mode, 200 cps in LQ (letter quality), and 333 cps in compressed mode. In 12-pitch, the speeds are even more impressive: 480 cps draft mode, and 240 cps letter quality.

NLQ (near letter quality), an option offered by some printer manufacturers, compromises between draft and LQ, running at speeds lower than draft mode but higher than that required for letter-quality print.

The letter quality of dot-matrix printers is not comparable to that of the daisywheel; the characters are not fully formed. However, the increased density and sharpness of characters from a 24-pin dot-matrix cause it to be ranked by most users as a viable alternative to the daisywheel.

Dot-matrix technology offers another important advantage over the daisywheel: It can "draw" curved lines. The grid of its dot-matrix printhead can be programmed to draw simple outlines, curves, circles, bars, horizontal and vertical lines, and even cross-hatch patterns for bar charts, pie charts, and maps. In brief, the dot-matrix printer handles graphics with relative ease.

Infinite Printers "Infinite" dot-matrix printers are in the experimental stage. These units use intradot scanning techniques to place a very large number of dots within a specific space on a printout. Proponents claim that infinite dot-matrix printers will produce true letter-quality output, as well as high-resolution graphics.

Optional Color Kits Taking technology one step further, many vendors are offering color kits as options for their 24-pin dot-matrix printers. By utilizing ribbons with four color strips (black, red, yellow, and blue), some have unveiled units which print in seven colors. The color strips are used singly or in combinations to create color variations.

Low Cost per Unit The final factor which has catapulted dot-matrix printers into the forefront of sales is their low cost. From a base of $300 to $400 for low-end machines and up to $2,000 or more for high-end models, dot-matrix printers are made to fit every user's budget.

In summary, dot-matrix printers deliver high-speed acceptable quality printout and high-resolution graphics at a cost comparable to or lower than their competitors. If prices continue to fall, these units should occupy an even stronger position in the printer arena of the future.

Non-impact Printers

Non-impact printers require no physical blow against a ribbon to transfer a character to paper. The printing technologies differ widely among the various types, however, so little can be said in terms of their common features. However, they are quieter, operating at a decibel level considerably lower than impact printers, and they are generally faster.

With the laser printer in the lead, the non-impact group is fast becoming a major force in the printer industry. Its *rate* of growth is keeping pace with less expensive models in the race for printer supremacy. Two other printers in the non-impact group—thermal transfer units and ink-jet printers—also serve the printing needs of many users.

Laser Printers The laser printer has been described as a hybrid printer and copier. Through a process called bit mapping, digitally encoded pages are sent to the printer from the computer, the address of each dot of an image bit-mapped internally. The printer then duplicates the image on paper.

Most laser printers share the same basic features, differing primarily in speed and resolution (number of dots per inch). The word *laser* is an acronym for *Light Amplification by Stimulated Emission of Radiation.*

The laser device emits a very intense, narrow beam of light formed of amplified, concentrated light waves. The beam carries the digitally encoded characters to a rotating mirror, where it scans a printing drum. The laser strikes the drum with an electrical charge, similar to that of a photocopier; the printer then transfers the image from the drum to the page.

The laser differs from the dot-matrix in that it accepts and stores the dot addresses for an entire page at once, while the dot matrix accepts output from the computer in chunks. Because they take a page at a time, laser printers need at least 1 megabyte of RAM storage to retain a page in temporary buffer memory.

Laser Print History

Historically, laser printers date from the first industrial model introduced in 1977 by the Xerox Corporation—the Model 9700. The 9700 utilized a print mechanism similar to Xerox photocopiers, the primary difference being that the 9700 accepted the digital image directly from the computer rather than from an optical scanner. IBM followed with the 3800, based on its own copier.

The first *commercial* laser was the Xerox 2700, introduced in 1981 at a consumer cost of $20,000; thousands of this model were sold. In 1984, Canon introduced its own printer engine which was incorporated into the most popular laser printers manufactured after that date.

Hewlett-Packard used the Canon engine in its LaserJet, the first affordable laser printer for most companies. The LaserJet pioneered laser printers for the office, amazing users by producing 40 pages per minute.

By the late 1980s, the demand for laser printers forced manufacturers to lower their prices in order to remain competitive. Reawakened interest in desktop publishing further fueled the demand. Eventually, desktop publishing and laser printers teamed to become a fast-paced growth industry.

Ink-jet Printers Ink-jet printers use tiny nozzles which direct a stream of electrostatically charged ink to the surface of the paper. A grid of ink sprays out from the printhead onto the page as letters or characters.

Problems with clogged nozzles which characterized earlier models have been largely resolved by improved technology. One solution to the problem is the solid ink-jet printer introduced by Dataproducts in 1987. The SI-480 of Dataproducts takes solid ink, heats it on demand, and shoots it out as a liquid. Upon hitting the page, the ink resolidifies.

Late-model ink-jet printers compete with laser printers in terms of font capabilities and the handling of graphics. Color models are also available.

Thermal-transfer Printers Thermal-transfer printers utilize a thermal ribbon with an underside coated with an ink that melts at high temperatures. Dot-matrix characters are formed via an array of electrodes (dots that form characters and lines). The electrodes transmit heat to the thermal ribbon, causing the ink to melt, then transfer the characters directly to the paper.

Thermal printers are quiet, they offer high resolution, and they can produce in color. But they are not particularly fast, and they are expensive to operate because of the high cost of the ribbon.

Choosing a Printer for Word Processing

The selection of a computer printer is directly related to the buyer's present and near-future needs. For example, if desktop publishing and quality documents are a primary concern, a laser printer is the obvious choice. If spreadsheet applications are important, a wide-carriage dot-matrix, or one of the new ink-jets, will fill the bill. An important issue in the decision is compatibility. Will the printer be 100 percent compatible with the software to be used with it? If the software and printer are purchased together, the dealer can demonstrate their compatibility by calling up certain printer commands from the software program.

Ergonomics—the science of human and machine compatibility—also deserves notice in the purchase decision; noise pollution can be a source of great discomfort to persons sitting nearby. Although acoustic hoods can reduce noise levels, a better option is the purchase of a machine whose sound level is several decibels below that which can cause discomfort. The variance in noise levels among printers of the same size and type is surprisingly broad. A listening test should be a part of the purchase decision.

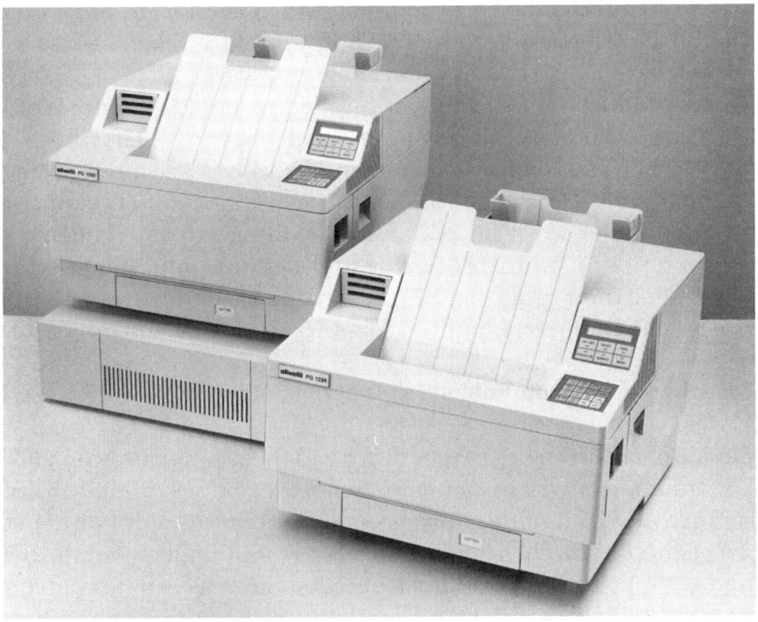

Figure 5-5 The Olivetti PG 1260 Laser printer has 35 resident fonts; the PG 1230, six. Both output 12 pages per minute. *Courtesy of Olivetti U.S.A.*

Purchasers should also use a reliable dealer, preferably one who will come on site to service the printers as needed after purchase. If this is not possible, a nearby authorized service center should be identified as a service representative of the vendor.

DESKTOP PUBLISHING

The term *desktop publishing* surfaced in the mid-1980s to describe a new technology designed for personal computers. Desktop publishing enabled *personal computer work stations* to produce documents rivaling in appearance those produced by professional printers.

Utilizing desktop publishing software, users can design and print newsletters, brochures, reports, and other publications with professional touches not unlike those of commercial print shops. Basic desktop features include: columnar layout of two, three, or more columns, line drawing capabilities, multiple styles and sizes of fonts, clip art to match many subjects, and import of scanned images, reduced or enlarged, to fit the place of insert.

Although still in its infancy as a technology, desktop publishing is one of the fastest growing segments of the computer industry. Its relationship to word processing, at first distant, has grown to a mutual cloning of each other's features, and to a possible future merger of the two into one "word publishing" technology.

MicroPro International Corporation calls its latest word processing release a "word publishing" package. Lifetree Software Inc. refers to its new word processing software as "personal publishing" software.

Other product line adjustments by major vendors include: Word Perfect 5.1 and Xywriter—both offering sophisticated page layout facilities, line art, graphics, and other desktop features in their latest word processing versions; and Lexisoft's Spellbinder Desktop Publisher, a page composition product wrapped around its Spellbinder word processor. Text-editing software is being replaced by a new generation of word processing and desktop publishing hybrids. Two factors have fueled their rapid growth: the emergence of desktop publishing software for personal computers, and reasonably priced laser printers.

Selecting a Desktop Publishing Program

Desktop publishing packages differ widely in sophistication and features offered. The administrative assistant must weigh the options carefully before selecting the package most suitable to the equipment and needs of his or her company.

To begin the search, he or she must know and understand the limitations of the company's computer system. Generally, the more sophisticated the software package, the higher its demands on hardware. For example, a hard disk, a high-resolution monitor, and a graphics display adapter are mandatory for most desktop publishing packages. If the company's computer system is a floppy disk/dot-matrix configuration, an entry-level package may have to suffice. While the resolution of images is less than impressive, the output may be adequate for in-house newsletters, training-program materials, and routine notices.

With more expansive computer configurations, the buyer's options are enhanced considerably. True desktop publishing quality is achieved through high-level packages, usually requiring a laser printer, a hard disk, megabytes of RAM memory, and graphics display monitors.

Clip art suitable for a variety of applications is included with most desktop

Figure 5-6 The Canon Express Desktop Publisher System includes three pieces of equipment: scanner, computer, and printer. *Courtesy of Canon USA, Inc.*

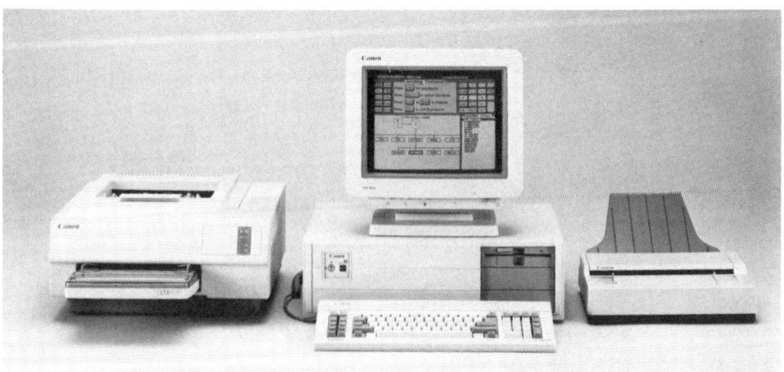

publishing packages, or can be purchased for a modest additional sum. Two leaders in the desktop publishing arena, PageMaker and Ventura, belong to this category. They produce professional-looking documents at a fraction of the cost charged by commercial printers. Style sheets and a generous selection of fonts account, in part, for their success.

Style Sheets and Fonts Style sheets allow the user to choose a design such as a book chapter or newsletter, and attach the set of design elements—number of columns and particular fonts—to the text. They help by bringing up the same style sheet every time one begins a new chapter or unit for example. No inconsistencies in format or font are allowed to creep into the publication.

A font is a particular size and weight of type. A font family describes the style of all those sizes and weights, such as Times Roman, Helvetica, or Courier. Font sizes range from 1 point to as high as 72 points. Fonts starting at 14 point are suitable for headlines.

Factors to Consider in Purchasing a Desktop Publishing Program

A critical question in choosing a desktop publisher is whether or not the program can "read" the word processing format of the document being imported to it. Format reading means more than reading the ASCII texts, stripped of any formatting information. It means reproducing the boldfacing, underlining, indented blocks, and other enhancements native to the word processing files it is accepting.

At the output level, the number and kind of printers supported by the desktop publisher is an important consideration. Most programs support popular laser printers but relatively few support dot-matrix printers. If a laser printer is not within the company's budget plans, the administrative assistant should make sure that the software does support 24-pin dot-matrix printers.

Since prices range from $100 or less for entry-level programs to over $1,000 for microcomputer-based systems, a wide range of choices is available. Somewhere between the two extremes—from entry-level at one end to high-level sophistication and cost at the other—is the just-right answer to a company's desktop publishing needs.

The administrative assistant should remember, too, that ease of learning may be a more important factor than price, since many hours of productive work-time can be lost by employees endeavoring to master the intricacies of a complex program.

Industry experts advise new users to start slowly with desktop publishing, since many features of the high-level programs may have little or no application to their own businesses. One way that the administrative assistant can determine which desktop features are most appealing and necessary for his or her company is to ask for sample printouts of various programs. The printout output should be produced with the same computer and printer hardware as that used by his or her company.

When the administrative assistant finds a program whose printouts are satisfactory, whose level of sophistication is high enough to handle company requirements, and whose price is fair, the purchase of the package can be recommended to company officials.

The Future for Desktop Publishing

Estimates vary widely on the direction of desktop publishing in the future. Some see it incorporating word processing as a subset of desktop publishing. Others see word processing packages incorporating more desktop publishing features, virtually eliminating the need for desktop publishing as a separate software application.

Since desktop publishing involves new vocabulary and skills, many users believe that it cannot be considered an extension of word processing. However, some mixing of technologies is already in place, and more is in progress. By the mid-1990s, the two technologies could evolve into a new medium, already referred to as *word publishing*.

SUMMARY

PC-based word processing is a prominent component of the electronic office. Word processing centers, once the heart of upscale electronic offices, have been replaced by one-on-one work relationships of executives and their administrative assistants.

With their personal computers, administrators and their assistants perform their own word processing chores, no longer depending on word processing centers to do it for them.

The responsibilities of the administrative assistant mount when attempting to evaluate market offerings in word processing software and trying to select the best word processor for the company's needs. To be considered are the features provided by the software package, the hardware restrictions imposed by the company's computer system, and the special needs of the primary users.

Printers, too, must be studied carefully to assure making the right choice. Impact and non-impact printers deserve consideration. The appropriate choice will become apparent as each printer is evaluated in the light of the essential and special features needed or desired by company users.

Optical character readers scan typewritten and printed materials to bring them into the electronic system. OCR technology enables a company to utilize electronic typewriters as well as word processors to manipulate and store data electronically. Image scanners import drawings into word-processed documents.

As desktop publishing software increases in popularity, distinctions between word processing and desktop publishing appear to be blurring. Analysts predict that the two technologies will merge into one medium in the not-too-distant future, creating *word publishing* as a replacement of both.

QUESTIONS FOR REVIEW

1. Describe the evolution of word processing from its primitive beginnings in the 1930s to its current status as an electronic staple in the office.
2. When and by whom was the term *word processor* first coined?
3. When did dedicated word processors begin to wane in popularity, and what precipitated their decline?
4. Give at least three benefits gained from the use of PC-based word processors as compared to dedicated word processors.
5. List some of the newest features which characterize full-featured word processing programs.
6. Describe the *essential* features which every word processor should have to be truly functional in today's electronic office.
7. Describe some of the typical hardware requirements of full-featured word processing programs.
8. Why is good documentation so important?
9. How can scanners save time and money for the company having a limited office equipment budget? Explain.
10. Why are dot-matrix printers so popular for both business and personal use?
11. Explain the disadvantages of daisywheel printers.
12. What two factors have contributed most to the growth of desktop publishing?

QUESTIONS FOR DISCUSSION

1. Which of the functions of the special or full-featured word processing packages would you like most to have at *your* fingertips? Explain your choice.
2. When a new word processing package is being considered for purchase, why is it important that the primary users be consulted about the selection? Is vendor support an important consideration in the purchase? Explain.
3. Desktop publishing has enabled companies to save many dollars in professional printing costs. In your opinion, how much, if any, impact is desktop having on the printing industry currently, or projected to have in the future?
4. OCR scanners scan typewritten and printed materials, reading them into a word processor for electronic editing, printing, and storage. Discuss the feasibility of having one word processor, one OCR, and eight to ten electronic typewriters in an office housing six administrators, and twelve secretaries, stenographers, and clerk typists. Would the dollar savings justify buying only one word processor but many typewriters, since OCR equipment can transform the typed materials into electronic media?

SUGGESTED ACTIVITIES

1. Set up a debate between two teams in the class to debate the issue of basic word processing packages versus full-featured ones.

   For: All major businesses should buy top-of-the-line word processing packages rather than the lesser known packages which are "feature poor" compared to their "big league" cousins.

Against: Basic word processing programs cost about 75 percent less than full-featured word processors, yet deliver the word processing functions that most users want and *use*. Therefore, it is foolish to spend extra dollars for something that may *never* be used.

2. Pretend that you are employed in a busy corporate office which produces a variety of documents (company newsletter, customer-appreciation brochures, sales flyers, and so on), some of which you have a hand in producing. You also process a heavy load of daily business correspondence.

   Consult a current comparison chart of word processors and check periodicals for evaluations of the newest word processing software. From the information gathered, select a word processing package which you believe will best fill your needs for both special applications and regular correspondence.
3. Form into groups of four or five each; each group investigate the pros and cons of one of the best-selling desktop packages. If possible, get copies of the software to demonstrate its merits to the class. Conduct a survey among class members afterwards to determine how each would rank the programs for quality of output, ease of use, and practicality for business applications.

REFERENCES

Desktop Publishing

ANTONOFF, MICHAEL, "DTP Software: Hardware and Features Choices," *Personal Computing* (June 1989), 115–120.

FOLEY, MARY JO, "PC Word Processing: The Era of New & Improved," *Datamation* (May 1988), 75–77.

METZNER, KERMIT, "Desktop Publishing: Pretty as a Picture," *Office Systems '88* (March 1988), 33–38.

KLEINMAN, LISA, "Now, Desktop Presentations," *Personal Computing* (January 1988), 91–93.

Scanners

BRIGGS, GEORGE, "Scanners Gain in Input Race," *MIS Week* (July 11, 1988), 35.

BURNACZ, JOANNE G., "Expand Your Horizons with a Scanner," *Today's Office* (August 1987), 12–18.

FEUCHE, MIKE, "Optical Character Recognition Takes a Step with New Pack," *MIS Week* (Augst 1, 1988), 23.

Word Processing

JENKINS, TOM, "Information Processing with the WP Connection," *Office Systems '88* (October 1988), 90–97.

JOHNSON, ROBIN, "Word Processing Software: Blazing New Trails," *Today's Office* (August 1989), 19–22.

MINICUCCI, RICK, "New WP Features Add Sizzle to Your Documents," *Today's Office* (March 1988), 24–29.

O'MALLEY, CHRISTOPHER, "Picture Perfect WordPerfect 5.0," *Personal Computing* (August 1988), 165–166.

GLOSSARY OF DESKTOP PUBLISHING TERMS

Ascender: Portion of a lower-case letter rising above its x height

Base line: Imaginary rule running under each line of type. Base lines touch the bottoms of most letters

Cap height: Height of the capital letters of a typeface

Character: Any letter, numeral, symbol, punctuation mark, or space between words

Compose: To set type

Composition: Type that has been set

Copy: All written material needing to be typeset

Copyfit: To use character counts and editing to plan so that type fits space allotted by the layout

Descender: Portion of a lower-case letter falling below its base line

Display type: Type of 14 points or over

Extended type: Characters wide in proportion to their height

Flush left or right: Type aligned vertically at the left or right side of the margin
Folio: Page number; low folio, the left-hand page; high folio, the right
Font: Complete set of upper- and lower-case characters of one typeface
Galley: Tray used to hold metal type assembled ready for printing
Galley proof: Proof of typeset copy
Gothic type: Type without serifs
Headliner: Machine that sets display type positioned individually by hand
Italics: Characters that slant to the right
Kerning: Letter spacing that makes letters appear better fitted together
Leader: Row of dots guiding the eye across a page
Leading: Amount of space between lines of type, expressed in points
Letter spacing: Amount of space between letters, usually adjustable
Page proof: Type output in page format complete with headings, rules, and numbers
Phototype: Type created by projecting light onto photosensitive paper
Point: Unit of measure equaling 1/12 of a pica and 1/72 of an inch; always used to express type size and leading
Repro: Type with corrections made and elements in position ready to reproduce by printing
River: Distracting pattern of white space running down through text type
Roman type: Type with serifs. Also type that is upright (not italic)

6
Management of Mail and Postal Services

The mailroom is an integral part of the communication channel which keeps business in touch with its clients and customers. Mailroom personnel collect, sort, and distribute incoming and interoffice mail to addressees company-wide; and collect, sort, post, and allocate costs to departmental units for mail addressed to external receivers. The final phase of their mail-handling procedures is delivery of the posted mail to the United States Postal Service for distribution.

Although the United States Postal Service (USPS) handles the bulk of a company's outgoing correspondence, courier services also play a role in the pickup and delivery of packages. The mailroom manager must be familiar with the services of both private couriers and the USPS in order to maintain an efficient operation.

The responsibilities of mailroom managers have grown to encompass an understanding of complex electronic devices as well as mechanized equipment to help them move the mail rapidly and efficiently. Concerns for employee health and well-being motivate their attempts to achieve an ergonomic balance in the process.

Terms in this chapter include:

- robotized letter carriers
- computerized manifest systems
- postal customer councils
- bar code readers
- priority mail
- "intelligent" inserters

MAILROOM MANAGEMENT

Figures from the United States Postal Service show that the volume of mail is mushrooming. The USPS processes over 160 billion pieces of mail annually, 95 percent of which is business related.

Add to this the additional millions delivered by private couriers, and it becomes clear why executives, particularly those with heavy mail volume, appreciate the contribution of cost-conscious mailroom managers to the company's overall profitability.

The current attitude of executives toward mailroom managers represents a change from the recent past. In the not-too-distant past, the mailroom was taken for granted as a mere clearinghouse for incoming and outgoing mail, its activities generating little interest on the part of anyone outside its immediate environs.

Viewed primarily as a necessary but unpopular cost of doing business, the mailroom was not recognized as a department which was amenable to positive change. Three factors reversed this negative view: (1) steadily rising postage rates, (2) high labor costs, and (3) an ever-rising tide of outgoing mail.

The need to find cost-cutting solutions alerted corporate executives to the need for effective mailroom management.

Rising Costs

Every two to three years for the past two decades, USPS has increased postal rates. In 1988, rates for first-class letters had reached 25 cents, an increase

Figure 6-1 Automated systems enable the mailroom staff to keep up with rising volumes of incoming and outgoing mail. *Courtesy of Pitney Bowes.*

of almost 14 percent over the previous rate. Other rates increased proportionately, to as high as 22 percent for some classes of service.

As in all departments, labor costs in the mailroom also escalated. To save dollars, management at first considered using fewer workers or replacing skilled employees with unskilled workers at lower pay scales. In the face of labor union resistance, however, the latter option could not be exercised.

With no control over postage rates, limited control over wage rates, and none over the mushrooming volume of mail deluging their departments, mailroom managers had to look elsewhere to satisfy company demands for efficient, cost-effective operations. They discovered a range of cost-containment options, many of which had already been tried experimentally and proven cost-effective. Most were classed in one of the following categories:

Automated mailing systems
New and updated equipment, designed for greater speed and accuracy
Newly designed mailrooms with ergonomic considerations given to furnishings, lighting, environmental conditions, and decor
Better utilization of USPS and courier services

Automated Mailing Systems

Computers have become an integral part of the mailroom functions in organizations large enough to staff fully operational mail-handling facilities. With the aid of computerized systems, all facets of the mail-handling process can be done with speed and accuracy far surpassing that achieved through manual procedures. For example, folding, inserting, weighing, and metering mail can be accomplished with speed and precision under computerized control.

Remote-controlled robotic systems can trim and fold letters, insert them into envelopes, and seal, meter, and stack them, without human interjection. Robotized letter carriers pick up and deliver the mail to company offices, following a fluorescent guidepath indicated on the hard floor or carpet. The robot carriers read operating instructions at each point of pickup, following orders given there. Some models are programmed to open doors or to board elevators. They also include certain safety features, such as beep tones and flashing lights to warn persons of their approach.

Automated mail systems also increase accuracy. In the past, mechanical scale readings were not always precise. However, *digital electronic scales* are very precise. Interfaced to postage meters and mail machines, the electronic scales weigh material with precision (some giving readings in increments of 1/32 or 1/64 of an ounce), selecting the most economical rate from a variety of couriers and the USPS, and affixing the postage.

Providing exact weights can reap savings as high as 30 percent, according to some estimates. Both USPS and business personnel tend to overpost mail that have borderline weights rather than risk the embarrassment of underposting them. With automation, weighing mail is no longer a hit-or-miss process. Some electronic scales also house internal microchips which accommodate postal rate changes as they occur.

Postage by phone is another trend in mailroom automation. *Postage-by-phone meters* provide a number of benefits. Users do not have to go to the post office to reset their postage meters. The meters use an electronic funds-transfer approach similar to the bill-paying services offered by many banks. Rental costs are only slightly higher than for conventional meters. Their automatic computer reports of meter and postage use also allow management to control and assess mailroom operations.

Computerized manifest or shipping systems provide accounting information for parcels sent via carriers such as the USPS, UPS, and overnight delivery services. These shipping systems automatically record complete and accurate accounts of all items shipped, thus eliminating much manual record keeping. They also provide documentation on the number of items shipped, individual and total costs, date and time of each shipment, and the name of the person to be charged in each department.

Automation has also upgraded the capabilities of postage meters. Available for as little as $15 per month, these *postage meters* can print postage and postmarks on thousands of letters per hour. One manufacturer provides a system which recharges a meter with postage by remote control. A telephone call to its data center resets the meter for the caller promptly.

Bar code readers are profitably employed in some mailrooms to sort incoming mail to 9-digit zips representing in-house departmental mail stops. Bar coding outgoing mail permits a finer sort in the postal system, thus speeding the delivery of business communications. Additionally, postage discounts earned by combin-

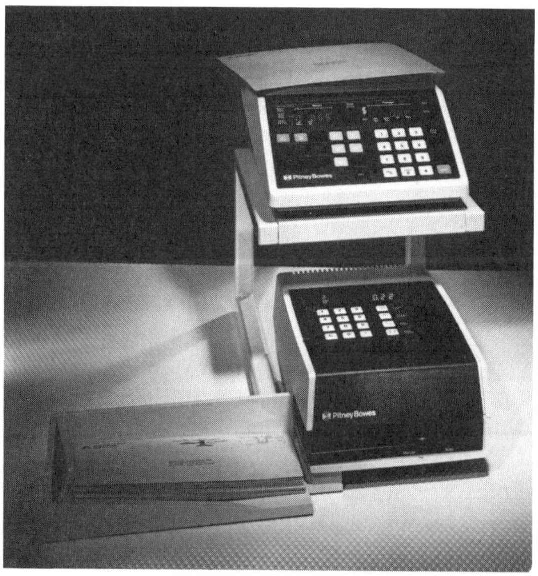

Figure 6-2 This automated desktop system features an electronic scale and a postage meter which can be reloaded by telephone. Rates are updated with a replaceable memory chip. *Courtesy of Pitney Bowes.*

ing ZIP + 4 and prebar-coded outgoing mail repay the investment in the company's bar coding equipment while it saves time and labor costs, too.

Labelers and inserters have also been automated for greater speed, accuracy, and cost savings. *Automated labelers*, for example, can presort mail by zip codes even when operating at speeds up to 30,000 documents per hour, and the presort operation can save as much as 5 cents on each first-class piece.

Handheld units can apply preprinted labels at a rate of 1,500 an hour. Ink-jet addressing systems, being used by some companies as an alternative to labels, print addresses and bar codes directly on envelopes at high speeds, to effect even greater savings.

Some high-speed inserting systems process 5,000 to 8,500 mailings per hour. *"Intelligent" inserters,* programmed to save postage costs, "decide" whether or not to insert another piece on the basis of weight and postage cost. If, for instance, one more insertion will call for additional postage, no insertion is made.

New and Updated Equipment

Equipment must be updated periodically to keep mailroom operations running smoothly. New devices, designed to speed operations or ease the burden of manual handling, also contribute to that objective. For example:

New bundling systems use plastic strips rather than rubber bands and strings to tie packages of mail.

Mail-extracting equipment separates mail by thickness, to sort standard bill payments from other incoming material.

Other equipment verifies that incoming envelopes are empty before being discarded.

An *accumulating printer,* interfaced with the postage scale, provides detailed audit trails and accounting information for managerial personnel.

Mail carts are upgraded with sorting bins to allow coarse sorting at time of pickup.

Modern plastics make products more durable and quiet, and decrease manufacturing costs.

To remain current, the mailroom manager must regularly scan trade periodicals and attend trade shows where new equipment is displayed. Only in this way can he or she keep the mailroom at top efficiency.

Design and Furnishings

While automated procedures and updated equipment are essential to the efficient processing of the mail, another facet related to productivity must not be overlooked. That is the workplace itself, its location and decor, and the effect these factors have on the personnel who work there.

A spirit of community with workers in other departments is fostered by a *centrally located mailroom.* Easily accessed by the regular mailroom "traffic," the

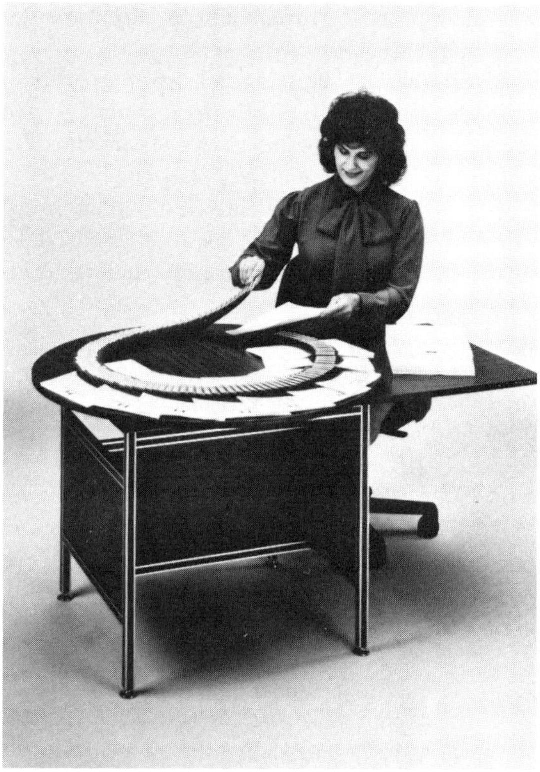

Figure 6-3 Ideal for small areas, the portable rotary sorter is just 36 inches in diameter, yet holds 112 polypropylene dividers. *Courtesy of Hamilton Sorter Co.*

central location allows all employees to socialize with each other, creating bonds of friendship and loyalty to the company.

Too often, the mailroom has been situated geographically distant from other departments, creating a situation wherein the employees feel cut off from other departments. Current trends place the mailroom in a centrally located position, accessible to all departments, with its employees active participants in company events and activities.

Appropriate decor is important to employee morale also. An attractive workplace, decorated with care and attention to detail, instills in the employees a sense of pride in their company. Studies have shown, too, that certain colors stimulate predictable psychological responses. Blue, for example, creates a cooling, quiet effect; red, vibrancy and drive; and yellow, a happy, upbeat mood.

Good lighting is essential in a mailroom. While overhead fluorescent lighting may be sufficient for the general area, *task lighting* is recommended for specific work areas, to reduce eyestrain.

For long stints at the computer station, employees must be provided *strong overhead lighting,* preferably incandescent, for steady uninterrupted light streams on the computer screen. The screen must have high resolution and be free of glare.

Computer operators must be cautioned, too, to take a break from their stations for a few minutes every couple of hours, to lessen the hazard of undue eyestrain.

Properly ventilated rooms are another imperative for employee health. *Central air conditioning* units are the surest means of getting healthful, cooling temperatures and adequate ventilation in the summer months. Central heating units, combined with central humidifiers, provide the same balance in the winter months.

Modular furniture in the mailroom saves space, promotes efficiency, and in the long run, generates savings through its flexibility. Modules are configured to fit a variety of needs and designed to suit the purchasers' current applications. If or when the applications change, the modules are rearranged to fit the new requirements. Modular units include file cabinets, book shelves, sorting racks, bins, countertops, and other functional items.

Courier Services

Over 70 percent of small-to-midsize companies regularly use overnight couriers. Courier-management services offer a selection of surface, air, or electronic alternatives to move mail. Temporary services provide in-house mail delivery management; and a number of "pack and ship" services cater to the small shipper.

Figure 6-4 Modular units are configured to match company requirements. This U-shaped wall unit is placed just above the work surface to speed and simplify the sort process. *Courtesy of Hamilton Sorter Co.*

SAMPLE MAILROOM DESIGNS

This sample design is typical of a small organization and occupies 160 square feet of floor space.

The L shape fine sort configuration in this mailroom has 132 oversize openings for incoming mail and combines the fine sort and dumping operations.

The outgoing area includes preparation, scale, postage sort and meter operations.

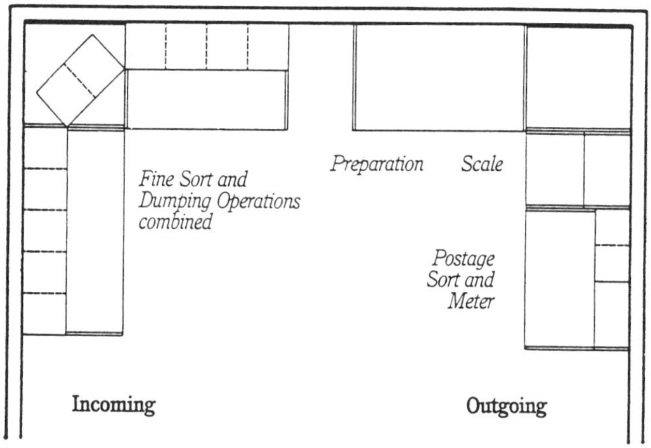

A larger organization might require a layout similar to the one illustrated here. This room is 15 feet wide by 17 feet long.

The incoming side is broken into three separate operations, dump, presort, and fine sort. The presort has 12 openings, one for each department, and the fine sort breaks these down even further to accommodate the 144 individuals within these departments.

The outgoing side has a branch sort with 48 openings, a scale area and a meter area.

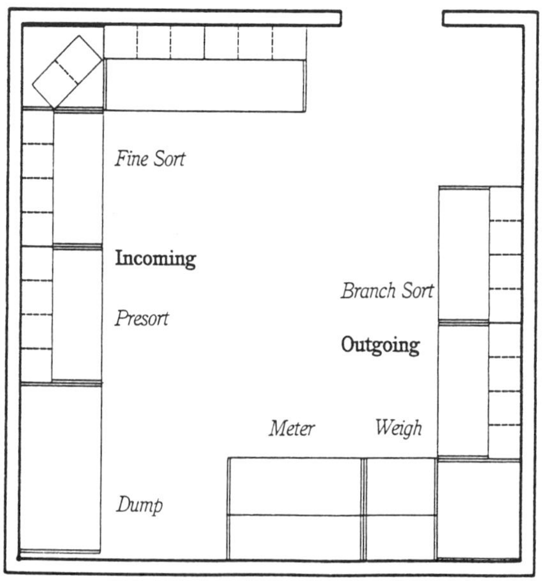

Figure 6-5 Sample mailroom designs. *Courtesy of Hamilton Sorter Company.*

As competition increases among courier providers, many are offering volume discounts and other incentives to lure new customers from competitors and retain the loyalty of their old customers. One nationally known carrier offers consultative services to companies having large volume mailings. They review a company's shipping applications and discuss alternatives to existing policies and procedures.

Before contracting with a courier for an extended period of service, the mailroom manager may opt for a limited-period service of one to two months to test the courier's competence and reliability. If the service is satisfactory, he or she may discover that contracting with outside service providers is a cost effective way to deal with certain aspects of mailroom operations.

THE UNITED STATES POSTAL SERVICE

One facet of management that directly affects the company's mailroom budget is the manager's knowledge and utilization of services offered by the United States Postal Service.

Despite the well-publicized weaknesses of the USPS, it remains the principal delivery channel for written communications in the United States. It is vital, therefore, that companies use the USPS services as cost effectively as possible.

The USPS does its part by making available to users information on all its special services and rates, including discounts available to volume mailers who perform some of the mail-handling duties otherwise performed by USPS personnel.

As an information channel, USPS offers a wide range of mailroom-related courses for customers who wish to know more about up-to-date mailroom procedures. They also sponsor lectures and seminars for in-house mailroom training, and provide self-training literature to customers who cannot attend their seminars.

Postal authorities claim that the seminars are as beneficial to the USPS as they are to their customers, inasmuch as better mail preparation at the company level results in better and faster delivery service by USPS workers.

For example, by bar coding their outgoing mail, businesses help the USPS perform a finer and speedier sort at the post office, thus speeding delivery of the bar-coded letters to their final destinations. By the same token, mailroom personnel can profitably employ bar-code *readers* to sort incoming mail to 9-digit zips (ZIP + 4), representing company departmental mail stops.

Prebar Coding and 9-digit Zip Codes

Companies who combine prebar-coded outgoing mail with 9-digit zips earn postage discounts which, over a period of time, not only pay for the bar code equipment, but continue to earn discounts while getting speedier mail-handling service from USPS.

The USPS is anxious to cooperate with businesses who wish to convert to the ZIP + 4 program; mailers can have their 5-digit zip-coded address lists converted to the + 4 digits free of charge. Mainframe computer users can obtain the ZIP + 4 Directory tapes free of charge; diskette users can submit their diskettes with a minimum of 300 addresses for the + 4 update. Printed lists of 5,000 or less also qualify for this free service.

Upon return of the updated lists or diskettes, the accompanying computer printout lists those addresses which could not be encoded. These are usually nonexistent or transposed street addresses which when deleted, clean the list, thus saving postage bills in future mailouts.

Postal Customer Councils

The combined efforts of the business community and the USPS have resulted in the formation of the Postal Customer Councils, a regularly scheduled forum designed for mutually beneficial dialogue between business and the USPS.

Members of the business community and postal officials meet in a common forum to discuss all aspects of the USPS. Here mailers can get their questions answered, have new programs explained, and voice comments and suggestions to the postal officials for improving service. At the same time, they can meet other

Figure 6-6 The nine-digit ZIP + 4 code shortens delivery time and generates discounts for volume users. *Courtesy of U.S. Postal Service.*

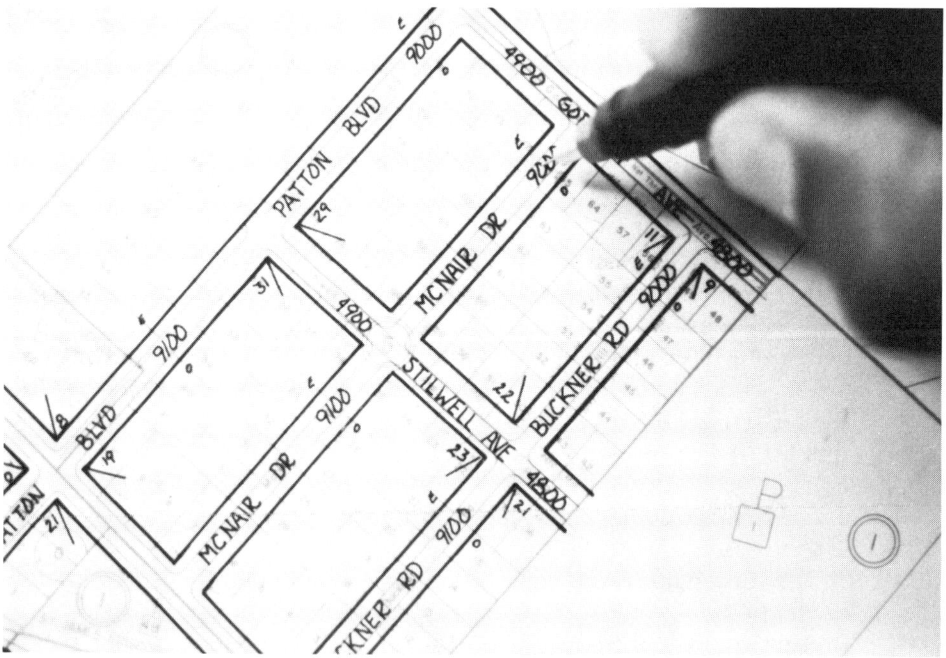

mailers to discuss matters of mutual concern. The result strengthens communication between postal management and business mailers.

Local councils are established on the basis of the postmaster's geographic area of responsibility, with membership open to anyone in that area. No annual dues are assessed, and members can participate through regularly mailed surveys and scheduled meetings.

Each council meeting typically includes a guest speaker and a seminar, the subject matter drawn from the results of annual questionnaires sent to members.

Begun in 1971, the response of the business community to the Postal Customer Councils has been enthusiastic. New local councils are established each year, generating greater understanding between the USPS and its primary users.

USPS Special Services

The wide range of special services offered by the USPS to both business and private mailers is too extensive to describe in detail here. Booklets published by USPS and listed at the end of this chapter detail other services, as well as current postal rates. Most are available free of charge from local post offices. Businesses avail themselves of many of the USPS special services, particularly the following:

Priority Mail Priority Mail is first-class mail weighing more than 12 ounces but no more than 70 pounds. In size, the priority-mail package cannot exceed 108 inches in length and width combined.

For one flat rate ($2.40 in 1990), any package weighing 2 pounds or less can be sent in just two days between major metropolitan areas, and three days everywhere else. The flat rate saves time in weighing packages and calculating postage.

Priority Mail envelopes and Priority Mail stickers, both available from USPS, assure preferential treatment from personnel at the post office.

Express Mail Next-Day Service This is the fastest service offered by USPS. Several options are available for delivery of letters and packages. Express Mail Overnight Service assures next-day delivery of an 8-ounce package for $8.75 and a 2-pound pack for $12.00. A 5-pound package is delivered for the flat rate of $15.25 (in 1990).

To use Express Mail Next-Day Service between major cities, mail must be deposited in an Express Mail collection box, generally by 5 P.M. for delivery the next day by 3 P.M. (weekends and holidays included). Destinations which can be reached overnight may be checked by using the Express Mail Network Directory, available at the post office.

Express Mail service comes with a money-back guarantee. A refund of 100 percent of postage is paid if the expressed mail is not at the destination post

Figure 6-7 Express Mail, one of many services offered by the U.S. Postal Service for prompt delivery of mail. *Courtesy of U.S. Postal Service.*

office by 10 A.M. the next business day, or delivery has not been attempted by 3 P.M. of the next day.

Various shapes and sizes of shipping containers are available for use with Express Mail, such as the "Overnighter Box," the "Overnighter Tube," and the "2-Pound Pak." Express Mail may also be certified, insured, and forwarded, if necessary.

Express Mail Reship Service gathers all the mail daily from one point and delivers it via Express Mail Overnight Service to the destination point in a single container. This eliminates piece-by-piece delivery and expedites delivery of time-sensitive mail. The service is especially convenient for heavy mailings between a corporate headquarters and its branch offices.

Certified Mail Certified mail provides a mailing receipt and a record of delivery maintained at the recipient's post office. A return receipt to provide the sender with proof of delivery is available for an additional fee.

Certified mail service is available only for first-class mail. No insurance coverage is provided against loss or damage for this service. (For valuables and irreplaceable items, one should use insured or registered mail.)

To use certified mail, the sender fills out Form 3800, Receipt for Certified Mail, and attaches it to the address side of the mail, together with the required postage.

Certificate of Mailing A certificate of mailing proves an item was mailed, but it does not provide insurance coverage for loss or damage. The post office provides the certificate for a fee, but no other record is maintained at the post office.

Registered Mail Registered mail is designed to provide extra protection for valuable or irreplaceable items, such as extremely important papers, documents, or items having a high monetary value. It is the most secure option offered by the USPS.

Registered articles require first-class postage and are controlled carefully by the USPS from the point of mailing up to delivery.

A receipt is issued by the post office when registered mail is accepted for mailing. Return receipt, postal insurance up to a maximum of $25,000, and restricted delivery services are available for an additional fee.

All packages and envelopes sent by registered mail must be sealed in such a way that items cannot be opened and resealed without showing signs of having been opened. Items that *appear* to have been opened and resealed cannot be registered. Good quality envelopes with heavy deposits of glue all the way to the edge of the flap are recommended.

Restricted Delivery Restricted delivery can be requested when purchasing return-receipt service. Restricted delivery means that delivery is made only to the addressee or to someone who is authorized in writing to receive mail for the addressee.

Restricted delivery mail *can* be delivered to an agent without written authorization from the addressee *if* the addressee is in one of the following groups:

officials of government agencies
members of the legislative and judicial branches of federal and state governments
members of the diplomatic corps
minors
individuals under guardianship

Return Receipts Return receipts are the sender's proof of delivery. They are available for mail sent COD or Express Mail, mail that is registered or certified, and mail that is insured for more than $25. The receipt shows who signed for the item and the date it was delivered. For an additional fee, the sender can request restricted delivery service.

Special Delivery All classes of mail except bulk third class can be sent special delivery. Special delivery is available on all days of the week, including Sundays and holidays, and after regular delivery hours, to customers served by city carriers or who reside within one mile of the destination post office.

The purchase of special delivery service does not always mean the article will be delivered by special messenger. It may be delivered by the regular carrier if the letter is available before the carrier departs for morning deliveries.

Special Handling Special handling service is available for third- and fourth-class mail only, including insured and COD mail. It provides preferential handling to the extent practical in dispatch and transport, but does not provide special delivery. Special handling does *not* mean special care of fragile items. Breakable items should be packed with adequate cushioning and marked *fragile.*

Collect-on-Delivery (COD) Service COD service may be used for merchandise sent to the addressee by first-, third- or fourth-class mail. The merchandise must have been ordered by the addressee and must not exceed $500 in value. The fees charged include insurance protection against loss or damage. COD service is not available for international mail.

Mailgram Service Mailgram service is an electronic message service offered in conjunction with Western Union. It provides next-day postal delivery for messages sent via Western Union to cities in the United States or Canada.

To send a Mailgram, the sender contacts Western Union by telephone or Telex/TWX and dictates the message to the operator; Western Union, in turn, sends the message, usually via Telex or TWX to the main post office of the destination city.

Local delivery is made to the recipient, along with the regular mail, on the next business day. A toll-free telephone number for sending Mailgrams is listed in telephone directories under U.S. Government, Postal Service.

Figure 6-8 Mailgrams, an electronic message service offered by the U.S. Postal Service in conjunction with Western Union. *Courtesy of U.S. Postal Service.*

Presorted First-class Mail First-class letters in mailings of 500 pieces or more qualify for a postage rate 4 cents per piece less than the regular letter rate if they are presorted and prepared according to specific requirements (21 cents for the first ounce in 1990). For properly presorted post cards, the rate is 2 cents less than the regular post card rate.

Basic requirements to qualify include an annual fee of $60; all pieces zip coded; 500 pieces minimum per mailing; weight per piece not to exceed 12 ounces; postage to be paid by postage meter stamps, precanceled adhesive stamps, or permit imprint; and each mailing to be accompanied by a properly completed Form 3602 or 3602-PC.

Complete details on properly presorted mail can be found in Publication 61, "Presort First-Class Mail," issued by the Postal Service and available at local post offices.

ZIP + 4 System As explained earlier in this chapter, the ZIP + 4 system offers a postage discount to volume users. Specifically, the discount is a half cent per piece *more* than the discount for Presort First-Class mailings of 500 or more pieces.

This system is based on the use of automated letter sorting equipment—optical character readers (OCRs) and bar-code sorters (BCSs). ZIP + 4 codes enable the Postal Service to sort the outgoing mail to specific streets, specific buildings, or even specific floors within a building.

The USPS claims that through ZIP + 4, volume mail is handled much more efficiently and accurately, thereby reducing costs and stabilizing postage rates into the future.

Figure 6-9 OCR-read area and bar-code-read area. *Courtesy of U.S. Postal Service.*

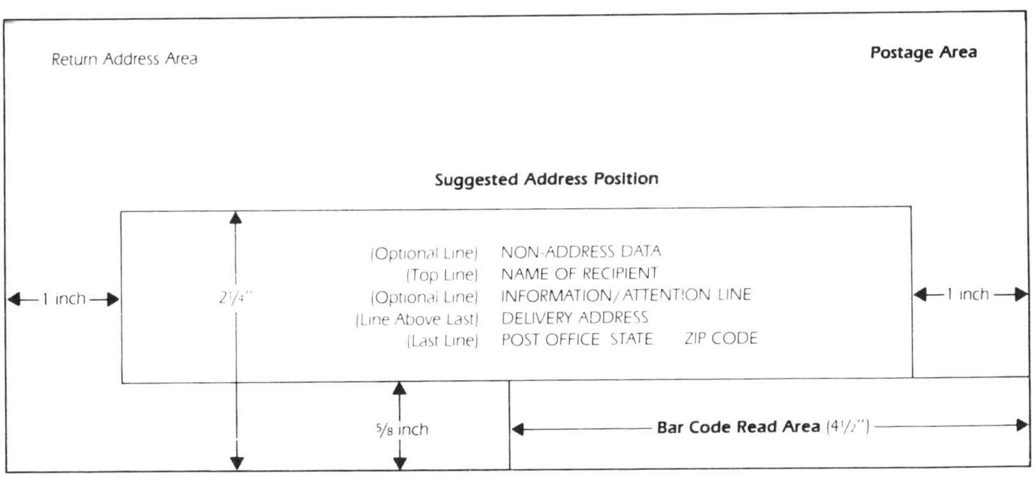

Last Line of Address Must be Completely Within White OCR Area

(Not Drawn to Scale)

The correct format for addressing envelopes for OCR and bar-code scanning is shown in Chapter 4. Brochures and flyers on ZIP + 4, available at local post offices, explain in detail how to qualify for this automated system.

ROLE OF THE MAILROOM MANAGER

Many factors are involved in developing an efficient mailing system, including, as discussed earlier:

A wide range of mechanized and electronic equipment

Modular furniture, configured to fit the specific needs of the mailroom

Strategic utilization of postal and courier services

Well-lighted, ventilated, and temperature-controlled work environments, ergonomically designed to safeguard employees from undue mental or physical stress

All of these factors contribute to a successful mailroom operation. However, one ingredient above all the rest is needed to pull the components together into a "clockwork" operation: capable management.

Although each person has his or her own style of management, guidelines for improving one's performance as a mailroom manager would almost certainly include these factors:

Well-executed procedures for expediting mail sort and distribution

Long- and short-range planning to coordinate with company plans for expansion and/or reorganization, if any

Accountability for expenditures for equipment and supplies, including allocation of costs to departments

Periodic training of new personnel for initial positions, and upgraded training for experienced personnel

Procedures

Procedures are rightly called the building blocks of good organization. Well-designed and *written* procedures, communicated to users in both verbal and written form, are vital to the expeditious handling of the mail.

Employees must master the step-by-step procedures which have proven effective in minimizing errors, increasing productivity, and alleviating stress for the workers.

Procedures include training in operation of the mechanized equipment and electronic devices which sort and meter outgoing mail, plus the sorting and distribution of incoming mail to company employees.

Manual procedures to follow in case of equipment malfunction are also a part of procedural training.

Planning

Long-range and short-range planning serve to unify the structure of mailroom organization. Current needs for personnel and equipment, plus projections for the near and distant future, take into consideration the 20 percent annual growth projected for mailroom operations into the twenty-first century.

Budget projections for additional equipment, personnel, and space to accommodate expanded work areas make up a major portion of five- to ten-year planning schedules.

Long-term goals affect current purchases of equipment. The make and style of electronic equipment purchased must allow for updates and improvements as technological advances occur.

Accountability

The mailroom manager must account to company directors periodically on the performance of the mailroom operation. This may be done monthly or quarterly. Accordingly, he or she must be alerted to strengths and weaknesses in employees' performance by periodic reports from them.

Employee performance reports normally include written evaluations by immediate supervisors, with productivity records and strengths or weaknesses of the employees receiving the major emphasis.

The accounting to company directors should include labor costs per mailing, postage expenditures by department, and total postage costs for the entire company.

Training

Training for newly hired personnel can take many forms, depending, in part, on the complexity of the job assignments, the budget allocations for training purposes, and the availability of competent training personnel.

On-the-job (OTJ) training is a common form of training for initial positions in the mailroom. Computer-aided instruction (CAI) is also increasing in popularity. Its low cost (no personal instructor required), its appeal to the trainees, and its success rate have made CAI the preferred choice of many training specialists.

Vendors also provide limited training programs for employees chosen to operate new or updated equipment. The trained employee then shares his or her newly acquired expertise with fellow workers.

For advancement to higher-level positions, formal training programs are sometimes offered in the mailroom as in all departments of the company. Programs vary, but they may incorporate formal courses offered by community colleges or universities within the area, or in-house courses taught by company personnel.

Attendance at postal conferences and Postal Customer Council meetings also provide valuable insights into customer concerns and the means to provide better service to them.

The Mailroom—Hub of Information Distribution

Paper remains the dominant medium for communicating information in business, with no evidence of its slackening in the near future. Although electronic communications are making giant strides in replacing manual communication methods, "hard copy" correspondence still predominates.

Unless or until the "paperless office" becomes a reality, the mailroom will retain its preeminence as the physical distribution hub of every major organization.

Recognizing its importance, informed company directors are elevating the mailroom to a place of prominence in the company structure. With its "renaissance," mailroom management is in turn recognized as a professional discipline, central to the overall success of company profitability.

SUMMARY

In spite of the availability of many electronic alternatives, the avalanche of written communications continues to mount. Mail volume is projected to grow 20 percent annually into the next century.

Although electronic mail in itself has not diminished mailroom volume, electronic equipment has speeded its processing substantially. Newly mechanized and electronic devices have streamlined the mail-handling process, enabling the mail department to become increasingly efficient and cost effective, contributing its part to the overall managerial effectiveness of its parent company.

Working with the U.S. Postal Service, business firms are earning substantial discounts on their postage by sharing mail-handling responsibilities with the USPS. In turn, the USPS is learning to work with business clients, listening to their concerns and suggestions for improvement at public meetings of Postal Customer Councils.

The councils, established nationwide in 1971 to provide a forum for the mutual exchange of concerns, are reaping benefits for both the USPS and business through mutual understanding and problem solving.

Company directors are recognizing the role of the mailroom manager in making the mail-handling operation cost effective. Because their contribution helps the company achieve profitability, mailroom managers are recognized as professionals by company officials.

QUESTIONS FOR REVIEW

1. Explain how robotics can automate certain phases of a company's mail-handling system.
2. Other than robotics, what other automated systems are being implemented into mailroom operations?
3. Define "intelligent" inserters. How do these devices save postage for users?
4. How do courier service providers contribute to efficiency and cost effectiveness in the mailroom?
5. In what ways will the Postal Service cooperate with businesses in helping them convert to the ZIP + 4 program?
6. Define priority mail. What conditions, in terms of size and weight, are placed on priority mailings?
7. Explain the term *restricted delivery*. Under what circumstances can an agent for the addressee take delivery of a restricted delivery mailing?
8. Can all classes of mail be sent special delivery? Will a special delivery mailing always be delivered by a special agent of the Postal Service? Explain.
9. What are Mailgrams? Are Mailgrams delivered with the daily mail by the regular letter carrier, or by special agents of the Postal Service when messages are received at the local post office?
10. Describe some of the training programs utilized in preparing new employees for positions in the mailroom and in upgrading employees to higher levels of responsibility.

QUESTIONS FOR DISCUSSION

1. In order to make mailrooms cost effective, a range of options is open to management. Of the four options discussed in this chapter, which do you consider most feasible for the small- to medium-sized business with a limited budget? Explain your position.

   Which of the proposed options can be implemented most quickly and with the least outlay of cash?
2. Present arguments for moving the mailroom from a remote location to a central place within the company's main facilities. Discuss how the geographic location of the mailroom can affect the following groups:
   a. mailroom workers
   b. office employees who frequent the mailroom
   c. company executives
3. Discuss the origin and purpose of Poster Customer Councils and their apparent success in establishing rapport with local businesses.

   How can the success of these councils be repeated in similar forums set up for the general public with postal officials? Are such forums practicable? If yes, who should initiate a movement in that direction, USPS representatives or persons representing the people? Explain.
4. In the hierarchical structure of a major corporation, at what level (of the following three) should the mailroom manager be placed? Justify your choice.
   a. top managerial level—second in command, or a vice president
   b. middle management
   c. supervisory

SUGGESTED ACTIVITIES

1. Arrange a class field trip to a local or nearby post office. Through preliminary telephone discussions with the Postmaster, plan to discuss or view:
   a. ZIP + 4 services offered to customers by the Postal Service
   b. OCR mail sort in operation
2. Arrange a similar field trip to the mailroom of a large business. Plan to discuss or view automated mail-handling systems, such as:
   a. digital electronic scales interfaced to postage meters
   b. robotic mail-handling systems that trim, fold, insert, seal, meter, or stack outgoing letters
   c. robotized letter carriers
   d. bar-code readers
   e. "intelligent" inserters
   f. other mechanized or electronic equipment which speeds the mail-handling processes
3. With the advice of mail handlers in small, medium-sized, or large businesses, design the ideal mailroom layout for a given business. Include the necessary equipment and furnishings, lighting fixtures, sound-suppressing room dividers (if any), and the ergonomic considerations necessary to create a healthful working environment.
4. If a Postal Customer Council exists in your city, ask to attend the next meeting. Assess the effectiveness of the meeting and give a brief report to the class.

BOOKLETS ISSUED BY THE U.S. POSTAL SERVICE

A Consumer's Directory of Postal Services and Products, Publication 201, (January 1987).

A Guide to Business Mail Preparation, Publication 25, (December 1985).

Address Information Products Directory—"Aids to Simplify Your Address File Maintenance," Notice 245, (January 1986).

Addressing for Automation—Notice 221, (May 1985).

Information Guide on Presort—First-Class Mail, Publication 61, (May 1987).

Postal Customer Council, A Partnership with Your Local Post Office, Publication 111, (October 1981).

Presort First-Class, Publication 61, (May 1987).

We Deliver, The Story of the U.S. Postal Service, Publication 1, (February 1986).

REFERENCES

BRACKETT, JOSH, "Scaling Down Mailing Costs," *Today's Office* (June 1989), 35–39.

FLEISCHER, RICHARD L., "ZIP + 4—Presort & Cut Costs," *Office Systems '88* (March 1988), 63–66.

LAVOIE, FRANCIS J., "The Mailroom: Meeting the Challenges," *Modern Office Technology* (August 1989), 78–80.

LONG, G. GORDON, "Mailrooms are Vital to Information Flow," *Office Systems '88* (January 1988), 84–86.

METZNER, KERMIT, "Space, People & Time are Mailroom Essentials," *Office Systems '89* (August 1989), 48–52.

7
Electronic Mail and Local Area Networks

INTRODUCTION

The term *electronic mail* (E-mail) encompasses a broad range of electronic communication systems, from computer-based message systems to speech-recognition technology.

Commonly identified with alternatives to written documents and manual delivery systems, electronic mail as discussed in this chapter focuses on the electronic alternatives to document handling by the U.S. Postal Service. It reviews E-mail as expressed in Telex and TWX, computer-based message systems, communicating word processors, voice mail, and facsimile transceivers.

Local area networks (LANs), a medium for transmission of internal E-mail, and wide area networks (WANs), for transmitting electronic mail to distant points, are reviewed in terms of their relationships to electronic mail.

Terms and acronyms in this chapter include:

WANs	teletypewriter
CBMS	modem
PC FAX	LANs
Star topology	Bus topology

ELECTRONIC MAIL

Until the late 1980s, the concept of electronic mail as a significant aid to communications was all but ignored by business. Off to a slow start, its potential for transmitting messages, images, voice, and data communications was recognized by only a few of the giant corporations and virtually none of the small- to mid-size businesses.

As information on E-mail increased and its varied applications became better understood, however, electronic mail began its rapid ascent to prominence.

Telex, TWX

Historically, electronic mail dates back to the invention of the telegraph by Samuel Morse in 1844 and the introduction of his teletype into this country in 1917. At one time, TWX and Telex systems were the most common form of message exchange in use other than that of the U.S. Postal Service.

Originally developed by American Telephone & Telegraph, the teletypewriter networks of Western Union were the largest public networks in the world. Although the two networks, Telex and TWX, were once competitors, both are now owned by Western Union. Each differs only slightly from the other; the teletypewriters differ in their keyboard arrangements, and TWX teletypewriters print somewhat faster than the Telex units.

TWX/Telex offer a relatively inexpensive medium of communications. Subscribers to the service type in a message on their teletypewriters, address it to the Telex or TWX address of the receiver and send it to the receiving terminal located at the recipient's address. Most units, having keyboards, are *transceivers;* that is, they can send as well as receive messages. Units without keyboards are receivers only.

One of the nicest features of TWX/Telex is that operators do not have to be present to receive an incoming message; therefore, messages sent after hours or between widely varying time zones are held until picked up during the next working day. They also have a store-and-forward capability which allows them to hold a message in storage until the receiving unit is free to receive the message.

A disadvantage worth noting, however, is the poor quality print and paper on which the messages are usually printed, making them unsuitable for communicating with customers and clients. For communications between branch offices of a parent company, however, the TWX/Telex communications are entirely adequate.

The units become an electronic convenience when computer terminals are networked with them. A communication originating from a computer can then be sent via the TWX/Telex networks just as readily as those originating from the teletypewriter keyboards. Companies with teletypewriters already installed, however, continue to use them as a relatively inexpensive means of communication.

Computer-based Message Systems (CBMS)

A CBMS can be described as a system for composing messages at a computer terminal and delivering the message to on-line mailboxes or addresses, to be read by recipients at their convenience. Output at the receiving end is displayed on the screen when the recipients check for their incoming mail.

Some public computer networks provide, for a monthly fee, a mailbox service for subscribers. The fee is usually based on the amount of time the subscribers utilize the service. To access the mainframe of the computer service, the subscriber must have communications software and a modem to connect his or her computer to the telephone. Modems are units which are attached to the computer and to the telephone lines to transmit computer signals over telephone wires. (See p. 164 of this chapter.)

The communications software is a versatile tool; its main function is to enable two or more computers to communicate with each other but its capabilities may extend beyond that function. For example, communications software may transfer files from one computer to another, dial busy telephone numbers repeatedly, and store frequently dialed numbers.

To send a CBM, the writer composes the message, then keys in the address or mailbox of the recipient, and the computer does the rest. The recipient has options, also. After reading the message, he or she can store it, print it, erase it, and/or send a response back to the sender.

CBMS are especially popular with employees who travel extensively. From their hotel rooms, employees who carry portable computers (usually with built-in modems) can contact and send messages to the home office electronically or retrieve any messages awaiting them at their desk terminals.

Communicating Word Processors

Since word processors must be compatible in order to communicate, word processing communications are usually restricted to internal use or to branch offices of the company.

The equipment needed to communicate with word processors in remote locations is the same as with CBMS; that is, communications software to connect the two units and a modem to transmit the text over telephone wires.

The process is fairly simple. As an example, consider a nationwide realty group in New York which is finalizing negotiations with potential buyers of a complex of commercial buildings. A tentative contract has been drawn up and the principals are ready to sign. However, before signatures can be affixed, approval must be sought from the top executives of the realty group in Los Angeles.

The contract is typed on the word processor in the New York office, then communicated via telephone wires to the Los Angeles office for review. A soft copy of the transmitted contract appears on the screen of the word processor in the Los Angeles office. The executives there read it, insert revisions or corrections, print a hard copy for their files and re-transmit the corrected version back to the New York office. Assuming that the potential buyers accept the revisions, the entire process may be completed the same day, perhaps within hours of the first transmission.

The beauty of communicating word-processed text is the ease with which revisions can be made or errors corrected at either end of the transmission. Also, at the remote station, as well as at the point of origin, duplicates of the soft copy can be stored on disk and/or printed at will.

Since most word processing is keyboarded on computers rather than on stand-alone processors, all the procedures which apply to computer communications also apply to word processing communications. That is, a computer-based message system (CBMS) is the basic system for transmitting and receiving word processing texts.

Voice Mail

Voice mail, or voice messaging as it is sometimes called, may be the greatest time saver of all forms of electronic mail. By reducing repetitive, time-consuming, and costly telephone calls, as well as futile attempts to make telephone contact between interested parties, voice mail provides a high level of communication efficiency.

Although the terms *voice mail* and *voice messaging* are often used interchangeably, voice mail is more accurately defined as one of two types: voice messaging and voice recognition. *Voice recognition,* though not fully matured as a marketable alternative to standard telephone systems, deserves special note as a technology whose time is near. *Voice messaging,* on the other hand, has become a major force in the electronic office as users recognize its convenience and efficiency.

Basically, voice messaging allows users to receive, send, store, annotate, and forward telephone messages. Typical systems have two facets: message recording and message retrieval. The recording begins when the number dialed is busy or goes unanswered by a human being.

At that point, the automated attendant answers the call with a greeting and a set of instructions to the caller for leaving a message or accessing another party. Typically, a system operates in one of four modes:

1. The automated attendant acts as a telephone operator, accepting calls and giving directions to the caller, including how to leave a message, or to enter an extension number to access another party.
2. The answering mode comes into play when the extension number dialed is busy or goes unanswered. Directions for leaving a message are given at this point.
3. The information center, or bulletin board, is where messages can be left for broadcast to multiple mailbox users. Subscribers to the system can call in from any phone to pick up messages broadcast on the bulletin board.
4. The voice mail mode allows subscribers to send or retrieve messages from the system. Each user's privacy is protected by an assigned password which is used to access the system and retrieve or send messages electronically.

When voice mail was introduced, the technology was limited to voice store-and-forward messaging only. A caller could leave a message on the system for the called party, or the owner could check to see if messages had been left. Messages were stored digitally in computer memory. As the technology matured, compression techniques made it possible to store more digitized messages than before, and the messaging software improved in quality. Costs plummeted also.

In the late 1980s, however, two factors catapulted voice mail into a place of prominence. One was the integration of voice mail with PBXs (private branch exchanges); the other was the integration of voice mail with personal computers.

Voice Mail and PBXs

Some PBX firms developed their own voice processing systems, offering them as add-ons to their basic PBX systems. Others offered one or more of the proprietary systems available from companies specializing in voice processing systems.

A minicomputer or mainframe typically handled the information exchange. Add-on features, such as call-forwarding frequently enhanced these systems.

Figure 7-1 Dictaphone Corporation's Connexions voice processing system forms a complete office systems network for improved interoffice and intraoffice communications. *Courtesy of Dictaphone Corporation, a Pitney Bowes Company.*

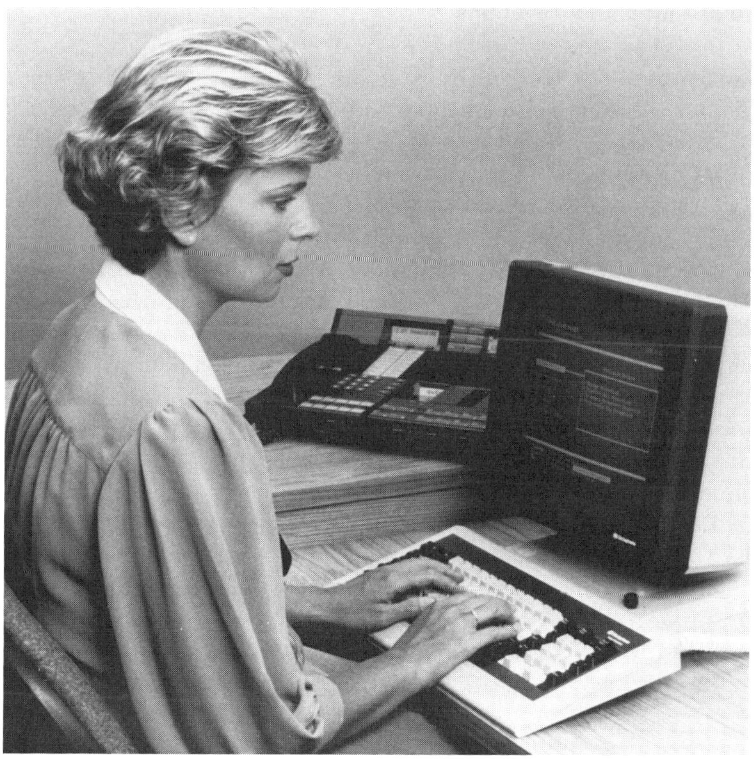

One advantage of coupling voice mail with a PBX system became immediately apparent: user-recorders could personalize their messages to their callers. For example, in contrast to the impersonal greeting and directives which callers usually received from stand-alone systems, PBX callers could get a personal greeting and friendly message from the person being called.

The add-on features of PBX systems are typically available as options on Centrex systems also, if local telephone companies are equipped to provide them.

Voice Mail and PCs

The integration of voice mail with personal computers helped voice mail to come of age. No longer a luxury reserved to large corporate users, voice mail became a standard component of the automated office when personal computers became standard equipment in offices of every size.

Vendors of automated office systems added voice-mail capabilities to their systems also. Logging onto such systems, users could request that their mailboxes display all messages addressed to them, including voice messages.

Only one type of voice mail remained a fledgling in terms of applications and acceptance by the general business community: voice-recognition, or speech-recognition, units.

Voice-recognition Systems

Voice or speech-recognition systems involve the computer's recognition and acceptance of human voice input. Widespread usage of speech-recognition systems is yet to be achieved, but as of the early 1990s, progress in that direction is proceeding steadily.

Two techniques involved in the technology include template matching and phonemic recognition. In the template method, a vocabulary of word patterns is stored in the computer's memory. When input from the user's voice matches the words stored in memory, the computer recognizes the sounds and responds to the commands given.

Impressive strides in template technology have taken place, particularly since advanced digital microprocessors have replaced the analog voice signals of earlier models. Except for special applications, however, the template method is still relatively slow and impractical for most business uses.

Phonemic recognition is based on 44 phonemes or sounds which are common to the English language. Like the template method, the phonemes are stored in memory for later activation by a human voice giving commands to the computer. On receiving the voice commands, the computer utilizes artificial intelligence and software-supplied rules of grammar to distinguish words and sentences from the sounds supplied.

In the opinion of most observers, the phonemic method of speech recognition shows great promise for the future. However, phonemics has yet to prove itself as a practical technology for many business applications.

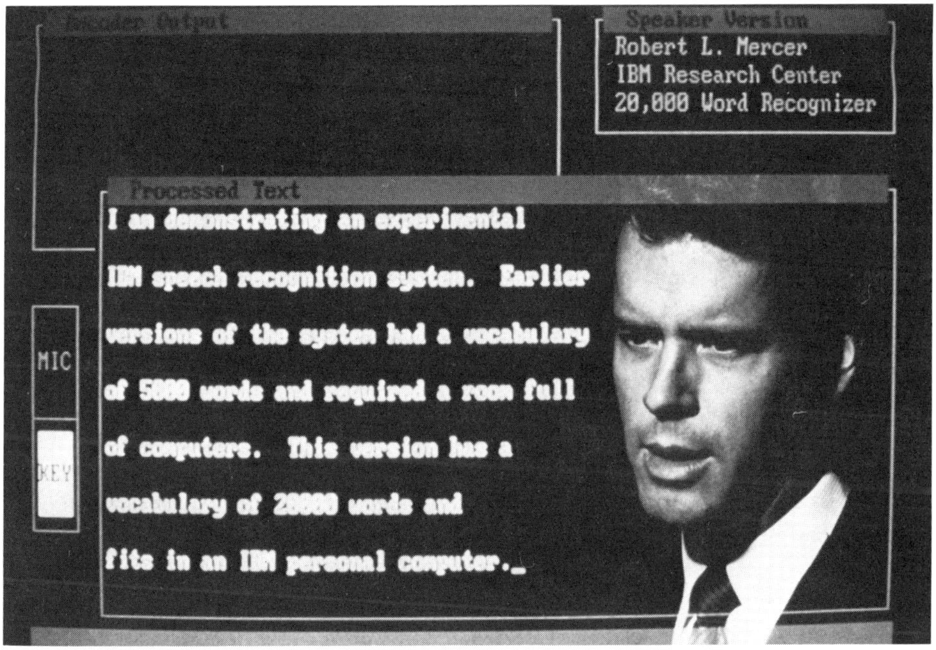

Figure 7-2 This experimental Speech Recognition System can transcribe sentences from a 20,000-word vocabulary with 95 percent accuracy. *Courtesy of IBM Corporation.*

Most speech-recognition systems are *speaker dependent.* That is, the speaker must "train" the computer to recognize his or her speech sounds. The length of the training session may be from a few minutes to over two hours. *Speaker-independent* systems require no pretraining by the user but their vocabularies are limited and users must pause between words.

Voice-recognition systems have experienced many setbacks in their relatively long period of development. However, vendors now have advanced systems on the drawing boards. When the demand for such systems swells significantly, research and development into this phase of technology will speed its ultimate success and acceptance.

Facsimile Transmission

The title of this document delivery system describes its method of communicating electronic messages. Facsimile machines transmit exact facsimiles of paper documents from one unit to another via telephone wires. The process is appropriately described as long-distance photocopying.

FAX machines have a long history, which, until the advent of microelectronics, was an uneventful one. Few people realize that the facsimile process was invented a year before Samuel Morse invented the telegraph. The first FAX mechanism was developed in 1842 by Alexander Bain, a Scottish physicist. In 1850,

Bain's device was replaced by a cylinder-and-screw mechanism developed by Frederick Blakewell. In 1902, Dr. Arthur Korn developed a photoelectric scanning system to transmit and reproduce photography; in 1907, he established a commercial picture-transmission system linking Berlin, London, and Paris, the world's first facsimile network.

During World War II, facsimile was used by the military to transmit maps, orders, photographs, and weather charts. Except for such special applications, however, facsimile machines were regarded as little more than an office curiosity.

In terms of speed, even teletypewriters, at a plodding 60 words per minute, outpaced the early FAX units; and the brownish paper output of FAX machines made teletypewriter output look good by comparison. FAX copies were rarely shared with anyone outside the company.

FAX, as it is known today, owes its recent development to three factors: the Bell Labs which took an active part in its "reincarnation"; the desktop units which caused business leaders to give the technology a second look; and the Japanese companies that recognized its market potential and perfected the process through microelectronics.

Developments in recent years have improved their speed and performance dramatically. Transmission time is measured in seconds rather than minutes and the reproduced copies are clear and distinct, in contrast to the fuzzy reproductions of earlier models. Simplicity of operation is also a key characteristic. Four steps are involved in the digital-facsimile process.

1. A scanner is used to scan the document in a raster pattern (left to right and top to bottom), creating an electronic image of the document.
2. The processor compresses the image in order to conserve bits (3.7 million bits are needed to describe an 8½ × 11-inch page).
3. A modulator converts the digital signal to an analog signal for transmission over telephone wires, and the addressee's telephone number is dialed.
4. At the receiving end, the tone is demodulated to a digital signal again; and the electronic image is restored and printed on the receiving FAX unit.

Four Groups of FAX

The International Consultative Committee for Telegraph & Telephone (CCITT) has defined four facsimile groups, numbered in the order of their introduction date and their level of sophistication.

Groups I and II Groups I and II were introduced in the 1960s. Group I reproduced images as a pixel map with about seven shades of gray and 96 pixels per inch. Transmission time for an 8½ × 11-inch page was six minutes. Group II units upped the speed to about three minutes per page, still too slow for an electronic environment.

The units sent and received analog signals only. Their low-resolution images and slow speed discouraged widespread acceptance by the business community. By the late 1980s, less than 100,000 I and II terminals were still in use.

Figure 7-3 The Ricoh FAX70E holds up to 57 pages in memory. Documents can be sent immediately or programmed to be sent later. When the 328-foot paper roll is depleted, documents are automatically routed to memory for later printout. *Courtesy of Ricoh Corporation.*

Figure 7-4 FAX machines have become a staple in the business office as more and more persons recognize the convenience of this type of electronic mail.

Group III Introduced in 1974, group III models are digital units, most units accepting and sending documents at 9,600 bps (bits per second). In fine mode, group III FAX machines effectively double the resolution of earlier models, creating images far clearer than that of the group I and II units. Transmission speed is one minute or less per page. Although the output is on thermal paper, the quality of the paper has so improved that little distinction can be made between the thermal and "plain" papers. Group III FAX units are the most popular of the groups in use today.

Group IV The most advanced of the four groups, FAX IV machines transmit images digitally within three or four seconds. Although group IV technology and speed are impressive, most data networks cannot transmit data at the speed of the FAX IV; therefore, the network transmission is not used. When access to high-speed networks is readily available, group IV units will attract more users.

PC FAX Boards

Personal computer and facsimile machines have much in common: FAX machines convert pictures and texts to digital data and transmit them to remote locations via telephone lines; personal computers convert text and graphics to digital data and *sometimes* transmit the information to remote locations via telephone lines.

The inevitable merger of the two technologies has taken place in the PC-FAX, primarily through PC-FAX boards. Benefits accrue to both systems. For example,

PC-FAX units are less expensive than separate stand-alone PCs and FAX machines.

Sending a message directly from one's computer is more convenient than sending it via the FAX unit in the next office.

High-resolution images are easier to obtain from a PC than from the FAX unit.

The text of the message can be edited by a word processing program stored in the computer.

The merged PC and FAX machines are part software, part hardware units. The hardware component is usually a FAX expansion board—essentially a specialized modem for sending and receiving FAX signals. It is inserted into an expansion slot inside the computer (although separate external units are also available). FAX boards are connected to telephone lines with standard telephone wire. The software is specialized communications software which controls various functions of the FAX board.

A scanner may be part of the system, also. Scanners allow users to send copies of hard copies to other computer users without first keying the document into the word processor. Vendors offer special discounts to purchasers who buy the scanner and the FAX board together. Personal computers equipped with a FAX and a scanner can do *almost* everything a regular FAX machine can do, except send documents directly from hard copy originals.

Another critical difference exists between the two machines: FAX machines accept and produce paper images only; a PC-FAX can send and receive computer files as well. A special benefit of the PC-FAX over the stand-alone FAX is privacy. One can send or receive messages from the privacy of one's computer station rather than utilizing the "public" FAX machine in the outer office.

To add an expansion board to one's computer, the user must remove the cover from the computer, then insert the FAX board into any available slot. A phone line, dedicated solely to the PC-FAX, should be connected to the unit to complete the hardware setup.

To set up the software, the usual procedure is to install the program on the hard disk, following the prompts for entering a name and phone number. By following the other prompts in like manner, the user can install the printer and scanner, both necessary for a complete system.

Some FAX programs are RAM-resident, enabling the user to send or receive FAX transmissions even while working on other application programs. This feature, of course, adds greatly to their versatility and convenience, making PC-FAX that much more desirable than stand-alone FAX units.

Information to be faxed can come from three sources: a file stored on disk, a scanner which scans an image or alphanumeric characters, or the screen image which can be sent to the FAX board instead of to the printer.

Choosing a FAX

With so many FAX machines on the market, choosing the best model to fit one's requirements becomes exceedingly difficult. Users and vendors make these suggestions to potential buyers:

Select a machine that is as automatic as possible and one your company won't outgrow.

Look for ease of operation and make sure the unit you select will be compatible with other machines in the office.

Order a separate phone line for your FAX.

Understand the limitations of the gray-scale feature. Although the gray-scale feature does wonders with sketches and artists' renderings, detailed photographs and color photographs still reproduce poorly, so this feature should not be the main reason for buying a FAX.

According to most experts, facsimile is in the vanguard of the electronic-imaging revolution and is considered by many to be the most dynamic device of the office-products industry today. One million FAX machines are expected to be in use by 1992.

Other Forms of Electronic Mail

TCOM Systems TCOM Systems, Inc. is an electronic mail service which takes mass correspondence from a company's computer, prints it at 25 sites around the country and deposits it in the local mail. Delivery is often the next day, but is guaranteed within two days. TCOM is a private-sector venture headed by William Bolger, Postmaster General when the U.S. Postal Service's Electronic Computer Originated Mail (E-COM) was initiated.

E-COM lost $99 million for the U.S. Postal Service between 1982 and 1985, more than $1.50 per letter handled. It was eventually shut down. Backers of TCOM claim that E-COM failed due to poor management; they (TCOM managers) vow they will not make the same mistakes. E-COM, they say, was delivering about 24 million letters annually at its peak; this, they claim, indicates that the market is "out there."

TCOM backers insist that the potential market for their electronic mail service is 9 billion pieces out of the 76 billion pieces sent annually by first-class mail. If they are right, more private ventures into the electronic mail market will emerge in time.

INTELPOST INTELPOST (International Electronic Post) service is an international facsimile message service available between the United States and more than 25 foreign countries.

Sponsored by the U.S. Postal Service, INTELPOST prints a black and white image of the mailed document and relays a FAXed copy of it to the destination city, using microwave and satellite channels as the transmission media.

The destination cities must have INTELPOST systems to receive the FAXed documents. Addressees at the destination city can pick up the documents at the post office or ask that they be mailed to them special delivery or with the regular mail on the following day.

LOCAL AREA NETWORKS

Cabling multiple electronic units into a company-wide network, local area networks (LANs) enable all the networked units to exchange messages electronically.

Growing annually at a moderate but accelerating pace, the LAN is defined as a data communications network spanning a limited geographical area, the primary purpose of which is to enable microcomputers and peripheral units to communicate with each other electronically.

The limited geographical area (from which the local area network derives its name) may range from the interior area of one office building up to a complex of several buildings linked by underground cables.

In contrast to micro-mainframe links, the networked units of a LAN ordinarily communicate with each other through a *server*—a microcomputer with large-capacity primary storage and a powerful processor. The server processes all transmitted messages between the networked stations, receiving and relaying the messages or commands to the stations designated.

In addition to exchanging messages, linked units can share resources, thus eliminating costly duplication of expensive equipment. For example, an expensive laser printer whose cost may be difficult to justify for a one-person work station can repay its initial investment rapidly if shared regularly by multiple users.

Many PC packages, now available in LAN versions, also effect cost-saving benefits. For example, a popular word processing package which costs $495 per package costs little more than $1,500 for the network version which accommodates 30 or more users. Besides improving a company's information system, LANs provide a central point (the file server) from which the company can manage security, data access, and data backup.

Installation and Access

Installation of a LAN consists of more than just plugging PCs into the cabling system and loading the network software. The file server must be prepared and the system software configured. Network management procedures must be determined and provision made for training users.

Once in place, accessing the network is fairly simple. Typically, the user dials into the network and enters a password. If the password is valid, communications begin. If the password is invalid, the user may be allowed up to three tries before the system disconnects. In some instances, the system disconnects after receiving the password, then calls back if the password is valid. Communications can then proceed.

Topology Patterns

LANs vary in topology patterns and the procedures (protocols) by which they transfer data. Each protocol uses a distinct topology; that is, the physical and logical layout of the cable connections. Ethernet, one of the first proprietary networks available for personal computers, uses a linear Bus topology.

Bus topology uses a straight-line cable connection which accommodates equipment of various makers, thus enabling users to network computers and peripherals from multiple vendors which are already in place. It is the least expensive to install of all architectural patterns.

Token Ring topology moves data from work station to work station on a ring of cabling. When a LAN work station receives a token (coded message), it is given permission to transmit. The work station "attaches" the message to the token; and the token "carries" it around the LAN to the designated receiver. Although all work stations can view the transmitted message, only the destination work station can accept it.

When the receiving station gets the message, it either generates another token, or the central network controller generates a new token. The entire process of generating and passing tokens around the LAN takes fractions of a second.

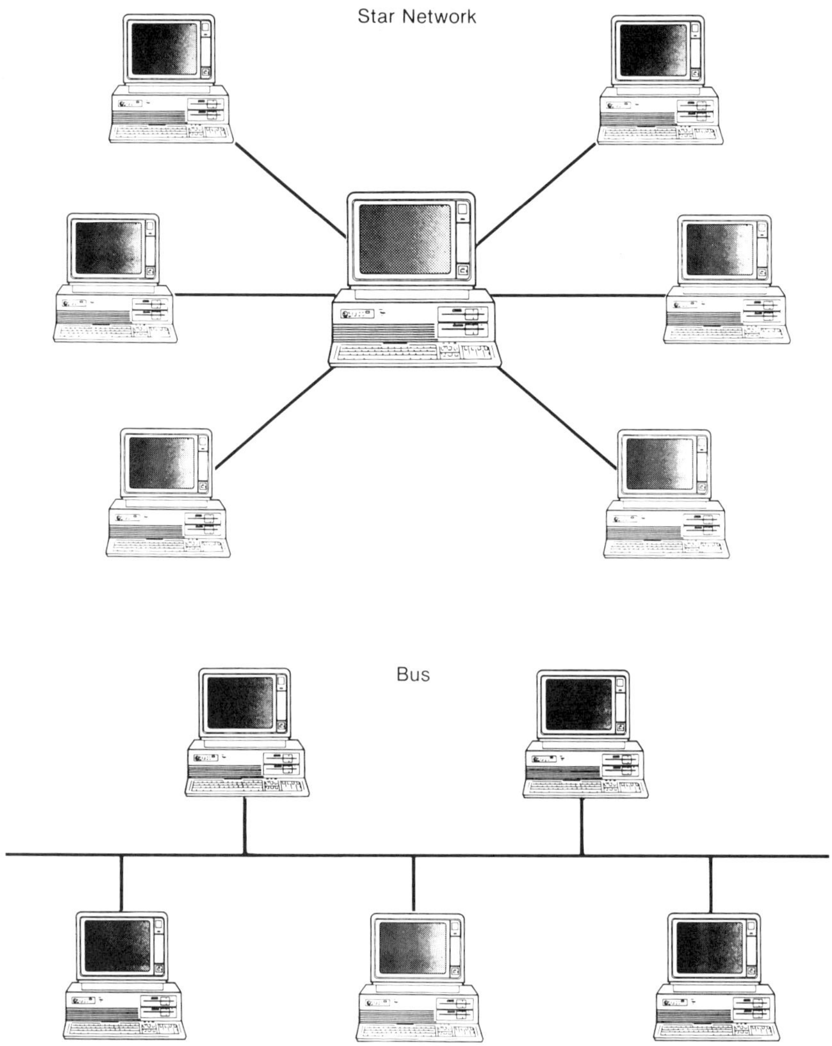

Figure 7-5 Two popular patterns of LAN topography, the Star and the Bus networks.

The Star topology links all work stations to its central work station, the hub, which in turn maintains connections among all units. Central control is easily established through the Star topology, but a disadvantage is that the entire system goes down when the central node fails. Local telephone exchanges utilize the Star topology. (See Star and Bus topology diagrams above.)

LANs—The Solution?

Under conditions where personal computers are already in place, a local area network is a relatively inexpensive solution to communication bottlenecks.

LANs are also an appropriate response to situations in which employees share the same accounting, billing, or other records; frequently swap files with each other; or wish to work on the same data simultaneously. It is conceivable that local area networks, paired with wide area networks, will predominate in the electronic mail sector of the electronic office by the mid-1990s.

WIDE AREA NETWORKS

Wide area networks (WANs) connect geographically dispersed offices. Through the use of telephone lines, microwave, and satellite transmission, WANs direct communications to all points of the globe. Three types of WANs exist: public, proprietary, and hybrid.

Public WANs are made up of the local telephone companies' and long-distance carriers' lines. The quality of service from public WANs is normally excellent and the cost is moderate. Except for high-volume users, therefore, public WANs are usually considered the most cost-effective method for communicating over widely dispersed areas.

Proprietary, or private, WANs are maintained by companies for their own exclusive use. Banking institutions, for instance, use private WANs for transferring funds between central and branch banks. Other institutions use proprietary networks for applications specific to their company needs.

Hybrid WANs are those which use a mix of both public and proprietary WANs in their communication networks. The hybrid represents a realistic approach to electronic communications by utilizing the efficient, moderately-priced links of the public WANs for communicating with customers, clients, and suppliers, while opting for the privately controlled proprietary WANs for internal messaging.

Satellite and Microwave Transmissions

In order to communicate between widely dispersed geographic areas, users have the option of terrestrial (land-based) transmission or space transmission. Terrestrial communications take place via wires mounted above the ground or laid underground, usually by a local or long-distance telephone carrier.

Space transmission is accomplished through radio waves beamed to satellites over 22,000 miles from the earth, or through microwave towers placed at equadistant positions (25 to 30 miles apart).

Microwave towers transmit communications via radio beams from one tower to the next along the destination path. The tower antennas are placed atop derricks 30 to 40 feet above the earth, with each microwave dish turned to receive signals from the preceding tower. Each signal is boosted by the receiving tower, then relayed to the next microwave antenna.

The distance spanned between towers is limited to line of sight; that is, it must not be obstructed by tall buildings, dense forestry, or hilltops that might interfere with the radio signals being transmitted between the towers.

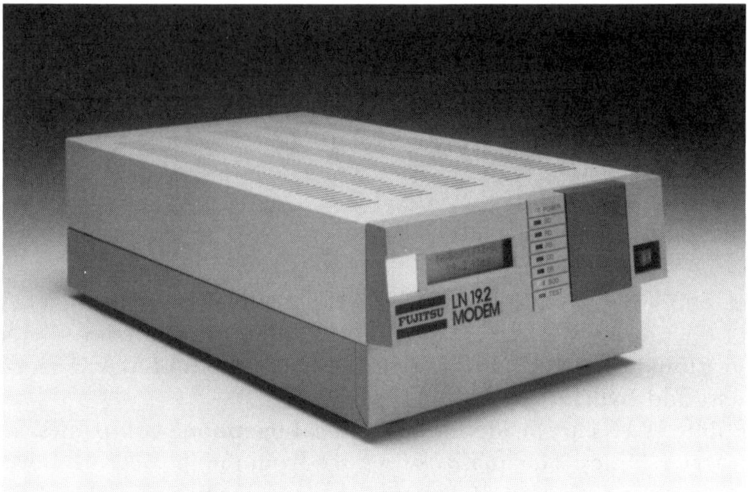

Figure 7-6 Fujitsu LN modems range in speed from 2,400 to 19,200 bits per second. *Courtesy of Fujitsu America Data Communications.*

Satellite communications extend microwave technology into space. Every type of communication transmitted electronically can be transmitted via satellite with speed vastly superior to land-based media.

Beaming signals from 23,000 miles above the earth, satellite transmissions offer bargain-rate communications, calculated on a cost-per-mile basis. The ease with which long distances can be spanned via satellite beams attracts growing numbers of users to satellite transmission services.

For example, one satellite pair of up/down links can connect two communicators on opposite sides of the globe within seconds. Terrestrial lines, on the other hand, might require a dozen or more land-based links, plus a transoceanic radio or cable link, to close the gap between the communicators.

The broadband capacity of satellite transmission also appeals to users. That is, every type of electronic communication, including voice and video transmission, plus textual and data communications, can be transmitted simultaneously via satellite up/down links. Consequently, the number of companies incorporating satellites into their electronic mail systems grows annually.

Modems for Converting Signals

All communications which utilize conventional telephone lines as their medium of transmission must be in the analog mode; that is, in the audio or voice mode for which telephone lines were originally designed.

Since most information emanating from the electronic office is computer generated and, therefore, in the digital mode, a device for converting digital signals to audio signals is necessary before transmission can take place over telephone wires. This device is the modem.

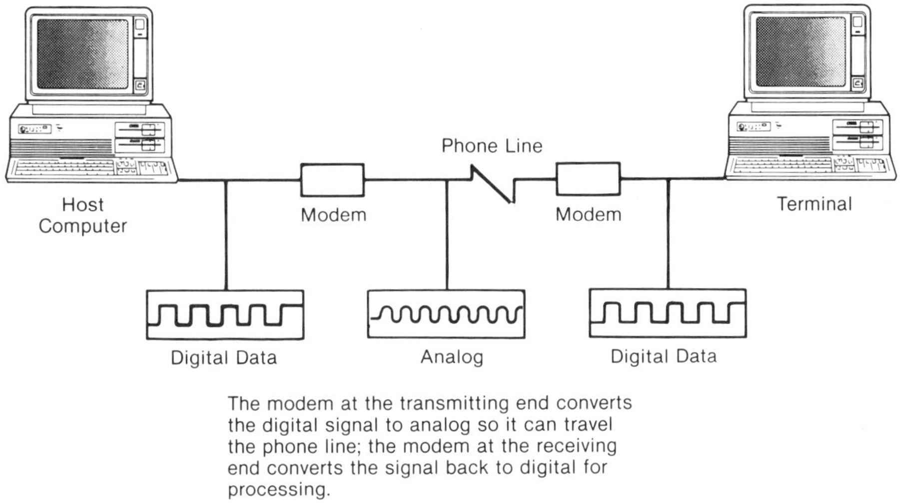

Figure 7-7 Using a modem to transmit digital data over analog telephone lines.

The word *modem* is coined from the two words *mod*ulate and *dem*odulate. In effect, the modem modulates a digital signal from a computer into an analog signal for the purpose of transmitting the data via telephone lines. It then demodulates the analog signal back to digital at the receiving end so that it can be read and processed by the receiving computer.

Modems can be inserted into personal computers as add-in boards or in the form of small boxes plugged into an external serial port of the computer. Con-

Figure 7-8 Productivity, an important goal for all businesses, is enhanced with the AppleShare file server, which lets work groups share and exchange information quickly and transparently over the AppleTalk network. *Courtesy of Apple Computer, Inc.*

nection to the phone is made through a port on the telephone designed for that purpose.

Modems can be used for several purposes. For example, files can be transferred from one computer to another at a distant location, users at home can contact the office via their computer and modem, and national information retrieval services can be contacted for any of a variety of services.

Prices of modems vary in direct proportion to their speed of transmission; the higher the speed, the higher the price. Add-in features also contribute to the higher-priced units. Built-in data encryption (to ensure data security), password security, automatic dial/automatic answer, and pulse and tone dialing are some of the features which command higher prices from buyers.

Purchasers must be aware, however, that the lower the speed of transmission, the longer the transmission time; therefore, the higher the telephone bill for long-distance communications.

SUMMARY

The term *electronic mail* embraces several technologies which enhance communications with the aid of electronics. Telex and TWX systems trace their origins to the invention of the telegraph by Samuel Morse and the introduction of his teletype machine in 1917. Cabled to computers, TWX/Telex units add the benefits of electronic convenience and speed for users.

Computer-based message systems are, as the name implies, based on computer-to-computer communications. CBMS are especially popular with business travelers who, through their portable computers and modems, can access their on-line mailboxes to check for messages received while away from the office.

Communicating word processors, like CBMS, communicate with the aid of special cabling and communications software. External communications are made possible through telephone links and modems which convert the digital signals to analog signals for the telephone-line transmission.

Voice mail provides efficient electronic communications through voice messaging and voice recognition. Voice messaging is basically a store-and-forward technology which, through its four-mode operations, can send, record, forward, access, and answer the mail communicated between the parties.

Voice-recognition systems utilize two technologies in their attempts at speech recognition: template matching and phonemic recognition. Most observers predict a promising future for the phonemic method if practical business applications materialize.

Facsimile transmission is a rapidly growing form of electronic mail. The introduction of FAX boards, which merge computer technology with FAX machines, has accelerated the fast-paced growth of this technology.

Local area networks (LANs) link computers and computer peripherals together into a totally integrated system. Joined with wide area networks, the two become a nationwide communication system, reducing time constraints of manual delivery systems to a minimum.

Satellite transmission systems speed communications between remote locations dramatically. Microwave systems play an important part also in beaming terrestrial messages via magnetic radio waves.

QUESTIONS FOR REVIEW

1. Name five types of electronic mail, briefly defining each.
2. Describe the beginnings of Telex/TWX systems.
3. Name some of the advantages of Telex/TWX systems.
4. Distinguish between *voice messaging* and *voice recognition.*
5. Two types of voice-recognition systems are being developed. Name and describe each.
6. With reference to voice recognition, what is meant by "speaker-independent" systems?
7. What three factors brought facsimile machines into a strong marketplace position?
8. Compare groups I and II facsimile units with group III. Which group predominates in business?
9. Name some of the benefits of PC-FAX machines.
10. Define the term *local area network.*
11. How do WANs add to the versatility and convenience of local area networks?
12. Describe the basic function of a modem and how its name was derived.

QUESTIONS FOR DISCUSSION

1. Some technologists have little faith in the future of speech-recognition systems. They believe that differences in speech patterns, accents, and voice tones of people from various geographic areas constitute impenetrable barriers for the computer in attempting to translate sounds into words.

   Discuss the logic of their position. Do you agree with them?
2. According to some users, each FAX machine should have its own telephone line. Discuss the wisdom of this suggestion.
3. Discuss the statement: *All* businesses should have LAN systems since electronic communications are basic to the electronic office.

SUGGESTED ACTIVITIES

1. From the local post office, obtain literature on INTELPOST. Share the information with the rest of the class. If possible, arrange for the local postmaster to visit the class and explain what impact electronic mail has had on the manual delivery systems of the Postal Service. Ask if the Postal Service has any plans for E-mail ventures in the future.

2. Through the campus library, conduct research to find the extent to which E-mail is utilized in business. Which industries have installed extensive E-mail systems, which *systems* are they using, and how well satisfied are they with the results?
3. Conduct library research on voice-recognition systems; determine the current status of this technology and what experts expect of this form of communications in the future.
4. Invite a regional FAX vendor to demonstrate a FAX transmission to the class; or plan a class visit to the vendor's place of business to view such a demonstration.

REFERENCES

Electronic Mail

GABRIELSON, HEIDI, "Videofax: a Merger of Familiar Technologies," *The Office* (September 1988), 32, 39.

HENRY, PAUL D., "The PC-FAX Merger," *Office Systems '88* (February 1988), 50–54.

JENKINS, TOM, "How FAX Grows with the Times," *Office Systems '88* (February 1988), 82–84.

LONG, GORDON, "FAX Growth Hinges on Needs," *Office Systems '88* (September 1988), 43–50.

MENKUS, BELDEN, "How Voice Messaging Is Used," *Modern Office Technology* (August 1988), 74–76.

MINICUCCI, RICK, "Getting a Fix on Personal FAX," *Today's Office* (January 1988), 21–26.

O'MALLEY, CHRISTOPHER, "Add FAX to Your System," *Personal Computing* (February 1988), 137–143.

ROETTER, MARTYN F. AND ARTHUR D. LITTLE, "Enhance Your PC's Communication Skills with a FAX Board," *Today's Office* (December 1988), 27–29.

SEYMOUR, JIM, "Stash a FAX in Your PC with an Add-In-Card," *Today's Office* (April 1988), 24–29.

Electronic Networks

BRACKETT, JOSH, "Modems Get the Message Across—Fast," *Today's Office* (October 1988), 48–50.

KAPLAN, JEFFREY M., "Managing Voice and Data with Wide Area Networks," *Today's Office* (June 1988), 26–31.

MILES, J. B., "A Network Server by Any Other Name," *Information Center* (September 1988), 17–20.

SCHULTZ, BRAD, "The Evolution of Arpanet," *Datamation* (August 1, 1988), 71–74.

STREHLO, CHRISTINE, "Network Systems are Growing Steadily," *Personal Computing* (August 1988), 126–131.

Case Problem 1 Unit II *Network Speeds Communications*

A distributor of electronic systems in the Northeast is proud of its electronic data communications system which enables the company to contact its dealers and distributors within minutes, rather than days, and at relatively low cost.

The company boasts a distribution network serving more than 300 U.S. cities plus 32 countries abroad. Business letters and memos were previously prepared with word processors and mail-list merges. With 110 names on the mailing list, the merging process took about an hour's time to complete; the letters were then printed, stuffed into previously addressed envelopes, sealed, and stamped. Dealers would receive the letter from two to five days later; the cost for labor and postage was over $200.

The WAN now handles these communications in this way: The letter is typed at a work station in the home office. A telephone number is dialed to link onto the WAN, and a command is given to transmit the letter to every dealer's electronic mailbox.

Minutes later, the communication is completed at a cost of about $72, a substantial saving over the former manual method of distribution.

1. Discuss the wisdom of this distributor's installing the electronic communications network. While the savings are significant, what's to prevent competitors from installing similar equipment and thereby erasing the competitive edge now being enjoyed?
2. Is privacy compromised through an electronic network? Explain.

Case Problem 2 Unit II *Dictation Changeover Causes Trauma*

A large service organization located in Minneapolis has recently made a company-wide conversion from live dictation to machine dictation/transcription equipment. Cited as reasons for the changeover:

Executives could use portable dictation units to dictate from wherever they were located—from their own homes after hours, or from convention sites in distant cities.

At the corporate level, less time would be consumed in the dictation process, as secretaries were freed to take care of other duties as executives dictated into the machines.

Better quality letters might also result, since dictators tend to give greater attention to framing messages for the machine than for one-on-one dictation.

The dictation units could serve a dual purpose, for example, doubling as recorders at company meetings, especially when the company wanted greater participation from *all* the staff.

Mallory, the office manager for the company, has some misgivings about dictating to a machine rather than to her efficient secretary of many years. She is frustrated with the depersonalized manner of dictating; the machine can neither "read back that last passage" nor inquire about the correct spelling of a proper name. In short, Mallory misses the one-on-one communication that had existed between her and her note-taking secretary.

1. Is Mallory's frustration justified? Should she have been consulted about the changeover before it was made?

2. If you were Mallory's superior, would you try to placate her by permitting her to continue to dictate live to her secretary? Why or why not?
3. Do you believe the company made a mistake in purchasing the dictation/transcription units? Explain your answer.

Case Problem 3 Unit II *McDonald's Grows with ISDN*

When McDonald's Corporation wanted to improve telecommunications with its 9,400 restaurants located in over 40 countries, it looked to AT&T for solutions. McDonald's main objective was to gain greater facility in reaching and conversing with its customers, without complicating the process with technology its users would find too difficult or impractical to use.

AT&T wanted to be sure that the system installed would accommodate the current needs of McDonald's while providing the basis for more sophisticated communications in the future. Accordingly, they installed the nation's first customer application of ISDN, the Integrated Services Digital Network.

ISDN supports digital phones, integrated voice and data terminals, facsimile, and access to the host computer of internal LANs. In other words, ISDN positioned McDonald's for much more than voice communications with its customers.

Thanks to ISDN, McDonald's now enjoys not only better customer service, but more current market information, better tracking of product promotions, more efficient inventory control, and reduced administrative workloads.

Explain how the enhanced communications capabilities of McDonald's can be translated into:

a. more successful sales promotions
b. greater uniformity of food products
c. better training of employees
d. lower turnover

UNIT

III

INFORMATION AND RECORDS MANAGEMENT: MANUAL AND ELECTRONIC

Records management in today's electronic office demands a diversity of skills and knowledge on the part of the administrative assistant.

Once restricted to paper records only, records management now entails increasing numbers of computer-generated records, stored magnetically on disks, tape, and micrographic forms to be stored in conjunction with the steadily mounting paper records.

All are merged into an integrated system of records and image management systems rivaling in complexity and importance that of any internal system of the electronic office.

8 Records Management: Objectives, Equipment, and Supplies

INTRODUCTION

The advent of computerized systems has not diminished the number and complexity of paper records handled in the electronic office. Incoming written communications from customers, clients, vendors, and government agencies show no sign of abatement; and outgoing letters of response continue to mount accordingly.

The development and implementation of procedures to handle paper-based records still ranks as a high-priority need, even in the electronic office. This chapter addresses issues pertinent to the development of such procedures. Topics explored include objectives of a records management program, selection of equipment and supplies, and the role of the records manager.

Terms introduced in the chapter include:

three-stage life cycle of records
vital-records protection
retention schedules
mobile files

OBJECTIVES OF A RECORDS MANAGEMENT PROGRAM

Defined as the memory or backup reference of an activity or event, a record can take many forms: paper; magnetic data on a floppy, hard, or optical disk; a microfilm image; a videotape; or an audio tape. The information contained in the record plus the current stage of its life cycle determine its inherent value to the organization.

Records management is the arrangement and maintenance of records in a well-organized fashion to facilitate their swift retrieval from current or inactive storage. Many large organizations have a centralized file system, with a full-time records manager in charge of the system. Many others, both large and small, prefer decentralized systems.

Centralized Files

Centralized filing systems provide two major benefits to company users: (1) the efficient management of records by full-time personnel devoted solely to the task; and (2) higher productivity of the personnel who use the records regularly.

Centralization provides better control, more consistent and accurate filing of records, and quicker retrieval of them by file clerks. Many companies install high-density mobile filing systems to accommodate all of their business records in a central storage area.

Decentralized Files

Decentralized systems have their advantages, also. Material that is frequently accessed by one person, or by a few people within one department, is more conveniently placed close to the work area, rather than in a central storage facility. Security for confidential material, such as classified personnel information, may be better protected if kept at the point of origin rather than within the company's central storage area.

Three-stage Life Cycle of Records

The development of an efficient records management system starts with a recognition of the three-stage life cycle of business records and the procedures needed to smooth their orderly passage from one stage to the next.

Stage 1 This is the period of active use when reference is frequent and immediate access is important. Records remain in the primary office, close to the users.

Stage 2 A period of semi-active use and storage, records are retained for occasional reference and/or legal purposes. Included are all records which are scheduled for permanent retention.

Stage 3 Except for certain vital records which require permanent retention, this stage includes all records which after a predetermined period of retention may be destroyed.

A well-managed record system facilitates the smooth passage of records through the three stages without loss or delay in locating any of the records in the process. Central to the accomplishment of this feat is the development, in writing, of a set of objectives for managing records.

OBJECTIVES OF A RECORDS MANAGEMENT PROGRAM[1]

Objectives of a well-managed program should include four components:

1. A vital-records protection program which safeguards records which are essential to company operations.
2. A records retention schedule that meets legal requirements and satisfies the company's administrative and fiscal needs.
3. A practical method of indexing and storing inactive records, and retrieving them quickly when needed.
4. An effective system for organizing, storing, and retrieving active records.

Records Inventory

Prior to implementing the four objectives established as the basis for good records management, company officials should authorize an inventory of all company records. An audit and count of all records in the office areas, storerooms, vaults, and warehouses should include computer printouts, disks, video and audio cassettes, and paper files.

Individual documents or file folders need not be inventoried. Rather, categories such as purchase requisitions, travel vouchers, and regional conferences can be inventoried and processed as groups. To facilitate and speed the process, the task may be divided among several employees, with one person appointed as chairperson to oversee the project to its successful conclusion.

Once the inventory is completed, companies may find that a substantial number of their records—in some instances, as many as one third—have no further value and can be destroyed. Other records have no immediate value and can be placed in off-site storage; and less than 50 percent of the inventoried records remain to be filed in the active files.

The next step in the process of organizing company records is to identify those records which are considered vital to the company's continued operations and to protect them from destruction in case of a major disaster.

Vital Records Protection A vital records program is oriented towards protecting records which are deemed vital for reconstruction of a business in the

[1]Susan Z. Diamond, "A Strategic Approach to Records Management," *Office Systems '87* (June 1987), 88–89.

event of a disaster that destroys vast numbers of records. Experts believe that only 1 to 2 percent of a company's records can be classified as vital.

A large expenditure of funds is not usually required to set up or implement such a program; rather, a common-sense approach to ferreting out the vital records is the most important first step in initiating such a program. The review process involves two sorts:

1. Sort #1 excludes all records which would *not* be essential to restarting the company's operations in case of a disaster.
2. Sort #2 excludes records whose information could be reconstructed from other sources.

From the remaining records, the truly vital ones are those which would be necessary to protect the company's legal and financial integrity in case of an accidental or natural disaster, sabotage, or civil disorder. For example, charters, deeds, pension and tax records, patents, contracts, inventory lists, accounts receivable, and property appraisals are considered vital records, to be afforded special protection against loss.

Vital records should be kept in a fireproof cabinet, safe, or vault. Duplicates should be stored at an off site storage area.

Some companies construct storage facilities in sparsely populated areas to protect against the possibility of large-scale disasters; others use underground installations to protect duplicates of their vital records.

Computer based records may be stored off site on backup tapes. Vital records which are *not* computer based may be stored off site on microfilm.

Properly identifying a company's vital records is so important that every effort must be made to avoid any inaccuracies in the process. Instead of assigning the task to only one person, many companies appoint a committee of three or four persons to perform this task, hoping thereby to get more thorough and accurate coverage.

RECORDS-RETENTION SCHEDULES

A records-retention schedule is basically a list of the types of records maintained in an organization, with timetables established to identify the length of time they must be retained in the active files.

In accordance with the guidelines set down in the schedule, inactive records are periodically purged from the active files and transferred to storage areas, usually off site, or are destroyed if they have no further value.

The schedule serves several functions for an active business. The four which follow help smooth a company's operations by retaining current files in accessible locations, available for fast retrieval as needed; and transferring outdated files to storage containers, indexed for later retrieval, if necessary.

In summary, a retention schedule enables a company to:

1. periodically purge unnecessary records from both active and inactive files
2. maintain current records for immediate retrieval
3. remove, index, and store inactive records to temporary or permanent storage in accordance with predetermined guidelines
4. ensure that, in compliance with laws enacted by Congress or state legislatures, legal and regulatory requirements are met regarding the minimum retention periods for designated records

Professional records managers customarily obtain three levels of clearance in setting up a retention schedule. This procedure gives a voice to the company's principal authorities and helps resolve any differences that may arise among the persons assigned to the task of setting up the schedule.

Retention schedules should do more than provide a timetable for transferring or purging files. Most record managers believe that schedules should also provide other information, such as the location of each record, the media on which they are stored (electronic, paper, film), and a detailed set of instructions and procedures for filing and retrieving the records.

An efficient method for combining inventory data with scheduled retention periods is the use of a two-part form. The form is first used to collect inventory data, then to establish retention periods for each type of record. An example of a "Records Inventory and Retention Control Card" follows.

FIGURE 8-1 Records inventory and retention control card. *Courtesy of Fellowes Manufacturing Company.*

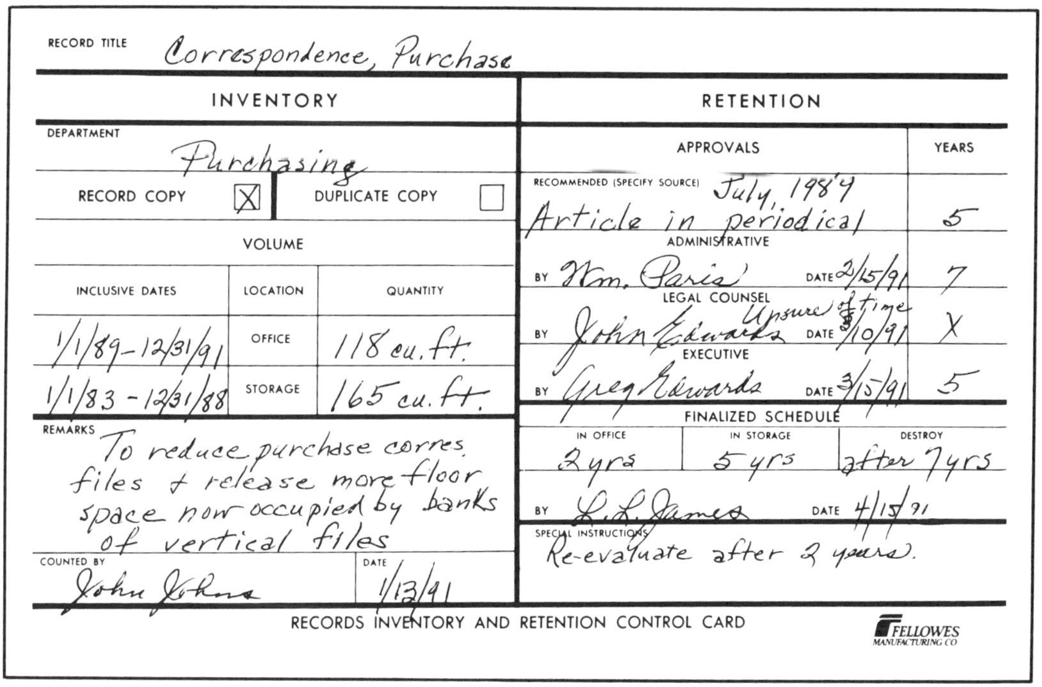
RECORD TITLE Correspondence, Purchase

INVENTORY

DEPARTMENT Purchasing

RECORD COPY [X] DUPLICATE COPY [ ]

VOLUME

INCLUSIVE DATES	LOCATION	QUANTITY
1/1/89–12/31/91	OFFICE	118 cu. ft.
1/1/83–12/31/88	STORAGE	165 cu. ft.

REMARKS To reduce purchase corres. files + release more floor space now occupied by banks of vertical files

COUNTED BY John Johns DATE 1/13/91

RETENTION

APPROVALS	YEARS
RECOMMENDED (SPECIFY SOURCE) July, 1989 Article in periodical	5
ADMINISTRATIVE BY Wm. Paris DATE 2/15/91	7
LEGAL COUNSEL BY John Edwards DATE 3/10/91 Unsure of time	X
EXECUTIVE BY Greg Edwards DATE 3/15/91	5

FINALIZED SCHEDULE

IN OFFICE	IN STORAGE	DESTROY
2 yrs	5 yrs	after 7 yrs

BY L. L. James DATE 4/15/91

SPECIAL INSTRUCTIONS Re-evaluate after 2 years.

RECORDS INVENTORY AND RETENTION CONTROL CARD

FELLOWES MANUFACTURING CO

Note that in the example, the record title is "Purchase Correspondence." Correspondence dated 1/1/89 to 12/31/91 is located in the office, and correspondence dated 1/1/83 to 12/31/88 is in storage. Remarks, signature of the inventory clerk, and date completed are on the left (inventory) side of the form.

The right side of the form (retention) provides for four recommended retention periods, one from each of the administrative division, legal counsel, and the executive department, as well as one unsigned entry based on information from a trade magazine.

A signed finalized schedule recommends two years' retention in the office, five years in storage and, after seven years, destruction of the correspondence. A "Special Instructions" section is also provided.

The retention schedule listing the finalized retention periods for all records is drawn up from the information shown on the inventory/retention cards. In a large firm, the schedule also classifies records by department.

The examples shown on this page and the next page typify the structure and layout of retention schedules drawn up for business and banking records.

The retention values assigned in the schedule should designate a specific

FIGURE 8-2 Sample retention schedule for business records. *Courtesy of Fellowes Manufacturing Company.*

SUGGESTED RETENTION SCHEDULE FOR BUSINESS RECORDS

For retention requirements established by Federal laws and regulations, see the current "Guide to Record Retention Requirements" published annually in the Federal Register which can be obtained at nominal cost from the Superintendent of Documents, U.S. Government Printing Office, Washington, D.C. 20402.

KEY:

"P" means Permanently, "O" stands for Optional, otherwise the figures represent the suggested number of years for retaining the records.

Accounting and Fiscal

Accounts, charged off	7
Accounts payable ledger	P
Accounts receivable	10
Accounts receivable ledger	10
Balance sheets	5
Bank deposit record	6
Bank reconcilement papers	8
Bank statements	8
Bills collectible	7
Bills of sale of registered bonds	3
Bill stubs	7
Bonds cancelled	3
Bonds registered	P
Bonds, sales or transfer	15
Budget work sheets	3
Building permits	20
Capital stock bills of sales	P
Capital stock certificates	P
Capital stock ledger	P
Capital stock transfer records	P
Cash books	25
Cash receipts & disbursement records	10
Cash sales slips	3
Cash slips	3
Charge slips	10
Check records	7
Check register	10
Checks, dividend	10
Checks, expense	10
Checks, paid & cancelled	9
Checks, payroll	7
Checks, voucher	6
Checks, warrants	P
Correspondence, accounting	5
Correspondence, credit & collection	7
Cost account records	7
Customer ledger	P
Donations	7

Administrative

Audit reports, internal	10
Audit reports, public & government	P
Audit work papers, internal	6
Classified documents: control, inventories, reports	5
Correspondence, accounting	5
Correspondence, advertising	3
Correspondence, credit & collection	7
Correspondence, engineering & technical	10
Correspondence, general	3
Correspondence, personal	6
Correspondence, production	2
Corespondence, purchase	5
Correspondence, sales & service	3
Correspondence, tax	20
Correspondence, traffic	6

SUGGESTED RETENTION SCHEDULE FOR BANK RECORDS

The following schedule is reproduced here through the courtesy of Bank Administration Institute, Rolling Meadows, Illinois. The Institute states that this schedule is only a guideline as many States have detailed regulations governing retention periods for bank records. Each bank should have its legal counsel approve its own retention schedule.

Type of Record	Suggested Retention Period
Administrative	
Attachments and/or garnishments	7 years after close
Note: Legal documents and copies of returns and correspondence should be filed with general correspondence after case is closed	
Bank examiners' reports	7 years
Note: These are the property of the supervisory authorities, whose approval should be obtained prior to destruction	
Charged-off asset records	5 years after close
Court case records (foreclosed real estate, etc.)	2 years after close
Insurance Records	
a) Schedules of fire and other insurance, also record of premium payments and of amounts recovered	6 years
b) Casualty liability policies expired—P.L. & P.D., O.L. & T., etc	6 years
c) Windstorm, fire, theft, etc., policies expired	2 years
d) Records of policies in force	3 years
e) Bankers blanket bonds	6 years
Minute books of meetings (stockholders, directors, committees, etc.)	25 years
Accounting and Auditing	
Accrual and bond amortization records	1 year
Audit reports	10 years
Audit work papers	optional
Bank call reports	3 years
Branch statements (daily)	2 years
Budget work sheets	3 years
Consolidated financial statements	permanent
Daily reserve computation	1 year
Difference record	2 years
Income and dividend report	3 years
Reconcilements of banks (due to) deposits	8 years
Reconcilement register (due from)	8 years
Reports to directors	5 years
Accounting and Auditing (Cont'd.)	
Reports to executive committee	5 years
Securities vault "in and out" tickets	1 year
Tax records	7 years
Note: Copies of schedules and returns to taxing authorities for tax purposes, notices of assessment by taxing authorities and documentary proceedings in appeal therefrom	
Capital	
Capital stock certificates, records of, or stubs of	permanent
Capital stock ledger	permanent
Capital stock transfer register	permanent
Dividend checks	10 years
Dividend register	6 years
Proxies	10 years
Receipts for stock certificates	permanent
Note: Where bank secures a receipt it is recommended that it be affixed to stub of certificate book	
Certificates of Deposit	
Certificates	5 years after paid
Ledger cards	permanent
Register	2 years
Checking Accounts—Individuals and Firms	
Account analysis	
Analysis work sheets or cards	1 year
Average balance cards	5 years
Interest computation records	optional
Service charge records	optional
Bookkeepers' daily list of checks charged in total (short lists)	2 years
Check book orders	optional
Checks paid (microfilm copy—front and back)	5 years
Copies of advices of deposit	6 months
Daily report of overdrafts	optional
Deposit tickets	10 years
Note: Return with statement after microfilming and retain microfilm 3 years.	
Individual ledgers (if no statement copy)	5 years
Individual ledger journals	6 months
Reports of accounts opened and closed	optional
Resolutions	5 years after recision or close
Signature cards	5 years after recision or close

FIGURE 8-3 Sample retention schedule for bank records. *Courtesy of Fellowes Manufacturing Company.*

date from which time is measured; for example, the end of the fiscal year or the first day of the fiscal year in which the documents are created or received.

Once in place, the schedule should be applied to records on a regularly scheduled basis—either annually or semi-annually—depending on the size of the business and the volume of records handled.

From time to time, the assigned retention periods should also be reviewed by persons in authority or by a records consultant. Based primarily on the company's experience with the system, such periodic reviews often afford businesses substantial cost reductions through the adoption of reduced storage periods for both active and inactive records. Changes in state or federal laws affecting the statutes of limitation, and the creation of new records, or elimination of old ones, also mandate periodic updates of the schedules.

Inactive Records: Indexing and Storing

Once in place, the economic benefits of the retention schedule become immediately apparent when inactive records are removed from primary office space and stored in a basement, warehouse, or other less costly storage area. Not only does the purging save space by the clearing of unnecessary files, it also saves time for file clerks and other office personnel who must rummage through outdated material to retrieve current records.

Before removing inactive records from the current file, the administrative assistant must develop an index to indicate where the records are to be stored and how to locate them for later retrieval. If the number of boxed records is small to moderate (500 boxes or fewer), a set of index cards can be used for each record series.

Each card and related box indicates the series title, location, and inclusive dates of the material contained therein. Descriptive data are also included when the title is too broad to properly identify all the documents within the box; and, in accordance with the timetables set by the retention schedule, dates of destruction are included, as well.

In cases where the number of inactive records is too great for a manual system, a computerized index may be utilized. For this purpose, a number of records-management software packages are available. In addition, standard database management software can be utilized for records indexing. (See Chapter 10, Electronic Storage and Imaging Systems.)

Due to the voluminous weight, a basement or ground floor is recommended for the storage site. The file structure usually consists of steel shelving and cardboard cartons designed specifically for legal and letter-size files, plus assorted sizes made to accommodate a company's individual needs.

Off-Site Storage

An alternative to storage in a company's own facilities is the use of commercial record centers for off-site storage of inactive records. Record centers specialize in the storage of business records and in some cases provide computerized indexing and retrieval of the records stored.

The service of these centers is especially appealing to businesses whose leasing costs run as high as $50 to $60 a square foot for primary office space. Utilizing this expensive space for the storage of frequently accessed records is justified, but for inactive records which may seldom, if ever, be retrieved, less expensive storage space must be sought.

Even basement warehousing in high-rent districts may be too high to justify the convenience of on-site storage. Accordingly, with increasing frequency,

FIGURE 8-4 A records storage area must have proper lighting and ventilation and adequate space and security against hazards of moisture, rodents, and fire. *Courtesy of Fellowes Manufacturing Company.*

businesses are choosing the low-cost alternative of off-site record centers to house their inactive records.

Some record centers claim that their clients save 30 percent to 40 percent over in-house storage in primary office space. One center estimates an average cost to its customers of $2.30 per cubic foot of storage per year. This compares with $40 per cubic foot for office space in many urban locations.

Many record centers employ computerized systems to organize, track, and control inventories; and they guarantee retrieval and delivery of documents within 24 hours.

One system, titled "The Safekeeper," allows clients to use a personal computer connected by a modem to mainframes in the center's 13 locations, so that clients can immediately find out the status of their records, and place orders for retrieval, delivery, or pickup. Information the customer provides is entered and cross-referenced. The cross-references include several headings to enable users to access the desired files without difficulty.

Destruction of Records

Stage 3 in the three-stage life cycle of records is the destruction of those records which have reached their predetermined period of retention. Except for vital records which for the security of the business must be kept indefinitely, all records eventually reach this stage. Their destruction is as much a part of the records management process as was their initial indexing and storage in primary office space.

However, in order to protect against the premature destruction of information erroneously classed as nonvital, the administrative assistant, in company with superiors, is encouraged to develop a fail-safe policy for monitoring this final activity. The policy developed for the destruction of fully aged records should include these procedures:

1. A list of records to be destroyed should be reviewed by one person assigned to this task. The person responsible must review the list with the appropriate persons in the company and with legal counsel to determine whether or not any action or litigation is pending for which the records may be needed.
2. A form to authorize destruction of records must be signed by a person in authority prior to their destruction.
3. The method of destruction to be used for each set of records should be indicated on the authorization form.
4. Written documentation of records destroyed must be retained for future reference; it should identify the records by title and date of destruction.

Shredders

As shredders become commonplace in business offices, more and more businesses routinely utilize this equipment to destroy old records.

Shredder equipment varies in size, style, and level of security offered. In size, shredders range from personal-use low-volume units which can shred up to 45 sheets at one time, to powerful high-volume machines suitable for continuous-shredding applications and paper feeds of up to 350 sheets per load.

The shredding capacity depends primarily on the horsepower of each system's internal mechanism. Desk-side units, for example, have 1.5 or less horsepower per system, while more powerful units range upward from there.

The three basic styles—straight-cut, crosscut, and confetti-cut shredders (disintegrators)—offer varying degrees of security, depending on the cutting mechanism each employs. Straight-cut shredders cut documents into strips only

FIGURE 8-5 High-volume conveyor-fed shredders for centralized operations. Capacities range from 750 lbs. of paper per hour to 3.5 tons per hour. *Courtesy of Allegheny Paper Shredders Corp.*

once; crosscut shredders cut them a number of times; and disintegrators provide the highest security of the three by reducing documents into minute particles (confetti) before emptying them into the dumpsters.

Cutter disks on straight-cut machines produce shreds in varying widths from 1/32-inch to 1/2-inch wide. The wider the cutting width, the less security offered by the unit, but the greater its speed of operation.

The trade-off between speed and security must be weighed by prospective buyers prior to their purchase of a straight-cut shredder. Although a 1/4-inch shred provides adequate security for most applications, especially when volume shredding is done, maximum security may require the confetti-like churning of a disintegrator.[2]

Capacity is measured by the number of sheets a shredder can accommodate at one time and by the types of materials it will accept. For example, some will accept, without jamming, cardboard, microfilm, microfiche, and offset plates, in addition to paper documents.

For businesses which store any of their documents on microfilm, therefore, this type of shredder deserves serious consideration when a purchase is being considered. A number of vendors also offer special-use shredders designed to meet the specific requirements of microform destruction.

In selecting the appropriate shredder for destroying dated records, therefore, buyers must evaluate at least three factors: capacity, speed, and level

[2]Tom Zanca, "Shredders Can Ensure Confidentiality," *Office Systems '88* (July 1988), 66.

of security provided by the units under consideration. Cost, as a function of the other three factors, may also be an issue but should not be the critical one.

FILING EQUIPMENT AND SUPPLIES

Filing Equipment for Paper Records

For paper records, the most popular filing cabinets are the lateral style and the traditional vertical three-drawer or four-drawer cabinets. Although vertical cabinets have dominated the office scene for decades, lateral files are rapidly replacing them as new offices open or old ones are refurbished.

Vertical files are upright letter- or legal-size files, usually of metal construction, having two to five drawers each. They are well suited to small- or medium-size offices since only one person at a time can access the files, and the storage capacity is limited.

Lateral files are similar to vertical files in that the folders inside stand upright and are usually, though not always, tabbed on top. They differ in that the drawers open from the side rather than from the front and they may have side tabs on the folders for quick identification and access to the files.

Metal side doors operate by sliding up and over the files when opened; they conserve space by utilizing only minimal extension footage when opened. When closed, they resemble bookcases, and are often used as work-station dividers in contemporary offices. Their attractive appearance and their utility as work-station dividers make lateral files especially appealing to office designers.

Alternatives to these two styles do exist, however. In addition to vertical and lateral styles, filing cabinets in use today include the following:

open-shelf files
horizontal (flat) files
center-hook files
automated files
mobile high-density files: manual, mechanical, and electronic

Open-shelf files offer extra economy in space usage. The shelves can vary in height to accommodate any size folder or other media and the shelving units may be configured in vertical units similar to bookcases, or in circular tiers which operate independently of each other from a center axis.

Files are tabbed at the side and are often color coded for easy access. Although controlled access is not normally associated with open-shelf filing, doors may be provided on components, providing some measure of security.

Horizontal (flat) files are used to store large documents in a horizontal (flat) position, without folding. Architectural drawings, maps, survey or land-use drawings are usually stored in horizontal files.

FIGURE 8-6 Vertical file cabinets serve a dual purpose as file cabinets and as pedestals for desktops. Glass blocks add another dimension in office decor and utility. *Courtesy of Steelcase.*

Center-hook files accommodate many types of media: letter- and legal-size papers, microfiche, diskettes, manuals, and audiovisual media to be hung on hanger-bars, similar to hangers in a clothes closet. Bulky items may be housed in binders, folders, or other containers.

Center-hook filing is especially efficient when it accommodates in one area all types of media relating to a given subject. Installation is fairly easy, also. Appropriately installed either on walls over work stations, or within shelf units, center-hook units can harmonize with any office design.

Automated files bring files to the operator mechanically. Keypad controls installed in front of the shelved folders allow the operator to bring the desired file folders to the front by correctly keying in coded instructions. The file or files desired are then retrieved quickly and easily. Automated files are labor-saving and time-saving devices which offer the added advantage of protection from unauthorized access to confidential records.

Mobile files are high-density storage systems composed of large vertical carriages mounted on parallel tracks. The carriages, housing records on shelves and in bins, racks, and other storage components, move horizontally along the tracks, creating access aisles only when and where records are requested.

Once the records are retrieved and the system is "at rest," the temporary "floating aisle" converts back to storage space, closing in the aisle with carriages realigned back to back.

Opening only one aisle at a time for accessing records, (and that on a temporary basis only), and utilizing all available vertical space from floor to ceiling, mobile systems are recognized as the most space efficient of all high-density systems. Three categories of mobile units are available: manual, electromechanical, and electronic styles.

Manual systems, operated by the operator's own strength, must be limited to low-volume collections of not more than 5,000 pounds in weight. Operators physically push or pull the rows of cabinets apart to open an aisle and access the records desired.

Electromechanical systems, designed for mid-volume use, are chain driven, much like bicycles. Up to 10,000 pounds can be moved with the chain driven mechanism.

Electronic systems handle high-capacity units at the touch of a button, or in the case of newer technology, with the use of light sensors. Users of the light-sensor units merely pass their hands across the beam of light to activate the sensor and open up the aisles.

Some electronic units do more than open aisles; they deliver the requested records to the operator's work station, as well. These systems contain a work surface on which a push-button index is located. The operator keys in the desired file, and the system locates the bin in which that file is stored, bringing it to the operator. This system can also be interfaced with a computer, making retrieval even faster and easier.

Desk-top filing equipment includes two major types: *card files* used for telephone numbers, addresses, business cards, and cross-indexed references; and *trays* housing folders temporarily retrieved from storage.

Tray units usually house file folders and correspondence in a horizontal position on top of the desk, but wall units serve the same function as the desktop trays by utilizing vertical space above the work area. Vertical wall units are hung from the wall for easy viewing and retrieval when needed.

Card files are designed for easy insert of new and updated information. Frequently anchored on spindles, the cards can be readily accessed without danger of misfiling or accidental loss. The designer's touch is evident in the stylish yet functional units offered by major manufacturers of desktop card files.

Filing Supplies

A well-stocked inventory of filing supplies is one of the earmarks of an effective records management program. As an extension of the records systems which they support, filing supplies are the "tools of the trade" for users.

Selecting the proper amount and kinds of materials needed to run the system continuously, without understocking or overstocking the supplies inventory, requires that the purchaser understand the level of activity within the system. A person familiar with the position will be able to answer the following questions without hesitancy:

How many people regularly access the records, and how frequently do they do so? (activity rate)

Will records be used internally only, or will they occasionally be shared with outside parties? (appearance and quality)

What is the expected life span of the files? (durability)

The activity ratio measures the frequency of access to the files. It is calculated by dividing the total number of references to a document or folder by the number of folders filed. For example, an activity ratio of 20 percent means that 20 references are made to every 100 folders in the file.

Records which are shared with parties outside the company should present an image of quality worthy of the company they represent. Plastic rather than traditional manila folders are recommended, with color-coded tabs to enhance their appearance and facilitate identification of the materials contained within each folder.

Durability is assured by the use of polyethylene or similar plastic folders designed to protect the contents for above-average life spans. Such folders resist the abuse of frequent and rough usage.

The folders and tabs chosen are directly related to the types of file transactions normally utilized. For example, correspondence files usually involve interfiling (documents added thereto on a continual basis).

Top-tab folders are best suited to this function because they allow the user to simply drop a document into the folder without having to remove it from its place in storage. Suspension folders are well suited to drop filing. Some manufacturers supply rails for suspension folders; others require them to be purchased as options.

Side-tab folders, combined with open-shelf filing and color coding, are best

FIGURE 8-7 A convenient storage system for floppy disks. *Courtesy of Atapco Office Products.*

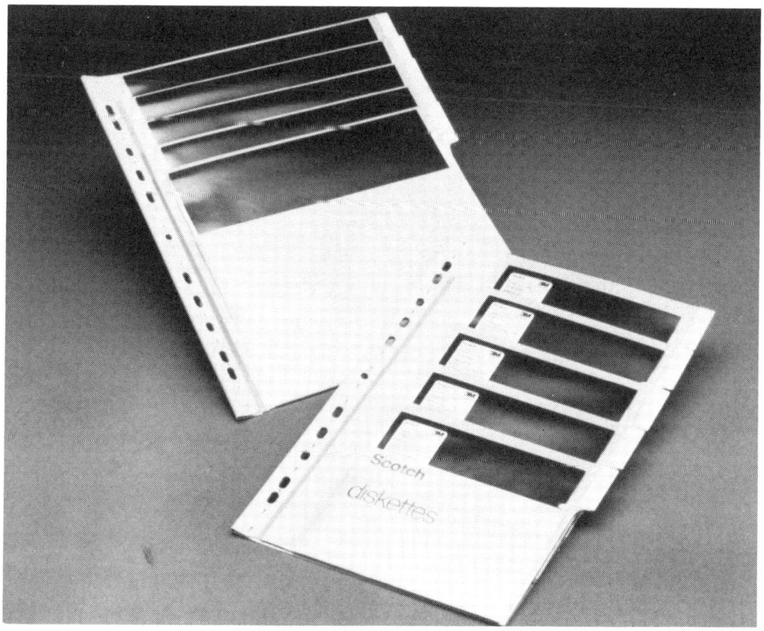

suited to files that must be removed from storage and examined in their entirety before documents are inserted or retrieved.

Color coding enhances readability and reduces the possibility of misfiling when files are removed from storage. Color coding is especially important to decentralized systems which allow all users access to the files, to retrieve and refile directly and regularly.

Studies have shown that color-coded documents are retrieved 60 percent faster than noncolored documents, and misfiles are reduced substantially when the files are returned to storage. When a misfile *does* occur, finding it is relatively easy because color "misfits" are easy to identify.

Filing guides divide files into sections or categories. They may divide a file alphabetically or by primary topic areas, with the primary topics placed in alphabetic sequence. Numeric, rather than alphabetic, guides protect sensitive material from illegal access by would-be violators.

In purchasing supplies, brand name may be an important consideration. Companies with well-established names usually stand behind their products. However, little-known companies which have not yet established themselves nationally may offer better service than a brand-name vendor whose service office is located in another city.

ROLE OF THE RECORDS MANAGER

Records management has been traditionally associated with the administrative services function of a business office. Clerical workers have often assumed the duties of coding and filing incoming records and retrieving them for managerial personnel when needed.

However, as business records continue their phenomenal growth in both type and quantity, management recognizes the need to place a person in charge of records who has formal training in the proper maintenance of records. The search usually turns inward first, to an employee who is familiar with company policy and company records.

Administrative assistants may be chosen for such a position. In most cases, their educational background, supervisory experience, and ability to work with people qualify them for the role. Normally, too, they have proven their ability to assume leadership in other projects and are ready and able to assume this new responsibility.

The initial development of a new program may, however, require the assistance of a committee to work with the administrative assistant in getting input from users throughout the company. Support from executives and managerial personnel is also necessary to ensure the program's acceptance by company personnel.

If appointed, the administrative assistant should be titled "Records Manager" and his or her former role reassigned to one who is able and ready to assume its responsibilities.

Except in very small operations, records management is a full-time position. No longer the province of clerical workers, it has become a major discipline within the electronic office.

Organizing, Storing and Retrieving Active Records

The last of the four objectives listed earlier in this chapter as central to a records management program concerns the organizing, storing, and retrieving of *active* records.

By definition, active records are those with which office personnel deal on a regular basis and which occupy "center stage" in the day-to-day flurry of business activity.

Located in the primary office area, these records are coded and filed for ready availability; then retrieved, used, and refiled repeatedly in the daily process of carrying on company operations.

The initial indexing, coding, and filing of active records at the inception of their life cycle is central to the success of the entire records management process.

For example, if filing guidelines are not followed consistently when new records are brought into the system, records could be misfiled or lost early on, causing confusion and delays throughout their life cycle. Therefore, this phase of records management—dealing competently with active records from their inception—is too important to be accorded a brief summary in the current chapter.

FIGURE 8-8 High-density storage units glide readily along tracks, enabling users to access records with ease. *Courtesy of Spacesaver Corporation.*

Rather, extensive coverage of generally accepted guidelines for indexing, coding, and filing business records is reserved to Chapter 10, which is devoted solely to this purpose.

Reorganization of a File System

Before adopting a new records management program, company officials must weigh the positive and negative elements associated with both the old and the new systems. Only after satisfying themselves that the positive aspects of the new system outweigh the negatives, and that the changeover is desirable, should they begin their search for a person to take charge of implementing the new system.

A cost-justification study will satisfy the first requirement; a review of personnel records to identify the most likely candidate to take charge, the second.

Cost Justification A cost/benefit analysis to compare current versus alternate record systems will enable company officials to determine the feasibility of installing a new system. Operating costs to be factored into the analysis should include equipment and supplies, salaries, space usage for the new system, and overhead.

One of the most costly components of the development costs may be the salaries of the analysts who evaluate the old system and design the new one. The preparation of new facilities will be a major cost factor also.

Benefits include more efficient and time-saving procedures, the salvage value of replaced equipment, and savings in floor space.

Although the qualitative benefits cannot be factored into the cost/benefit analysis directly, they may in the long run make the changeover more beneficial than the cost/benefit analysis reveals. Intangibles such as improved employee morale and job satisfaction are impossible to quantify.

SUMMARY

Paper documents remain the primary communications media for most offices. An effective system for managing records through their three-stage life cycle—from active to inactive to disposal status—is vital to the smooth operation of every business, large or small.

Central to good records management is an understanding of its four objectives: protection of records vital to the company's continued operations in case of disaster; the development of a records retention schedule fitted to the company's goals; economical methods for storing and retrieving inactive records; and practical systems for organizing and storing active records.

Equipment and supplies for various styles of storage from traditional vertical file cabinets to electronically controlled mobile files offer users an array of options from which to choose.

Prior to the adoption of a new records system, management should commission a cost-justification study to analyze the cost/benefit ratio to be realized from the system under consideration. If benefits appear to justify the costs anticipated, a person to initiate and head the new system must be selected.

The administrative assistant is a likely candidate for this role. Educational background, knowledge of company records, and experience in dealing with people usually are the qualifications required of a Records Manager.

QUESTIONS FOR REVIEW

1. Describe the three stages of a record's life cycle. Do all records go through the three cycles?
2. Describe what is meant by records classed as vital to a company's continued operations in case of a major disaster. What percentage of a company's records are usually classed as vital?
3. Which records are called active and why is it important that active records be coded and filed correctly from their inception into the system?
4. How can a company benefit from a thorough inventory of its records?
5. Define *retention schedule.* Name at least three benefits that accrue to the company with an up-to-date retention schedule.
6. What are some of the advantages of employing a commercial record center to store inactive records off site?
7. Why should written authorization be provided before the destruction of records which are no longer needed by the company?
8. Name and describe three basic styles of shredders. How do they differ in capacity and type of documents they will shred successfully?
9. Describe the basic structure of mobile files.
10. What is meant by *activity ratio* and how is it measured?
11. How do color-coded labels on file folders aid in decreasing the number of lost or misfiled records?

QUESTIONS FOR DISCUSSION

1. In the initial stages of a company's changeover to a new records management system, the person assigned to the task of developing and implementing the new system is often assisted by a committee of three or four other employees. List, in rank order, three ways that *you believe* the committee can best serve the interests of the company and the responsible person by smoothing the transition to the new system. Explain your choices and your ranking.
2. In setting retention periods for certain records, which persons in a company should have input? For example, who should help determine how long to retain these documents:
   a. copies of your company's annual reports
   b. sales receipts for microcomputer purchases
   c. routine correspondence with customers
   d. medical records on employees' annual physical exams performed by the company physician
   e. expired fire and accident insurance policies

3. In the 1970s, it was predicted that the "paperless office" would become a reality within a decade. In your opinion, why has this not yet happened? Did the visionaries totally misread the signs of electronic inroads into future communications or were they just ahead of themselves?
   If you believe that their vision was right but their calendar wrong, when do you expect communications to become almost totally electronic? Explain your position.

SUGGESTED ACTIVITIES

1. Collect materials on different brands and styles of shredders; explore catalogs of office supply stores and vendors to get pictures and information on special features, capacities, prices, and types of cutter disks (crosscut, straight-cut, and confetti-cut) offered in the models shown. Compare prices and features of the shredders shown and select one for *your* office.
2. Discuss the security and privacy issues which have made the manufacture of shredders a growth industry.
3. Interview the person in charge of records management in a local or area company. Focus on retention schedules and their importance in the overall system of managing records. Ask how their retention periods are determined and how often the schedule is updated. Ask how they store inactive records (on or off site?) and how they dispose of inactive records when their retention periods have expired.
4. If a commercial record center exists in or near your city, call to see if the class can tour their facility. If a visit is not feasible, ask that a representative of the center come to speak to the class explaining the purpose and objectives of a commercial record center.
5. From ads in periodicals and catalogs of vendors and office supply stores, collect pictures and information on file cabinets and mobile units just as you did for shredders. Compare features and prices and select filing equipment for *your* office.

REFERENCES

DIAMOND, SUSAN Z., "A Strategic Approach to Records Management," *Office Systems '87* (June 1987), 88–93.

FERNBERG, PATRICIA M., "Office Shredders Carve Their Niche," *Modern Office Technology* (November 1987), 84–90.

JONES, ART, "Records Management Now & in the Future," *Office Systems '88* (May 1988), 100–103.

LANGEMO, MARK, ED. D., CRM, "How Long Must You Keep Your Business Records?" *Office Systems '88* (April 1988), 40–45.

LANGEMO, MARK, ED.D., CRM, "Records are too Costly to Remain Uncontrolled," *Office Systems '86* (June 1986), 93–98.

Records Management Handbook with Retention Schedules, Fellowes Manufacturing Company, Itasca, Illinois, 1986.

SIRAGUSA, GAIL, "A Manager's Guide to Document Filing Systems," *Administrative Management* (November 1985), 26–29.

ZANCA, TOM, "Shredders Can Ensure Confidentiality," *Office Systems '88* (July 1988), 64–68.

9

Paper-Based Records: Filing Systems and Procedures

INTRODUCTION

The administrative assistant plays a major role in the management of paper records in an office. Primary responsibilities usually encompass the following:

1. Inspection and preparation of paper documents for active storage
2. Organization of efficient procedures to insure that
   a. records are filed correctly and consistently, in accord with the rules of the filing system adopted by the company
   b. misfiles or lost records are kept to a minimum

Alphabetic systems, the most popular of the filing systems used today, are reviewed in this chapter, with typical business applications illustrating the indexing and coding rules. Subject, geographic, and numeric filing systems are also described.

Administrative assistants must also organize the myriad of papers which cross their desks each day. Several options available for this purpose are also described herein.

Terms introduced include:

indexing/coding of documents
middle-digit numeric systems
ARMA International

PREPARATION AND STORAGE OF RECORDS

The administrative assistant usually follows a standard set of procedures in preparing documents for storage in the active file. Whether the filing system used is numeric or alphabetic, the preliminary steps vary little from one system to another. Prior to filing, each document is examined carefully to determine its proper placement in the files. In the examination process, each document is inspected, indexed, coded, cross-referenced, if necessary, sorted, and labeled. Only then is the document ready to be filed in the appropriate file cabinet. Studies have shown that such uniform procedures speed the filing process and reduce misfiles.

Inspection and Release

The first step in preparing materials for filing is the inspection of each paper to see that related materials are stapled together in date order, with the most current date on top; that no paper clips or pins are attached; that damaged records are reinforced; that small clippings are taped or glued to larger sheets; and that large documents are folded to fit the dimensions of a file folder.

Following inspection, the documents may be released for filing. The release-for-file indicator may be a rubber-stamped "for file" notice, or the initials of an executive or administrative assistant, or a message code indicating that the document is ready for filing. For obvious reasons, "file" copies of outgoing correspondence do not require a release mark; they are created as a file reference.

Indexing and Coding

The *indexing* process is one of decision making. The decision maker must determine the key word or number which most logically identifies the document's place in the files. The key word could be a geographic location, a proper name, or a subject; a number would probably refer to an index file of predetermined codes which identify document categories.

The importance of careful indexing cannot be overstated. Illogical indexing and coding probably account for more misfiles than any other factor because the errors follow the documents' entry into the system to their "retirement" to inactive status and final dissolution.

Coding is the process of putting the indexing decision into writing. The reader/examiner identifies the key word or number by which the document will be filed and underlines it in colored pencil or writes it at the top of the document.

For example, in geographic filing of incoming correspondence, the city or state in the letterhead may be underlined or circled; with subject filing, the subject word is underlined in the document, or written at the top of the page, or both; in number filing, the number assigned to the document is written in the upper right corner of the page.

Cross-referencing

Cross-referencing is necessary only when a file can be logically filed in more than one location, as in the correspondent's home city, and by the type of product manufactured. In such cases, the document is filed according to the caption by which it is most likely to be requested, and a cross reference is made, captioned by the second title. The cross-reference directs the user to "see" the original file.

Cross-references for card files use cards of the same size and weight as the regular cards; they may, however, be of a different color. Cross-references for correspondence may be card indexes or letter-size sheets. Instances which suggest the use of cross-references include:

Subject filing (cross-referenced by name of company or correspondent)

Marital name changes (Leona Brown becomes Mrs. Paul Simon), or marital versus legal name (Mrs. Paul Simon, or Leona Simon)

Full names versus initials or acronyms (Desktop publishing or DTP; American Telephone & Telegraph or AT&T)

A fail-safe device for the person who indexes most company documents, cross-referencing is a necessary tool for simplifying the search for elusive files.

Sorting and Labeling

The written code at the top of documents indicates that they are now ready for filing. To save the time and energy file clerks often expend in shifting back and forth between cabinets filing unsorted papers, the stack of documents is sorted sequentially into related groups. If the stack is large, two or three sorts may be necessary to organize the papers.

For example, the first sort might gather the documents into groups initialized by the first seven letters of the alphabet—A to G, then H to N, O to U, and so forth; the second sort, by alphabetized sequence within each group. Numeric filing follows the same basic procedure, using numbers instead of the alphabet.

Labels

In typing labels, certain conventions are usually observed. Whether for the sake of expediency or custom, most typists follow an established pattern of line placement on file folder labels. The *primary reference* occupies the first line on the label; searchers are thus enabled to find their files more promptly. In a geographic file of the 50 states, for example, Illinois would be a primary reference, typed on the first line on the label.

The *secondary reference,* if any, occupies the second line on the label. For

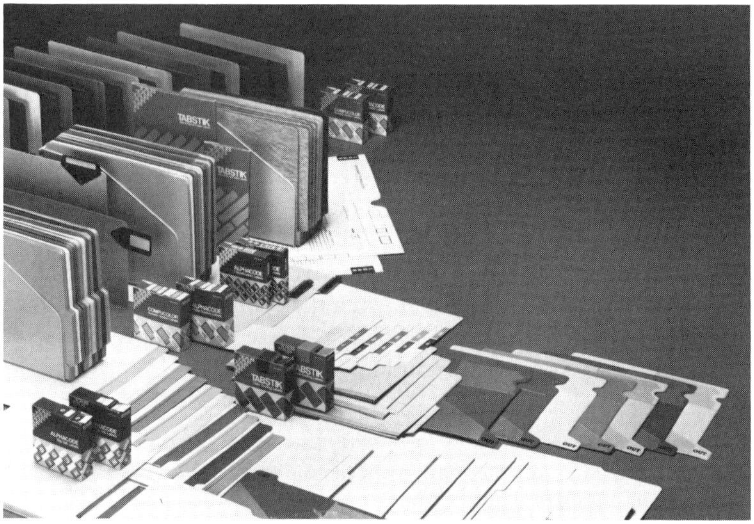

FIGURE 9–1 A variety of filing supplies are necessary for paper-based records.
Courtesy of TAB Products Company.

example, in a geographic file, Springfield, as a secondary reference under Illinois, would be written on the second line.

Abbreviated names are spelled out in full unless the person or organization is better known by the abbreviation than by the full name. IBM is a good example.

Upper- and lower-case letters are preferred in typing labels. Generally believed to be easier to read than "ALL CAPS," the upper- and lower-case letters add one more simplification to the process of filing and retrieving files easily and quickly.

Suggested Handling Procedures

Certain procedures are suggested to "fine tune" records preparation and filing. The following suggestions will streamline the process.

1. Batch the "to-be-filed" records together for filing at a specified time each day. Choose a time when interruptions are least likely.
2. Sort the folders and documents into related groups for faster processing.
3. When labeling new folders, stagger the tab cuts so that all labels can be easily seen by the user.
4. Leave space in each drawer or shelf for expansion.
5. Place the most recently dated materials in the front of the folder.
6. Divide groups of folders by appropriately labeled guides. File all folders behind the guides in numerical or alphabetical order.

7. Provide a miscellaneous folder for each guide, making it the last folder in each section. File in the miscellaneous file any records which are not expected to generate more correspondence. Make a new individual folder when correspondence adds up to three or more documents.
8. Divide folders when contents exceed the width of the widest expansion score at the base of the folder.
9. When inserting sheets in a filed folder, lift the folder slightly so that the inserted sheet can drop completely into it.
10. To avoid a serious accident when working with vertical files, open only one drawer at a time.

Charge-out Methods

To keep files readily available for users, and to minimize the risk of loss, a charge-out method is usually installed. Although several systems are in current use, most follow the same basic procedures.

When an item is removed from a folder, a substitution card is put in its place. The card gives the name of the user, a description of the material removed, and the date removed. In an emergency, the file can be recovered and returned promptly.

When an entire folder is removed, an outguide or an outfolder may replace the missing folder in the file drawer. In some instances, the central filing department does not release original files to anyone, but *does* make photocopies of the requested materials for persons with the proper identification.

The larger a company, the more important are formal charge-out procedures. Substantial losses can and do occur when companies become lax in safeguarding their records.

To Guard against Misfiles

1. Use large type on the tab headings. Labeling devices can be purchased which imprint title labels in large, bold print. Chances for misreading and misfiling are thus reduced.
2. Use file-drawer guides to separate the files into sections.
3. Stagger both the guides and the folders by their tab positions (1/5 cut, 1/3 cut, and so on) so that the tabs do not obscure one's vision of other files.
4. Color code files to identify groups more readily.
5. Periodically purge the files to remove unnecessary "baggage."

Searching for Misfiles

1. Check alternative spellings of proper names. Examples: Smith/Smythe, Allen/Alan, Johnson/Johnston, and Bryce/Brice.
2. Look for transposed names. Example: Scott, Patrick, rather than Patrick, Scott.
3. Check folders in the vicinity of the lost file; a careless user may have returned the file to an adjacent folder by mistake.
4. Check cross-references, if any, for related titles.

Confidential Files

In major organizations, certain records are treated as classified information. The confidential nature of the information may relate to personnel data, new-product data, or legal strategies planned for a pending court hearing. For example, biographical information on employees, including medical records, marital and family status, age, and salary earned should be protected from curious eyes. Information on the progress of new products must be kept "under wraps" until fully developed and patented, and information related to a pending court case must not be divulged prior to the judicial hearing.

For the sake of security, these confidential records are usually housed within the related department, with the administrative assistant charged with protecting them from unauthorized users. Charge-out procedures, if allowed at all, are restricted to authorized personnel only.

ALPHABETIC FILING SYSTEMS

Alphabetic filing systems are the most popular of all systems for filing paper records. Less complex than other systems, they answer most filing requirements with sufficient precision and flexibility to handle a variety of records.

Deceptively simple, however, alphabetic systems accommodate wide variations in users' interpretation of indexing and coding rules. In fact, surveys have shown that prior to 1985 no nationally accepted rules existed for indexing and filing records alphabetically, and that indexing and coding rules were almost as numerous and varied as the companies using them.

A set of standards developed by the Association of Records Managers and Administrators (ARMA International) sought to reduce confusion by simplifying and clarifying the rules governing the usage of alphabetic systems. ARMA shares its set of guidelines with all interested parties, in the hope that its guidelines will gain support from the public as the national standard for all alphabetic systems.

Based on the premise that ease of retrieval is of paramount importance, ARMA published seven simplified filing rules which they suggest for consistency in manual filing.

Included in ARMA's Alphabetic Filing Rules are some major changes from traditional filing practice. The changes affect the filing of some compound words, numbers which are not spelled out, abbreviations, acronyms, and some governmental titles. While no organization is obliged to accept their proposed standards, ARMA suggests that each company document and communicate its indexing and filing rules—whatever their source—to personnel who regularly file and/or retrieve company records. Such action will result in increased consistency in filing procedures, with a corresponding decrease in misfiles.

Seven Simplified Filing Rules[1]

(A filing *unit*, by ARMA's definition, is a number, letter, word, or any combination of the three used in indexing and filing. One or more units makes up a filing *segment*; i.e., the total name, subject or number being filed.)

1. Alphabetize by arranging files in *unit-by-unit order and letter-by-letter within each unit.*
2. Each filing unit in a filing segment is to be considered. This includes prepositions, conjunctions, and articles. The only exception is when the word *the* is the first filing unit in a filing segment. In this case, *the* is the last filing unit. Spell out all symbols, and file alphabetically; e.g.,
   # (pound, or number)
   , (comma)
   $ (dollar)
3. File "nothing before something." File single-unit filing segments before multiple-unit filing segments.
4. Ignore all punctuation when alphabetizing. This includes periods, commas, dashes, hyphens, apostrophes, etc. Hyphenated words are considered one unit.
5. Arabic and Roman numbers are filed sequentially before alphabetic characters. All Arabic numerals precede all Roman numerals.
6. Acronyms, abbreviations, and radio and television station call letters are filed as one unit.
7. File under the most commonly used name or title. Cross-reference under other names or titles which might be used in an information request.

Applications of the Simplified Filing Standard Rules[2]

1. *Personal Names:* Use the last (surname) as the first filing unit, the first name or initial as the second unit, and subsequent names or initials as successive units. (Rule 1)

	AS FILED			
AS WRITTEN	*Unit 1*	*Unit 2*	*Unit 3*	*Unit 4*
Jackie E. Adkins	Adkins	Jackie	E	
Mary Ann Bacon	Bacon	Mary	Ann	
Judy Barford	Barford,	Judy		

[1]ARMA International, *Standards Program, Alphabetic Filing Rules,* Prairie Village, Kansas, 1986, 1.

[2]Indexing rules defined by ARMA, based on the *Simplified Filing Standard Rules;* illustrative examples furnished by the author.

2. *Personal Names with Prefixes:* Surnames which include a prefix are filed as one unit whether the prefix is followed by a space or not. (Rules 1 and 4)

	AS FILED			
AS WRITTEN	*Unit 1*	*Unit 2*	*Unit 3*	*Unit 4*
Robert J. Cinq-Mars	CinqMars	Robert	J	
Louis Clay-Mendez	ClayMendez	Louis		
Alphonse M. Di Pietro	DiPietro	Alphonse	M	

3. *Personal Names with Personal and Professional Titles and Suffixes:* Suffixes are not used as filing units except when needed to distinguish between two or more identical names. When *needed,* a suffix is the last filing unit and is filed as written, ignoring punctuation. (Rules 2, 3, 4, 5, and 6)

	AS FILED			
AS WRITTEN	*Unit 1*	*Unit 2*	*Unit 3*	*Unit 4*
R. Blaise	Blaise	R		
Robert Blaise	Blaise	Robert		
Robert T. Blaise	Blaise	Robert	T	
Robert T. Blaise, Ph.D.	Blaise	Robert	T	PhD
Robert T. Blaise, 3rd	Blaise	Robert	T	3
Robert T. Blaise, II	Blaise	Robert	T	II

4. *Personal Names Which are Hyphenated:* Ignore the hyphen and file the two words as one unit. (Rule 4)

	AS FILED			
AS WRITTEN	*Unit 1*	*Unit 2*	*Unit 3*	*Unit 4*
Jo-Lynn Edmiston	Edmiston	JoLynn		
Jan E. Haney-Powell	HaneyPowell	Jan	E	
Diane M. O'Brien-Kuhn	O'BrienKuhn	Diane	M	
Lee-Ann D. Connelly	Connelly	LeeAnn	D	

5. *Pseudonyms and Royal and Religious Titles:* Pseudonyms are filed as written. Personal names which start with a royal or religious title and are followed by *only* a given name(s) are filed as written. (Rule 7)

AS WRITTEN	AS FILED Unit 1	Unit 2	Unit 3	Unit 4
Father Bob	Father	Bob		
Sister Maria Regis	Sister	Maria	Regis	
Father Philip Bryce	Bryce	Philip	Father	
PeeWee Herman	PeeWee	Herman		
Rev. Thomas Long, S. J.	Long	Thomas	Rev	S J
Marge Sanders, CPA	Sanders	Marge	CPA	
Kermit the Frog	Kermit	The	Frog	

6. *Nicknames:* When a person commonly uses a nickname as a first name, file using the nickname. Cross-reference from the given name only if necessary. (Rule 7)

AS WRITTEN	AS FILED Unit 1	Unit 2	Unit 3	Unit 4
Dizzy Dean	Dean	Dizzy		
Bubba Charles Younger	Younger	Bubba	Charles	
Founch Jeff Gordon	Gordon	Founch	Jeff	
Marney Margaret Edwards	Edwards	Marney	Margaret	
Slugger Jim O'Toole, II	O'Toole	Slugger	Jim	II

Business and Organization Names

1. *Business and Organization Names:* These are filed as written according to the Simplified Standard Rules and using the business letterhead or trademark as a guide. Names with prefixes follow the examples shown for Personal Names with Prefixes. (Rules 1, 2, 3, 6, and 7)

AS WRITTEN	AS FILED Unit 1	Unit 2	Unit 3	Unit 4
A&P Foods	A	and	P	Foods
AAA Auto Club, Inc.	AAA	Auto	Club	Inc
C W Dandy's	C	W	Dandy's	
Caesar's Pizza	Caesars	Pizza		
D&W Drive-In	D	and	W	DriveIn
De-Lorean's Body Shop	DeLoreans	Body	Shop	
Fat Albert's	Fat	Alberts		
The Royal Inn	Royal	Inn	The	
WAND Television, Inc.	WAND	Television	Inc	

2. *Place Names in Business:* Each word/filing unit is treated as a separate filing unit. (Rules 2 and 4)

	AS FILED			
AS WRITTEN	*Unit 1*	*Unit 2*	*Unit 3*	*Unit 4*
Oklahoma Natural Gas Co.	Oklahoma	Natural	Gas	Company
St. John's Hospital	StJohns	Hospital		
Paris Power & Light	Paris	Power	and	Light
Hanft Jewelry Store	Hanft	Jewelry	Store	

3. *Compass Terms in Business Names:* Each word or unit in a filing segment containing compass terms is considered a separate filing unit. If the term includes more than one compass point, treat it as written. (Rules 2 and 4)

	AS FILED			
AS WRITTEN	*Unit 1*	*Unit 2*	*Unit 3*	*Unit 4*
North East Estates, Inc.	North	East	Estates	Inc
South Eastern Oil Co.	South	Eastern	Oil	Company
South-East Foods, Inc.	Southeast	Foods	Inc	
South Western Coal Co.	South	Western	Coal	Company

Governmental and Political Designations

1. *State and Local:* State, county, parish, city, town, township, and village governments and political divisions are filed by their distinctive names. The words "county of," "city of," and so on, if needed, are added for clarity. If "of" is not part of the official name as written, it is not added. (Rules 2 and 7)

	AS FILED			
AS WRITTEN	*Unit 1*	*Unit 2*	*Unit 3*	*Unit 4*
Coles County Department of Public Aid	Coles	County	Public	Aid
City of Mattoon	Mattoon	City	of	
State of Illinois Department of Health	Illinois	Health	Department	

2. *Federal:* Eliminate "Department of" and file by their distinctive names. (Examples shown in indexing order.)
   a. United States Government Coast Guard
   b. United States Government Internal Revenue Service
   c. United States Government Soil Conservation Service

Alphabetic Variations

The majority of all filing in business and professional offices is based on the alphabet. Alphabetic filing systems are reliable, direct, and easily understood by most users. In addition to the alphabetic systems previously illustrated, in which all files are sequenced alphabetically by *name*, two other systems based on the alphabet are widely used: *subject* files and *geographic* files.

Subject filing systems differ from alphabetic *name* sysems in that the captions refer to topics rather than to names of people or companies. However, within the structure of the *subject* system, alphabetic filing rules are usually applied.

Probably the most difficult aspect of subject filing is determining the *logical* heading for file captions. The captions must be the logical choice of most users. A cross-reference index is necessary for all files which have multiple caption possibilities. The index is welcomed by users who sometimes experience the frustration of looking for a file under the wrong caption. To find the file, the user consults the cross-reference index to discover the captions under which the file may be stored. As an example, the following cross-reference index lists four popular software packages which are used as cross-references for the primary subject, "Word Processing."

DisplayWrite	See Word Processing
Multi-mate	" " "
Word Perfect	" " "
Word Star	" " "

In subject filing, each main heading has at least one subhead. For example, the subject "Professional" might have these subheads:

Organizations
Conferences
Awards

The subheads may be further divided into specific titles or subjects related to both the main title and the subhead. For example, the subhead "Organizations" may be subdivided as follows.

Professional
  Organizations
    Delta Pi Epsilon
    National Business Education Association
    Office Systems Research Association

Each major subject heading is identified by a primary guide labeled in bold letters. The subhead, if any, is also introduced by a labeled guide. Labels on the folders which follow the guides include the main heading, the subheading, and the title of the file. Example:

Professional — Organizations
DPE Membership

When a subject filing system is properly installed, several captions of headings and subheadings are usually visible in the opened file drawer, with folders properly filed directly behind their related guides. Color coding is often used to help distinguish the file classifications.

Since the secret to successful subject filing lies in the logical selection of titles, greater consistency is usually achieved through having just one person assume responsibility for setting up and maintaining the filing system.

Geographic filing systems arrange records alphabetically by geographic location. Supported by a card file cross-reference which indexes companies, customers, or clients by name, geographic systems are convenient for businesses having a strong geographic orientation. Travel agencies, sales distributorships, political organizations, and some government agencies adopt geographic systems as the most logical form of storage for their records.

In a geographic system, the filing sequence begins with the largest geographic unit recognized in the system and descends sequentially down to the smallest unit. For example, a sales organization operating from its headquarters in Tulsa, Oklahoma, with regional headquarters handling groups of states throughout the country, might have its geographic system set up in this way:

1st level:	Eisor Corporation Corporate headquarters
2nd level: Regional Headquarters	Eastern Division Western Division Midwest Division . . . etc.
3rd level: States within the Midwest Region	Illinois Missouri Kansas Oklahoma
4th level: Cities within Oklahoma	Bartlesville Oklahoma City Tulsa

As in subject filing, each folder reflects the names of the divisions above it. For example:

Midwest: Oklahoma
Tulsa

As in subject filing, each record is arranged alphabetically within its classification.

NUMERIC AND OTHER FILING SYSTEMS

Numeric filing systems index records in numeric order. Government agencies which record data on citizens by their social security numbers, banks which identify their accounts by account numbers, and lawyers which identify their clients and cases by number find numeric systems the logical choice for indexing and storing their records.

A numeric system is easy to administer and use; each new file is simply assigned the next number in sequence. An alphabetized card index is used as a cross-reference; on each card is written the name of the customer or client corresponding to a numbered file, plus the number assigned to him or her. The user first goes to the alphabetically indexed card file to get the assigned number of the file for which he or she is searching, then to the file cabinet for the desired file folder.

Terminal- and middle-digit systems are based on a series of assigned code numbers read from right to left with the terminal digits or middle digits read as a unit of two or three numbers. For example, in the sequence *82-35-50* the terminal digit is 50, the middle digit, 35.

The number groupings can represent sections, files, types of documents, or some other category of the filing system. Numeric systems are suitable for large mail-order firms and for very large filing systems.

Other Systems

Alphanumeric systems are numeric systems to which letters are added to clarify or expand the entries in the system. The Dewey Decimal System for classifying library holdings is an alphanumeric system.

Chronological systems are of two types: follow-up or *tickler* files which keep track of activities by date; and *chron* files which are daily logs of all correspondence prepared in the office. Chron files are explained on page 208 of this chapter. Tickler files are used by the administrative assistant and others as reminders of pending events.

ORGANIZATION OF DESKTOP PAPERS

The day-to-day activities processed in every office require that the administrative assistant organize an efficient method for dealing with the steady flow of papers passing through the office every day. Depending on the nature of the business, the papers may include:

inquiries, complaints, or orders from customers
correspondence to and from clients, customers, and vendors
records of telephone calls made and received

vendor ads to review
bills to process
periodicals to file or toss
reports to complete
memos, letters, and reports to read
folders to return to central files

All of these papers need to be *put* somewhere—for a few minutes, or for the day or week while awaiting appropriate action. Good organizational plans provide a place for each type of document; the administrative assistant sees that each document is put "in its place."

Some solutions which have withstood the "test of time" in dealing with the daily round of activities include such practical devices as daily "logs," desk-drawer files, in/out boxes, chronological folders, and desktop card files. Without such aids, the harried office worker might never get the day's paper work organized and his or her desk cleared.

Daily Logs

A log book is used for recording daily events in the office, such as long-distance calls made or received, special mailings sent, telegrams sent or received, executive visitors received, and similar activities. Each event is recorded with a description, time and date, and, when appropriate, with comments added.

FIGURE 9-2 "Designer 2" collection of desktop accessories. *Courtesy of Rubbermaid Corporation.*

FIGURE 9-3 "New Traditions" desk accessories. *Courtesy of W. T. Rogers Company.*

In/Out Boxes

Metal or plastic trays, usually stacked in tiers of two, three, or more, are placed at the worker's station for the purpose of temporarily stashing incoming or outgoing papers. Typically, the trays are labeled "in," "out," and "hold" to signify their principal purpose. Nevertheless, they may serve purposes other than the temporary storage of papers enroute into or out of the office.

On a limited basis, the boxes may also be used for storing stationery, forms, envelopes, and current periodicals for brief periods. In such cases, the trays should be labeled appropriately.

Desk-drawer Files

Popularly utilized to store forms, stationery, manuals, and other frequently used supplies, desk-drawer files offer convenience and efficiency. For persons who prefer a noncluttered work surface, desk-drawer files are also frequently used in lieu of in/out boxes for temporary storage of incoming/outgoing correspondence.

Since the desk-drawer file is used solely by the worker occupying the station, it can be organized to suit that person's convenience.

Chronological Folders

A temporary chronological file (chron file) is used to file copies of correspondence sent to central files. Bound by a ring binder at the side or at the top, the carbon copies or photocopies of the letters are filed by date in chronological order with the latest date on top.

The copies are used as reference by the department originating the letters. They verify, for instance, that a letter has been sent to central files, the date sent, and the information contained in the letter. The chron file makes it unnecessary to consult central files or to request copies be sent back to the department when information is needed. The chron file does *not* substitute for central files, however; copies are retained in the chronological file only temporarily, then destroyed.

Card Files

Card files are one of the most popular desktop devices used by the administrative assistant to organize information referred to often. Typically, card

FIGURE 9-4 Card file expands to hold 500 cards. *Courtesy of Rolodex, Inc.*

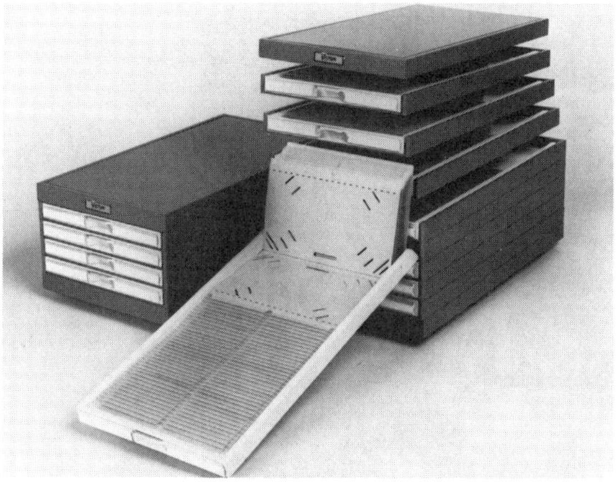

FIGURE 9-5 Two styles of visible record systems: card trays and folder-bound format. *Courtesy of KARDEX Systems, Inc.*

files supplement a standard filing system, and are used as an index to the standard system.

Available in many styles, card files are designed to fit the three standard-sized cards: 3 × 5 inches; 4 × 6 inches; and 5 × 8 inches. The most popular styles are portable wheel files, visible files, box files, and rotary files.

Portable wheel files hold slotted cards and guides of all standard sizes. Both cards and guides can be easily removed from the wheel to delete outdated information. A small wheel holds as many as 1,000 cards; larger wheels hold many times that many.

Visible files provide the reader with information visible at a glance. Placed in see-through pockets, the information may be viewed on a narrow strip of paper or card stock, or on a card. In some types, the cards are filed horizontally; in others, vertically. One part of the card or paper strip, however, is always visible. Visible files often employ colors to aid in classifying the records and making the search/retrieval process easier and quicker.

Visible card files are used extensively in situations where the time factor may be crucial; for instance, patient records in hospitals are often kept on visible

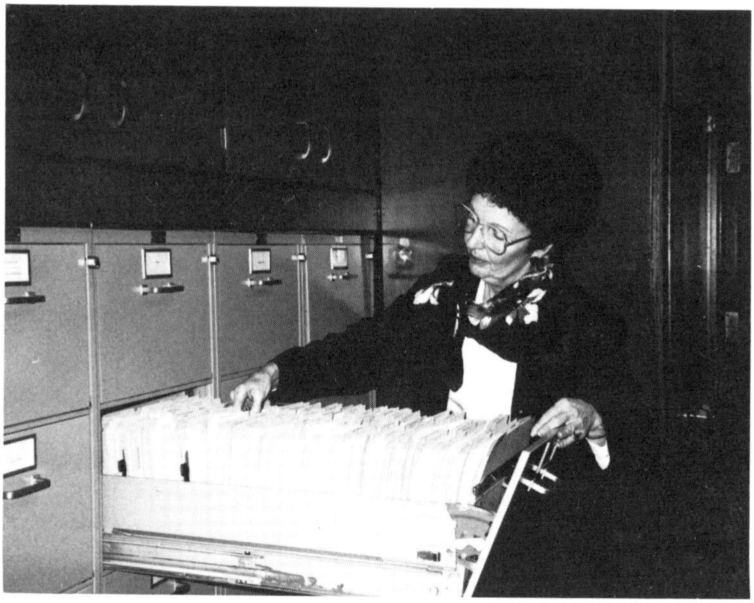

FIGURE 9-6 Consistent, uniform procedures for managing paper records are essential to an effective records management program. The administrative assistant plays an important role in establishing such procedures.

card files. Visible card files are also useful for extensive inventories, such as hardware supplies.

Box files date back to the beginning of record keeping, but are still prized as valuable filing aids for the busy executive or administrative assistant. The metal or cardboard boxes come in the three standard horizontal sizes of 3 × 5, 4 × 6, and 5 × 8, and in depths to fit the customers' needs.

Rotary files come in both desktop and floor models. Each desktop model is mounted on a rotary wheel which can be pivoted manually from the knob on its side. In addition to cards which are hole punched and attached to the unit by a rod, the rotary files also accommodate loose-leaf binders. Motorized card files are constructed to rotate vertically or horizontally.

SUMMARY

Uniform procedures of inspecting, coding, sorting, and labeling documents are usually followed by the administrative assistant prior to filing documents in their respective file cabinets or shelves. When the procedures are followed consistently, the retrieval process is speeded, and misfiles are reduced dramatically.

Alphabetic systems in use today include the direct, or name, method which indexes documents by the names of companies, customers, clients, or items filed;

plus two variations of the direct method—subject filing and geographic filing—both of which employ the alphabet in their sort and file procedures. The subject method sorts files alphabetically by topic, and the geographic method sorts alphabetically by geographic area.

The Association of Records Managers and Administrators (ARMA International) has published a set of guidelines for indexing and filing documents which it proposes as a standard for business and industry. Its seven simplified filing rules were developed in response to the filing inconsistencies ARMA discovered in a survey of business filing practices.

Variations of alphabetic systems are seen in subject and geographic filing, each of which is useful for special businesses and professions. Numeric, alphanumeric, and chronological systems are also appropriate for certain applications.

QUESTIONS FOR REVIEW

1. What steps are involved in the process of examining documents prior to their filing?
2. In what instances is it wise to cross-reference files?
3. List seven of the ten handling procedures suggested in this chapter.
4. Explain how the charge-out methods a company adopts can affect the company's rate of file losses.
5. Name three means of guarding against misfiles.
6. Describe four devices which help organize desktop papers.
7. Card file equipment comes in various styles and sizes. Describe some of the most popular designs used in business today.
8. Explain the difference between "direct" (or "name") alphabetic systems and subject filing systems.
9. What is a filing unit?
10. Define numeric filing systems.

QUESTIONS FOR DISCUSSION

1. ARMA International proposes certain standards for filing records which if adopted nationally would improve filing consistency from one company to another, and probably cause a substantial reduction in the number of misfiles and lost files. In your opinion, should ARMA's guidelines be mandated by the federal government? Explain your position.
2. New clerical workers should be given thorough instruction in the company's filing procedures so that they can become adept in handling the filing duties with ease and accuracy. In your opinion, what is the best means of imparting this knowledge to the newcomers?
3. Some companies believe in a centralized filing system; others prefer a decentralized system. List the pros and cons of each.

SUGGESTED ACTIVITIES

1. Arrange the units of the following personal names *alphabetically* in proper indexing order.

	INDEX ORDER OF UNITS			
Name	*Unit 1*	*Unit 2*	*Unit 3*	*Unit 4*
Mrs Brenda Litteken				
M Litteken				
Marie A Litteken, R.N.				
Michael Litteken				
Michael L Litteken				

2. Index the following business names *alphabetically* and in proper indexing order.

	INDEX ORDER OF UNITS			
Name	*Unit 1*	*Unit 2*	*Unit 3*	*Unit 4*
Taco Bell				
The Decatur Herald				
WEIU Radio, TV				
The Floor Show, Inc.				
Rockome Association of Commerce				

3. Arrange in alphabetic order and index the units of the following governmental agencies.

	INDEX ORDER OF UNITS			
Name	*Unit 1*	*Unit 2*	*Unit 3*	*Unit 4*
Tulsa County Dept of Housing				
State of Pennsylvania Dept of Health				
U.S. Government Dept of Education				
City of Tulsa				

REFERENCES

ARMA International, *Alphabetic Filing Rules,* Standards Program, ASN 2-1986.

JENNINGS, LUCY MAE, *Secretarial and Administrative Procedures,* 3rd ed., pp. 412–431. Englewood Cliffs, NJ: Prentice Hall, 1989.

OLIVERIO, MARY ELLEN, and WILLIAM R. PASEWARK, *Office Procedures and Technology,* pp. 520–537. Cincinnati, OH: South-Western Publishing Company, 1988.

10
Electronic Storage and Imaging Systems

INTRODUCTION

Although paper-based filing systems may never be totally replaced, a growing number of businesses are integrating one or more electronic components into their storage/retrieval systems. A variety of options are available:

> Database management systems (DBMS) digitize records on magnetic tape or disks and store them in structured patterns for users to access electronically.
>
> Electronic imaging systems use laser beams to store massive amounts of data, graphics, and pictures on optical disks. Scanners, another form of imaging, convert text and images to digital format to allow for storage in electronic format.
>
> Micrographics miniaturizes records on film. COM (computer output microfilm) units create microfiche for storage of multi-page records on 4 × 6-inch microfiche. Coupled with computer-assisted retrieval (CAR) systems, microfiche records are retrieved electronically at the user's command.

The administrative assistant must remain current with state-of-the-art electronic storage alternatives to paper-based systems. Any of these media may replace the *bulk* of paper records in the future.

Acronyms in this chapter include:

CD-ROM	WORM
COM	CAR
DBMS	FMS

ELECTRONIC STORAGE SYSTEMS

An important component of the electronic office, electronic filing is broadly defined as the storage of documents in digital or optical format. Files stored electronically are luring a growing number of users away from paper-based systems.

The decision whether or not to change from a manual system to an electronic one depends in part on the size of a company's business operations, the volume of paper work done, and the financial resources earmarked for the purchase or lease of storage equipment.

Companies may choose to automate totally or to automate only parts of the record-handling procedures. They may also limit the transition, initially, to select departments, rather than integrating records of the entire company in the changeover.

The administrative assistant will work with superiors in assessing the feasibility of a changeover and the extent to which the company should commit itself to a new electronic system. An assessment of the company's volume of documents processed daily and the frequency of user access to the filed documents should be considered.

Answers to the following questions will provide additional insights:

Under the current system, what is the average ratio of misfiled documents?
Is access to the current files restricted, or do all personnel have access?
How quickly are documents supplied when called for?
How much can the company afford to invest in a new system?

Advantages usually associated with an electronic filing system include:

Faster and easier access to stored records
A gain in floor space
Fewer misfiles
Accessibility of records via a communications network
Improved productivity per worker

Paper-intensive industries, including banks, insurance companies, and universities, usually experience a marked improvement in speed and efficiency when they switch to an electronic storage system. Manufacturing firms and low-volume paper users experience substantial, though less dramatic, improvements.

Some companies find that a mix of more than one electronic media suits their purposes, with different divisions of the company utilizing different media. Ultimately, the objective of a good "fit" in the storage media chosen is an overall improvement in the processing of records, with a consequent improvement in productivity.

Types of Electronic Storage Systems

Currently, the following are the most popular media employed by business and professional offices for the electronic storage and retrieval of information.

Database management systems (DBMS) with the database records stored on magnetic disks or tapes

Computer-assisted storage and retrieval systems, using micrographics—a form of filmed miniaturization of records on microfiche, aperture cards, or reels

Image-based systems utilizing optical disks for high-density storage

DATABASE MANAGEMENT SYSTEMS

A database management system is defined as a collection of electronically stored records, organized according to a set of attributes common to all the records. Database software with user-friendly programs coupled with well-designed user-training programs have made electronic databases the favored mode of storage for businesses of every size. Thousands of businesses and professional offices utilize database management systems to store all their records.

Hard (fixed) disk drives were instrumental in making the shift from paper-based records to databases especially practical for small to mid-size offices. Prior to the advent of hard disks, the storage capacities of desktop computers were not sufficient to accommodate the memory requirements of large databases. Fixed disks, with their generous storage capacities, made the shift to electronics a practical alternative, not only for large corporations but for smaller businesses as well.

The source documents for data entry into a database may be a collection of invoices, customer accounts, price lists, or names of sales personnel and their volume of sales completed during a given time period. When the data are logically classified into records—for example, the names of the salespeople, and secondary attributes, such as the sales territories and volume of sales in each—the information gathered from the processed data provides insights into the company's level of sales per territory and the performance of their salespeople in each territory.

With such information in hand, company officials can detect weak links in recent ad campaigns, concrete evidence supporting (or failing to support) seminars for sales personnel, and comparative data on the success rate of newly hired personnel. Data thus become information which managers utilize in decision making.

Database Models

In order to select the most appropriate database for the company, the administrative assistant must know what models are available, then evaluate each

Relational Database

NAME, LAST	NAME, FIRST	HOME CITY	MAJOR
CARTER	LOIS	ROCKFORD	AIS
CHISM	BRUCE	CHICAGO	AIS
COREY	PATRICIA	CHICAGO	DP
GREGG	JANICE	ROCKFORD	MGT
HACKETT	GENE	ROCKFORD	DP
PIERCE	WALTER	CHICAGO	MGT

Hierarchical Database

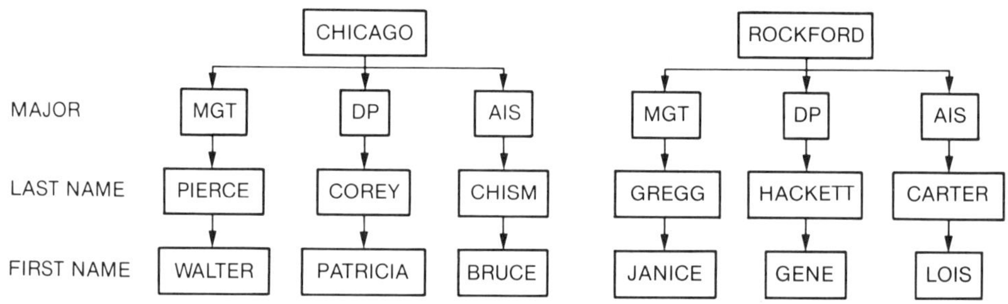

FIGURE 10–1 An example of the contrasts between the relational and the hierarchical database structures: Note how the data are recorded in tabular form in the relational structure, and in a tree-like top-down fashion in the hierarchical pattern.

in terms of the company's needs. Currently, three types dominate the market: the hierarchical model, the relational model, and the file management system (FMS).

The hierarchical model is essentially a tree-structured pattern, in which higher-order pieces of information are linked through branches to lower-order ones. One level may point to several branches below it, but each lower branch may have *no more than one* upper-level connection in the hierarchy.

Resembling the organization chart of a company, data items are ordered in top-down fashion, creating logical links between the items. (See Figure 10–1 for an illustration of the hierarchical model.) Speedier response to users' search-and-retrieve commands is a characteristic of the hierarchical model. However, additions and deletions demand a somewhat higher level of expertise than that required of relational database users.

Designed primarily for mainframe applications, the hierarchical model is used by IBM in many of its mainframe database systems. Because its pattern does not fit most mini- or microcomputer applications, however, it is not as widely known or used as the relational models.

The relational model has a wide following of microcomputer users and is used increasingly on minis and mainframes, too. Like its counterpart, the file manager system (FMS), the relational model is set up in tabular form as a two-dimensional array, similar to a spreadsheet. Each row or "tuple" (to rhyme with couple), represents a record (person or thing), and each vertical column, one of its attributes.

Because of their familiar tabular styles, file managers and relational models are relatively easy to understand and use. The most significant difference between the two is that a relational database can merge related files while the FMS cannot. Relational databases also have some programming features not found in the FMS models.

Although a relational database is conceptualized as a table, it is formally a mathematical set that can be manipulated by algebraic operations, such as JOIN and PROJECT. JOIN links two tables to produce a third table. PROJECT extracts columns from one or more tables and uses them to produce a new table. Using PROJECT, JOIN, and other algebraic operations, it is possible to manipulate or extract any information in the database.

File Management Systems (FMS)

Like the relational database, *file management systems* are arranged in tabular format, with attributes shown in vertical columns, and records in horizontal rows. Additions and deletions of data are made in the same fashion as those of relational databases. Unlike relational databases, however, a file management system does not "relate" to other files; that is, it cannot merge information of one file into another, even if the two files are "related."

When FMS systems were introduced, they were also very limited in terms of the number of records they could handle and/or the number of fields allowed per record. However, current file management systems are no longer flat in performance or capacity. File Management Systems offered by major software developers now incorporate three major improvements over their predecessors: power, simplicity of use, and increased capacity—for more fields per record and more records per file.

Power is demonstrated in added features which allow for searching, sorting, calculating, extracting, and reporting; simplicity, in the extensive use of menus rather than sequential commands to access most functions; and increased capacity, in the thousands of records they will accommodate, with room for hundreds of fields in each. For example, five current FMS systems have a capacity of 65,000 records, a number that is difficult to outgrow for most organizations.

Speed is there, too. Searching out a series of records in some of the "new breed" of file managers takes two to three seconds. Compound instructions (e.g., all students earning a 3.5 GPA with a major in marketing and a minor in data processing) are processed routinely within seconds. Most FMS software also includes a simple word processor for memo writing.

A major advantage of both relational and file management models is the ease with which they can be changed. Attributes (fields) can be added or deleted without affecting any other parts of the structured tables; likewise, data can be readily added, deleted, or altered without affecting other records in the database.

Both models operate logically under these constraints:

1. No row (record) can exactly duplicate any other. (One would be superfluous.)
2. An entry that is unique for each row (record) must be present in at least one column or combination of columns; the column heading for this column, or group, is the key which serves as a marker for search operations.
3. Each cell must have one and only one entry; the entry may be zero.

Using an excerpt from a larger database, Figure 10–1 illustrates the relational and hierarchical database structures.

Magnetic Media for Storing Electronic Information

The familiar diskette which introduced thousands to computer usage still ranks as one of the most popular storage media for microcomputer users. Hard disk usage has grown to accommodate the increased memory demands of new software, and magnetic tape remains the medium of choice for storing the records of large-volume users.

Although emerging technology in optical disks points to a shift toward that medium in the future, industry leaders maintain that magnetic disks and tapes will retain their position of strength into the foreseeable future.

Diskettes Inexpensive and convenient to use, diskettes are popular with microcomputer users. Made of magnetically coated plastic, they are smooth surfaced at the time of purchase. By a command of the computer's operating system, they are formatted into concentric tracks, with pie-shaped sectors subdividing each track.

Two sizes currently dominate the market: the 5¼-inch floppy and the 3½-inch rigid microdiskette. The floppy diskettes have a capacity ranging from 360 kilobytes to a high-density 1.2 megabytes; the 3½-inch diskettes, from 720 kilobytes to 1.644 megabytes. The primary advantages of diskette usage are convenience and low cost. The disadvantages are limited storage capacity and vulnerability to environmental hazards and magnetic fields.

Diskette Protection To protect diskettes from environmental hazards and human error, users should practice certain precautions before, during, and after sessions with the computer. The following practices are suggested:

For diskette safety, *do*:

1. Label diskettes with a felt-tipped or other *soft*-tipped pen to prevent damage to the disk surface.
2. Label the diskette sleeves as well as the diskette labels with identifying information.
3. Keep diskettes in their protective sleeves when not in use.

4. File diskettes in a vertical position.
5. Store with each diskette a printed directory of its files. Keep it current.
6. Maintain a "healthful" environment for stored diskettes—free from excessive dust, humidity, and extreme temperatures.
7. Guard against bending, touching, or dropping the diskette. Take *special* care to avoid touching any exposed areas.

Other guidelines to follow:

1. *Do not* eat, drink, or smoke at the computer station.
2. *Do not* place diskettes on or near a magnetized field.
3. *Do not* place cleaning solvents near the diskettes or drives.
4. *Do not* carry diskettes under heavy objects, such as textbooks, to protect them from unknown hazards.
5. *Do not* force diskettes into disk drives; use a gentle but persistent touch, instead.
6. *Do not* leave diskettes in closed automobiles during extreme weather conditions.

Hard (Fixed) Disks

Like diskettes, hard (or fixed) disks store data magnetically in tracks and sectors. Their storage capacities are measured in megabytes and gigabytes. (One megabyte is 1 million bytes; one gigabyte is 1,000 megabytes or 1 million kilobytes.)

The disks have a hard rather than flexible base. In addition to high-storage capacity, fixed disks provide speedy access to stored programs. The disks are contained in a head-disk assembly (HDA) which is hermetically sealed. Air within the HDA is continuously circulated and filtered. Unlike the read/write head on the floppy disks which actually contacts the surface of the diskette when reading or recording data, the read/write head of the hard disk rides on a thin film of air thousandths of an inch away from the disk's surface.

Removable hard disks come in a sealed container that slides into the computer. Most popular are the 3½-inch hard disks mounted on expansion cards (boards) that fit into the back of the computer. Users can install the boards themselves.

Cartridge disks, which are easy to remove, come in a hard shell that slides into the computer or into a separate unit. Software can then be easily transferred from one computer to another. Many workers take their cartridge disks home after work to continue processing them on their home computers.

Unfortunately, storing files on hard disks does entail some risks. Power surges, blackouts, and even a moderate blow to the computer can cause the disk to "crash," thus destroying weeks or months of work. The data lost may be irreplaceable, or cost more to replace than the investment in the computer itself. Fire and theft are other potential hazards.

Periodic backup is the only solution to potential software losses, whatever the source. How often one should back up the originals depends on two important factors: the value of the information stored, and the frequency with which it is accessed and/or updated.

For additional protection, the backups should be kept in an off-site location, or, at minimum, in another part of the building which is safe from environmental hazards.

Magnetic Tape *Magnetic tape* was the dominant storage medium for many years until the hard disk "revolution" triggered a slowdown in tape sales. However, the hard disk phenomenon eventually enlivened the tape market as a backup media for hard disk storage.

Magnetic tape cartridges, resembling audiocassettes in appearance, have varying storage capacities, depending on tape length, number of tracks, and recording density.

Some cartridges have a capacity of 134 megabytes on 600 feet of 1/4-inch tape; others vary in capacity from 10 megabytes to 150 megabytes. Recent advances in technology have affected the storage capacity and access speed of tape cartridges:

1. Tapes which store two gigabytes (2,000 megabytes) on a tape cartridge have been introduced. The recording technique used in these high-density tapes rotates the write head in a diagonal pattern across the full width of the tape in order to utilize *all* of the tape for information storage.
2. Information stored on the cartridge may be accessed randomly rather than sequentially. This provides users with search-and-retrieval speed rivaling that of magnetic disks.

FIGURE 10-2 Each tape cartridge in the IBM 3480 magnetic tape subsystem features self-threading tape drives, high-density storage, and high-speed search functions. *Courtesy of IBM Corporation.*

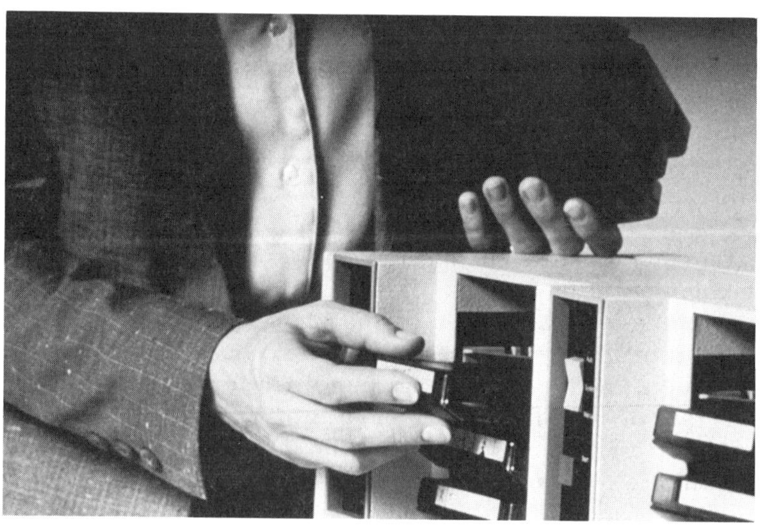

New Magnetic Technology Researchers are constantly searching for more efficient ways to store records magnetically. Two new products recently introduced are the stretched disk and hard-disk expansion boards.

The *stretched disk* is classified as a cross between a hard disk and a diskette. The present 5¼-inch version has a capacity of around 12 megabytes, with future technology aiming at the 100 megabyte range.

The *hard disk expansion board* fits into a single expansion slot of a microcomputer. These boards offer 20 megabytes or higher storage and can be easily installed by the user.

ON-LINE INFORMATION SERVICES

Over 400 organizations provide on-line bibliographic database and other information to subscribers of their services. Their on-line storage is accessed by subscribers who pay a monthly or usage fee for access to the information.

Business organizations are the biggest users of the on-line databases. For example, the Global Report, a round-the-clock information service for senior executives, specializes in international news and analysis of world events. The report is created especially for senior executives, bankers, and investors.

The Dow Jones News/Retrieval, established in 1974, provides information on business and investing services, stock quotations, market averages, and general information.

NewsNet is directed at executives, managers, lawyers, and information specialists. Its editors peruse articles from 300 business newsletters. They also channel full-text articles from ten wire services, including USA Today, UPI, AP, and the PR Newswire. NewsNet reports stock prices, continually updating prices on stocks listed on the New York Stock Exchange and the American Stock Exchange.

CompuServe offers a wide range of information services to subscribers, including tax tips from the Internal Revenue Service, stock market reports, news, weather, executive news services, and foreign reporting and commentary on world events.

Using the services of these and other information services may prove very helpful to the administrative assistant. Major research can be conducted and reports written or revised from information accessed at the computer keyboard, and business decisions based on current market conditions are made with greater confidence.

To connect with these electronic databases, three components are necessary: a telephone, a computer, and a modem to link the computer to the telephone line. To utilize the system, the user dials the telephone number of the service, then responds to the monitor's requests for a user ID and password. When accepted by the computer, the user selects from the menu the area of service he or she wants. No advanced computer skills are required.

MICROGRAPHICS

Micrographics is the photographic miniaturization of records on film. The format of the film used varies from one application to another, in accord with the objectives of the companies utilizing the micrographic procedures. Current choices include three basic microforms, with two variations:

1. 16mm and 35mm film reels
   a. film cartridges and cassettes
   b. film jackets
2. aperture cards
3. microfiche

The microform chosen depends on the volume of information being miniaturized, the physical characteristics of the source documents, how frequently the information is to be accessed, and how frequently it is to be updated, if at all.

Microimaging techniques benefit users in many ways. Used in place of paper records, microfilmed records reduce costs for storage, mailing and distribution, and filing equipment. Office space requirements and access time to retrieve documents are also reduced, while security against natural disasters and privacy violations is increased. (The master copies are kept in storage; user requests, after being validated, are met by duplicate copies only.)

Micrographic Formats

Film reels represent one of the earliest types of microfilmed documents. Sequentially paged documents are photographed and stored on rolls of film, providing space savings of at least 90 percent over that required to store paper documents. Libraries were among the first users to recognize the potential savings in shelf space to be realized by the use of film. The reel is most suitable for long-term storage of vital records and for semi-active records. Files stored on reel tape are retrieved sequentially, in contrast to those stored on magnetic disks which are retrieved randomly by track and sector.

Film cartridges and cassettes offer greater convenience than reeled film. When combined with automated indexing, they can be retrieved by computer through a computer-assisted retrieval (CAR) system.

Cartridges have a single core and must be rewound before removal from the viewing equipment. Cassettes have two cores and need not be rewound.

Microfilm jackets have a transparent plastic container with channels for film insertion. The inserted film (16mm or 35mm) comes from reels of film or from filmstrips. When filled, the jackets are manually filed in drawers or cabinets.

Aperture cards contain an opening (aperture) for insertion of one or more images on a 16mm or 35mm card. The generous space available on an aperture card makes updating or changing of images a fairly simple process. Frequently

FIGURE 10-3 Microfiche are stored in cabinet drawers designed especially for them. *Courtesy of Russ Bassett Corp.*

used for engineering purposes, aperture card drawings and specifications accompany the image(s) shown in the aperture.

Microfiche, the most common of the three basic microforms, is a rectangular sheet of 105mm film of approximately 4 × 6 inches in size. Microimages having a reduction ratio of 24X (1/24 the horizontal and vertical measure of the original document), are displayed in frames in a grid pattern. Each frame images one page; approximately 450 pages can be imaged on one microfiche.

The convenient postage-card size of the microfiche makes it easy to duplicate. Fiche can be produced as original camera film from a computer output microfilm (COM) recorder, or as a duplicate from a film jacket or another fiche.

Updatable microfiche are made by special film that permits the fiche to be returned to the camera and additional documents added. Depending on the system, documents can be added to the fiche for up to 20 years. Adding an image to a fiche takes about eight seconds and can be verified by the operator immediately after it is added.

Updatable fiche are suited to documents to which information is added periodically. Insurance policies which must be changed periodically to reflect changes in family situations, or personnel files which must be changed as employees' status within the firm changes are documents that are well suited to storage on updatable fiche.

Ultrafiche were developed by the National Cash Register Company. They represent a space-saving factor even more dramatic than that offered by microfiche. Ultrafiche use a reduction of 90X or more. A 4 × 6-inch ultrafiche with a reduction ratio of 90X can display more than 1,000 sheets of a document. As with microfiche, ultrafiche are randomly accessed when combined with a CAR system.

Holofiche are the latest form of ultrafiche. By recording in binary code, holofiche can image up to 20,000 pages on a 4 × 6-inch fiche. For storing great quantities of information, such as that generated by the Federal Government, holofiche represent substantial cost savings over other storage media.

Cameras for Microfilming Documents

The three types of cameras used for microfilming text, data, and graphic images are planetary, rotary, and step-and-repeat cameras.

Planetary cameras are used primarily to photograph materials which do not "feed" automatically into a rotary camera device, such as oversized records and bound volumes. The planetary lens and film are positioned above a flatbed on which the records are held stationary, by either manual or mechanical means.

Using 16mm or 35mm film, planetary cameras produce film rolls or aperture cards. The slower operation and feed mechanisms allow for more precise lighting adjustments than is possible with rotary camera systems. Consequently, they produce higher-quality reproductions. A trade-off in speed, however, is exacted.

Rotary cameras use a set of motorized rollers to transport each film-ready document into and out of the range of the camera lens. They are utilized primarily to film standard-size documents, such as bank checks, that can be filmed at a rate of hundreds or thousands per hour.

Some models can film both sides of a document simultaneously. High-volume copying, not precise detailing, is the primary purpose of rotary cameras. High rates of speed are characteristic of the rotary.

Step-and-repeat cameras are a variation of the planetary model. Used primarily to produce microfiche in a patterned grid of columns and rows, the 4 × 6-inch standard microfiche is produced by moving the lens across the film in a step-by-step process.

Updatable microfiche require a specialized type of step-and-repeat camera which exposes and develops one or more frames at a time, or voids pre-existing frames. Microfiche can therefore be updated or added to without refilming an entire document. Depending on the system, documents can be added to the fiche for up to 20 years.

Readers and Reader/Printers

For small to mid-size companies which choose to use service bureaus for their microfilming services, cameras are not a necessity. Readers, however, *are* necessary in order to read the filmed output.

Most readers are designed for specific film formats, e.g., microfiche, aperture cards, or roll film. The type of film used in the organization, therefore, determines what type of reader the company should buy. Some manufacturers do offer models with optional attachments to read additional formats, however.

Basically, all readers magnify the filmed image on a lighted screen, lit from behind so that the operator sees through the screen to read the image.

Reader/printers produce a paper copy of the filmed image. Good quality output can be expected from reader/printers for about the same cost per page as that of photocopiers reproducing from hard copy. In addition to cameras, readers, and printers, fully equipped micrographic systems require processors to develop the film, duplicators to make single or multiple copies of microforms,

FIGURE 10-4 Designed to read and print COM and source document fiche, jackets, and 16mm roll film, the RP-503 reader-printer is compact enough to sit atop a desk. *Courtesy of Minolta Corp.*

jacket fillers to insert film into jackets, and aperture card fillers to mount the 35mm images onto the aperture card.

Cost Effectiveness of Micrographics

Investment in a micrographics system requires a substantial commitment in time and dollars. Before making such an investment, the administrative assistant and his or her principals must consider whether the payback will justify the cost. Several factors should be taken into account, including space utilization, the volume of records to be miniaturized, and the level of activity in records usage.

The major benefit of micrographics is the amount of space it saves for other office functions. Although savings in space can be phenomenal, the dollar savings realized from the additional square footage are only significant if space is at a premium, or is extremely costly. This is not always the case.

In most instances, the location of the facility in an urban or nonurban setting is the telling factor in setting the "price" for space—as a premium item which costs dearly, or a relatively inexpensive "nonitem" which does not warrant a shift to miniaturization to hoard its usage.

If the company records are very active; that is, if records are continually accessed, passed around for discussion and review, updated, and refiled on a day-to-day basis, the organization is *not* a good candidate for a micrographics system. Micrographics are best suited to records which are handled infrequently and with few updates, if any.

If the volume of stored documents is relatively small, micrographics will not enhance the company's efficiency rating, nor contribute to the convenience of records users. The volume of records converted to miniaturized format must be large enough to justify the expenditure in time and money.

In what instances *do* micrographics offer substantial payback to its installers? Typically, companies which are prime candidates for a micrographics system are those which have tried unsuccessfully to cope with three major problems: (1) a high volume of paperwork to be processed; (2) an urgent need for long-term storage for many documents; and (3) a demand for better utilization of floor space in company offices.

Such organizations are ripe for the substantial gains provided by micrographics systems. The cost effectiveness of the installed systems, however, depends in part on the severity of the problems addressed and in part on the system itself—how smoothly it functions, once in place.

Micropublishing and Microfacsimile

The publication of documents on microfilm rather than on paper is already well established. Libraries of educational institutions, as well as public libraries, have from the first been heavy users of micrographics.

Microfilmed media are also used by governmental agencies and professional societies in the publishing of thousands of books, reports, and conference proceedings. Private telephone and address directories for members of societies and organizations are published on microfiche or ultrafiche.

Microfacsimile technology is a merger of micrographics and facsimile machines. From microfilm input, the unit outputs hard-copy facsimile. Several vendors offer such systems.

Computer-Output Microfilm (COM)

COM is the microform generated internally by a computer from a digitized "photograph" of computer data. The data are passed from the computer to the COM recorder (a camera device) in somewhat the same manner as data are transferred from a computer to a printer. The output is either a roll of microfilm or a microfiche.

An estimated 8,000 COM recorders have been installed in the United States. Most major mainframe installations have COM; and slow but steady growth is also evident in organizations with microcomputers only, where COM service firms are employed to convert the company's diskettes to microforms.

COM offers a number of benefits. First is output speed: COM prints reports onto film more than twenty times faster than typical line printers. Second, the heavy cost of paper production and distribution is eliminated through the COM-generated microfiche. (A 900-page report can be reduced to two 4 × 6 inch microfiche.) Third, with a local area network in place, information from the COM fiche can be dispatched promptly and efficiently to any computer station on the network.

Finally, the automated retrieval of the microformed records is made possible through the combination of COM with computer-assisted retrieval (CAR) systems.

Computer-Assisted Retrieval (CAR) Systems

A major advance in micrographic storage is computer-assisted retrieval (CAR). CAR technology facilitates both finding and retrieving stored fiche or cartridges through the integration of cameras and readers with computer hardware and software.

CAR systems maintain full copies of documents on microfilm, while the index to those documents is stored in a computer file. Thus, CAR provides both economical long-term storage and rapid access to information.

Automated microfilm systems incorporate the camera operation as a part of the index entry. The operator enters the correct index information (ID) into memory as the documents are filmed, and the camera "blips" the film at that point so that it may be retrieved later when needed.

A range of automation levels is available. On the low end are local standalone configurations that pinpoint film locations from an indexed database with keyed-in ID information, but require cartridges to be manually retrieved and inserted into readers or reader/printers.

FIGURE 10-5 Any indexed film can be located by this menu-driven CAR system, with the image brought to the user within seconds in the format specified (to printer, to screen, to a spreadsheet, or similar applications). *Courtesy of Minolta Corp.*

On the high end are fully automated systems that can search through remote microfilm archives, scan and digitize appropriate frames, and transmit images *electronically* to work stations for quick viewing on users' monitors or immediate printout on their printers.

The Future for Micrographics

The future for micrographics in the electronic office seems assured. Microform usage shows no signs of abatement; rather, it has grown steadily since its introduction to the business community.

Even as newer technology (for example, optical disks) piques the interest of potential users, loyal microform users reassert their allegiance to microfiche and other micrographic formats as the most practical media for their business applications.

Analysts predict that as equipment costs decrease, the user base of micrographics systems will broaden. Small to mid-size companies, along with their larger counterparts, will swell the ranks of businesses who have selected microforms as a feasible alternative to banks of space-eating file cabinets. Installations of computer-generated microforms coordinated with CAR systems may become the norm rather than the exception.

ELECTRONIC IMAGING AND OPTICAL DISKS

Electronic image management (EIM) deals with the imaging of documents in order to incorporate them into the users' electronic filing systems. Two types of EIM currently dominate the optical environment: optical disks, in the form of CD-ROMs (compact disk—read-only memory) and WORMs (write-once, read-many-times).

Scanners, as OCRs (optical character readers) and image scanners, also belong to the image processing field. Their function is to convert noncomputerized images or documents to digital format, ready for storage in an electronic filing system—on optical or magnetic media.

Industry leaders predict an even more flourishing future for optical disks than that experienced by magnetic media. Described as image processing, the technology is demonstrating remarkable capabilities. For example, optical systems store immense quantities of data, are not subject to disk drive crashes, and are not affected by hostile environments, such as air pollution, sound vibrations, salt air, or electrical storms.

To illustrate the immense storage capacity of optical disks, the administrative assistant can compare them with hard (fixed) disks. The memory capacity of fixed disks begins at about 20 megabytes and currently stretches to over 100 megabytes. Optical media *start* in the range of a *few hundred megabytes* of storage, going up from there. Capacities of both are, of course, continually soaring.

Optical Disk Technology

Evolved from television videodisk technology, optical disks can store both digital and analog data, as well as pictures, graphs, and drawings. The disk is described as having three layers, two of which are glass or plastic, and the third a mineral alloy.

Laser beams record the information on the disks by burning pits into the surface or, alternately, raising bubbles on the surface. Once recorded, the information remains permanently stored, since the pits or bubbles are not readily erased. The technology is not suited, therefore, to storage applications which require frequent revisions, such as word processing documents.

Compared to magnetic storage, optical storage offers a huge increase in density. A single 12-inch optical platter stores as much as 2.3 gigabytes; that is, almost 200,000 pages of text and images. Two billion bytes is comparable to 80 file cabinets of paper records or 60 reels of standard magnetic tape. One company recently marketed a 14-inch optical disk which stores *6.8 gigabytes* (6,800 megabytes) of information.

Storage life on optical media is estimated to be more than 30 years, far surpassing the life expectancy of conventional magnetic tape. Unlike magnetic disks, optical disks cannot "crash" since no read/write mechanism "reads" the stored data etched on the surface.

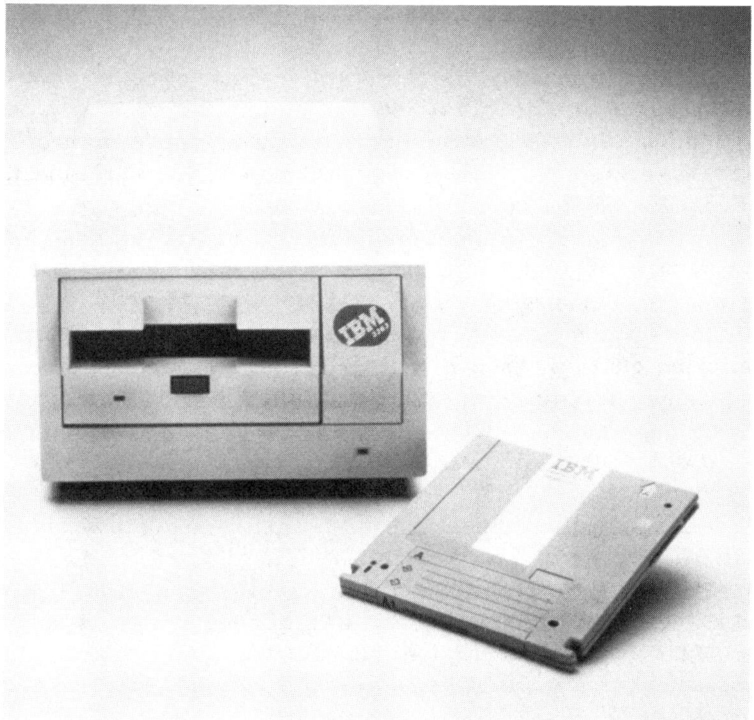

FIGURE 10-6 With the optical disk drive, data can be written once and read many times on the removable 3363 Optical Disk Cartridge. The cartridge can contain up to 200 megabytes of data, over 500 times the capacity of the standard 360 Kbyte disk. *Courtesy of IBM Corporation.*

CD-ROMs and WORMS

The optical disk format can be either CD-ROM (compact disk—read-only memory) or WORM (write-once, ready-many-times).

A standard *CD-ROM* stores the equivalent of 1,500 double-sided floppy disks. Especially valuable for storing bibliographic data, CD-ROMs are replacing indexes in libraries. Users can access an incredible amount of information quickly and easily. From their CD-ROM–equipped computer stations, users can access data from periodicals, newspapers, and conference presentations.

Many subjects are available, including stock performance, tax advice, business and other bibliographies, and legal databases. CD-ROMs also combine video with audio in producing training modules.

WORMS cannot be erased, but they are designed for the user to write thereon his or her own data. Most WORM disks are in the 5¼-inch and 12-inch formats, but a 3½-inch disk is being readied for market by several manufacturers. A "jukebox" for storing platters vertically is also available.

Erasable Storage

The newest addition to the optical media market is the erasable drive. Combined with erasable media in the form of a removable cartridge, the erasable unit is an attractive alternative to large-capacity fixed disks.

The removable cartridges provide users with security not available in fixed disks, with the added convenience of greater storage through use of additional cartridges. They also make suitable backup media.

Erasable drives began shipping to distributors in late 1988 and early 1989. The cost is comparable to 600-megabyte and 700-megabyte fixed disks.

The Future for Optical Disks

In the near term, the most practical office application for optical disks may be large updatable databases available by subscription. Current subscribers to information retrieval systems may find it less expensive to subscribe to CD-ROM databases than to spend $40 to $125 an hour accessing an on-line information service.

WORM disks are positioned to replace paper and microfiche for some applications, particularly for archival uses and as backup for hard disks.

For storing large amounts of data, CD-ROMs are predicted to be the way of the future. WORMs and erasable drives are also attracting the attention of paper-intensive industries. Prices on erasable media and WORMs are decreasing, matching the already lowered prices of CD-ROMs. As a result, more activity will be seen in all types of image processing.

OCR and Image Scanners

With the advent of desktop publishing and optical disk technology in recent years, scanners have come to fill an important niche in the electronic office. *Image* scanners record the location and density of each bit of information making up an image, such as a graph, line drawing, or a photograph, and converts this information into computer-understandable code.

Optical character readers (OCRs) read *textual* materials and digitize the text for incorporation into a word processor. Like all computer-coded text, the scanned text supplied by the OCR can be readily edited and/or revised by the computer operator in the same way that keyboarded entries can be edited via the word processing software.

When first introduced, scanners were of the OCR type exclusively, incapable of handling graphics, and in fact could read only a limited number of typefaces. Today, most scanners are both image and character readers. They also allow the user to specify to which format the scanner should output; for example, to a popular word processor, such as Word Perfect, or to a spreadsheet.

FIGURE 10-7 TDC's Docuscan 2600 scans both sides of page in one pass at speeds of less than 2 seconds per page. *Courtesy of TDC.*

CONVERSION TO AUTOMATED RECORDS

Converting from a paper records system to any form of electronic storage is a major undertaking. To be successful in effecting a tension-free transition, the administrative assistant must carefully plan, with superiors, the implementation of the system chosen. Their principal concern must be for the personnel who may inwardly resist adapting to the new system.

Employees' apprehensions about the new technology may be alleviated in part by a gradual phasing in of the chosen system. Conversion may be attempted with one department at a time, with the newly trained persons assisting in the changeover. If the newly adopted system involves micrographics, the company may hesitate to commit a substantial investment in cameras and peripheral equipment. If so, a service bureau may be employed to photograph and record the documents on microfiche, with the company purchasing a reader/printer only.

When the time is ripe for higher-level automation, the system can be integrated with a computer-assisted retrieval system, and/or brought totally in house.

A major benefit of microfilm is that it is acceptable in courts of law. Another is that the degree of implementation into micrographics may be tailored to the company's needs and financial resources. A company-designed manual for new users of the system will ease the transition. Manuals cut down on the costly learning-curve period and relieve the supervisor of additional training sessions after the employees' hands-on introduction. At minimum, the manual should include conventional step-by-step directives for use of the system, with examples using company records, a glossary of commonly used terms relating to the media being used, and a reference manual which details all the major functions and commands.

SUMMARY

Misplaced files, slow access times, and diminishing floor space cause managers to look to electronic storage and image management systems to solve their records management problems. Three popular options are:

1. *Database management systems:* A database is excellent for organizing information pertinent to customers' accounts, salespersons' territories, or the company's accounts payable. With each record identified by fields of data and mathematical values calculated by preset commands, the database is ideal for organizing and storing this type of information. Magnetic disks and diskettes are a popular form of electronic storage for databases.
2. *Electronic image management (EIM):* Optical disks utilize laser beams to store massive amounts of both video and alphanumeric data to optical disks. Current usage of CD-ROMs focus on relatively permanent data, such as bibliographic indexes and training manuals. Scanners, another form of EIM, incorporate non-computerized textual and graphic materials into the electronic mainstream via word processors or other software programs.
3. *Micrographic systems:* Micrographic storage miniaturizes records on film, usually in the form of microfiche. Paper-intensive industries, such as government agencies and insurance firms, are the most likely candidates for micrographics, although many other industries are also switching to micrographics to replace their paper records.

QUESTIONS FOR REVIEW

1. Name and define the three types of electronic storage media discussed in this chapter.
2. Name the three database models described in this chapter. Which model is probably the most used in business?
3. How does an FMS differ from a relational database?
4. List at least five precautions to observe in protecting diskettes from contaminants and damage.
5. Name five types of microfilm media. Which is used most often?
6. What is meant by updatable microfiche?
7. What equipment is found in a fully equipped micrographic system?
8. What institutions have made regular use of micropublishing technology since its inception?
9. Describe some of the benefits of COM, the microform generated from digital data within a computer.
10. Give three advantages of optical disks over magnetic media.

QUESTIONS FOR DISCUSSION

1. Considering the array of options available in the field of records automation, what advice would you offer company officials in choosing the "best" electronic medium to automate their company's records?

2. Discuss the similarities and the differences between file management systems (FMS) and relational databases. In the light of recent improvements in FMS programs which lessen the differences between the two, do relational databases, in your opinion, deserve to rank as superior to FMS? Justify your position.
3. Optical disk technology is perceived by many developers as the storage medium of the future, primarily because of its phenomenal storage capacity and its immunity to environmental hazards. Do you agree with the opinion of some that ODs will replace magnetic media and micrographics totally at some point in the future? Why or why not? What factors weigh in favor of, or against, this possibility?

SUGGESTED ACTIVITIES

1. Design a database for your class, with each student in the class a "record" in the database. Collect from each student identical types of academic and personal data. List the information in tabular form (as in a relational database or a file management system).

   Each piece of information will be classed as a field and placed in vertical columns, opposite the students' names listed in the first column. Suggested fields and their column titles follow. (Others may be added or substituted.)

   Field names: first two columns:
   - Name of student (last, first)

   Third and succeeding columns
   - Date of birth (year)
   - Month of birth
   - City of birth (or city/state in two fields)
   - Major area of study
   - Current courses
     (elect three or four courses to list, each a separate field)
   - Name of advisor
   - Anticipated graduation (year)
   - Anticipated graduation (month)
   - Career goal (administrative assistant, office manager, and so on)
   - Beginning salary expectations (annual)
   - Salary expectation (annual) five years hence

   Upon completion of the preceding design, transfer it to a software database, such as Lotus 1-2-3, d-base III, or any off-the-shelf database software package.

   Manipulate the data to extract mini databases, such as all students taking accounting, data processing, and administrative procedures; or all students having the same career goal; or a mix of more than one criteria—say, all administrative assistant careerists who plan to start at salaries of $20,000 or more when they graduate.
2. Plan another database, using different types of records, such as restaurants in town and the menus of each, airlines serving your area and the direct service they provide to other cities, or video rental stores in your area. Work with the data as in the preceding activity, mixing criteria and extracting mini databases from the originals.

REFERENCES

Image Processing and Optical Disks

BRIGGS, GEORGE, "Experts See Electronic Imaging as Boom Industry," *MIS Week* (November 30, 1987), 10.

DICKEY, SAM, "CD-ROM: A World of Information on a Disk," *Today's Office* (July 1988), 30–32.

DUDEK, VIRGINIA, "Optical, Magnetic Storage Compete for Markets," *MIS Week* (October 10, 1988), 10, 37.

DYKEMAN, JOHN, "Optical Disk, A Technology on the Move," *Modern Office Technology* (June 1988), 81–88.

FLYNN, MARY KATHLEEN, "IBM Enters Image Processing Arena," *Datamation* (August 1, 1988), 80–82.

GOFF, LESLIE, "New Storage Options Bring Power to Users," *MIS Week* (July 11, 1988), 26–35.

HONAN, PATRICK, "What's New in Optical Storage," *Personal Computing* (February 1989), 111–118.

KADOR, JOHN, "New Technology Fights Data Center Paper Glut," *Software Magazine* (January 1989), 54–60.

SANTARELLI, MARY-BETH, "CD ROM in the Information Center," *Information Center* (March 1988), 18–21.

Magnetic Media and Electronic Filing

BURNACZ, JOANNE G., "Sizing Up Diskettes," *Today's Office* (May 1988), 18–24.

WEILERSTEIN, KENNY, "Magnetic Media, More for Less," *Office Systems '88* (August 1988), 23–28.

Micrographics

AVEDON, DON M., "Meeting Your Need for Micrographics," *Office Systems '88* (April 1988), 48–52.

JONES, VIRGINIA A., "The Correct Focus for Micrographics," *Office Systems '88* (September 1988), 82–87.

DATABASE GLOSSARY

Database: A collection of related information organized in a structured way for the purpose of further computer operations

Export: To transfer information from a database to another software program

Field: The primary unit of a database structure; a named area, such as "CITY," that can receive an entry in each database record

File: In a database, a grouping of records or parts of records that are logically related

Import: To transfer information from another software program file to a database

Key Field: The field by which a database is ordered

Merge: To combine data from one database into another

Output: Data displayed, printed, or stored to disk; especially data retrieved from a database and assembled in a meaningful fashion

Record: A collection of all field data for a single subject

Scan: To browse through information in a database

Select: To retrieve from a database only those records that meet certain criteria

Sort: To arrange selected records in a particular order

Structure: The framework of a database field. It contains such information as field length, field type (character, numeric, indicator or date), field names and database description. It doesn't include the actual information entered into the fields.

Case Problem 1 Unit III *Microstored Records Save $Millions*

Efficiency and productivity have increased at the headquarters of a beer distributor since they installed an advanced micrographics system at their corporate headquarters.

From the corporate office, master records for all their breweries and subsidiary plants are maintained on microfilm. When a problem develops on a production line in one of the plants, engineers look up drawings of equipment to guide on-site technicians.

Before the computer-driven, microfilm handling and CAR system was installed, the company's engineers had to sift through paper records stored in dozens of file cabinets in order to refer to previous projects. A single lookup could take an hour's time. Now, engineers have instant access to more than a million records, and a lookup on the microimage terminal takes three minutes.

Since the new system was put into place, the payback, based on speed of retrieval and security of the microfilmed information, has justified the investment many times over.

1. Assume that when the computer-driven micrographics system was installed, the young engineers at the company welcomed the change with enthusiasm, but engineers who had been with the company for many years resisted the changeover; they had felt comfortable with the manual filing system and saw no need for a change. They were apprehensive when the changeover was proposed, then implemented, in spite of their misgivings.

   How would you as a company executive have handled this changeover so as to alleviate the anxiety felt by some of your engineers, especially older engineers who had demonstrated their loyalty to the comapny over many years of service? Would you have adopted a hard line "adapt or leave" stance?
2. Give suggestions on how to effect a *smooth* transition from traditional to automated procedures which apply to most business applications.

Case Problem 2 Unit III *Mobile Units for Efficient Storage*

A large U.S. manufacturer of household appliances was running out of floor space; its voluminous records had expanded to the point that two to three rooms on every floor of its ten-story building were filled with eight-drawer file cabinets.

Not only were retrieval rates slowing down and misfiles increasing, but the weight of the heavy file cabinets on the building's wooden floors created a safety hazard. A committee was formed to explore solutions to the problem. The committee's proposal, eventually adopted by company officials, incorporated three principal features: (1) a centralized storage facility, (2) housed in the basement of corporate headquarters, (3) utilizing electric mobile-shelf units for storage.

The storage units would consolidate all files in one place, with access to records limited to Central Records employees. The reinforced concrete basement floor would solve the problem of excess weight on wooden floors; the shelved file records would simplify retrieval; and the use of full-time personnel would improve access retrieval rates.

Only one problem confronted the planners: the morale of the employees scheduled to move to the basement. The employees envisioned themselves as isolated from other employees in dark, nonwindowed, damp and musty settings, typical of those most often associated with basements.

Corporate officials were dismayed to discover employee resistance to a move they considered essential to company safety and efficiency. They pondered how to solve the employee morale problem without retreating from their resolve to make the move to centralized storage in the basement.

1. What solution would you propose to company officials to solve this morale problem?
2. Can the human factor of employee morale be met without sacrificing the safety and space efficiency the company is seeking? If so, explain how you would blend the two into a feasible solution.

Case Problem 3 Unit III *Scanners Track Paper Files*

The insurance industry is one of the most paper-intensive industries in the world. Although many companies are converting paper documents to some form of magnetic media or film, industry leaders maintain that paper still occupies the lion's share of stored records and will continue to do so, at least into the foreseeable future.

Accordingly, users look to manual systems for records control in order to achieve the same efficient retrieval speed as that provided by magnetic media. One Philadelphia-based insurance company has adopted bar coding and handheld laser scanners to smooth the paper flow at its corporate headquarters. To put its system into operation, the company first consolidated each of its region's thousands of policies under a single roof; then it bar coded each policy.

By scanning the files' bar codes at the end of each day of use, the files' locations can be accurately tracked. With over a million pages of documents tracked regularly, the company has been gratified by the increased retrieval speed and the lowered number of misfiles since the bar coding went into effect. Company officials and all records users are pleased with the results.

If bar coding and handheld scanners are the solution to one company's tracking system, they could be the answer for others, as well. Until paper records are totally replaced by other records media, users must opt for *some* form of paper control.

Records Management Specialist Nelda Brown is dismayed to read of this insurance company's response to an overcrowded records management system. Nelda believes that micrographics is the proper solution to overcrowded file cabinets.

Justify Nelda's point of view as you understand it. If you do *not* agree with Nelda, justify the position of the insurance company officials who have opted for bar coding and scanning paper documents for more efficient filing and retrieval of records.

Case Problem 4 Unit III *"Print-on-Demand" Forms Systems*

The cost of preprinting and storing paper forms is exceedingly high for a paper-intensive industry, such as insurance or banking. When a form must be revised and the earlier versions scrapped, the cost can escalate quickly. Hence, the impetus to create forms electronically; no excess storage of forms is necessary, and updates may be made without wasting paper or time.

Electronic-forms creation is made possible through software packages designed specifically for the design and creation of forms tailored to individual companies' needs. Several software packages currently marketed offer buyers alternatives from which to choose. For example, Xerox Corporation offers FormBAse for IBM PCs; Antic Software offers FLEXFORM Business Templates; and Softview, Inc. offers FormSystem.

1. Place yourself in the position of records manager in a mid-size company with heavy reliance on forms. You believe that your company could profit from an electronic-form system. How would you investigate the quality of software packages designed for this purpose? Would you ask for a tryout period prior to purchase of a package?
2. What criteria would you set up in choosing the package which best fits your company's forms-management requirements?

UNIT

IV

ADMINISTRATIVE SUPPORT SERVICES

Some services performed by the administrative assistant relate primarily to one major office system, such as business communications, and are conveniently classed under that system's umbrella of activities.

Others support the needs of every department in the company. Classed administrative support services, these services vary widely from one department to another. The administrative support services detailed in Unit IV of this text include technology and applications of reprographics and photocomposition in the business office (Chapter 11), the skills involved in learning and using telecommunication systems effectively (Chapter 12), the correct procedures for conducting meetings in accordance with established rules of order, and a look at the options available in teleconferencing (Chapter 13), plus the procedures involved in making travel arrangements for both domestic and international travel (Chapter 14).

11 Reprographics and Photocomposition

INTRODUCTION

In the electronic office, paper copies of contracts, invoices, reports, and similar documents are frequently critical to the smooth operation of the office. Multiple copies are often shared with managerial personnel, the support staff, plant operatives, and customers.

Accordingly, reprographics, the science of reproducing acceptable paper copies, has its special niche in today's office systems. Photocopiers, offset duplicators, and photocomposition systems make up the lion's share of reprographics equipment. A review of the technology of each enables administrative assistants to assess their practicality in serving their companies' special needs.

Terms in this chapter include:

phototypesetters	duplexing
bursters	blue erase
decollators	image overlay
thermal copiers	xerographic copiers

REPROGRAPHIC SYSTEMS

Reprographic systems commonly employed in business can be grouped into four classifications: photocopiers, electronic copier/printers, offset duplicators, and photocomposition (phototypesetting) machines.

Each type has its own purpose and design, but lines of distinction setting off each type become easily blurred. For example, some duplicators employ photocopying processes, and some photocopiers are described as copier/duplicators.

Photocomposition, traditionally associated with commercial printing establishments, is in a class by itself. Its specialized and expensive equipment provides a professional-quality output exceeding that of any other reprographics system.

Offset duplicators have been an office fixture for many years, while electronic copier/printers are a fairly recent addition. The photocopier is conceivably the most indispensable piece of equipment in offices today.

PHOTOCOPIERS

Photocopiers have become a fixture in business offices of the twentieth century. They are as numerous today as typewriters were prior to the advent of microcomputers.

Conventional copiers range in size from small desktop models, identified as personal copiers, to large copier/duplicator models offering many special features. The wide range in prices and optional features makes the selection of the most appropriate copier difficult. However, the selection usually entails a review of the models available, and of company copying requirements.

Xerographic Copiers

Indirect electrostatic copying (xerography) does not require specially-coated paper. The indirect process utilizes a drum which is *negatively* charged by two electrical wires. When the drum is exposed to the original, the white areas of the original (blank areas) reflect light on the drum, neutralizing the negative charge on the blank areas of the drum, leaving only the image negatively charged.

Dry toner, *positively* charged, is brushed onto the *negatively* charged area of the drum (the image). When the paper, now electrostatically charged, comes in contact with the drum, it attracts the toner from the drum in the form of the original image. Heated rollers fuse the toner onto the paper as it passes through, creating a copy of the original document onto the copy paper.

Xerographic copiers, known as plain paper copiers, currently dominate the copier market. Accommodating almost any kind of plain paper and using dry toner, these models are convenient to use and inexpensive to operate.

Fiber Optic (Electrographic) Copiers

Fiber optic copiers use an electrographic process. The electrically charged drum is exposed to the original through fiber optic strands. The strands of glass transmit information in pulses of light directed by laser beams. The invisible image captured on the drum by exposure to the original is transferred to the copy paper, where it is developed. The paper then contacts the toner particles which are attracted to it in the form of the image by static electricity. The image is thus duplicated on the paper.

The future for fiber optic copiers seems assured. The units are smaller than conventional copiers and said to be more reliable, as well as less expensive, than conventional copiers. Their processing rate is somewhat slower, however, since the light source remains stationary while the copy paper passes beneath it on a moving platen.

Thermal Copiers

Thermal copiers use heat-sensitive paper, lifting the image from the original as it passes over a drum under thermal heat. A copy is made by inserting the original and one sheet of thermal paper into the copier.

Processing speed is not one of the strengths of a thermal copier; nor is its long-term storage value. The copies turn dark after long periods of storage. Most users, therefore, opt for thermal copies only when one or two copies are needed for immediate use, or when other copiers are not available.

Special Features of Photocopiers

Duplexing is the process of making copies on both sides of a sheet from one- or two-sided originals.

Edge erase erases the edge and gutter (center) on the photocopied image of a bound volume. (A faint image of these borders frequently mars the reproduced image of the text or graphics being copied).

FIGURE 11-1 This compact copier does five-color single-tone copying, and simplifies maintenance with consumable toner cartridges. *Courtesy of Sharp Products.*

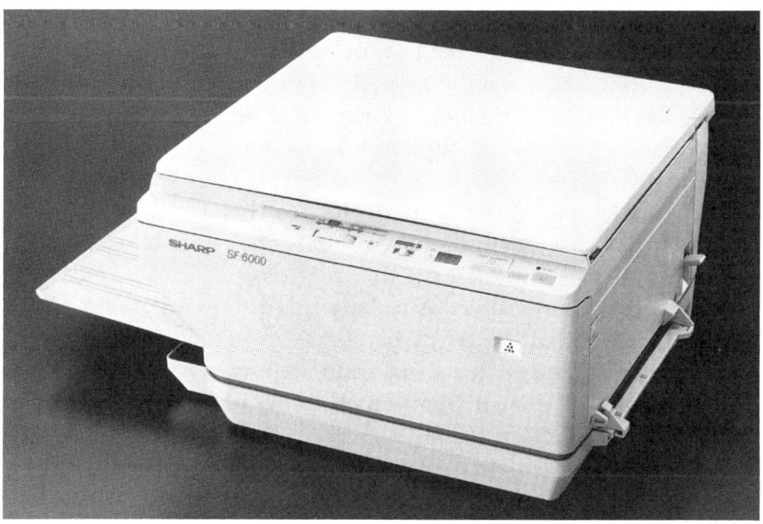

FIGURE 11-2 Canon's NP 9330 "intelligent" laser copier uses digital image processing and laser technologies to copy slides or negatives as well as paper originals, and can reduce or enlarge images up to 800 percent. *Courtesy of Canon, USA, Inc.*

Blue erase capability allows editors to edit copy with blue pens or pencils. Blue erase makes the copier insensitive to blue markings, thus giving editors the freedom to write comments and correct errors without fear of their markings being detected and copied by the photocopier.

Image shift makes it possible to move the image to the right or to the left. This feature is important when the copied papers are to be bound at the left and extra space is needed to accommodate the binding.

Image overlay accommodates two images being copied on the same page, one over the other. Used to create special effects, image overlay enjoys an extra dimension when a color unit is used in the copying process.

Multifunction memory enables the operator to program sequential copying steps into the copier to be called up for frequently run jobs. For example, the steps might include reduction ratios to be used, duplexing commands to be followed, and the number of copies to be run.

Photo mode sets the copier for maximum contrast, eliminating shadow tones, or reducing contrast and providing greater tonal gradations. This feature is useful when pictures are frequently copied.

Job interrupt allows the copier to be interrupted during a multipage run so that another job may be completed. After the interruption, the first job continues without a machine reset or interruption in the number count of copies already run.

Job separate eliminates the time spent in manually separating jobs or sets. The copier separates sets in the exit tray by automatically inserting a sheet of paper between sets.

Automatic document feed permits a stack of originals to be automatically moved to the copy position.

Automatic collation collates documents automatically. Some microprocessor-controlled collators are bidirectional, collating from top to bottom, or bottom to top, for greater speed and accuracy.

Copier control features monitor use of the copier by authorized personnel only. Authorized users are assigned a numeric code which they must enter into the machine in order to operate it. The machine also records the number of copies made by each user.

Reduction in size up to 50 percent of the original may be had in the reduction mode. Two 8½ × 11-inch sheets may be copied in the maximum reduction mode onto a single 8½ × 11-inch sheet.

Automatic job recovery causes a lighted message to appear on the control panel telling the operator to check the paper path should a problem arise in the operation of the machine.

Machine diagnostics assist a service representative in making machine adjustments and in anticipating service requirements.

Copying in Color

One attribute of photocopiers which attracts the immediate attention of potential buyers is color. Customers complain that black and white duplicates of colored originals are not "true" duplicates. In response to their demands, manufacturers are producing color copiers at a pace matching the consumers' rising interest.

Copy quality continues to improve on both black and white and color copiers as vendors vie for the competitive edge. Some offer additional features on special models, such as full-color prints from slides, color negatives, and transparency film as available options. During the 1990s, color units are predicted to comprise 80 percent of the total copiers sold.

Size and Volume Categories

In terms of size, cost, and number of copies duplicated per month, copiers are classified into four groups:

Personal copiers. These copiers are designed for small offices with limited need for copying, and for home users. Usage is limited to under 1,000 copies per month; the initial investment is under $1,000, also.

Convenience copiers. With a capacity for greater volume and speed of operation than the personal copiers, these units have much broader usage in the business market. Typically, the convenience copier has a capacity of 20,000 copies per month.

Copier/duplicators. Requiring an investment of $10,000 or higher, these units copy (or duplicate) up to 75,000 images per month.

Duplicators. Because these units can reproduce more than 75,000 copies per month, they are called duplicators rather than copiers. Speed is around 51 cpm (copies per minute) and initial investment costs run around $75,000.

Choosing an Office Copier

Vendors currently market copiers offering a broad array of options and models from which to choose. Understandably, the potential buyer may be overwhelmed by the wide selection. Joseph Gianascoli, chief executive officer of Copy Data Group, offers some tips in getting and maintaining the best model copier for one's own company.[1]

1. Determine how you will use the machine before you actually buy it. Do not be enticed by bells and whistles you don't need and probably won't use.
2. Buy the right size machine for your needs. If you do 50,000 copies a month or less, you will probably want to get a desktop copy machine. If you do more than 50,000, you should be looking at a duplicator.
3. Consider your future needs. For an individual looking at a machine that can do 3,000 to 5,000 copies a month, look instead at a machine that has the capability to expand its volume 15 to 20 percent.
4. Think about replacement in three to five years. Today's machines are obsolete sooner than they used to be because of technology.
5. Consider your service requirements. In many offices, there is only one copier. If it goes down, you have to depend on the dealer to get it up and running again promptly.
6. Look for a dealer with good service and reputation. Ask others in the community about their experience with the dealer.
7. Find someone in the office who can perform minor preventative maintenance. Look for a company that can train your employees on the little intricacies of keeping your machine up and running.
8. Ask for a demonstration. Once you've identified the top two or three dealers, invite them to your office to demonstrate the equipment. Many dealers will even leave the equipment for up to a week. For smaller units, there is usually no charge.

Monitoring Copy Usage

To guard against unauthorized use of the machines, copiers can be equipped with an autotron. The autotron, a device issued only to authorized personnel, must be inserted into the copier to operate the machine. It records the number of copies run and charges the proper department for copying costs.

[1]Joseph Gianascoli, as quoted in the *St. Louis Business Journal* (January 1988), 16.

Another form of control is achieved through the establishment of centralized copy centers. Full-time operators do all the copying jobs from authorized requisition forms which accompany each order.

Copyright Infringements

Under federal law, authors of copyrighted material have the *exclusive right* to publish, *reproduce,* or display their work. Without the express permission of the author (preferably given in writing), no one else is free to reproduce the author's writing or to distribute copies of them to other persons.

Serious penalties can be imposed for copyright infringements: a year's imprisonment and a $25,000 fine for each violation. Alternative penalties include injunctions against further copying or distributing by the guilty party, and the right of the author to recover punitive statutory damages, as well as court costs and legal fees. Because photocopiers are available and convenient to use, however, users risk "getting caught" by copying materials regardless of copyright restrictions. For example, a manager reads a useful article in a professional journal, and photocopies it for distribution to the entire staff, instead of obtaining reprints. The manager may not realize that many periodicals grant permission to reproduce articles for conference handouts and training materials.

However, a distinction is noted between infringement and the doctrine of "fair use," which allows limited copying or quotations without permission. The factors which determine "fair use" relate to purpose: that is, is the copying done for educational, commercial, or nonprofit purposes? Other factors: What is the ratio of copied material to the written text as a whole? What effect does inclusion of the copyrighted material have on the value of the text as a whole?

Improper copying can result in liability even where copyright protection does not apply. For example, confidential client data must be protected from illicit copying; and training manuals accompanying copy-protected software must be respected.

Centralized Reprographic Systems

Copying facilities are commonly centralized in medium-to-large firms, with one or more high-speed copiers operated by specially trained personnel. Convenience and economics are two of the factors which dictate this type of arrangement.

For example, large jobs are handled easily and quickly on high-speed copiers, and quick turnaround time is assured to the executives who order the jobs. Convenience copiers, stationed throughout the firm, are also freed to handle small jobs without the undue delay of big-job tie-ups.

Cost per copy is usually lower on high-speed systems than on convenience copiers. A copy which costs 5 cents on a convenience copier may run only 2 to 3 cents on the high-speed machines. Full utilization of the equipment in a centralized station also yields a higher return per dollar invested.

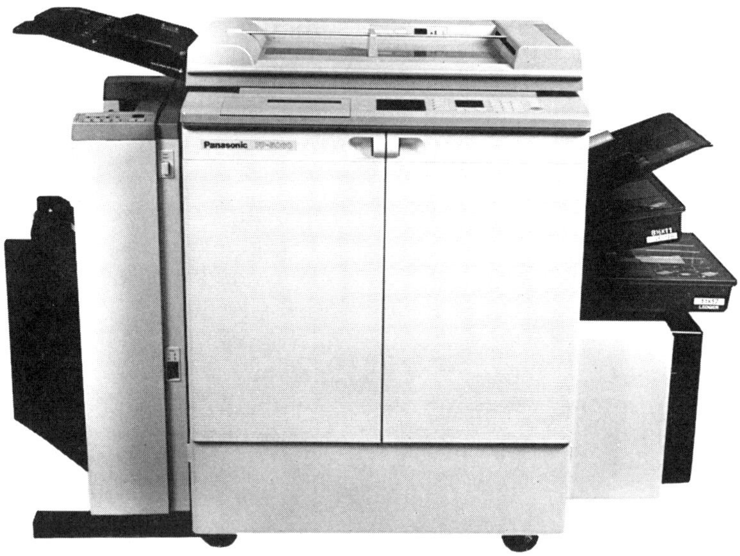

FIGURE 11-3 The FP-5060 produces one- or two-sided copies from two-sided originals and features a 2,000-sheet and two 500-sheet cassettes for high-volume jobs. *Courtesy of Panasonic Communications & Systems.*

Decentralized Systems

In decentralized systems, convenience copiers are placed in departments throughout the company. Executives and administrative assistants work at their own pace, making copies as needed on departmental equipment. Confidentiality is protected, too, when access to classified information is restricted to designated persons only.

Typically, however, companies blend both systems. Large jobs are handled by the copying center; small ones, by departmental personnel.

ELECTRONIC COPIER/PRINTERS

Electronic (intelligent) copier/printers accept commands to copy and print documents directly from computers and word processors electronically linked to them.

Soft images (those projected on the computer screen) are relayed directly to the copier/printer via copy/print commands. As input is received, it is formatted and stored in the memory storage area of the copier. When ready to be printed, a low-powered laser beam scans the document and transfers the image to paper. Output may be printed, transferred to other electronic units, or stored on magnetic media for future use.

Text and illustrations can be reformatted and printed in a variety of formats suitable to special applications. Some units can also mix hard copy originals with the soft text and graphics sent from the computer.

Recognized for their speed and quality output, "intelligent" copier/printers have forged a solid niche in mid- to large-sized companies, replacing or sharing with conventional copiers the photocopying functions of the electronic office.

Supplies for Reprographics Equipment

Two factors contribute to a renewed emphasis on quality supplies for reprographics equipment: (1) the technological changes in the equipment which demand more stringent specifications for supply items in order to function smoothly, and (2) the users' demand for supplies that match the high quality of the equipment in which they have invested so heavily.

Three very necessary consumables for reprographics users are toners, developers, and paper.

Toners All copiers use toner to develop the latent image. Dry toner is used in most copiers and is either monocomponent (single element) or dual component. Dry dual-component toner produces good-quality copies and is used in machines at all volume levels. However, copiers using dual-component toner require the purchase of toner and developer, each packaged separately. The expected copy yield for each of these consumables is provided by the manufacturer.

Developers Because of their fine size and light weight, the toner particles require a carrier to transport them to the photoconductor. The carrier, or developer, consists of glass or resin-coated aluminum or steel beads, usually ten times larger than the toner particles. When the developer mixes with the toner, the friction which occurs causes them to cling together; then both the toner and the developer are transferred to the photoreceptor where the image of the original is made.

Cartridges Cartridges containing both toner and developer have simplified the care and upkeep of photocopiers. Neatly packaged in throw-away cartridges, the toner/developers make the copying process simpler and cleaner for the users. The cartridges also simplify the use of color when desired. By a simple swap of cartridges, users can designate different colors for different runs.

Copier Paper Appearance of the copied document is related directly to the quality of the copy paper used. The paper should have a good finish and should function well, not causing jams or paper "sawdust" build-up.

The paper weight should not exceed the copier specifications, usually a maximum of 24#. Paper moisture content should not exceed 5 percent; otherwise curling or jamming may occur. Moisture rates of less than 4 percent can cause static build-up, resulting in double-sheet feeding.

Brightness, a measure of light reflectivity, determines the whiteness of the

FIGURE 11-4 This copier-duplicator automatically selects the appropriate paper format and reduction ratio for documents of varying sizes. Options include accent or spot color, a stapler, and a 15-bin sorter. *Courtesy of Kodak Corporation.*

paper. Good bond paper has a brightness of 80 to 90 percent; lower-grade papers, 70 to 75 percent.

Opacity level determines how well the paper absorbs the image without "show-through." The paper must be sufficiently opaque for two-sided copying without an image show-through on either side.

To reduce costs, volume buying of reprographic supplies is usually recommended. However, when changing paper brands, experienced users also recommend making a trial run of the new brand before committing the company to a volume purchase. At least 500 sheets should be run through the photocopier to test its imaging quality and its compatibility with the machine under normal operating conditions. If the run is satisfactory, a large-quantity order may be placed.

Ideally, *all* reprographic supplies should be tested on site before a purchase commitment is made. The vendor's availability for service and/or additional supplies should also be assured prior to purchase.

Binders, Bursters, Decollators

Binders Binders for printed materials serve three purposes. They:

1. project an image of professionalism to the customer or client
2. protect the content of the materials within the binder
3. enable users to label and file the bound set of materials.

Types of Binders Binders are designed to match their special purposes. For example, for long-term storage, pressboard binders are designed with riveted steel channels and heavy hinges. Some have sliding hook mechanisms which retract for shelf storage and extend for suspension filing. They can be shelf-filed or filed on suspension frameworks inside a vertical or horizontal file cabinet.

Some binders, designed for reports, are coated with a special, moisture-proof acrylic coating to protect them from the wear and tear of frequent handling and excessive moisture in high-humidity areas.

Clear binders, made of a clear overlay of plastic, wrap around the front, spine, and back of the document, creating outside pockets where artwork, photography, or reference material may be inserted.

Top-ring binders are best suited for *unburst* printouts which require constant updating. Reports are quickly inserted or removed by rotating rings around a lock-in slot mechanism.

Square-ring binders are the best choice for frequently used *burst* reports. Square rings are spaced for the appropriate-sized punched sheets. A label holder on the spine allows for easy shelf filing and identification.

Binder indexes help users classify data and retrieve information from files quickly. Computer printouts easily fit into binder indexes, with insertable index tabs keeping information neatly organized. Sized to fit virtually any binder, all indexes provide quick, easy access to data, making it simple to retrieve information.

Bursters Bursters provide a fast and easy way to detach stacks of continuous computer forms. Single-ply, multipart, or carbon interleaved continuous tractor paper can be separated and stacked at speeds up to 72 feet per minute with an electric burster. The tractor-hole margins are also trimmed from both sides of the sheets as they are separated.

Some electric models also feature static bars to help eliminate electrical charges from forms, as well as foam-lined housing to ensure quiet operation. With a "footprint" of approximately 2 square feet, the electric bursters also offer convenience and speed of operation.

Manual bursters are time and cost savers. Operated by a manual crank, the bursters can accommodate forms up to 15 inches wide and 12 inches in length.

Decollators Decollators separate carbon or carbonless multipart forms of almost any weight into separate stacks. The units send the individual parts of the forms into different directions, assembling the separated parts into neatly aligned stacks. For small jobs of 200 copies or less, a desktop decollator, costing under $500, is usually adequate.

Larger models, costing around $1,200, are necessary for heavy-duty use when full boxes of forms must be separated. Both desktop and larger models are electric, although some manual units are still seen in older offices. Desktop models, costing under $500, operate around 55 to 100 feet per minute; larger decollators, at speeds up to 450 feet per minute.

OFFSET DUPLICATORS

Offset duplication, sometimes called *multilith* or *lithography,* is a cost-effective method of printing documents in house. As many as 2,500 copies of an original can be run from a paper master, or up to 50,000 copies from an aluminum plate. A variety of masters are available, with the length of the run usually determining the type of master selected.

Presensitized aluminum plates run up to 50,000 copies.

Photodirect masters, produced by camera processors, can run 10,000 copies.

Xerographic masters produced on photocopy machines are usually limited to 5,000 copies.

Direct-impression masters produced by a typewriter or impact printer have a maximum run of 2,500 copies.

Copies are frequently difficult to distinguish from originals when offset lithography is used. The multilith accepts almost every type of paper document for reproduction, including typewritten or handwritten pages, drawings, charts, graphs, and even photographs.

Tabletop models of offset printers range in speed from 3,500 to 7,000 copies per hour; console models, up to 10,000 per hour.

Commercial Offset Printing Service

Companies vary in their handling of large-volume printing/duplication tasks. Many large companies routinely process such jobs on in-house offset printers; full-time operators handle the orders on a requisition basis.

Other companies prefer to employ the services of local print establishments to handle all print/duplication tasks exceeding a set figure.

The decision whether to send out a job for commercial processing or to handle it internally depends on a number of factors, including the speed and capacity of the company's offset press, and the level of expertise demonstrated by company employees in producing high-quality output.

PHOTOCOMPOSITION AND PHOTOTYPESETTING

In-house printing at its highest level is seen in documents printed by a photocomposition system. The capacity to utilize the technology of photocomposition to print/duplicate documents in house is derived primarily from the merger of computer technology with professional printing techniques and equipment.

The all-inclusive term, *electronic publication,* incorporates multitechnologies to create professional documents *in house.* The concept and terminology are familiar to many persons and identified by many titles. The following four titles are commonly used interchangeably:

Desktop publishing systems (not to be confused with desktop publishing packages which are microcomputer-based) are generally tied into mini or mainframe systems.
Photocomposition (including phototypesetting)
Computer-aided publishing (CAP)
In-house printing/(publishing)

Microcomputer-based desktop publishing is discussed in detail in Chapter 5. Numerous software packages support microbased desktop publishing. Although its memory and processing speeds are somewhat limited when compared with desktop publishing systems, DTP microbased packages are adequate for many business applications.

Desktop publishing systems, however, offer greater speed, higher-resolution monitors, and more professional output than the microbased units. Hence, their descriptive title, *computer-aided publishing,* sets them apart from the smaller DTP programs.

Desktop publishing systems, focused on in this chapter, are comprised of three parts: (1) an input computer work station with a monitor, keyboard and mouse or other graphic design tools; (2) a graphics scanner for inputting art and photographs; and (3) output devices such as a laser printer and/or a phototypesetting machine.

When the three elements are combined, the desktop publishing or photocomposition system thus created is rightfully dubbed computer-aided publishing (CAP). Many companies now produce their forms, letterheads, manuals, promotional brochures, and similar material on their own desktop publishing systems. Their reasons for doing so include:

1. Rapid turnaround. Rush jobs can receive immediate attention. Even low priority jobs are accorded more prompt attention by company employees than can normally be expected from outside contractors.
2. Tighter reins on security. Sensitive or classified documents are monitored closely via internal control systems.
3. Space savings on paper supplies. Frequent printing of letterheads, forms, manuals, and other high-volume paper supplies eliminates the need for voluminous inventory storage; hence, the savings in storage space.
4. Lower cost per print run.

Two Phases of Publication

The publication of textual and pictorial information involves two phases: prepress activities and duplication or printing. *Prepress* activities include writing the copy, adding the pictorial material such as graphics, clip art selections, or electronically scanned photographs and drawings, typesetting the text, and designing the layout. The second step is the actual *printing* or *duplication* of the work after the first-step processes are finished.

Many companies prefer to contract with outside printers for the second phase of the operations. As costs for equipment continue their downward spiral, however, ever increasing numbers are opting for a completely in-house operation, including the printing or duplication of the documents created.

Phototypesetting

After the text is created and the pictorial additions selected, the type is set from the source document. The process of phototypesetting the text and designing the layout determine the appearance and reader appeal of the publication.

Phototypesetting or photocomposition is the process of using a keyboard and photographic unit to transfer typed text to a film image. *Traditional* phototypesetting machines require a large, dedicated work space and several operators.

Today, most users have turned to electronic typesetting and layout. Processed by computer, camera-ready output is produced readily with considerably less stress than that imposed by traditional typesetting machines. The electronic process is both cost effective and flexible; fewer employee working hours are involved, and fewer keying errors are made. The computer also facilitates rewrites as needed.

Phototypesetters which are run from computer keyboards store the text in electronic memory, usually on magnetic disks or tapes, until ready for printing or updating. As in word processing, the text can be called up from memory and editorial changes made at will.

The process of setting type is much the same as that of typing on a typewriter or a word processor. The operator sits before a keyboard and screen and types the documents, inserting codes to specify formats and type styles. If, after typing, the document is saved to a magnetic disk, the disk is then fed into the photographic unit where images of the typed characters are projected onto photosensitive film or paper. The media are then developed and processed chemically.

The finished product is a clear, sharp publication-quality image of the text. In terms of appearance or readability, no other media approaches its professional quality. For annual reports, company brochures, and sales promotion letters, phototypesetting is the printing medium of choice by most major businesses.

Advantages of Photocomposition

The two biggest advantages of photocomposition are its high-quality output and its production speed. It also conserves paper by condensing documents into fewer pages. Many types of word processors can be linked to the photographic unit, allowing multiple users to take advantage of the photocomposition technology. Storage diskettes from microcomputer software can also be used as input into the phototypesetting process.

Designing a Layout for Photocomposition

A page layout is a diagram or arrangement of the job to be printed. It includes the text, graphics, headlines, and scanned photographs, if any. It can be designed for one page, or for an entire document. As with phototypesetting, it may be handled in house or sent out to a professional layout designer. Ideally, as employees' skills in the utilization of phototypesetters and printers advance, their eye for good layout design will sharpen, too, allowing this facet of the publishing process to move in house, as well.

Trends for the Future

Businesses with medium to large printing needs are turning in increasing numbers to the in-house concept of computer-aided publishing. Although the investment in photocomposition units is substantial, the advantages of publishing documents under the watchful eye of company supervisors make the CAP concept especially appealing. Turnaround time is reduced considerably, and confidential or classified materials are not compromised by being shared with persons outside the company.

The economic advantages of in-house publishing may also become apparent. Studies have shown that the capital outlay for equipment can be repaid within a relatively short time due to the savings generated by in-house production of multiple print jobs.

SUMMARY

Administrative assistants and their superiors have several options from which to choose in selecting a duplicator or photocopier for their companies. A review of current vendor material on photocopiers reveals that several models—thermal, xerographic, and fiber-optic—offer capabilities unique to each system. Special add-on features are also available.

Some auxiliary equipment, including binders, bursters, and decollators, is recommended for heavy users of the equipment. These materials speed the copying process or add a professional touch to the output without adding significantly to the overall cost.

For volume duplicating, electronic copier/printers and offset duplicators are available. Photocomposition of outgoing documents may be used in conjunction with either. The phototypesetting of documents (photocomposition) is attracting more and more users as they recognize applications for its superior print quality. Brought in house, the system is variously described as computer-aided publishing, in-house printing/publishing, or desktop publishing.

QUESTIONS FOR REVIEW

1. Name and describe four classifications of reprographic systems commonly used in business.
2. Of the three classes of copiers described in this chapter, which is the most popular in terms of number of units used in business offices? Explain.
3. Define each of these value-added features of photocopiers:

duplexing	image overlay
edge erase	photo mode
blue erase	job separate
image shift	multifunction memory

4. Explain the concepts of centralized and de-centralized systems as applied to reprographics.
5. Give two names (other than offset) sometimes used to describe offset duplication. What level of print quality can be expected from offset duplication?
6. Name some prepress activities described in this chapter.
7. How is electronic typesetting superior to traditional typesetting?

QUESTIONS FOR DISCUSSION

1. The monitoring of copier usage in a large organization can be a sensitive issue. Many employees view the use of the company's photocopier for personal copying a minor "perk" they deserve, so long as they don't overdo it. Signing their name or using an autotron to account for each copy they make is to them somewhat of an affront; after all, they reason, they only copy two or three pages at each session—hardly enough "to be noticed," much less monitored—by company officials.

   Do you agree that companies should discontinue their monitoring of photocopy usage by company employees? Why or why not? How can a company initiate a monitoring program without arousing resentment on the part of the employees?
2. "Information is valuable property which should be treated with the same precautions as financial assets." Discuss this statement in the light of copyright infringements often disregarded by copiers of articles, book excerpts, and other copyrighted materials.

   How can a company protect itself from charges of copyright infringements due to the illegal copying of copyrighted documents by its employees?
3. Current trends point toward more in-house publishing of company brochures, promotional materials, and sales literature. Photocomposition units, purchased by businesses, are being operated by company personnel in lieu of sending materials out to be printed.

   What do you perceive as the current impact of this trend on the printing industry as a whole, and what do you foresee as the long-term effect of this trend if it continues into the future?

SUGGESTED ACTIVITIES

1. Choose from the following activities the one(s) most practicable to pursue in your locale:
   a. Arrange an appointment with a local print shop to view a phototypesetting machine in operation.
   b. Visit your campus newspaper shop to observe the typesetting and running of the campus newspaper (if done on campus).
   c. Invite a professional printer to speak to your class about the printing industry as a whole and/or within your geographic area. Ask that he or she speak particularly to the issue of desktop and in-house publishing and the anticipated impact (if any) of these trends on professional printers.
2. Conduct a campus-wide survey of administrative offices and departments using photocopiers. Develop a questionnaire similar to the following one to determine the brands and models of photocopiers in use, the level of satisfaction users experience in operating them, and the extent to which each one is used.

   Upon completion of the survey, compile the results in a formal report and share it with administrative officials of your college or university.

QUESTIONNAIRE: PHOTOCOPIER USAGE ON CAMPUS

1. Brand/model of copier in use ________________
2. Date put into operation ________________
3. Operated by:
   ________ Assigned operator   ________ Individual users
4. If operated by individual users, is usage monitored by:
   ________ Autotron   ________ Coded no. assigned to users
   ________ Signature/Dept to be charged   ________ Not monitored
5. Approximate cost of the photocopier ________________
6. Suggested maximum usage per month to insure warranty continuance by the manufacturer ________________
7. Special features on this model (please check):
   ________ duplexing   ________ automatic feed
   ________ collating   ________ job interrupt
   ________ enlarging   ________ reducing
   ________ job separate   ________ other (specify)
8. Level of satisfaction: (Check one for each attribute)

	Fair	*Good*	*Excellent*
Copy quality			
Ease of operation			
Speed of operation			
Performance dependability			
Vendor cooperation as to:			
Service			
Training of operators			

9. Would you purchase another copier of this brand and model? Explain your answer.

REFERENCES

BRINDZA, STEPHEN, "Advancing Technology Hones in on Printing," *Modern Office Technology* (October 1988), 102–106.

CADY, PEG, "How to Learn the ABCs of Desktop Publishing," *Office Systems '88* (October 1988), 82–88.

FERNBERG, PATRICIA M., "Color Copying Meets a Spectrum of Needs," *Modern Office Technology* (March 1988), 46–48.

GIANASCOLI, JOSEPH, *St. Louis Business Journal* (January 1988), 16.

HANSON, RICHARD E., "Today's Advances Make Smarter Copiers," *Business Communications* (May 1988), BC7–BC12.

"How to Choose an Office Copier," *St. Louis Business Journal* (January 1988), 16.

LIPPIN, PAULA, "Full Line Covers the Marketplace," *Modern Office Technology* (August 1988), 37.

MCCOOEY, EILEEN, "Copiers Show Their True Colors," *Today's Office* (July 1988), 17–23.

12 Telecommunication Skills and Technology

INTRODUCTION

Studies show that more contacts are made with clients and customers via the telephone than by any other communications media. Administrative assistants who diplomatically process all incoming and outgoing calls for their employers contribute immeasurably to their success by building good relations with the public.

Another facet of effective telephone usage is equally essential. The administrative assistant must understand, from the user's point of view, the technology of current telecommunications systems. As the technology advances, this becomes an ever increasing challenge. Two facets of telephone usage are, therefore, addressed in this chapter: diplomacy and skill in the use of the telephone, and an understanding of current telecommunications technology. This includes telephone systems, telephone equipment, and services and options.

Terms in this chapter include:

Centrex	PBX
LANs	CBX
WATS	ISDN

EFFECTIVE USE OF THE TELEPHONE

The broad extent to which telephones are used in communicating with customers, clients, and the public in general makes it imperative that they be used effectively.

FIGURE 12-1 Effective telecommunications begin with dependable equipment and knowledgeable, courteous users. *Courtesy of Siemens Information Systems, Inc.*

Communications consultants agree that employees who understand state-of-the-art telecommunications equipment and use it wisely build untold good-will for their companies. They state that the knowledge and skills required are an understanding of the telecommunications systems installed on their premises, no matter how complex, and a courteous demeanor in placing outgoing calls or in responding to incoming calls, regardless of the frustrations met in either.

Although both facets are important, courtesy must be paramount. Regardless of the equipment in use, courtesy is always in style. And, like all worth-while skills, it needs to be cultivated.

Telephone Courtesy

Courtesy can be expressed in many ways, directly or indirectly. Basically, courtesy means putting oneself in the caller's shoes and anticipating his or her needs, often before they are expressed. For example, to expedite calls, clarify doubts, and make oneself perfectly understood to callers, the telephone user must:

Identify oneself and the company immediately to all outside callers.

Keep a log of all incoming calls; notebooks designed for this special purpose are available.

Return to callers placed on hold every 30 or 40 seconds when the hold is unduly long.

Arrange to have one's telephone answered when temporarily away from the phone.

Avoid slang words or expressions.

Enunciate clearly.

Speak in a moderate tone of voice.

Offer assistance to callers who cannot reach the party they want. Try to put them in touch with someone else who can help them, or ask "May I have Ms. Smith call you upon her return?"

Listen carefully to the caller, concentrating on what he or she is saying.

Take messages accurately and completely. A complete telephone message includes the name of the caller and his or her telephone number, the name of the party being called, the date and time of the call, the message itself and the name of the person who took the call.

Screen calls with the utmost tact. Callers are easily offended by persons who intercept their calls, for whatever reason. Many consultants frown upon *all* screening of telephone calls, claiming that screening insults callers and wastes the time of both parties.

Handling Complaints Listen patiently to persons who file complaints; they may have valid cause. Know what the company policy is regarding complaints and respond accordingly. Do not let anger or other negative feelings creep into your voice; show empathy for the caller's problem and try to help by putting him or her in touch with the person in the company who can resolve the problem.

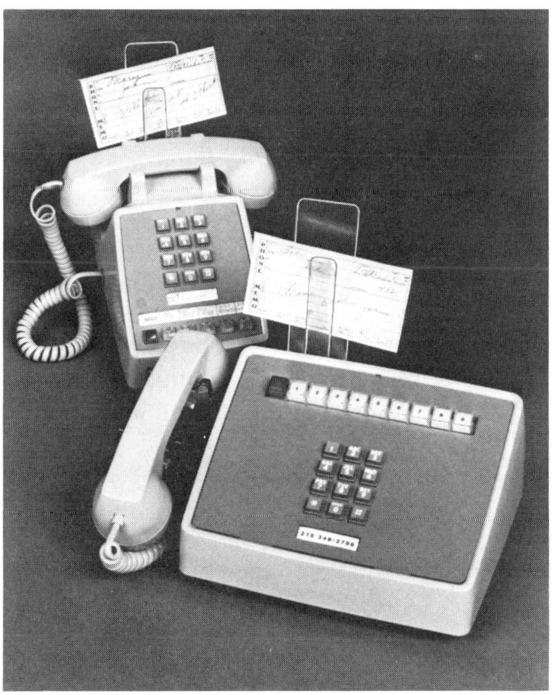

FIGURE 12-2 Visual reminders of telephone messages, such as this "call back" message holder, remind users to return important calls. *Courtesy of R&D Products, Inc.*

Multiple Calls Don't panic if several calls come in at once. Give the first person priority; politely excuse yourself from the phone and put the first caller on hold. Complete the second call if it can be done quickly; otherwise, return to the first caller. Then return to the second caller *after* the first call is completed.

Transferring Calls Before transferring a caller, the administrative assistant should ask the caller's permission to do so; then he or she should give the caller the name and telephone number of the person to whom the call is being transferred. If accidentally disconnected, the caller will then know whom to contact on the next call.

Efficiency, courtesy, and skill in the use of telecommunications equipment leave a lasting, positive impression on callers. They also impress company officials who observe the talents of the administrative assistant and others who handle this duty in a consistently courteous and efficient manner.

TELECOMMUNICATION SYSTEMS

The telephone was once a voice-only communication device; transmission of communications other than voice was not envisioned by most users. During the 1980s, however, the role of the telephone in transmitting *all* types of communications changed dramatically. At that time, the telephone evolved into a telecommunications *system*, sending and receiving voice messages, FAX documents, word processing texts, video, and computer data to and from all points in the world.

Managers and their assistants were suddenly faced with the problem of selecting telecommunication systems geared to their current and future needs. They looked to consultants for technical advice, or they set up committees to explore their options.

Systems and Options

Choosing the most practical system for each company's communication needs is not an easy task. A managerial task force, including the administrative assistant, is often assigned to the task. The administrative assistant, therefore, must know and understand the practical aspects, including the cost effectiveness, of each of the several options available, from POTS (plain old telephone service) to glittering fourth-generation digital PBX systems. Basically, the options can be reduced to three: purchase a PBX, lease Centrex, or buy specialized equipment that works with Centrex to enhance the voice/data capabilities.

Private Branch Exchange (PBX)

A PBX allows internal calls to be routed over a company's interior wires, minimizing the number of trunk lines needed to handle outside traffic. Newer

PBX systems are small, fast, and run on less electrical power than their predecessors.

They perform telecommunication functions similar to the way mainframe computers handle data-processing requirements. Electronic keys on the system's telephone instruments signal the computer to perform a selected task, and the computer responds.

Technically, the PBX is an electronic switch which routes voice calls over established circuits from one point to another, either through in-house lines or outside services, such as local or long-distance lines.

Software programming and call-handling features such as LCR (least cost routing) and ARS (automatic route selection) ensure that costs are kept to a minimum.

Special Features of PBX

Not only does the PBX offer outstanding quality in terms of voice transmission, but the special features it provides can save time and frustration for users. For example:

> *Voice messaging* alerts an employee that calls came in while he or she was away. When callers cannot reach the called party directly, they can leave a message by accessing a message-reminder push button. This causes a message to appear on the receiver's screeen showing the caller's number and time of call.
>
> *Call-forwarding when busy (CFWB)* forwards calls to selected alternative extensions when a busy signal is received.
>
> *Forward all calls (FAC)* forwards calls to another extension when the person is away from his or her desk.
>
> *Speed dialing* allows frequently dialed numbers to be programmed into the phone's memory for recall at the press of a button.

Additional functions similar in practicality to the preceding ones are introduced from time to time, enhancing the efficiency and cost effectiveness of the installed systems.

Since most PBXs are priced on a per-line basis, averaging around $750 to $1,000 per line, a system handling 50 extensions with ten additional trunk lines costs between $45,000 and $60,000. Built on a modular concept, systems can be expanded or contracted as the company's needs change. Hybrid-model PBXs perform some functions on the premises and others in the central station of the telephone company. For example, the company may handle interdepartmental calls internally, but use central-office lines (Centrex) for certain other functions.

Centrex Systems

Centrex is a regulated service provided by the local phone company under authority of the Public Utilities Commission and the Federal Communications Commission (FCC). Centrex performs the switching functions in equipment

FIGURE 12-3 At Illinois Consolidated Telephone Company, operators process calls from "state-of-the-art" computerized stations. *Courtesy of Consolidated Communications Inc.*

located in the telephone company's central office. It is leased to customers with no option to purchase.

Several advantages accrue to users of Centrex systems, making it the choice of many companies, especially those in the small-to-mid-size category. These include:

Reliability. The telephone company has the workers and resources to keep the system "up" at all times; for the sake of their reputation as a service organization, they keep the equipment in good repair.

Availability. Service is available 24 hours a day, every day of the year.

Capacity. As the company's needs grow (or diminish), the telephone company can expand or contract lines and service to accommodate the changing volume of user traffic.

Maintenance and repair. The telephone company must care for its own equipment; the customer utilizing the Centrex equipment is not responsible for upkeep and repair.

No capital outlay is necessary on the part of the customer to get "up and running" with a Centrex system.

No overhead expenses are incurred for insurance, maintenance contracts, and utilities.

More features are promised for the future by telephone companies offering Centrex systems.

Price rates are being reduced in order to remain competitive with PBXs.

Add-on Features: Centrex/PBX/POTS

For those offices which need to upgrade their telephone service but do *not* need a change in their basic communication *system*, a wide variety of telephone add-ons are available at modest cost. Some are designed for Centrex or PBX only, but many fit "Plain Old Telephone Service" (POTS) systems as well.

Representatives of local telephone companies can provide details and cost estimates of these added services. The following list includes the most popular options:

Call processing systems fill in for a human operator, saving callers the frustration of getting a busy signal. A human-like voice "talks" to callers, giving them instructions, or sending their calls to appropriate departments. Some intercept calls enroute to busy extensions and direct callers to voice message boxes instead.

Voice mail is closely related to call processing. Callers leave electronic messages for the called party to retrieve at his or her convenience.

Call accounting records all calls by user and department name. The records incorporate all relevant details, including the date, time, and maker of each call, the length of the call, and the department to be charged for each.

Automatic call distribution shares incoming calls among a number of answering phones so that calls are served in order of receipt.

Class-of-service restrictions limit access to certain functions and external networks on a station-by-station basis.

Direct-inward dialing (DID) permits incoming calls to bypass the attendant and ring directly at a specific station.

Direct-outward dialing (DOD) permits stations to ring outside numbers without assistance from the attendant.

Hunting routes calls automatically to an alternate station when the called station is busy.

Call-waiting display tells the attendant the number of calls waiting to be answered.

Conference enables the attendant to establish a call with more than two parties.

Direct-paging access provides paging zones through the telephone system by push-button operation.

Store and repeat allows the caller to store the last number dialed so that a push button can be accessed later when retrying the same number.

Local Area Networks

Businesses which regularly transmit data information among their departments may find a local area network (LAN) the answer to their internal information exchange needs. LANs use on-site electronic switching equipment to transmit data over relatively short distances, such as from one office to another within the same building, or between adjacent buildings. The LAN private networks allow for sharing of both data and equipment among related users. Shared equipment may include computers, printers, terminals, and "intelligent" photocopying machines.

One of the advantages of local area networks is that they do not interfere with ongoing voice communications being transmitted on separate lines. LANs not only speed up data communications, but they alleviate the crowded telephone lines already burdened with heavy voice traffic. (See Chapter 7 for more information on LANs.)

Integrated Services Digital Network (ISDN)

Called the wave of the future in telecommunications, integrated systems combining all forms of communications—voice, data, and video—are now marketed by telecommunication vendors.

The ISDN enables customers to plug into any electronic outlet. The network transmits information sent by the customer to a receiver on the same network in a manner similar to a telephone communication. Current ISDNs vary widely in price and capability ranges, giving the buyer several options from which to choose.

Fully developed standards for ISDNs are not expected until the mid-1990s. By that time, fully compatible communications of all types may become a reality.

When to Upgrade Systems

When communications problems develop and solutions are not readily found, administrative assistants and their principals may perceive them as signals to consider an upgrade in their telephone systems. Some telltale signs of dissatisfaction with the current system are these:

Complaints from customers and clients about frequent busy signals
Grumblings from employees about difficulty in getting outside lines
Clerical and stenographic workers overburdened with telephone answering and message taking
Complaints from sales personnel and others frequently out of the office who fail to get their calls.

Such complaints suggest a change in systems. Which system the company officials choose—PBX, Centrex, or Centrex with added features—depends on the traffic level of telephone communications, the legitimacy of the complaints received, and the cost of a newly installed system.

A telecommunications consultant, preferably one without a proprietary interest in *any* system, can propose alternative solutions for the problems being experienced, including a cost/benefit ratio for each of the proposed solutions.

Fees paid to professional consultants net a handsome return if the consultants are thorough and objective in their research. An effective telecommunication system is more than a luxury to a going business; the business cannot flourish for long without it.

Computerized Branch Exchange (CBX)

The electronic version of the private branch exchange (PBX) is the computerized branch exchange (CBX) or the private automated branch exchange (PABX).

Both the CBX and the PABX offer more advanced capabilities than those offered by the private branch exchange. They merge readily with local area networks (LANs) and they provide more sophisticated monitoring systems than the PBX systems offer.

Many private branch exchange systems retain their current PBX titles even though they have upgraded to a computerized exchange status. In the future, however, as more PBX systems are computerized, the term *private branch exchange* will likely be supplanted by the more accurate *computerized branch exchange (CBX)* or *private automated branch exchange (PABX).*

TELEPHONE INSTRUMENTS AND SERVICES

A standard fixture in every office, the irreplaceable telephone has gone through major changes in recent years. Not only is it a more versatile instrument than before, but it is also a more stylish one. Telephones now come in decorator styles and colors to match each office decor, from Victorian to contemporary.

Touch-tone Telephones

The rotary-dial telephone which used pulse signals to contact the called party has become an anachronism in most offices, supplanted by the push-button tone-dial instrument. The touch-tone telephone holds a place of prominence in business, not merely as a speech-communications instrument, but as a medium for transacting business in an orderly fashion.

For example, touch-tone telephones are used to transmit messages between computers, and to store and forward voice messages via electronic mail. Touch-tone telephones equipped with built-in memory processors and programmed key commands respond to callers' requests or give them directions. In short, the integrated circuitry of the microchip, merged with touch-tone technology, has elevated the telephone to a multi-use telecommunications instrument.

Peripheral instruments, such as answering machines and paging devices, add another dimension to telephone communications.

Answering Machines

An inexpensive solution to the problem of unanswered calls and misplaced messages is the answering machine. Widely accepted by both business and home users, two factors have fueled its growing popularity: the steady decline in prices of the units, and the upgraded features of the latest models. Since the mid-1980s, price declines have averaged 400 percent or more, and add-on features have made the units appealing to buyers.

For example, the use of microcassettes to replace standard cassettes in answering machines has made it possible to reduce the bulkiness of the earlier models. Today's 2-pound machines have the same recording capacity as yesterday's 40-pound units.

Microprocessor chips have also facilitated the addition of such features as time-and-date stamping, voice-synthesized prompts, and screening of calls. In addition, the chips enable VOX (voice-activated recording) to eliminate blank spaces on the cassette tape; CPC (calling-party control) to detect when the caller hangs up, so as to automatically reset the machine for the next call; and call forwarding to call the user at a preset phone number when a message has been received.

Paging Devices

Paging devices, or beepers, signal users with a beep, telling them that a call or message is waiting for them. A given telephone number is then dialed by the user to receive the message. Late models can display the calling number, or even a short message, to advise users of the urgency of the call.

FIGURE 12-4 This numeric display pager, weighing just 3 ounces, holds in memory up to 120 digits, or 12 separate messages of 10 digits each. *Courtesy of NEC America, Inc.*

Pagers are a relatively inexpensive means for keeping in touch with one's office; hence, their popularity with busy executives or professionals who must be away from their offices frequently or for long periods of time.

Cellular Telephones

Cellular telephones are mobile units designed primarily for automobile installation. Although relatively expensive, cellular phones are no longer the special perk reserved for limousine riders. For "on-the-road" businesspersons, these mobile telephones have become an integral part of business life.

The name *cellular* derives from the antenna networks placed in hexagonal cells adjacent to one another in large cities. These antennae provide the power for the radio signals sent to and from the phones. As drivers move from one cell to another within the cellular maze, the user is switched from cell to cell so that no loss of power is detected by the users. Almost all models offer certain standard features such as last-number recall, a phone directory memory for storing frequently dialed numbers, and an electronic lock for security.

More expensive models also include an auxiliary alert mode that flashes the headlights or blows the horn to indicate an incoming call to users away from the vehicle and a cumulative timer to keep track of actual calling time.

FIGURE 12-5 Cellular telephones enable sales personnel to keep in touch with corporate headquarters and with customers. *Courtesy of Audiovox Corporation.*

Cellular phones can be purchased, leased, or rented. An outright purchase requires a sizable cash outlay; prices range from just under $1,000 to more than $4,000, depending on model, features, options, and installation costs.

Rental plans offer the most flexible option in month-to-month rentals. Rental fees typically range from around $20 to $100 per month, including maintenance and insurance. This does not include monthly cellular access charges or airtime usage charges, which can be substantial.

For potential buyers, however, some vendors allow users to apply a percentage of the monthly rental fee to the purchase price of the equipment. Leases, another option, allow users to spread payments over a number of years.

The Videophone

Although the first "picturephone" was unveiled by AT&T in the early 1960s, its potential has never been realized. There is evidence, however, that the talk/see phone may be poised to make its move. Mitsubishi introduced its Luma 1000 videophone in 1986, the first unit to send black and white still images over ordinary phone lines.

Image Data Corporation offered a unit which could send or receive a high-resolution, still picture in seven seconds. The basic package, meant for industrial use, included a photophone, a camera, and a diskette system that would store up to 70 pictures, any of which could be transmitted at the touch of a button.

To transmit *moving* images, fiber optic transmission lines are required. Experts predict that when sufficient fiber optic lines are in place, live full-motion video will be transmitted readily at affordable prices. Then the true picturephone envisioned in the 1960s will become a reality.

Special Services

Telephone companies offer special telecommunication services to customers whose business connections are scattered over a wide geographic area. For additional fees, which vary with the extent and type of service offered, subscribers can add these to their basic services. Among the most popular are:

800 toll-free service for incoming calls
WATS lines for outgoing calls
private (tie) lines
FX (foreign exchange) service

Toll-free (800) Calls Toll-free service for incoming calls is a discounted long-distance service which encourages incoming calls through an "800" telephone number. Offered to persons in selected geographic areas, 800 numbers are now so numerous that telephone directories listing 800 numbers are available. Cost to the subscriber is based on units of use and the geographic zones from which calls are received. For users, the service is free.

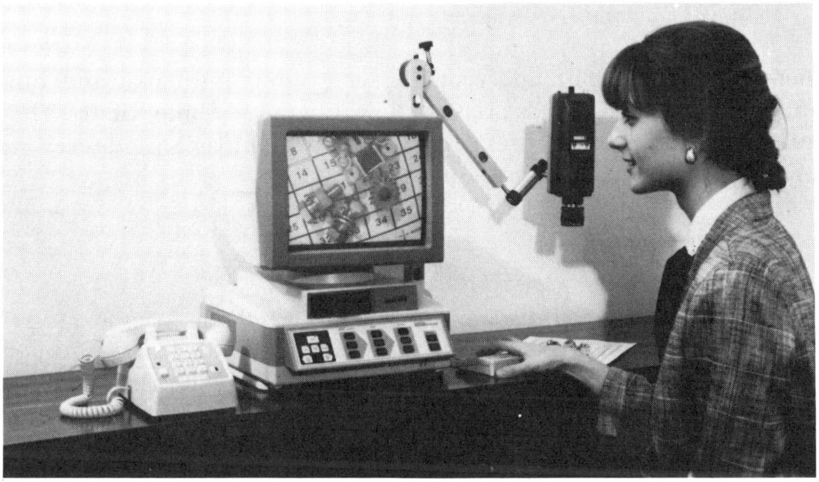

FIGURE 12-6 This Imagephone brings personnel together for problem-solving and planning sessions. Pictures are sent by transceiver to an Imagephone in another building or city at a rate of 9,600 baud. The user selects the images to be viewed. *Courtesy of Interand Corporation.*

Wide-area Telephone Service (WATS) For outgoing calls, another discounted service, WATS, is available to high-volume subscribers. Like the 800 service, wide-area telephone service is based on geographic levels.

The broadest geographic level covers all 50 states plus Puerto Rico and the Virgin Islands. Charges to the subscribers are based on volume of usage, geographic level, and the time and day of week on which calls are made. Volume of usage determines the savings, if any, gained from WATS lines.

Private Lines Private "tie" lines provide subscribers with exclusive use of telephone lines between predetermined points. For a fixed monthly charge, subscribers tie intracity or intercity branches of their businesses together through privately leased lines, thereby gaining unlimited exclusive usage of the lines.

Tie lines can also be extended to foreign branches and to other frequently called business locations. Convenience is the principal benefit of leased lines, but dollar savings can be substantial if the volume of usage is high.

FX (Foreign Exchange) Service Customers of large retail, wholesale, or mail-order firms may be able to dial certain firms with a local telephone number, even though the firm itself is located out of the city. This toll-free service is made possible through an FX (foreign exchange) service to which the companies subscribe for a given fee.

Calls are charged to the subscribers at a discount, based on volume of calls received and the distance spanned in each call. Frequently, the toll-free numbers are listed in the customers' local telephone directories, along with other local businesses.

LONG-DISTANCE TELECOMMUNICATIONS

Long-distance telecommunications involve intercontinental and other international calls, as well as calls originating within the 50 United States. The administrative assistant must understand the procedures for placing and receiving *all* calls, within the country and outside it.

International Calls

Thanks to direct-distance dialing, over 100 countries around the world can now be dialed direct without the delay and added cost of an operator's assistance. All that is necessary is a directory of the country and city telephone codes plus the local telephone number of the person being called in the destination city.

The caller dials 1 to bypass the operator + the three-number international access code + the two-number country code + the city code + the local telephone number. For example, to dial Great Britain (code 44) one can dial as follows:

1 + 011 + 44 + 1 + ______________ (local number)

The caller must be especially aware of time zone differences when placing international calls. For example, calls made to England from the Eastern time zone of the United States will reach England five hours later. Hence, a call made from New York at 2 P.M. will reach England at 7 P.M., well after closing hours.

If a directory is not available, or if the caller needs assistance, AT&T offers a toll-free International Information Service at 1–800–874–4000. Other carriers offer similar assistance.

Operator-assisted Calls

Long-distance calls made within the United States can be divided into two classes: operator-assisted calls and direct-distance dialing (DDD) calls.

Operator-assisted calls are necessary when the caller places a person-to-person call; when he or she calls collect; or charges the call to another number; or (in some cases) uses a credit card for billing. In each case, the proper procedure for the caller to follow is this:

1. Dial zero to get the operator.
2. Without waiting for the operator, dial the area code.
3. Then immediately dial the telephone number.

Wait for the operator to come on the line, then continue as follows:

4. For a person-to-person call, tell the operator the name of the person to whom you wish to speak.

5. For a collect call, give your name (for approval of the charge by the person at the receiving end of the call).
6. If the call is *not* to be charged to the telephone in use, tell the operator what telephone number to charge.
7. Give the operator the credit card number if the call is to be so billed.

Major airports and some other public reception areas offer special telephones for credit card users. By inserting the card into a slot, then dialing zero and the telephone number, the calling party dials direct, with the billing automatically charged to his or her credit card.

Special assistance from the operator can be had, however, by dialing zero, then waiting for the operator to respond. Professional or technical assistance is then available.

Information Assistance from Operators If assistance from the operator is needed in getting the called party's telephone number, users may dial the prefix 1 plus the area code and 555-1212 for information. This will connect them with the operator at the destination area code; the operator will ask what city they are calling. The user provides the name of the destination city, then asks the operator for the telephone number of the called party. If the area code is *not* known, the user calls a local operator to obtain the area code number, and then proceeds as before.

Most telephone directories now include a map of the code numbers assigned to areas throughout the United States. Users should look to this source before contacting the telephone operator to obtain this information for them.

Direct-distance Dialing

By dialing 1 and the area code, rather than 0 and the area code, when calling a point outside one's area code, the user bypasses the operator and makes direct telephone contact with the receiver. This is known as direct-distance dialing (DDD).

If the call is made to a point *within* one's own area code, the procedure is simply to dial the prefix 1 and the telephone number, *not* including the area code number.

Station-to-Station and Person-to-Person Calls Direct-distance dialing is often equated with station-to-station calling since the telephone charges begin immediately when the telephone at the destination point is answered. However, station-to-station calls may also be made with operator assistance; that is, when the caller elects to speak to anyone who answers the telephone.

In contrast, person-to-person calls generate charges only when the person designated actually speaks to the caller; or, when a substitute for the called party is accepted to take the call in his or her place.

Person-to-person calls are more expensive per message unit than station-to-station calls; however, they are cost saving when the called party is absent and no charge is made for a "wasted" call.

"Operator 6" Calls When party A calls party B, and party B is out, party A may leave an "Operator 6" message for party B. This means that A asks B to return the call by asking for "Operator 6." "Operator 6" is a coded message that automatically bills the toll charges to A, the person who originated the call.

Choosing a Long-distance Carrier

Choosing the carrier best suited to the company's needs requires of the administrative assistant careful consideration of several factors. A good place to start is a cost comparison of the services offered by each carrier. To get a realistic estimate of the monthly service and toll charges the company can expect from a carrier, the administrative assistant must first review the company's telephone usage patterns.

For example, exploring answers to the following questions will reveal the company's typical pattern of long-distance usage:

What is the average number of long-distance calls made each month?
How many calls are less than 3 minutes in length?
What is the average length and cost per call with the current carrier?
What area codes are most frequently called?
Are most long-distance calls made out of state or within the company's home state?

With this information in hand, the administrative assistant can examine and compare competitors' rates with those of the company's current carrier.

Since rate structures vary from one carrier to another, a careful scrutiny of carrier charges is necessary. For example, some carriers initiate charges when a call is answered; others begin billing as soon as the call is dialed. Some carriers charge on a per-minute basis, beginning with the first minute; others, on a per-minute basis only after the first three minutes of telephone usage.

All carriers round usage times upward, from six seconds to 30 seconds per call; for users with a pattern of high-volume short-call usage, the difference in cost over a month's duration can be significant.

Substantial cost reductions, however, may depend primarily on the volume of calls made. High-volume users of long-distance service find that carriers with reliable WATS service save them substantial amounts through low-cost WATS lines. Low-volume users, on the other hand, save more by ignoring the WATS service carriers and dailing their calls direct.

Quality of service is another major factor to consider. Users may have to accept a trade-off of high-quality, reliable service for the lower per-unit cost of some carriers. Extraneous noise, voice distortion, transmission delays, and frequent redials are typical complaints of users of lower-priced carriers.

In the final analysis, the most reliable means for evaluating a carrier's service is hands-on usage of the service. Depending on the policy of the carrier in question, a trial period may be feasible. If a tryout period is arranged, a minimum of one to two months will be necessary to gauge the potential benefits, if any, to be gained by changing carriers.

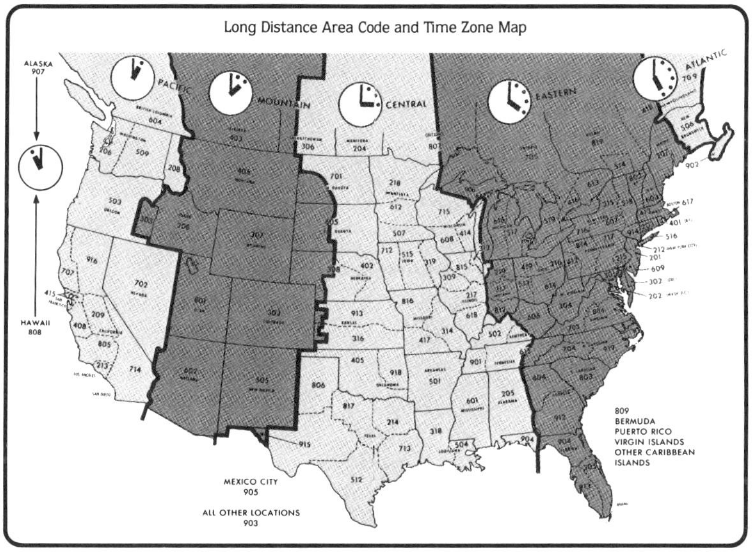

FIGURE 12-7 A map of the area codes and time zones enables the administrative assistant to plan the timing of long-distance calls. *Courtesy of Consolidated Communications Inc.*

SUMMARY

The telephone is one of the most widely used devices in the electronic office. The broad extent to which this instrument is used to communicate with customers, clients, vendors, suppliers, and the general public mandates that all users, especially the administrative assistant, become skilled in its use.

Two facets of telecommunications skill contribute to the effective use of the telephone: an understanding of the technology incorporated into the system, and diplomatic skill in its usage.

Diplomacy in dealing with callers of all types, even the most difficult, is an acquired skill. It can be developed through practice. Knowledge of telecommunication systems is equally important. With information readily available, the administrative assistant can acquire this expertise also.

Special services offered by telephone companies include 800 numbers to encourage incoming calls, WATS for discounted long-distance calls, and private tie lines for frequent usage between designated points.

QUESTIONS FOR REVIEW

1. This chapter suggests many ways of showing courtesy to telephone callers. List as many as you can recall.
2. Explain how to handle the panic situation of multiple calls coming in at one time to an operator.

3. Explain the concept of Centrex.
4. What is a PBX? A CBX?
5. How does a PBX compare with Centrex in terms of reliability and service?
6. Define each of the following terms and acronyms:
   a. Voice-messaging
   b. Speed dialing
   c. WATS
   d. ISDN
   e. LAN
7. Explain the cell concept of cellular telephones.
8. Explain the procedure for dialing direct to a telephone in England.
9. How does one dial the information operator in another city to get a party's telephone number?

QUESTIONS FOR DISCUSSION

1. Answering machines appear to be a mixed blessing; all callers are answered (although not by a human being) and the called party receives recorded messages of callers who respond to the prompts. However, some persons resent answering machines and will hang up rather than leave a message when prompted to do so. What solution do you suggest to solve this problem?
2. If complaints regarding frustrating telephone service have been escalating in recent weeks, how would you, as a company official with enough clout to do something about it, evaluate the complaints insofar as they suggest a telephone system upgrade?
3. Explain the statement: *Courtesy can be expressed in many ways other than the proverbial "please" and "thank you" expressions.* How important is telephone courtesy in developing and/or maintaining a desirable public image?

SUGGESTED ACTIVITIES

1. Contact a cellular telephone user or owner. Invite the person to visit your class and share with students his or her experiences in using the cellular telephone. Question the user on usage costs, reliability of the equipment and service, frequency of use, and benefits of usage in his or her profession.
2. Visit the local telephone company to view operators handling computerized calls. Observe the speed and efficiency of the operators. Ask supervisors what add-on features the company offers customers (speed dialing, call-forwarding, call-waiting, and so on).
3. Obtain permission to visit a local bank, merchandising operation, or department store and observe their telephone system in operation. Share your findings with the store or bank officers, offering suggestions, if appropriate.

REFERENCES

DAVIDSON, JEFFREY P., "Caring about Your Callers," *Office Systems '88* (October 1988), 22–25.

GLAGOW, STEVE, "Functions to Look for in Telephone Systems," *Office Systems '88* (June 1988), 22–24.

LAVOIE, FRANCIS J., "Today's Telephone System: Sophisticated & Affordable," *Modern Office Technology* (November 1988), 76–78.

PECKMAN, KIM, "What's the Latest Twist in Telephone Upgrading?" *Office Systems '88* (November 1988), 70–75.

ROSENBERG, ARTHUR M., "Can We Talk?" *Modern Office Technology* (February 1988), 40–48.

TOTTY, PATRICK, "Be Careful, Be Selective in Buying a Telephone System," *The Office* (September 1988), 86–89.

13
Arranging Meetings and Teleconferences

INTRODUCTION

One of the major support services the administrative assistant provides an employer is assistance in planning company meetings. Whether held in company headquarters or many miles distant, meetings are an integral component of business communications.

The administrative assistant must understand not only the logistics of organizing a meeting efficiently, but how to conduct one in the absence of the presiding officer. In these instances, he or she must observe the usual rules of order followed in formal meetings, while facilitating free discussion among the participants.

Teleconferencing, the "electronic meeting" which is replacing some travel to distant meetings, is making its impact felt also. Thousands of business firms utilize teleconferencing services regularly. An understanding of the structure and terminology of teleconferencing is, therefore, another of the requisites of the contemporary administrative assistant in the electronic office.

Terms in this chapter include:

ad hoc conferences	freeze-frame video
virtual conferences	full-motion video

ORGANIZING EFFECTIVE MEETINGS

Most organizations would find it difficult to function for long without the informational exchange provided by regularly scheduled meetings. From informal get-togethers of a few employees to formally structured business meetings called by company officials, meetings are a necessary component of successful business operations.

Some meetings are very effective, some totally ineffective, with most falling somewhere between the two extremes. The ideal meeting may be defined as one which facilitates discussion by all participants on issues set forth in the agenda, encourages amicable exchange of opposing views on issues raised, remains within its stated time frame, and provides for definitive closure on issues discussed, thereby accomplishing its stated objectives.

The level of effectiveness of most meetings is directly related to the time and effort its organizers spend in planning every detail. Good planning promotes good meetings.

Administrative assistants often play a major role in planning company meetings, from informal staff meetings held regularly in the company's conference room to the annual stockholders' meeting called by corporate executives. On rare occasions, the administrative assistant's role may be more than supportive; he or she may have to conduct a meeting in the executive's absence. To prepare for such occasions, the skills covering every aspect of organizing and conducting effective meetings must be mastered.

On-site Meetings

The locale for regularly scheduled staff meetings varies little from one meeting to the next. Choosing a meeting site means simply reserving one of the meeting rooms far enough in advance to be assured of its availability. Planning involves tasks spread over three time frames: before, during, and after the meeting.

1. *Before the meeting*
   a. Scheduling the date and time
   b. Planning the agenda
   c. Contacting the participants
   d. Arranging the room setting
   e. Preparing visual aids and equipment, if needed
2. *During the meeting*
   a. Starting on time
   b. Taking of minutes (by the secretary)
   c. Following parliamentary procedures
   d. Facilitating discussion
   e. Reducing conflicts
   f. Wrapping up discussions for good closure
   g. Adjournment
3. *After the meeting*
   a. Distributing copies of minutes
   b. Following up on assigned tasks

In planning their meetings, administrative assistants will find the following suggestions helpful in carrying out the preceding tasks.

Before the Meeting

Scheduling the Date and Time The meeting should be scheduled well in advance of the date proposed. This gives participants the opportunity to reserve the appointed time slot and, if necessary, to rearrange their schedules.

Planning the Agenda Agenda items should include unfinished items of previous meetings, followed by new items for discussion and/or action, listed in order of priority. Information relevant to the agenda items should be prepared in advance and duplicated for participants, if appropriate.

Contacting the Participants *Written* notice of the scheduled meeting should be sent to participants several days prior to the set date. Included in the notice should be a copy of the planned agenda and an invitation to suggest additional agenda items if so desired.

Arranging the Room Setting Prior to the meeting, tables and chairs should be arranged so that participants can see and speak to each other freely. A special effort should be made to give each person enough space to feel at ease and view the chairperson as the focal point of the gathering. If customary, notetaking materials can be provided.

Preparing Visual Aids If films, slides, or other video materials are to be shown, a screen positioned to reflect the visuals in the best possible light must be in place, ready to use. Projectors for showing the visuals must, of course, be in place also.

During the Meeting

Starting on Time One of the simplest, yet most effective, methods for starting a meeting off right is to start it on time. The presiding officer establishes his or her authority by beginning the meeting at the time scheduled. Busy persons for whom time is a precious commodity appreciate the leader who values their time as much as his or her own. Starting (and ending) meetings on time also sets the tone for effective discussion and closure of the issues presented.

Taking Minutes The secretary appointed to take minutes should sit near the presiding officer. Verbatim notes are not necessary except when recording motions; however, the minutes should reflect all facts pertinent to each issue discussed, plus the conclusions drawn or decisions made on each.

When writing motions, the full name of the person making the motion is to be recorded as well as the exact words he or she uses in phrasing it; the name of the person seconding the motion must be recorded also.

FIGURE 13-1 Two screens enable more viewers to see the projected images, thus enhancing the speaker's presentation. *Courtesy of 3M Corporation.*

Formats used for the printed minutes are not standardized; however, the following elements shown on p. 285 are included in the recorded minutes, regardless of the format used.

Following Parliamentary Procedures Until thoroughly acquainted with the basic rules of parliamentary procedure, the presiding officer may want to keep a procedures manual at hand for ready reference. Some of the formalities explained in a manual are:

- Kinds of motions
- Proper wording for a motion
- When a second is needed
- When a motion can be amended
- Required vote to pass specific motions:
  - Majority
  - Two-thirds
  - Rule of the chair

Group title

Date Time

Names of persons present (and absent, if the group is formally structured)

Minutes of former meeting read by ____________

Motion to approve minutes as read (or as corrected) made

by ____________

Seconded by ____________

Old business (if any)

____

Discussion ____________

Action taken ____________

New business

____

Discussion ____________

Action taken ____________

Date set for next meeting ____________

Signed ____________

Name/Secretary

____

Date

Elements of Recorded Minutes

Types of voting:
- Voice
- Show of hands
- Roll call
- Ballot
- General consent

Procedures for presenting an item of business before a group and securing a vote:
- Rising and addressing the presiding officer
- Recognizing the speaker
- Presenting the motion
- Seconding the motion
- Stating the question
- Discussion or debate
- Putting the question
- Voting on the motion
- Announcing the vote

Miscellaneous procedures for:
- Referring business to a committee
- Suspending standing rules
- Debating an issue
- Handling nominations and elections

The terms used in parliamentary procedures can be intimidating to the uninitiated. However, they do become familiar with extended use.

Facilitating Discussion To develop a climate for group discussion, the presiding officer may direct questions or raise issues which stir participants to express opposing points of view. In the lively exchange which often ensues, he or she must facilitate discussion by encouraging input from all the members, keeping all parties on course when or if they digress to irrelevant issues, and attempt to bring the discussion to successful closure after all have aired their views.

Reducing Conflict Tempers sometimes flare when the issue under discussion affects the participants personally. On such occasions, the presiding officer must make every effort to maintain the peace and to resolve the differences separating the disputing parties. By prevailing on the members' objectivity, he or she may succeed in maintaining harmony and keeping the meeting on track.

In any event, the presiding officer holds the unenviable position of arbiter or peacemaker when discussions become heated. Unless brought under control, the disputants' conduct may cause the meeting to abort without its achieving the desired goals. Experienced leaders offer these suggestions for preserving harmony when tensions and tempers appear to be mounting:

Inject (delicately) some light-hearted humor.

Suggest that the thorny issue be discussed further *after* the meeting.

Put off a decision until further research can be done on the issue.

Call a 5-minute break to defuse tempers and relax.

To preclude arguments, some leaders suggest that new ideas be discussed with a few persons prior to the formal meeting. The idea may be proposed to two, three, or more persons; upon their acceptance of it as worthy of discussion, it may be formalized for discussion and review by the entire group.

In general, controversial issues are difficult to resolve; on frequent occasions they may not be resolved at all. A discreet presiding officer may postpone public debate on sensitive issues for an extended length of time, since time itself is often an ally in resolving problematic issues.

Wrap-up and Adjournment Efficient wrap-up and closure are important. Meetings tend to lose their force when discussion of agenda items suffer from overkill. Members grow impatient, lose interest, and tune out the proceedings. Two safeguards against the onset of boredom are:

1. A fast-paced meeting in which each agenda item is in turn addressed, discussed, and resolved or set for continuance at a later date, all in due order and within reasonable time limits.
2. On-time adjournment. Participants discuss agenda items more eagerly, realizing that the adjournment time will be honored. Failure to complete discussion of all items may require the unpopular alternative, further meetings.

FIGURE 13-2 One of 52 conference rooms at the headquarters of Quaker Oats Company. Conferees appreciate the circular glass exterior, recessed lighting, and decorative muted colors of the conference setting. *Courtesy of Quaker Oats Company, Chicago.*

After the Meeting

Distributing Copies of the Minutes Minutes should be printed as soon as possible, ideally within 24 hours after the meeting, with copies distributed to all members, including absentees.

Follow-up If at the meeting task assignments were given or responsibilities were voluntarily assumed by participants, follow-up communications are in order. To those who volunteered their services, the reminder includes a special note of appreciation. To all, the written follow-up serves as a reminder of what they have been asked to do or have volunteered to do and by what date reports are due on their activities.

CONFERENCES AND CONVENTIONS

Companies which regularly sponsor large meetings at sites away from the home office often hire a full-time meeting planner or coordinator. The coordinator makes the arrangements for all company-sponsored off-site meetings, including trade shows, seminars, conferences, and conventions.

Administrative assistants are normally exempt from planning complex off-site conferences, but as assistants they may well be asked to help their principals do so. The following suggestions are designed to make the job easier for them.

Stay within the budget limitations for the convention. Selection of the site and the planning of meals depend in large part on the amount of money budgeted for the event.

Choose the site carefully. The accommodations and food are essential components of a successful conference.

If spouses of the participants are to attend, plan some special activities specifically for them.

As the time approaches, recheck every detail of the event. A successful conference is as much a result of good planning as good speakers and sessions.

Selecting a Site for the Conference

Look carefully at the food service. The quality of the food and the ambiance of the dining facility are important to conference-goers.

Check the size and appearance of the sleeping rooms. Look for conveniences, too, such as express checkout service.

Designate a particular person at the proposed facility as liaison with the company group; turn over to him/her the information necessary to make the meeting successful.

Negotiate prices. Rooms are usually negotiable; food is not. Expecting too large a discount for a block of rooms, however, can be counterproductive. If the site proves to be very pleasing to the attendees but the facility has lost money, a return engagement may be out of the question.

Prior to the conference, visit the property unannounced and unidentified. Remain alert to the competency and attitude of the hotel staff toward you.

Consider a conference center as the site of the company's conference. They have become the favorite meeting places for many planners.

Conference Centers

Traditional meeting facilities provide participants with a businesslike atmosphere and basic services. Today, however, in addition to the basic services offered by traditional centers, *conference centers* supply many high-tech services, such as personal computers, FAX transmission, and teleconferencing facilities.

As customized meeting facilities, conference centers also specialize in accommodating relatively small groups; for example, 10 or 12 sales representatives, 50 to 60 management trainees, or an association of 300 educators. Although prices for the centers range somewhat higher than their hotel counterparts, their basic charges typically include all meeting and guest rooms, meals, recreational facilities, and audiovisual equipment.

Computer and video capabilities are a specialty of conference centers. PC hookups in meeting rooms, guest rooms, and lounges are provided as part of the basic package in most conference centers. Additional high-tech equipment is available for a nominal rental fee.

If the conferees include many nationalities, conference centers may provide simultaneous translation of different languages so that all attendees can participate in the sessions.

FIGURE 13-3 Elegant furnishings, paneled walls, and effective visuals characterize this well-appointed executive conference room. *Courtesy of Quaker Oats Company.*

Convention Bureaus

Convention bureaus work with companies who are interested in bringing conventions to their cities. They endeavor to make the planning process as hassle-free as possible, in the hopes of generating more business from the companies in the future.

The bureaus advise planners on the types of facilities available in their cities and which are most suitable for their planned activities. Working as liaisons between the meeting planners and the staffs of proposed meeting sites, bureau personnel try to negotiate a package that is agreeable to all parties.

Novice planners find convention bureaus to be especially helpful in their first planning attempts. Veteran planners, too, repeatedly turn to the services of convention bureaus to arrange favorable facilities at reasonable rates.

TELECONFERENCES

Teleconferencing, or the use of telecommunications to conduct *electronic meetings*, is currently enjoying explosive growth in business centers throughout the world. Defined as the meeting of three or more persons at multiple locations via telecommunication systems, teleconferencing offers several advantages over traditional meetings. For example:

Teleconferences tend to be shorter and better organized than face-to-face meetings.

Decisions are made more quickly due to the ready availability of key personnel.

Productivity is improved as travel time is reduced.

Travel costs are reduced.

Broader opportunities for employees' education and training are made possible.

Expert resource people, not otherwise available, are brought in to update and motivate managerial personnel.

Mini sales meetings are one of the most common applications of small-scale teleconferencing. Brainstorming sessions are another.

Forms of Teleconferencing

Four forms of teleconferencing are currently available. Each has its place in the business or professional world, with the choice largely depending on at least three factors: (1) the application to be made of the technology; (2) the frequency of use anticipated; and (3) the financial investment the user cares to make in the equipment or servicc.

The four forms of teleconferencing are, in order of cost and complexity:

1. Audio (voice only)
2. Audiographic (voice plus visuals)
3. Virtual, or computer-based conferencing
4. Videoconferencing

Audio Conferencing

Probably the most accessible and the least intimidating of all forms of electronic meetings, audio conferencing is the most widely used of all four forms.

Similar to both the telephone conference call and upscale videoconferencing, the audio conference differs significantly from both in at least two ways. In comparison with traditional conference calls, the audio conference accommodates greater numbers of people than the conference call; and the audio conference requires the services of a "bridge" to interconnect all circuits attached to it.

In contrast to videoconferencing, the technology and equipment involved in audio teleconferencing is far less complex; and an audioconference is less costly to arrange than a videoconference.

The "bridge" used in audio conferences is a special kind of switch which enables persons on the circuits to speak and listen to one another. The bridge acts as a leveler, to balance the sound levels of the various circuits. It also blocks contention among the speakers so that no more than one person can access a "talking path" at one time.

Three types of network bridges are in use:

1. a dedicated or permanently wired network of locations spanning relatively short distances.
2. a telephone-company network linked by an operator at the phone company's call-out bridge; the operator calls the conferees to assemble them for the conference.
3. a "meet-me" bridging network with call-out and call-in capabilities, using one of several vendors' bridging devices. Each participant calls in on long-distance phone circuits to "meet" others via the conference bridge.

The bridge of the "meet-me" network automatically connects the participants, without the use of an intervening operator. Its greater speed and lower cost make the "meet-me" bridge preferable to operator-assisted bridges, which it is gradually replacing.

In terms of size, audio bridges typically serve 15 to 20 participants, although 50 to 100 can be accommodated. As with face-to-face meetings, the success or failure of an audio teleconference is due in part to the leadership of the moderator.

The moderator's duties are twofold: to assure all participants the opportunity to be heard, and to achieve the objectives of the meeting. Ideally, the objectives are set forth in the agenda, with copies distributed to the participants a few days prior to the meeting.

Arranging an audio teleconference is not difficult. Two approaches are used. In the first, the operator assigned to the bridge contacts the participants; as they respond, each is connected directly into the teleconference. If the bridge is a part of a PBX, the PBX operator acts as the bridge operator.

In the second approach, the participants themselves call the assigned number; as each is identified to the bridge operator, he or she is connected to the teleconference.

In the first instance, the teleconference organizer pays whatever telephone charges are involved; in the second, all participants pay their own long-distance telephone charges.

Organizations which do not have their own dedicated bridge can contract with a bridging network for a nominal per-hour fee. The bridging service provides all the necessary equipment, including speaker phones and microphones, plus the services of the bridge operator.

The bridge operator answers the participants' incoming calls and identifies each caller to the group. The operator may also monitor the meeting if requested to do so, announcing the "arrival" of latecomers to the network, screening uninvited callers from the conference, and urging soft-spoken members to speak up when their voices fail to carry well.

For meetings which do not require the personal presence of the participants, audio teleconferences are an efficient alternative to traditional face-to-face meetings. When the traditional meetings involve travel and hotel costs, audio conferences are also a very cost-effective alternative.

Audiographic Teleconferencing

Audiographic conferences add another dimension to audio conferencing: limited visuals or graphics. For example, electronic blackboards, telewriters, and facsimile machines provide real-time visual interaction between locations to complement the voice transmissions being exchanged.

Electronic Blackboards Diagrams which are written on the surface of the electronic blackboard are automatically digitized, then transmitted via telephone lines to the designated receiving station. There they are reproduced, exactly as written, on the receivers' computer screen. If hard copies are desired, a printer attached to the computer can print copies of the screen graphic.

Telewriters Telewriters are similar to electronic blackboards. The telewriter system uses an electronic table, the surface of which is the size of a standard piece of typing paper. With an electronic pen, the user draws an image on the tablet. The image is digitized, then transmitted via telephone lines to the receiving station where it is reproduced electronically on the screen.

Facsimile Machines The facsimile machine is frequently incorporated into audiographic conferences. The facsimile scans and converts documents into electronic signals, then transmits the signals to a facsimile unit at the receiving station. As the signals are decoded, a hard copy of the original document is reproduced on the receiving facsimile (FAX).

Audio conferencing has become a standard medium of communication in many companies. Its low cost and simple installation make it a feasible alternative to traditional face-to-face meetings. Some companies combine traditional meetings with audio conferencing. They find that the combination of the two increases the effectiveness of their meetings without crippling their budgets.

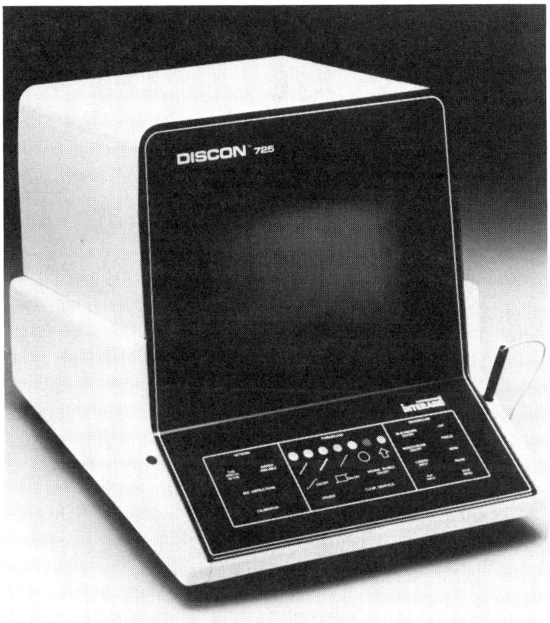

FIGURE 13-4 The DISCON 725 is an integrated teleconferencing system designed for the small conference room or desktop. Images that can be captured by a video camera can be shared by decision makers at remote stations. Touching a stylus to the graphics display, users can also draw directly onto the video image and transmit graphics to viewers. *Courtesy of Interand Corp.*

Computer-based Conferencing

A lesser-known form of electronic conferencing is the computer-based form, also known as *virtual* conferencing. Patterned after electronic mail, computer-based conferencing enables people to communicate with one another at different times in different places via computer networks. Senders and receivers need not be on the system at the same time.

As in electronic mail, conferees in a virtual conference log on when convenient, and the digitized text is transmitted via a computer store-and forward message processing system. Users access the central host computer via a telecommunications network to send or receive messages.

Although virtual conferencing and electronic mail are similar, the two differ in the way they are used. Electronic mail users typically send messages on a one-time basis to *one* intended receiver; the recipient receives and responds to the sender's messages, then opts to save or not to save the message on his or her own system.

In a computer conference, however, messages are saved for the duration of the conference so that *all* participants can share and/or respond as they choose. Conferees do not have to interact simultaneously. Although many individuals in scattered locations interact electronically via the computer, communication takes place only when the participants choose to access the central host computer where the messages are stored. In other words, participants schedule their own participation.

Virtual conferencing provides communications for a fraction of the cost of face-to-face meetings, at least when the persons taking part are widely scat-

FIGURE 13-5 A small-group teleconference in progress. *Courtesy of Colorado Video, Inc.*

tered. It also allows for interim research on complex issues between communications.

Video Conferencing

The most sophisticated and costly of all forms of teleconferencing, video conferencing currently enjoys a higher growth rate than all others. While audio still represents the largest overall segment of the market, the growth of video in the corporate world is characterized as explosive.

In terms of transmission types, three major forms of video conferencing are in use:

Private broadcast: the use of one-way video broadcast presentations to large audiences, with limited interaction.

Video meetings: two-way interactive conferencing, usually between small groups in specially equipped meeting rooms.

Desk-to-desk: two-way interactive video communications between individuals or small groups using desktop terminals.

Private broadcast is used extensively to deliver corporate communiqués or training to employees. News releases or regularly scheduled company programs are made available to employees, either through company-owned installations of satellite networks or through networks leased from communication firms specializing in satellite broadcasts.

Hewlett-Packard, IBM, Kodak, J. C. Penney, TRW, and General Motors are examples of major corporations with private broadcast networks. VSAT (Very Small Aperture Terminals) technology, a recent development in the growth of private networks, is employed by large corporations to transmit data among their branch offices or stores.

For example, thousands of VSATs, or low-cost small earth stations, have been installed by K-Mart and other retail firms to transmit corporate communications, new product announcements, and training for new employees. With modifications added, the terminals can also receive one-way full-motion video.

Video meetings have become an affordable medium since methods of compressing video signals were improved during the 1980s. Compressed signals reduce the data rates required for an acceptable video image, thus reducing the capacity needed to transmit video images and the cost of doing so. Consequently, full-motion video has become a reality for companies of medium to large size.

Video codec equipment, the coder/decoder equipment needed to perform the signal compression, has been reduced in cost from around $250,000 in 1980 to $12,000 or less in 1990. Growth in video meetings is likely to follow as more companies recognize their benefits.

Desk-to-desk video becomes a reality as phone systems are changed from analog to digital technology. An international standard for ISDN (integrated service digital networks) provides 64,000 bits per second to the desktop computer. This is an adequate data rate for bringing limited-motion video and audio to personal computers. Video transmission of limited motion thus becomes feasible for the small screen.

Experiments in desk-to-desk video are being tried in situations formerly considered inappropriate for video applications. For example, job interviews are being conducted via desk-to-desk video technology; corporations conduct initial interviews with job candidates through a college placement network. Following the on-screen interview, companies select the candidates they would like to invite to their headquarters for a face-to-face interview. The screening process thus saves the company time and travel costs by narrowing its employee search to the most likely prospects.

Slow-scan Video

Video conferencing is available in two formats: slow-scan or freeze-frame video, and full-motion video. Slow-scan video transmits still images of the conference participants. The images, taken by a television camera, are digitized by a codec (coder/decoder) which converts an analog signal into a digital signal, then compresses the signal and transmits it over the telephone network to comparable equipment at the receiving location.

At the destination, the signal is reconverted into an image and displayed on a computer terminal equipped for TV-like reception. The viewers receive a series of still images rather than full-motion video.

Freeze-frame technology does not require expensive transmission media.

FIGURE 13-6 Freeze-frame broadcasting allows viewers to study images in detail and to print hard copies of visuals while they remain on screen. *Courtesy of Colorado Video, Inc.*

The narrow bandwidths normally associated with audio transmission are adequate for freeze-frame images as well. Consequently, the cost of transmission is comparable to that of normal audio communications.

To transmit the images, the slow-scan video transmits one image, then retransmits it seconds later, showing only the changes which have occurred since the previous transmission.

While this technology lacks the impact of full-motion video, it is adequate for many applications, and is in fact preferable in some instances to full-motion video. For example, the transmission of charts, graphs, engineers' drawings, and similar materials, one frame at a time, allows viewers to study each frame individually as it comes into view. An additional benefit is that a printer attached to the receiving unit can produce a hard copy of the image as it remains in view on the screen.

Slow-scan video is less complex and less costly than full-motion video. Minimal investment in equipment is required, and a short training period enables users to master its transmission techniques. These two factors add to the appeal of slow-scan video.

As long as potential users perceive no need for full-motion video but do recognize the advantages of video over audio conferencing, the slow-scan or freeze-frame video will retain its position as a viable form of teleconferencing.

Full-motion Video Conferencing

Full-motion video is top-of-the-line conferencing. The most sophisticated, complex, and expensive of all forms of teleconferencing, it is nonetheless the fastest-growing segment of the teleconferencing options. Two forms of transmission exist: one-way and two-way video.

One-way Full-motion Video One-way conferencing transmits both audio and full-motion video signals from a central location to multiple receiving stations. The receiving stations can see and hear the full-motion transmissions from the central location but can only transmit audio, not video, signals back to the central site.

One-way video conferencing, also known as *ad hoc* or *broadcast* conferencing, is often utilized for a single event, rather than on a regular basis; hence, its ad hoc descriptor. Ad hoc conferences are effectively used to assemble widely dispersed persons for impromptu meetings. As with all video conferencing, the economic benefits depend in part on the number of people who are reached through the medium. The more persons served, the more justified the cost.

Non-economic advantages are readily apparent. The ability to reach all interested parties at one time has at least three benefits:

1. The communicated information and related discussion reach all the parties at one time, eliminating the need for repeated communications.
2. Misunderstandings, due to second-hand misinformation to absent parties, is eliminated.
3. Issues needing clarification are discussed and questions are answered during the conference, quelling doubts or misgivings which might otherwise arise.

Ad hoc video conferencing is very effective, especially when the message is urgent. A classic example is the case of the Johnson and Johnson Tylenol scare.

Within hours of the initial news that tampering with the Tylenol products had occurred, a nationwide video conference was underway, with Johnson and Johnson officials explaining their case to the press. In this instance, video conferencing was a powerful force in helping the pharmaceutical firm maintain its customers' loyalty and trust.

Satellite transmission is one of the key components of ad hoc conferencing. Growth in this form of conferencing can be expected as more satellites are launched and the competition among leasing firms escalates, effecting a reduction in service charges.

Two-way Full-motion Video Two-way full-motion video conferencing accommodates both audio and full-motion video signals to and from the distant sites; that is, all parties involved in the conference can be seen as well as heard.

To be truly effective, the conference rooms at each site should be fully equipped with two or three television cameras, special lighting, and large screens. Multiple microphones and speakers, telephone equipment and cables, digitizing and compression equipment, and conference tables and chairs are equally important. Acoustical safeguards, such as heavy draperies and sound-proof interiors, complete the fully-equipped installation.

Cost estimates on fully-equipped installations vary widely, but the digitizing equipment alone may cost tens of thousands of dollars. Furnishing and modifying the dedicated facility can cost thousands more.

The capital investment in dedicated facilities is therefore beyond the means of many organizations. However, costs appear to be leveling off, with equipment costs coming down substantially since dedicated facilities were first introduced. Transmission costs are dropping also. Codecs, which compress the digitized signals for transmission over telephone wires, are down 30% to 50% since 1988.

Nevertheless, the less costly one-way video has outpaced the two-way video since both options were introduced. Observers believe, however, that the disparity between the two forms will lessen, with the two-way form of video conferencing becoming dominant by the mid-1990s.

The Role of Teleconferencing

Teleconferencing has become an accepted form of communication in business. Audio, ad hoc, computer-based, and full-motion video satisfy needs unmet by conventional meetings. Teleconferencing is not meant to replace traditional meetings, however; some situations call for the personal contact of face-to-face meetings. Rather, the role of teleconferencing is to support and complement traditional meetings.

Teleconferencing plays its most significant role by enabling participants from all parts of the globe to meet and converse without leaving their home posts, to see and listen to a renowned speaker otherwise unavailable to them, and to stretch limited budgets by reducing travel expenditures.

Meetings: Summary of Functions

Meetings, whether electronic or conventional, are vital components of business operations. In summary, their principal functions are to:

Keep employees well informed
Keep management in touch with problems and progress within the organization
Maintain the company's competitive position in the market
Help the company remain current with technological advances
Assist company officials in responding to changes in public trends and tastes

SUMMARY

Successful meetings are the result of good organization and effective leadership. Administrative assistants play an important supportive role in planning and implementing them. In some instances, their roles may be more than supportive; they may be asked to preside at meetings on behalf of their superiors.

Serious meeting planners structure meeting plans into three time frames: before, during, and after the meeting, scrutinizing each in the light of the most effective procedures to follow.

Planning large-scale conferences and conventions may be a part of the administrative assistant's responsibilities. On such occasions, he or she can utilize the advisory services of conference centers and convention bureaus, usually provided without charge.

Teleconferencing is a technology which the administrative assistant must come to understand and support. Gaining adherents daily from business and professional organizations, teleconferencing is firmly established as a technology with current and future applications.

Although all forms of teleconferencing show promise of explosive growth, traditional meetings will not necessarily decrease in number or importance. Rather, they may be enhanced with the additional input of renowned speakers who join the real-time meetings via a teleconferencing linkage.

GLOSSARY OF TELECONFERENCING TERMS

Ad hoc video conference: One-way full-motion video conference, usually called for a specific event.

Audio conference: A voice-only teleconference; no visuals.

Codec: A coder/decoder device which converts an analog signal into digital form for transmission, and reconverts it at the signal's destination.

Earth station: The antenna and associated equipment used for transmitting and receiving communications via satellite. Some earth stations transmit and receive; others receive only.

Freeze-frame video: The transmission of sequential video images, usually about 30 seconds apart, to receiving stations of teleconferencing networks. The frames are "frozen" prior to transmission and sent as still pictures. Freeze-frame video is less expensive to transmit than full-motion video images.

Point-to-multipoint video conference: All sites receive video images but only one site can send them. The audio component is usually bidirectional.

Point-to-point video conference: Two sites of a teleconference, each of which is able to transmit as well as receive both audio and video communications.

Teleconference: Electronic meeting transmitted over telephone wires shared with three or more people located at two or more sites.

Video compression: A means of reducing (compressing) the information to be sent over a telecommunication system, in order to reduce the costs of transmission.

Video conference (full motion): A video conference in which full-motion video plus audio are transmitted to the receiving sites. The signal can be one way on video with two-way audio; or two-way for both video and audio signals between sites.

QUESTIONS FOR REVIEW

1. Describe the ideal meeting in terms of at least four factors which typically characterize it.
2. One way of organizing all details of an upcoming meeting is to structure the planning into three time components: before, during, and after the meeting.
   a. What issues must be addressed by the administrative assistant *before* the meeting?
   b. What issues must be addressed *during* the meeting?
   c. What follow-through activity should be taken care of *after* the meeting?
3. If the administrative assistant is asked to make the arrangements for an upcoming corporate convention, what information must be had in order to do a thorough and effective job?
4. Convention bureaus make the meeting planners' work much easier. Explain.

5. Teleconferences provide certain advantages to users which are not available through traditional meetings. Name as many advantages as you can.
6. Name four types of teleconferencing.
7. Briefly describe each of the four types of teleconferencing.
8. What part is played by the "bridge" used in audio conferences?
9. Describe three types of audiographic devices.
10. How does slow-scan differ from full-motion video?
11. What is ad hoc conferencing? How may it be used?
12. What equipment is required for full-motion video conferences?

QUESTIONS FOR DISCUSSION

1. Which of the following do you believe has the most impact on a meeting's effectiveness?
   a. a definitive wrap-up of each agenda item as the discussion closes on each item
   b. beginning and ending the meeting on time as scheduled
   c. following up on assigned projects after the meeting
2. *Convention bureaus are a meeting planner's best friend.* Explain this statement. Should a meeting planner utilize the services of the same convention bureau year after year if the company's annual conference is held in the city of that convention bureau? Why or why not? Defend your position.
3. Some observers predict that before the year 2000, teleconferences will have replaced most, if not all, meetings involving participants' travel to distant points. Economic factors, they say, preclude the heavy expenditure of hotel bills, airfares, and expensive restaurants funded by company budgets, when electronic meetings held on site afford the same benefits.

   Do you agree with the prediction? Employees who have enjoyed the perks of traveling on company expense accounts are the ones most affected by a change to teleconferencing. How do you perceive their reaction to company policy which would eliminate all but emergency travel at company expense?

SUGGESTED ACTIVITIES

1. Ten or more students may select ten major cities in the United States. Then write to the Convention Bureau in each city asking for information on the services they offer to meeting planners bringing a major convention to their city. Do not leave the false impression that you are planning a convention in their city; explain your status as a student working on a project to explore the services of convention bureaus.

   When all letters have been written and the responses received, gather with your fellow students to compare notes. Record the results of your mini-survey in tabular form so that the services of each city's convention bureau may be compared with that of others. Discuss your findings.
2. Use your school library to conduct a periodical research on the current costs of equipping a room to transmit and receive full-motion videoconferencing. Gather pictures from periodicals or other sources on room layout for the conference room.
3. Most computer-based communications relate to electronic mail, not electronic meetings. Explain the difference between electronic mail and electronic meetings, especially with regard to computer-based systems.

REFERENCES

BRACKETT, JOSH, "Computer Conferencing: The Right Choice for Anytime, Anyplace Meetings," *Today's Office* (November 1988), 53–58.

"How to Choose a Meeting Site," *St. Louis Business Journal,* (January 1988), 44.

"How to Plan a Corporate Convention," *St. Louis Business Journal,* (January 1988), 48.

MEEKS, BROCK N., "The Quiet Revolution," *Byte* (February 1987), 183–186.

14 Travel Plans: Domestic and International

INTRODUCTION

In the American economy, travel is an integral component of business operations. In large organizations, a full-time director may head a department devoted entirely to travel for the company. More frequently, the travel function is delegated to an employee who handles the responsibilities part time in conjunction with other duties. The administrative assistant is often assigned this task.

The function of the travel director is to obtain for company travelers the best accommodations possible within the budgetary restraints imposed. In many organizations, business and professional trips extend beyond national boundaries, encompassing international as well as domestic travel.

Domestic travel focuses primarily on booking airline reservations, hotel accommodations, and car rentals. International travel requires a thorough understanding of regulations on import duties imposed by other countries, of procedures for obtaining passports and visas, and of the most expedient way to exchange American dollars for foreign currencies. A well-formulated travel policy spells out the procedures for handling these and other related issues.

Terms in this chapter include:

- business-class fares
- visas
- passports
- The Source
- CompuServe
- letters of credit

DOMESTIC TRAVEL

American businesses spend over $100 billion annually on travel. With the press of inflation, the figure could double by the mid-1990s. Many companies nevertheless view travel as an investment which yields handsome dividends in terms of company growth and expansion. Influential contacts, broader markets, and increased sales are the rewards and motivation for most business travel.

In companies where travel is extensive, management must delegate the travel-related responsibilities to a qualified director. Depending on the extent of travel involved, the director may devote full time or part time to the job.

If the company's operations warrant travel abroad, the director's duties include international as well as domestic travel arrangements. In most instances, however, domestic travel occupies the "lion's share" of the director's time and energy, since twice as many business trips are made to cities within the continental United States as to cities in all foreign countries combined. The travel director, therefore, must be thoroughly schooled in all aspects of domestic travel arrangements.

For example, a routine but serious responsibility of the director is to find suitable hotel accommodations for company travelers, often at a moment's notice, and at a reasonable rate.

Corporate Accounts with Hotels

According to hotel sales personnel, many large corporations fail to establish corporate accounts with the hotels their employees regularly frequent, even though doing so would save them substantial sums.

Through negotiated rates, prearranged accounts with hotels can generate thousands of dollars in annual savings. Studies reveal that the average discount for corporate accounts ranges from 7 percent to 20 percent. The travel director who is concerned with escalating costs should calculate the savings that would result from a negotiated reduction of 10 percent on the company's annual hotel bill.

Booking Hotel Reservations

A directory of toll-free telephone numbers lists all the major hotel and motel chains throughout the country. To reserve a room, the administrative assistant or the travel director dials direct to the number listed and provides the following information to the operator:

1. Name of the hotel to be contacted. (In large cities, multiple hotels of the same chain are often available.)
2. Names of the parties for whom the rooms are being reserved.
3. Date and time of arrival, plus length of planned stay.
4. Size of rooms desired: single, double, or suite.
5. Name of the company to be charged.

6. Name of the convention being attended, if applicable. (Convention rates may apply.)

A written confirmation of the reservation including the cost of the rooms being reserved should be requested. If the hotel has a courtesy car to meet incoming passengers at the airport, the name of the airline, the flight number, and the arrival time of the travelers should be provided to the hotel reservation clerk.

Most hotels now reserve special floors or sections of the hotel for nonsmokers. If any of the travelers request nonsmoking rooms, the reservationist should be informed so that the travelers' preferences can be accommodated.

If travel plans are cancelled, the reservations should be cancelled as promptly as possible and a cancellation number requested from the hotel.

Available by subscription, the *Hotel/Motel Redbook* is a ready reference for regular users of commercial travel. The directory contains the names, addresses, and telephone numbers of the major hotels in major cities, with a description of services provided by each. *The Official Hotel and Resort Guide* and *Leahy's Hotel-Motel Guide* are similar directories.

AIRLINE TRAVEL

Cost Containment

Air travel is one of the major components of travel expense. The cost-conscious administrative assistant or travel director, anxious to stay within budgetary constraints, looks for ways to reduce costs without inconveniencing travelers. The following suggestions come from travel directors of many industries.

When feasible, the company should choose one airline as its official choice for commercial air travel. Volume discount fares may be negotiated with the airline if the company uses its services frequently. If the company does not rate volume discounts regularly, it may still qualify for group rates when several employees travel to a meeting together. Discounts may run as high as 30 percent.

The timing of reservations can also lead to substantial cost reductions. A recent analysis of ticket costs showed that a reservation booked three or more days before travel had a 70 percent probability of being discounted. The discount probability dropped to 30 percent for reservations made two days prior to travel.

Except for company executives, first-class service should be disallowed. Instead, consider business class. It is less expensive than first class and almost as comfortable. Business class is available on international flights, on transcontinental flights of some airlines, and on most flights using widebody planes.

Coping with Delays and Overbookings

Two common complaints of frequent air travelers are late plane arrivals and departures and overbooked passenger flights. The root of the problem is fairly clear. Airline carriers competing for passengers duplicate each other in scheduling flights for prime departure times. During promotion periods, they also offer low fares for prime-time flyers.

Both lures result in congested air traffic which delays arrivals and departures at the airport gates, and overbooked flights which necessitate "bumping" of some passengers. To alleviate the problem, travelers should:

1. Avoid traveling on Friday and Sunday evenings when congestion is high.
2. Avoid rush hours—early morning and early evening.
3. Take carry-on luggage only.
4. Request a boarding pass when making the flight reservation.
5. Arrive at the airport early.

If a flyer is bumped despite having arrived at the gate before check-in time, he or she is entitled to compensation or some type of accommodation by the airline. In some cases when one is forced to make an overnight layover at a city not on his or her itinerary, the airline must pick up the hotel bill. But when the airline is not at fault—for example, if bad weather is the culprit—the airline is not held responsible for delays and need not accommodate inconvenienced travelers. For the sake of good customer relations, however, they usually do accommodate them in some way.

Two publications explaining the rights of airline passengers are available from government agencies:

Fly-Rights: A Guide to Air Travel in the U.S. is available for $1.00 from the Superintendent of Documents, Consumer Information Center, Dept. P-165, Pueblo, Colorado 81009.

Facts & Advice for Airline Passengers costs $2.00 from Aviation Consumer Action Project, P.O. Box 19029, Washington, D.C. 20036.

FIGURE 14-1 Air travel is the transportation of choice of most busy executives. *Courtesy of American Eagle Airlines.*

Reading Airline Timetables

Proficiency in interpreting the airlines' timetables enables users to review the options they have in the flights scheduled for their intended destination and to choose the one they prefer.

Having made their selection, they also save time with the reservations clerk when they call to reserve a seat on that specific flight. (A second choice and perhaps a third should be chosen in case the preferred flight is fully booked.)

Timetables are supplied by the airlines free of charge to the public. Due to fluctuating patterns of passenger traffic, flight times and schedules are subject to frequent change. Therefore, new timetables are published several times a year with the caveat, "subject to change without notice," plainly printed on or near the cover.

In addition to the scheduled flights, the timetable usually includes helpful additional information. For example, excerpts from one airline's timetable are shown at the end of this chapter. Included in the timetable are:

1. An alphabetical listing of the codes used in the timetable and how to interpret them when reading the tables
2. Maps of its airport hubs, designating the terminal name, the gates—by number and concourse—used by the airline
3. The location of the main lobby and ticket counters in the airport.

Reserving a Flight

Prior to calling the travel agent or airline to make a reservation, the administrative assistant should have at hand the following information:

The traveler's departure and return dates

The name of the airline and flight number preferred (if familiar with the airline's latest schedule of flights) or the time of day the traveler prefers to fly

The class of service desired. Basically, three classes are usually available: coach, or economy, class—the least expensive of the three classes; first class which for considerably higher fare offers special amenities, including more comfortable and roomier seating; and business class offered on selected flights for slightly more than coach fare, with amenities similar to first class.

The traveler's preference for the smoking or nonsmoking section and for window or aisle seat

The method of payment to be used. If the company maintains a charge account with the airline, the account number must be provided; if a credit card is to be used, its number plus expiration date must be given. If boarding passes are issued at the time of the reservation, these should be requested also.

If car rental service is desired, the rental agency and type of auto preferred should be specified. The airline representative will relay the information to the rental agency.

Where the ticket is to be obtained: at the airline office, the travel agency, the airport, or via the U.S. Postal Service.

Arranging for Rental Cars

Upon arrival in the destination city, travelers may need to arrange for ground transportation if they will travel extensively in and around the city. Car rental agencies which rim the airport provide this service.

In selecting a dependable rental car, travel consultants make the following suggestions.

Consider first the reputation of the agency for good service and dependable automobiles. The major agencies which advertise nationally have more to lose through poor service than do the regional or local agencies. If you lack information on any other agencies, the majors may offer the closest thing to "satisfaction guaranteed."

If the company maintains an account with a particular rental agency, the traveler may be obliged to use that agency's service. A corporate discount may offset any difference in price between the corporation's agency and the budget agencies' low rates.

Travelers who must monitor expenses closely and who do not enjoy corporate discounts should shop the minor as well as the major agencies for the best price that can be negotiated without sacrificing quality and dependability.

Check insurance coverage. It is unsafe and sometimes illegal to drive a car without minimum liability coverage. Several companies offer no fewer than four different kinds of insurance: the collision damage waiver, liability insurance, personal effects coverage, and personal accident insurance covering medical bills and death benefits.

If the traveler is covered, however, by the company's insurance, additional coverage is not necessary. Also, if one's personal insurance covers collision in a hired or non-owned car, the driver has adequate protection. Renting a car abroad is an exception, however; travel outside the United States requires double-checking for adequate insurance protection.

TRAIN TRAVEL

Amtrak passenger rail service has brought about a reemergence of travel by train. Businesspeople are rediscovering the comfort of traveling at a slower pace. They also appreciate the convenience of boarding from a downtown train station, rather than from a distant airport many miles outside the city. Amtrak's services principally shuttle people between major metropolitan areas located within close proximity of each other, such as Baltimore and Washington, D.C.

Longer train trips have certain advantages as well. The comparatively slow-paced train ride enables executives to catch up on their reading or prepare a presentation while they relax in the comfort of a passenger or lounge car. On some routes they can enjoy a full-course meal; on others, snacks and soft drinks. Upon arrival at the destination stations, they are just a taxi ride away from local hotels.

FIGURE 14-2 Amtrak takes travelers to the "heart" of downtown. *Courtesy of Amtrack.*

East-Midwest Routes

New York/Washington...Pittsburgh...Fort Wayne...**Chicago**

Train Name ►				The Penn-sylvanian	The Broadway Limited	The Capitol Limited		The Capitol Limited	The Broadway Limited	The Penn-sylvanian	The Penn-sylvanian
Train Number ►				47	41	29		30	40	46	246
Days of Operation ►				Daily	Daily	Daily		Daily	Daily	① ExSu	② Suonly
Train Service ►				☕ (403)	Ⓡ ✕	Ⓡ ✕		Ⓡ ✕	Ⓡ ✕	☕ (403)	☕ (403)
	Mile	Symbol	▼	READ DOWN			▲	READ UP			
Connecting Train Number						171/161		642			
(Amtrak)											
New York, NY – Penn. Sta. (ET)	0	🚗	Dp	7 45A	2 25P	1 20P	Ar	4 45P	4 25P	6 52P	9 28P
Newark, NJ – Penn. Sta.	10	♿ 🚗		8 01A	R 2 40P	1 35P		4 27P	D 4 02P	D 6 32P	D 9 09P
Metropark, NJ (G.S. Pkwy. Exit 131A/B)	25			8 14A						6 17P	
New Brunswick, NJ	33	⊘ (80)		8 23A						6 09P	
Princeton Jct., NJ (Princeton (57))	49	⊘ (80)		8 38A						5 57P	
Trenton, NJ	58	♿ 🚗		8 48A	R 3 20P	2 09P		3 45P	D 3 18P	5 45P	8 34P
North Philadelphia, PA	86	⊘		9 11A						5 21P	8 10P
Philadelphia, PA – 30th St. Sta.	91	♿ 🚗	Ar	9 23A	R 3 57P	2 40P	Dp	3 09P	D 2 20P	5 11P	8 01P
Connecting Train Number				168	542				171/161	185	647
Washington, DC – Union Sta. (ET)	0	♿ 🚗	Dp	6 20A	1 20P	5 55P	Ar	12 52P	4 39P	7 33P	9 50P
Baltimore, MD – Penn Sta.	40	⊘ ♿ 🚗		6 58A	1 58P				3 48P	6 45P	9 05P
Philadelphia, PA – 30th St. Sta.	135	♿ 🚗	Ar	8 11A	3 09P		Dp		2 40P	5 37P	7 53P
Philadelphia, PA – 30th St. Sta.	91	♿ 🚗	Dp	9 45A	R 4 20P		Ar		D 2 20P	4 47P	7 36P
Ardmore, PA	99	•		(78) 9 58A						(78) 4 33P	(78) 7 23P
Paoli, PA	110	⊘		(78) 10 13A	(46) 4 46P				D 1 52P	(78) 4 20P	(78) 7 10P
Downingtown, PA	122	⊘		10 26A						4 06P	6 56P
Lancaster, PA	158	♿ 🚗		10 58A	(46) 5 28P				(47) 1 09P	3 33P	6 23P
Harrisburg, PA	195	♿ 🚗	Ar	11 38A	(46) 6 10P		Dp		(47) 12 30P	2 55P	5 45P
(Conrail)											
Harrisburg, PA	195	♿ 🚗	Dp	11 39A	(46) 6 20P		Ar		(47) 12 22P	2 54P	5 44P
Lewistown, PA	256	•		12 59P	7 28P				11 10A	1 42P	4 32P
Huntingdon, PA	292	•		1 37P	8 07P				10 30A	1 04P	3 54P
Tyrone, PA	312	•		2 05P						12 37P	3 27P
Altoona, PA	326	♿		2 22P	8 52P				9 43A	12 16P	3 06P
Johnstown, PA	365	♿		3 21P	9 56P				8 41A	11 16A	2 06P
Latrobe, PA	402	•		4 06P						10 31A	1 21P
Greensburg, PA	412	•		4 15P	10 49P				7 46A	10 20A	1 10P
(CSX)											
Rockville, MD	17	•				6 17P		12 10P			
Harpers Ferry, WV	56	•				6 59P		11 28A			
Martinsburg, WV	74	•				7 21P		11 06A			
Cumberland, MD	147	•				9 01P		·9 41A			
Connellsville, PA	238	•				11 16P		7 06A			
McKeesport, PA	282	• ♿				12 15A		6 05A			
(Conrail)											
Pittsburgh, PA – Amtrak Sta.	443	♿	Ar	4 59P	11 37P	1 12A	Dp	5 35A	7 02A	9 40A	12 30P
			Dp		11 52P	1 27A	Ar	5 17A	6 47A		
Canton–Akron, OH	545	♿			1 56A	3 31A		3 02A	4 32A		
Crestline–Mansfield, OH	632	• ♿			3 45A	5 20A		1 22A	2 52A		
Lima, OH	704	♿			5 02A	6 37A		11 59P	1 29A		
Fort Wayne, IN	763	♿			(63) 6 14A	(63) 7 49A		(63) 10 58P	(63) 12 28A		
Warsaw, IN (ET)	802	• ♿			(63) 6 53A	(63) 8 28A		(63) 10 07P	(63) 11 37P		
Valparaiso, IN (CT)	867	• ♿			(52) 6 56A	(52) 8 31A		(52) 8 02P	(52) 9 32P		
Hammond-Whiting, IN	896	♿			(52) 7 31A	(52) 9 06A		(52) 7 27P	(52) 8 57P		
Chicago, IL – Union Sta. (CT)	911	♿ 🚗	Ar		8 22A	9 57A	Dp	7 00P	8 30P		

Amtrak Thruway Bus Connection—Chicago, IL/Rockford, IL... Madison, WI

Connecting Train Number	Mile	Symbol			41	29/51		30	40/50		
Chicago, IL (CT)	0	🚗	Dp		9 45A	12 15P	Ar	4 10P	7 40P		
Rockford, IL	85	•	Ar		12 10P	2 40P	Dp	2 10P	5 20P		
Madison, WI (CT)	140	•	Ar		2 10P	4 40P	Dp	12 01P	3 10P		

FIGURE 14–3 Train schedule for east-midwest routes. *Courtesy of Amtrak.*

To read the Amtrak timetable in Figure 14–3, follow the down arrow to read the "enroute to" cities; and the up arrow for the return trip.

INTERNATIONAL TRAVEL

International travel arrangements mirror those of domestic arrangements insofar as airline reservations are concerned. As for hotel reservations, if neither the travel director nor the traveler is familiar with the country being visited, a travel agency should be employed to make the reservations.

Other travel preparations distinguish international from domestic travel, however. Visas, passports, customs regulations, and exchange of American dollars for foreign currency are major considerations when preparing for a trip outside the United States.

Passports

According to the U.S. Bureau of Consular Affairs, United States citizens need passports to depart or enter the United States and to enter most foreign countries. Exceptions include short-term travel between the United States and Mexico and Canada.

For many Caribbean countries a birth certificate or voter registration card is acceptable proof of U.S. citizenship. However, a valid U.S. passport is the best travel documentation available and, with appropriate visas, is acceptable in all countries.

The demand for passports becomes heavy in January and begins to decline in August each year. However, after those months, periods of high demand for passports can occur. The State Department therefore suggests that travelers apply several months in advance of planned departure dates whenever possible. If visas are needed also, allow additional time.

In applying for a passport for the first time, the applicant must complete and present in person the Passport Application, Form DSP-11, at one of the federal passport agencies or at one of the several thousand federal or state courts or the U.S. post offices authorized to accept passport applications.

Documentation required to obtain a passport is the completed DSP-11 form plus proof of U.S. citizenship. Acceptable proof of citizenship is a certified copy of one's birth certificate, obtainable from the Bureau of Vital Statistics in the state of one's birth.

If the birth certificate is not available, the "best secondary evidence possible" is required. This may include a baptismal certificate, a hospital birth record, or other documentary evidence such as family Bible records, newspaper files, and insurance papers.

Persons applying must also give proof of their own identity. A valid driver's license or a government (federal, state, municipal) identification card are acceptable documentation. A social security card is *not* acceptable. A 2-inch × 2-inch recent photograph, in black and white or color, must also be presented. As of 1990, the charge for a ten-year passport was $42.00.

Visas

Visas are endorsements or stamps placed in the passport by a foreign government, permitting the person to visit that country for a specified purpose and a limited time; for example, a three-month tourist visa.

In most instances, the traveler must obtain necessary visas before leaving the United States. Passport agencies cannot issue visas, but the embassies or consulates of the countries to be visited do.

Many travel agencies keep a supply of visa applications on hand for the more popular destinations. Once the application is completed, travelers should send it to the embassies, along with the passport, a self-addressed envelope, and the consular fee ($10 to $20). Some embassies also require a photo and a copy of an airline ticket.

A publication of the Bureau of Consular Affairs lists the entry requirements for U.S. citizens traveling to most foreign countries and where and how to apply for visas and tourist cards. Although the publication is updated annually, the bureau suggests that travelers verify the latest visa requirements with the appropriate embassies.

In major cities where embassies and consulates are located, visa service companies are in operation to help travelers get visas quickly. For a fee, couriers from the visa companies make daily rounds of the embassies and, in some cases, are able to obtain visas on the spot. The average cost is $30 per visa, plus consular fees.

This individualized service is especially valuable when multiple visas must be obtained. Without the visa service company, the traveler would have to submit a passport, then wait for a visa to be issued. When the first visa was received, the traveler would then send the passport to the next embassy on the list and wait for the visa again. Depending on the number of visas needed, the process could take several weeks to complete.

Business travelers often turn to visa service companies because of stringent entry requirements. Whether they deal with a service company or apply directly to the foreign consulate for their visas, authorities suggest they apply well in advance of their scheduled departures.

Immunizations

Under the international health regulations adopted by the World Health Organization, a country may require international certificates of vaccination against yellow fever and cholera. It is not necessary to be vaccinated against a disease to which the traveler will not be exposed, and few countries refuse to admit travelers who have no proof of the necessary vaccinations. However, it is wise to check requirements before departing the United States.

An increasing number of countries are establishing regulations regarding AIDS testing, particularly for long-term residents and students. Checking with embassies or consulates will provide current information on AIDS and other communicable diseases. No immunizations are required to return to the United States.

Customs

Foreign-made personal articles brought from abroad are subject to duty and tax unless the traveler has acceptable proof of prior possession. Documents such as a bill of sale, insurance policy, jeweler's appraisal, or receipt for purchase may be considered reasonable proof of prior possession.

Watches, cameras, tape recorders, and similar articles which may be readily identified by serial number or permanently affixed markings may be taken to the customs office at the port of departure for registration before leaving the United States. The certificate of registration provided will expedite free entry of the items when the traveler returns.

DEPARTMENT OF THE TREASURY
UNITED STATES CUSTOMS SERVICE

CUSTOMS DECLARATION

PRESENT TO THE IMMIGRATION AND CUSTOMS INSPECTORS

FORM APPROVED OMB NO. 48-R0386

EACH ARRIVING TRAVELER OR HEAD OF A FAMILY MUST WRITE IN THE FOLLOWING INFORMATION. PLEASE PRINT

1. FAMILY NAME	GIVEN NAME	MIDDLE INITIAL

2. DATE OF BIRTH *(Mo./Day/Yr.)*	3. VESSEL, OR AIRLINE & FLT. NO.
4. CITIZEN OF *(Country)*	5. RESIDENT OF *(Country)*

6. PERMANENT ADDRESS

7. ADDRESS WHILE IN THE UNITED STATES

8. NAME AND RELATIONSHIP OF ACCOMPANYING FAMILY MEMBERS

9. Are you or anyone in your party carrying any fruits, plants, meats, other plant or animal products, birds, snails, or other live organisms of any kind?	☐ YES	☐ NO
10. Have you or anyone in your party been on a farm or ranch outside the U.S.A. in the last 30 days?	☐ YES	☐ NO
11. Are you or any family member carrying over $5000.00 (or the equivalent value in any currency) in monetary instruments such as coin, currency, traveler's checks, money orders, or negotiable instruments in bearer form? *(If yes, you must file a report on Form 4790, as required by law.)* Note: It is not illegal to transport over $5000 in monetary instruments; however, it must be reported.	☐ YES	☐ NO

12. *I certify that I have declared all items acquired abroad as required herein and that all oral and written statements which I have made are true, correct and complete.*

SIGNATURE:

NON-CITIZENS ONLY >	13. U.S. VISA ISSUED AT *(Place)*	14. VISA DATE *(Mo./Day/Yr.)*

The laws of the United States require that you **declare ALL articles acquired abroad** *(whether worn or used, whether dutiable or not, and whether obtained by purchase, as a gift, or otherwise)* which are in your or your family's possession at the time of arrival. **Repairs made abroad also must be declared.**

Nonresidents may make an oral declaration. **Returning Residents** may make an oral declaration if the total price of articles declared *(price actually paid or, if not purchased, fair retail price in country where obtained)* is not more than the sum of $300 per person. Otherwise **You Must List In Writing On The Reverse Of This Form All Articles And Repairs Acquired Abroad Which You Are Now Bringing Through Customs.** *(See additional instructions on reverse.)* If you are arriving *(directly or indirectly)* from American Samoa, Guam, or the U.S. Virgin Islands and are having articles sent from these possessions, you must list **ALL acquired articles** *(accompanied and unaccompanied).*

All your baggage *(including handbags and hand-carried parcels)* may be examined. **False Statements Made To A Customs Officer Are Punishable By Law.** Consult "U.S. Customs Hints" and your inspector for full information.

INSPECTORS' USE ONLY

STAMP NOS.	
NO. PCS BAGGAGE EXMD.	TIME COMPLETED
INSPECTOR	
DATE	BADGE NO.

CUSTOMS FORM 6059-B (11-24-78)

FIGURE 14-4 Sample customs declaration form. Used to declare articles purchased while abroad.

Driver's Licenses and Permits

If the traveler plans to rent a car while abroad, a driver's license or permit will be necessary. Some countries do not recognize a U.S. driver's license; however, most countries accept an international driver's license. One can be obtained at the local office of an automobile association. Applicants must present two passport-size photographs and a valid U.S. driver's license.

Certain countries also require road permits in lieu of tolls for using their divided highways. Fines may be levied on drivers who have no permit. A check with the appropriate embassies before departure from the Unites States is recommended.

Return Transportation

The traveler should reconfirm his or her return reservation with the airlines at least 72 hours before departure. The State Department recommends that, whenever possible, the confirmation be in writing. If the confirmation is done by telephone, the traveler should record the time, day, and the agent's name who took the call.

Reconfirming the reservation is a precaution; a traveler whose name does not appear on the reservations list has little recourse in asserting his or her rights and may very well be stranded.

Train Travel

Rail service in European countries is fairly extensive. Train passengers must care for their own luggage; therefore, traveling "light" with no more than two bags is recommended. Sleeping accommodations are available on some of the routes but only to persons who hold reservations. Since the number of sleeping cars is limited, early reservations should be made. A Eurail pass entitles passengers to first-class travel through 16 countries. Travelers who wish to purchase one must do so prior to leaving the United States. The passes are available at Amtrak stations.

Insurance

Persons traveling out of the country should have adequate medical protection in case of a serious illness or injury. Short-term medical and hospital insurance for coverage abroad can usually be procured from the company's regular insurance carrier at reasonable rates.

Travel Funds and Foreign Currency

Before leaving for a trip abroad, the traveler may want to obtain foreign currency for each of the countries to be visited. For around $10.00, the travel direc-

FIGURE 14-5 Eurail passes accommodate foreign visitors to most of the European sector. Tickets must be purchased prior to leaving the United States.

tor can order packets of foreign currency through a travel agency or bank. Before purchasing large sums, however, the latest exchange rate for that currency should be checked with a local bank or broker.

When abroad, the traveler can exchange dollars for the local currency as needed. Because banks allow the most favorable rates of exchange, they should be the traveler's primary source of funds; usually, banks charge no commission for the purchase of local currencies.

If the traveler needs cash during off-hours or Sundays when the banks are closed, he or she can tap one of the automated teller machines (ATMs) located throughout the world. The machines dispense local currency at the most favorable exchange rate—the wholesale rate used in interbank transactions. Typically, the ATMs provide operating instructions in both English and the local language. Limits and fees vary with each bank, but a charge of 75 cents to $1.50 for each withdrawal is common.

Visa cards, MasterCards, and cash or credit cards issued by U.S. banks access the ATMs in different parts of the world; some ATMs accommodate Visa only; others, MasterCard only; and fewer yet accept bank cards. To be on the safe side, travelers should have more than one of the three types of cards with them at all times. The traveler's personal identification number (PIN) should be jotted down before departure from the United States, in case such withdrawals become necessary.

Traveler's checks are good insurance against theft. Sold in denominations

FOREIGN CURRENCY UNITS

When you buy or sell products or services in the United States, you use U.S. currency, namely dollars, or some fraction of dollars in the form of coins. On the other hand, when you buy or sell products in foreign countries, you must use their money—the currency of the country with which you are conducting business.

The following is a list of selected countries and the names of their currency units.

COUNTRY	CURRENCY UNIT
Australia	dollar
Austria	schilling
Bahamas	dollar
Belgium	franc
Canada	dollar
China, P.R.	yuan
Denmark	krone
France	franc
Germany, F.R.	deutsche mark
Greece	drachma
Hong Kong	dollar
India	rupee
Ireland	pound
Italy	lira
Japan	yen
Korea, Rep. of	won
Malaysia	ringgit
Mexico	peso
Netherlands	guilder
New Zealand	dollar
Norway	krone
Portugal	escudo
Saudi Arabia	riyal
Singapore	dollar
South Africa	rand
Spain	peseta
Sri Lanka	rupee
Sweden	krona
Switzerland	franc
Thailand	baht
United Kingdom	pound
USSR	ruble

FIGURE 14-6 Selected countries and the names of their currency units. *Courtesy of Federal Reserve Bank of Richmond.*

of \$10, \$20, \$50, \$100 and \$500, they are issued solely to the persons who purchase them. The traveler should keep with him or her at all times (preferably *not* in a wallet), a list of the checks issued, by number and amount, in case any are lost or stolen. A duplicate list should be left at the company office.

Money orders are sold by banks, post offices, express companies, and telegraph offices; their primary purpose is to provide ready cash as needed by travelers. American Express cardholders can obtain a special PIN number to buy traveler's checks. This number and an American Express card are used to obtain up to $500 in American Express traveler's checks from ATMs throughout the world.

The credit cards, including MasterCard, American Express, Visa, and Diner's Club, permit holders to charge practically any service or goods to a personal or company charge account. For reimbursement purposes, printed records of the charges should be kept; these will be needed to validate expenses upon the traveler's return.

If the traveler will need substantial sums of money while abroad, a letter of credit may be obtained from a local bank prior to leaving the country. The letter, addressed to a foreign-city bank, permits the user to withdraw funds from that bank when or if necessary. The amount that can be withdrawn is limited to the amount stated in the letter of credit.

Safety Abroad

The Bureau of Consular Affairs issues several publications dealing with travel to other countries, including one on how to enjoy a *safe* trip abroad. Publication 9493 from the bureau is intended to narrow the chances of an unhappy *incident* while abroad. Its suggestions are divided into four parts: before you go; precautions while traveling; protection against terrorism; and assistance abroad.

Before You Go

Learn about the places you plan to visit. Familiarize yourself with local laws and customs in those areas.

Lock your luggage and put your name and address inside each piece.

Don't take anything you would hate to lose. Leave at home all unnecessary credit cards, expensive jewelry, or irreplaceable family objects.

Photocopy your airline ticket, passport, driver's license, and credit cards you take with you. Leave one set at home and keep another with you in a separate place from these valuables.

Leave a copy of the serial numbers of your traveler's checks at home; take another with you separate from the checks themselves and, as you cash in the checks, keep a tally of which ones remain unredeemed.

Leave a copy of your itinerary with family or friends at home should they need to contact you in an emergency.

Find out from your credit card company what your credit limit is and be sure not to exceed that amount on your trip. Americans have been arrested in some countries for innocently exceeding their limit.

Precautions While Traveling

Carry traveler's checks instead of cash. Don't flash large amounts of money when paying bills. Only countersign traveler's checks in front of the person who will cash them and be sure your credit card is returned to you after each transaction.

Get a claim check for each piece of luggage you check. Don't leave your bags unattended in public. (Traveling light will help.)

Keep hotel and car keys on your person.

If any of your possessions are lost or stolen, report the loss immediately to the police. Keep a copy of the police report for insurance claims and as an explanation of your plight.

Also report the loss of traveler's checks to the nearest office of the issuing company; airline tickets to the airline company or travel agent; and passport to the nearest U.S. Embassy or consulate.

Keep a low profile. Dress and behave conservatively.

Try not to travel alone at night. Let someone know when you expect to return, especially if out late at night.

Keep your hotel door locked at all times. Meet visitors in the lobby.

If possible, book a room between the second and seventh floors—above ground level to prevent easy entrance from outside and low enough for fire equipment to reach.

Make a note of emergency telephone numbers you may need. Learn a few phrases in the local language so you can signal your need for help, the police, or a doctor.

Protection Against Terrorism

Schedule direct flights if possible.

Minimize the time spent in the public area of an airport. Move quickly from the check-in counter to the secured areas.

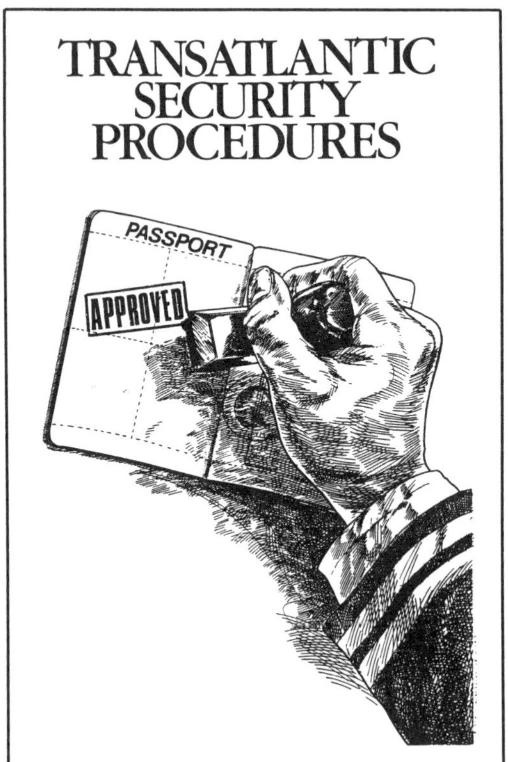

FIGURE 14-7 Security precautions must be taken when traveling abroad. *Courtesy of American Airlines.*

In High-risk Areas

Register with the U.S. Embassy on arrival.

Leave no personal or business papers in your hotel room.

Make a mental note of safe havens, such as police stations, hotels, and hospitals.

Report any suspicious activity to local police and the nearest U.S. Embassy or consulate.

Don't take a cab which is not clearly identified as a taxi. Select your own cabs at random.

If possible, travel with others.

Assistance Abroad

U.S. consular officers are located at U.S. embassies and consulates in most countries abroad. Officers can advise you of any adverse conditions in the places you are visiting and can help you in emergencies.

The embassy will facilitate the issuance of a new passport should yours be lost or stolen.

Should you find yourself in any legal difficulty, contact a consular officer immediately. They can provide lists of local attorneys and help you find legal representation.

If you become destitute overseas, consular officers can help you get in touch with your family, friends, bank, or employer and inform them how to wire funds to you.

A list of key officers and addresses for all U.S. embassies and consulates abroad is published and updated three times a year. A single copy may be ordered for $4.25 from the Superintendent of Documents, Washington, DC 20402.

A list of passport agencies in key cities of the United States follows.

Passport Agencies

Boston Passport Agency
Room E123, John F. Kennedy Bldg.
Government Center
Boston, Massachusetts 02203-0123
Recording: 617-565-3934-7
Public Inquiries: 617-565-3930-3

Chicago Passport Agency
Suite 380, Kluczynski Federal Bldg.
230 South Dearborn Street
Chicago, Illinois 60604-1564
Recording: 312-353-5426
Public Inquiries: 312-353-7155

Honolulu Passport Agency
Room C-106, New Federal Bldg.
300 Ala Moana Blvd.
P.O. Box 50185
Honolulu, Hawaii 96850
Recording: 808-541-1919
Public Inquiries: 808-541-1918, 1920

Houston Passport Agency
One Allen Center
500 Dallas Street
Houston, Texas 77002-4874
Recording: 713-229-3607
Public Inquiries: 713-229-3600

Los Angeles Passport Agency
Room 13100, 11000 Wilshire Boulevard
Los Angeles, California 90024-3614
Recording: 213-209-7070
Public Inquiries: 213-209-7075

Miami Passport Agency
16th Floor, Federal Office Bldg.
51 Southwest First Avenue
Miami, Florida 33130-1680
Recording: 305-536-5395
Public Inquiries: 305-536-4681-3

New Orleans Passport Agency
Postal Services Building
Room T-12005
701 Loyola Avenue
New Orleans, Louisiana 70013-1931
Recording: 504-589-6728, 29
Public Inquiries: 504-589-6161-3

New York Passport Agency
Room 270, Rockefeller Center
630 Fifth Avenue
New York, New York 10111-0031
Recording: 212-541-7700-7709
Public Inquiries: 212-541-7710, 7719

Philadelphia Passport Agency
Room 4426, Federal Bldg.
600 Arch Street
Philadelphia, Pennsylvania 19106-1684
Recording: 215-597-7482
Public Inquiries: 215-597-7480, 7481, 7486, 7487

San Francisco Passport Agency
Suite 200, 525 Market Street
San Francisco, California 94105-2773
Recording: 415-974-7972
Public Inquiries: 415-974-9941-9948

Seattle Passport Agency
Room 992, Federal Office Bldg.
915 Second Avenue
Seattle, Washington 98174-1091
Recording: 206-442-7941-3
Public Inquiries: 206-442-7945-7

Stamford Passport Agency
One Landmark Square
Street Level
Stamford, Connecticut 06901-2767
Recording: 203-325-4401-3
Public Inquiries: 203-325-3538, 3539, 3530

TRAVEL-RELATED RESPONSIBILITIES

A corporation which logs thousands of miles annually in the course of normal business operations exacts more of its travel staff than hotel reservations and airline ticket purchases. The administrative assistant or the travel director may be expected to:

complete itinerary forms for employee travelers, furnishing copies to the travelers, their supervisors, and the travel department

review expense accounts of returned travelers, approving for reimbursement those expenditures which fall within the guidelines set by company policy

assist in the development of a travel policy and implement it with fairness and consistency among company travelers

utilize professional assistance when necessary; e.g., drawing on the expertise of travel agencies and their on-line information on air fares and flight schedules

evaluate current electronic procedures in managing travel functions; for example, the cost, convenience, and financial benefits (if any) of subscribing to an on-line travel information service

Travel Itineraries

A travel itinerary consists of two types of information: a day-by-day appointment schedule, and travel information (flights scheduled and hotel accommodations reserved).

Having scheduled the flights and made the hotel reservations for each traveler, the travel director will have little difficulty in drawing up an itinerary

EISOR CORPORATION
Tulsa, Oklahoma

Travel Itinerary—Ralph Redman
January 17–19, 1991

Thursday, January 17

10:30 A.M.	Depart Tulsa International Airport American Airlines Flt #346.
11:50 A.M.	Arrive Chicago, O'Hare Accommodation: Palmer House Hotel
2:30 P.M.	Appointment: Thomas Hays, President Hays & Owen Manufacturing Company
6:30 P.M.	Dinner with Hal Gearhart (Telephone to confirm: 555-3412)

Friday, January 18

10:15 A.M.	Appointment: Harry Knorr (Confirm with secretary: 555-2390)
12:30 P.M.	Lunch with Attorney Harry James James & John, Attorneys-at-Law Meet in lobby of Palmer House (Review real estate papers)
3:30 P.M.	Conference with Geraldine Paxton, broker Paxton and Adams, Inc. (Discuss stock split, company shares)
7:00 P.M. (approx.)	Dinner at home of sister, Jane (Call her for transportation)

Saturday, January 19

11:45 A.M.	Depart Chicago, American Airlines, Flt 367 (Luncheon flight)
1:15 P.M.	Arrive Tulsa

Sample Itinerary

of this travel information. Drawing up an appointment schedule for each day is more challenging. The challenge lies in collecting all the information on scheduled appointments in each city—from the traveler or his or her supervisor—then verifying the information with the travelers before they depart. A sample itinerary is shown on p. 321.

Expense Reports

Upon the traveler's return, an expense report must be filed; otherwise, the traveler will not be reimbursed for dollars spent on company-related business. Forms are usually provided for these reports, with columnar headings matched to the types of expenses usually incurred.

Some companies give their employees a per diem allowance; that is, a designated amount of dollars per day for meals. This policy has at least two advantages; it gives each traveler a fair allowance while it discourages exorbitant spending, and it eliminates the need for continual recording of expenses for each meal eaten. To calculate reimbursement for meals, the traveler has only to report the number of days traveled.

To facilitate the preparation of the expense report, the traveler should retain copies of the hotel bills and the airline tickets used, plus receipts for any other expenditures needing documentation for reimbursement. With all the information at hand, a secretary usually completes the expense report form and passes it on to the traveler for signature.

The travel director, having confirmed that all claimed expenditures are valid, signs his or her approval. A check for the reimbursement due is then drawn up and presented to the traveler.

Using a Corporate Travel Service

In lieu of a travel director or a travel department, many large corporations now employ a corporate travel service to manage all of their travel arrangements. A corporate travel service offers several benefits to its clients. For example, employees at the travel service are professional persons who know the travel field well and can execute requests for reservations quickly and efficiently; and the travel service offers computerized travel information as well as on-line reservations.

Agency officials suggest that when looking for a corporate travel service, companies get references from personal travelers and from other corporations using the agencies. They suggest, too, that companies explain the extent of their air travel and hotel usage when they approach agencies to take their accounts. Honest negotiations can only take place when both parties are aware of the others' needs and capacities.

Agency officials also suggest contacting the American Society of Travel Agents. ASTA does not rank agencies, but can tell if an agent has been reported for unethical behavior. Some agencies provide corporate clients with periodic man-

FIGURE 14-8 Travel agencies book hotel reservations, reserve rental cars, and provide on-line flight information, at no fee to users.

agement reports. The reports list the financial details of trips made by each company employee, including the cost of the airline ticket, the name and price of the hotel used, the car rental agency used, and the make and size of car rented.

These reports enable management to adjust the travel budget as needed and to compare costs of various airlines, hotels, and car rental agencies. They can also be used as negotiating tools to get special rates from all three.

When business travel is very extensive, the use of a corporate travel service may be the answer for large companies. Maximizing the travel dollar may require professionals, fully devoted to the travel profession, to get the highest return on the dollars invested

On-line Travel Services

In lieu of operating a full-time travel department or contracting with a corporate travel service to handle its travel operations, businesses have a third option: the use of a computer-based information retrieval network which incorporates a travel division in its catalog of available services.

An electronic information service focused on travel can be administered by fewer persons than traditional travel departments because most of the work is done by the computer and its tapped information base. Many national networks offer their subscribers travel information, as well as financial forecasts and news commentaries.

CompuServe, Genie, Prodigy, The Source, Dow Jones News/Retrieval, Delphi, and Dialog Business Connection are some of the leading information networks which provide electronic versions of Dun and Bradstreet's *Official Airline Guide* (OAG).

Users can view on the computer screen up-to-date listings of domestic air fares and flight schedules. Several networks offer even more, including online travel agencies to handle surface travel and electronic ticketing. For example, CompuServe and The Source offer these travel services.

CompuServe Through its *Travelshopper,* CompuServe enables users to access TWA's airline reservation service to check and book flights, select seat preferences, and arrange for tickets to be mailed, issued by travel agents, or held for pickup.

The *Official Airline Guide, Electronic Edition* offers schedules for over 1.5 million direct and connecting flights worldwide; it includes dates, times, fares, and aircraft type. The user can make reservations on any airline through Thomas Cook Travel.

CompuServe's *A–Z Worldwide Hotel Guide* lists accommodations at 27,000 hotels worldwide; its "Travelvision" gives highway directories for automotive travel throughout the United States, Mexico, and Canada.

The *Visa Advisors Service* provides information required for entry to most foreign countries; and the *Department of State Advisories* reviews travel conditions abroad—hotel shortages, political unrest, and a list of embassy addresses.

The Source Like CompuServe, The Source electronically projects information from the *Official Airline Guide* on screen, plus national and international hotel listings. Reservations can be booked through Thomas Cook Travel.

The Source also provides the star-rating system of Mobil Oil Corporation for 16,000 hotel accommodations in the United States and Canada, plus the star-rating system of the *Mobil Restaurant Guide* for restaurants in 1,600 U.S. and Canadian cities.

Accu-Weather describes weather conditions and forecasts, including the condition of regional highways during the winter months. For international travelers, *Currency* provides daily closing spot exchange rates for 35 currencies.

To access these information retrieval services, the company must subscribe to the service, paying an annual or usage fee, the amount depending on the length of usage time. Equipment needed is a computer, a telephone, a modem to hook the computer to the telephone, and communications software.

Information Retrieval Services: A Select Few

Bibliographic Retrieval Services
1200 Rte. 7
Latham, NY 12110
(518) 783-1161

CompuServe, Inc.
5000 Arlington Centre Blvd.
P.O. Box 20212
Columbus, OH 43220
(800) 848-8199

Dialog Information Services, Inc.
3460 Hillview Ave.
Palo Alto, CA 94304
(800) 3 DIALOG

Orbit Search Service
8000 Westpark Dr.
McLean, VA 22102
(800) 421-7229

Dow Jones News/Retrieval
P.O. Box 300
Princeton, NJ 08540
(800) 257-5114

The Source
1616 Anderson Rd.
McLean, VA 22102
(800) 336-3366

The Travel Director

When a company maintains an in-house travel department, the role of the travel director is obvious. As department head, the full responsibilities of company travel rest on his or her shoulders. When the company is small and the amount of business travel does not warrant a full-time director, however, the responsibilities are delegated on a part-time basis to another employee. As stated earlier, that person is often the administrative assistant.

To carry out travel tasks efficiently while continuing to shoulder other responsibilities, the administrative assistant must develop a set of job guidelines. Drawn up with the approval and assistance of company officials, the guidelines describe explicitly the boundaries of the travel-related duties and responsibilities.

Typically, travel directors act as liaisons between the company and its travel agencies, interpret the company's travel policy when issues are in need of clarification, negotiate discounts with hotels and rental car agencies, and keep track of changes in the travel industry which may impact on the company's travel budget.

Travel Policy

A well-formulated travel policy provides guidelines which cover who and under what circumstances persons can fly first class or business class, limitations on meal expenses, documentation required for expenses incurred, requirements for specific prior approvals of certain travel arrangements, and restrictions on how many key personnel can fly on the same plane.

Travel policies should have as a major objective that of accommodating the travelers. For example, first-class fare on a "red-eye" (late night) flight from coast to coast is often the same as coach fare on a daytime flight. Therefore, if a traveler prefers to make a return trip earlier than planned, flying more luxuriously on the first class "red-eye," the travel policy should be flexible enough to accommodate this request.

Although a travel policy requires top management's participation, no policy should be formulated without input from the employees, especially the frequent travelers who will be most impacted by its provisions when the policy is put into effect. Without such input, management may find it difficult to put a new or revised policy into effect, especially if it differs substantially from long-established practices of the past.

Using this timetable:

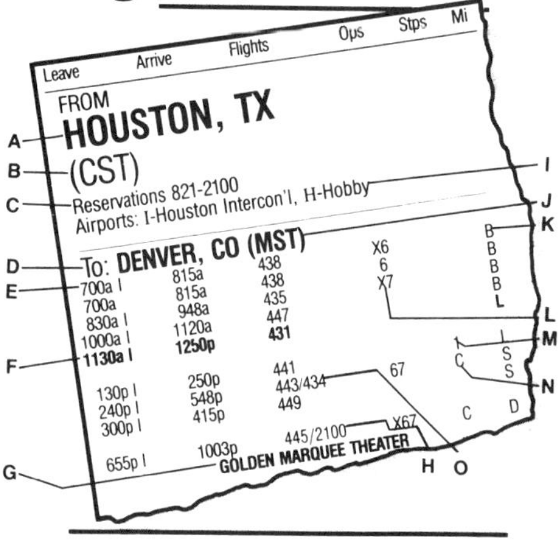

(The above is for reference only — it is not an actual schedule)

A Originating City.
B Time zone in originating city.
C Reservations phone number.
D Destination City.
E Leave: departure time from originating city shown in local time.
F Wide body 747, DC-10 or Airbus on at least one segment indicated by boldface type.
G Flights designated with GOLDEN MARQUEE THEATRE will show a first run feature film on at least one segment in all cabins of service. Coach passengers traveling within the U.S. will be charged a $4.00 headset rental fee.
H *Flight Number ranges listed below indicate a Continental code shared flight operated by the carrier reflected.
- 950-967, 970-997, 3300-3399—Express/Britt—Continental Airlines/Air Micronesia
- 2000-2499—Continental Express/Rocky Mountain
- 2500-2799, 3000-3025, 4400-4999—Continental Express/Britt Airways
- 3200-3299—Southern Jersey Airways
- *3400-3599, 3650-3999 3600-3649 Continental Express/Bar Harbor City Express
- 8900-8949—Continental/SAS-Scandinavian Airlines System

I Airport symbol: when more than one airport serves the same city or area.
J Time zone in destination city.
K Meal Service—
- **B** Breakfast
- **L** Lunch
- **D** Dinner
- **S** Snack

L Days of Operations
- **X** Except
- **1** Monday
- **2** Tuesday
- **3** Wednesday
- **4** Thursday
- **5** Friday
- **6** Saturday
- **7** Sunday

M Number of intermediate stops on a direct flight.
N Indicates one or more connecting flights.
O / indicates a change of plane and flight number.

Schedules in this timetable are subject to change without notice.

CONTINENTAL AIRLINES

FROM **ACAPULCO, MEXICO** (CST)
Reservations 4-69-00

To	Lv	Ar	Flts	Ops	Stps	Ml	Notes
ALBUQUERQUE, NM (MST)	140p	750p	868/1299		C	S	A/C Departs At 1355
ALEXANDRIA, LA (CST)	140p	625p	868/*2570	X6	C	S	A/C Departs At 1355
	140p	625p	868/*2526	6	C	S	A/C Departs At 1355
AMSTERDAM, NETHERLANDS (GMT + 1)	**140p**	**250p**	**868/4**		C	D	A/C Departs At 1355; Chg A/C At LGW; CO/HV Joint Operation
ATLANTA, GA (EST)	140p	955p	868/294		C	D	A/C Departs At 1355
AUSTIN, TX (CST)	140p	615p	868/1089	X7	C	S	A/C Departs At 1355
	140p	615p	868/1091	7	C	S	A/C Departs At 1355
BATON ROUGE, LA (CST)	140p	923p	868/594	X6	C	S	A/C Departs At 1355
BEAUMONT/PT. ARTHUR, TX (CST)	140p	710p	868/*2714		C	S	A/C Departs At 1355
BOSTON, MA (EST)	140p	1126p	868/1086		C	S	A/C Departs At 1355
CHICAGO, IL (CST) Airports: O-O'Hare M-Midway C-Meigs Field	140p	752p O	868/1052	X6	C	S	A/C Departs At 1355
	140p	752p O	868/1062	6	C	S	A/C Departs At 1355
CLEVELAND, OH (EST)	140p	1038p	868/1128		C	D	A/C Departs At 1355
COLLEGE STATION, TX (CST)	140p	720p	868/*2578		C	S	A/C Departs At 1355
COLUMBUS, OH (EST)	140p	1117p	868/1082		C	S	A/C Departs At 1355
CORPUS CHRISTI, TX (CST)	140p	645p	868/*2507		C	S	A/C Departs At 1355
DALLAS/FORT WORTH, TX (CST)	140p	624p D	868/1107		C	S	A/C Departs At 1355
DENVER, CO (MST)	140p	632p	868/1275	X6	C	S	A/C Departs At 1355
	140p	632p	868/1052	6	C	S	A/C Departs At 1355
DETROIT/WAYNE CO., MI (EST)	140p	1110p	868/1681		C	D	A/C Departs At 1355
EL PASO, TX (MST)	140p	615p	868/1299		C	S	A/C Departs At 1355
FT. LAUDERDALE, FL (EST)	140p	953p	868/68		C	D	A/C Departs At 1355
GULFPORT/BILOXI, MS (CST)	140p	955p	868/*2582	X6	C	S	A/C Departs At 1355
HOUSTON/HOBBY AIRPORT, TX (CST)	140p	525p H	868/*3009	X6	C	S	A/C Departs At 1355
HOUSTON/INTERCONTINENTAL AIRPORT, TX (CST)	140p	400p I	868		0	S	A/C Departs At 1355
INDIANAPOLIS, IN (EST)	140p	953p	868/1082		C	S	A/C Departs At 1355
JACKSONVILLE, FL (EST)	140p	956p	868/1188		C	S	A/C Departs At 1355
KANSAS CITY, MO (CST)	140p	910p	868/152		C	S	A/C Departs At 1355
LAFAYETTE, LA (CST)	140p	625p	868/*2794	X6	C	S	A/C Departs At 1355
LAKE CHARLES, LA (CST)	140p	630p	868/*2558		C	S	A/C Departs At 1355
LAREDO, TX (CST)	140p	635p	868/*2525	X6	C	S	A/C Departs At 1355
	140p	635p	868/*2577	6	C	S	A/C Departs At 1355
LAS VEGAS, NV (PST)	140p	654p	868/1193		C	D	A/C Departs At 1355
LONDON/GATWICK, ENGLAND, UK (GMT) Airport: Gatwick Airport	**140p**	**950a**	**868/4**		C	D	A/C Departs At 1355; GOLDEN MARQUEE THEATRE
LOS ANGELES, CA (PST) Airport: L-Los Angeles Int'l	140p	616p L	868/1093		C	D	A/C Departs At 1355
MIAMI, FL (EST)	140p	852p	868/494		C	D	A/C Departs At 1355
MINNEAPOLIS/ST. PAUL, MN (CST)	140p	921p	868/532		C	D	A/C Departs At 1355
MOBILE, AL/PASCAGOULA, MS (CST)	140p	1025p	868/*2656	X6	C	S	A/C Departs At 1355
NEW ORLEANS, LA (CST)	140p	616p	868/267		C	S	A/C Departs At 1355
NEW YORK, NY & NEWARK, NJ (EST) Airports: E-Newark L-La Guardia	140p	950p E	868/584	X6	C	D	A/C Departs At 1355
	140p	950p E	868/412	6	C	D	A/C Departs At 1355
	140p	1002p L	868/502	X6	C	D	A/C Departs At 1355
	140p	1043p E	868		1	D	A/C Departs At 1355
	140p	1112p L	868/126		C	D	A/C Departs At 1355
OKLAHOMA CITY, OK (CST)	140p	820p	868/130		C	S	A/C Departs At 1355
OMAHA, NE (CST)	140p	847p	868/114		C	S	A/C Departs At 1355
ORLANDO, FL (EST)	140p	1000p	868/488		C	D	A/C Departs At 1355
PENSACOLA, FL (CST)	140p	952p	868/527	X6	C	S	A/C Departs At 1355
	140p	952p	868/1113	6	C	S	A/C Departs At 1355
PHILADELPHIA, PA/WILMINGTON, DE (EST)	140p	1050p	868/194		C	S	A/C Departs At 1355
PHOENIX, AZ (MST)	140p	710p	868/1045		C	S	A/C Departs At 1355
ST. LOUIS, MO (CST)	140p	839p	868/896		C	D	A/C Departs At 1355
SALT LAKE CITY, UT (MST)	140p	730p	868/485		C	S	A/C Departs At 1355
SAN ANTONIO, TX (CST)	140p	622p	868/107		C	S	A/C Departs At 1355
SAN DIEGO, CA (PST)	140p	651p	868/489		C	D	A/C Departs At 1355
SAN FRANCISCO, CA (PST)	**140p**	**800p S**	**868/483**		C	D	A/C Departs At 1355; GOLDEN MARQUEE THEATRE
SEATTLE/TACOMA, WA (PST)	140p	834p	868/891	X6	C	D	A/C Departs At 1355
SHREVEPORT, LA (CST)	140p	650p	868/*2655	X6	C	S	A/C Departs At 1355
	140p	650p	868/*2516	6	C	S	A/C Departs At 1355
TAMPA/ST. PETERSBURG, FL (EST) Airport: T-Tampa Int'l	140p	946p T	868/88		C	S	A/C Departs At 1355
TUCSON, AZ (MST)	140p	657p	868/177		C	S	A/C Departs At 1355
TULSA, OK (CST)	140p	1005p	868/291		C	S	A/C Departs At 1355
VICTORIA, TX (CST)	140p	705p	868/*2611	X6	C	S	A/C Departs At 1355
WASHINGTON, D.C. (EST) Airports: D-Dulles N-National	140p	914p N	868/412	X6	C	D	A/C Departs At 1355
	140p	1036p N	868/454		C	D	A/C Departs At 1355
	140p	1049p D	868/140		C	D	A/C Departs At 1355
WEST PALM BEACH, FL (EST)	140p	950p	868/90		C	D	A/C Departs At 1355
WICHITA, KS (CST)	140p	813p	868/1072		C	S	A/C Departs At 1355

FIGURE 14-9 Excerpt from an airline timetable, with explanation of the codes used. (Flight schedules shown subject to change.) *Courtesy of Continental Airlines.*

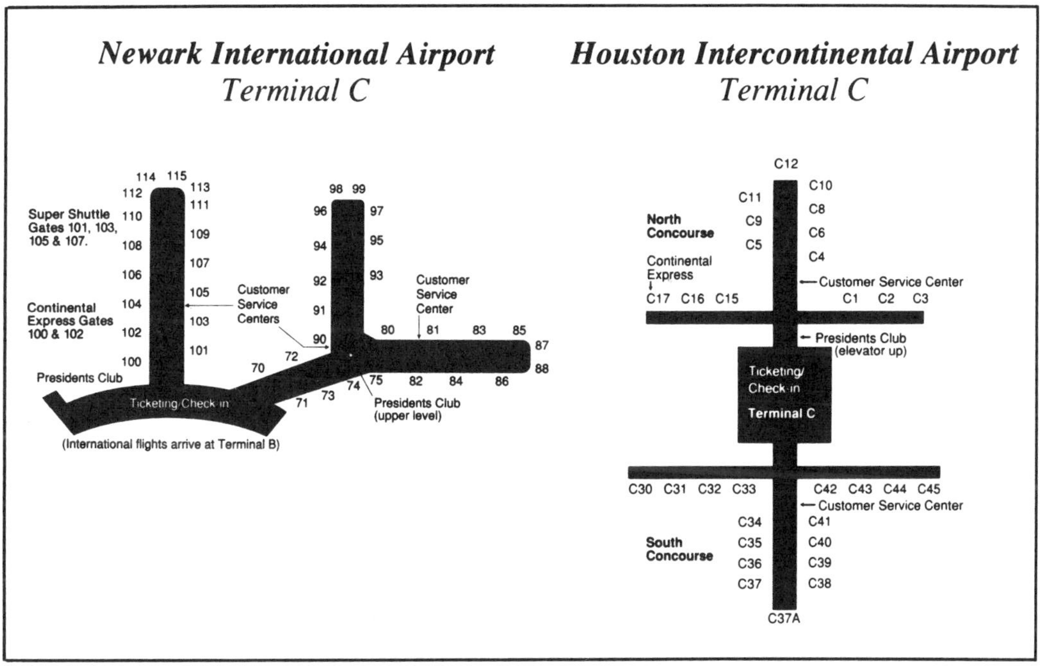

FIGURE 14-10 Airport hub maps and diagrams of the Houston and Newark airport terminals. *Courtesy of Continental Airlines.*

SUMMARY

Travel is an integral component of American business operations. Organizations which do a massive amount of travel each year may assign a full-time or part-time travel director to administer the travel function.

As a part-time position, the job is often assigned to the administrative assistant, who assumes the responsibilities in conjunction with other duties.

An alternative to the travel director's position is a corporate travel service hired to make travel plans and issue airline tickets for all company travelers.

Another alternative is the on-line travel services available to subscribers of information retrieval services. On-line services offer convenience and speed to users through prompt ticket issuance, with or without a travel agent acting as agent.

The issuance of passports and visas, the exchange of American dollars for foreign currency, and special concerns for travel safety apply especially to international travel. The Bureau of Consular Affairs issues helpful booklets addressing these important issues in detail.

Developing a travel policy and seeing to its proper implementation is another responsibility of the travel director. Maintaining the policy with periodic reviews and updates is necessary to keep the policy current.

QUESTIONS FOR REVIEW

1. List in order of importance the information that should be given to the hotel reservations clerk when calling to reserve a room for a traveling employee.
2. Which directories are the most used references for information on hotels and motels in major cities?
3. Name the three classes of air travel available on large aircraft and explain the distinctions between them.
4. When is a passport *not* required to enter or leave the United States?
5. Where may an applicant present a passport application when he or she is applying for the first time? That is, what places are authorized to accept the passport applications?
6. Explain what a visa is and why it is necessary to have the necessary visas when visiting foreign countries.
7. What is a visa service company? What worthwhile service do these companies perform for their customers?
8. How can ATMs (automated teller machines) diffuse the panic of tourists who suddenly find themselves out of cash—on a weekend or holiday—while vacationing in a foreign country?
9. What is a letter of credit? When might one be necessary for a traveling executive?
10. Which federal bureau is concerned with the safety of American citizens traveling abroad?

QUESTIONS FOR DISCUSSION

1. Large organizations which do extensive traveling often contract with one major airline as the primary carrier of their company's business travelers. Discuss the positive and the negative aspects of this arrangement.
2. The Bureau of Consular Affairs offers a catalog of safety precautions to travelers abroad, including protection against terrorism. How important is it to observe such precautions? In your view, is the bureau stirring up needless fears and unrest?
3. Discuss the role of the travel director in a large organization. When the travel director's job is a part-time one, is it a fitting addition to the duties of the administrative assistant? Why or why not?
4. How can a printed travel policy clarify the company's position on travel-related issues and reduce problems stemming from a "no-policy" position.

SUGGESTED ACTIVITIES

1. Visit a local travel agency. View their on-line reservation service. Inquire about their computer information service. For example, does it provide information on weather conditions in other states and countries? Does it list hotel accommodations? Ask the agents to contrast their present computerized form of reserving airline space with former precomputer methods.
2. Invite a representative from a large corporation to the class to speak on the extent of travel in his or her company and how the travel function is administered. Learn how the travel responsibilities are handled, whether this is a part-time or

full-time job, and who in the company is assigned to this job. Is a corporate travel service employed to handle the responsibilities?

3. Obtain an airline flight schedule and plan a coast-to-coast business trip for one or a group of employees. Type the travel itinerary, including all the necessary information as to departure and arrival times, flight numbers, class of service, and food service included on each flight.

   Add to the itinerary the hotel accommodations reserved, rental cars reserved, if any, and appointments scheduled at the destination cities. Add any comments deemed appropriate.

4. Write to three or more of the information retrieval services listed on page 324, asking for a current catalog of their retrieval services, including subscription and usage prices. Compare the listings and rank them in terms of services offered and prices charged.

REFERENCES

BONNANZIO, JOHN G. F., "Focus on Services," *Industrial Distribution* (February 1987), 76:48–50.

DILLON, RAY D., BETTY C. HORN, and THOMAS S. DUDICK, "Business Travel Expenditures: A Plan for Controlling Costs," *Journal of Accountancy* (October 1986), 162:146.

"How to Choose a Corporate Travel Service," *St. Louis Business Journal* (January 1988), 46.

HUMPHREY, SUSANNE M. and JOHN B. MELLONI, *Databases: A Primer for Retrieving Information by Computer*. Englewood Cliffs, NJ: Prentice Hall, 1986.

JENNINGS, LUCY MAE, *Secretarial & General Office Procedures*, 3rd edition. Englewood Cliffs, NJ: Prentice Hall, 1989.

KEATING, MICHAEL, "Knowledge at Your Fingertips," *Modern Office Technology* (September 1987), 110–114.

SEGAL, TROY, "Rental-Car Insurance: Don't Get Taken for a Ride," *Business Week* (January 19, 1987), 106.

TAYLOR, ALEX, III, "Why Car Rentals Drive You Nuts," *Fortune* (August 31, 1987), 74–78.

U.S. government publications:

Your Trip Abroad, Publication 8969.

Fly-Rights: A Guide to Air Travel in the U.S. ($1.00) Supt of Documents, Dept P-165, Pueblo, CO 81009.

Key Officers of Foreign Service Posts, Supt of Documents, Washington, DC 20402.

ZIGAS, DAVID, "Don't Go Abroad Without Your Trusty Cash Card," *Business Week* (July 20, 1987), 179.

Case Problem 1 Unit IV *Automated Routing of Toll-Free Calls*

A national distributor of computer-related products had a major telecommunications problem. As many as 70,000 callers per month failed to complete their toll-free calls to the company due to overcrowded lines; and of those that were completed, the average "hold" time was 15 minutes.

The company had eight toll-free (800) lines available to handle customer service inquiries, with all calls routed through the company's PBX operators, then to the appropriate customer service representative. Frequently, however, callers were using the 800 number to call departments other than customer service, thus jamming the 800 lines; or callers wanting customer service dialed inappropriate telephone numbers to reach the service they wanted.

As a result, the company was losing touch with a broad base of potential customers, and its current customers were not receiving the level of service they had been promised. Something had to be done.

To solve the problem, the company installed a call-processing system which would automatically route each incoming call to the proper department. Incoming calls were separated into five categories based on the callers' inquiries: customer service, special services, warranty information, parts, and orders.

Within the first few weeks, approximately 90 percent of the previously misrouted calls were eliminated, the average hold time was reduced to 90 seconds or less, and customer satisfaction soared. Company officials estimated that the automated routing system paid for itself within the first few months.

1. Put yourself in the place of one of the callers who had been foiled in his or her attempts to reach this company by its 800 number. What would your reaction have been?
2. Other than the installation of an automated-routing system, what other options might the company have tried to solve this problem?
3. If you were asked by your employer to investigate the installation of a call-processing system, where would you start? Who would you contact? What kind of information would you seek?

Case Problem 2 Unit IV *The "Phone Doctor" Has a Big Practice**

One day, Nancy Friedman of St. Louis became so angry at the poor telephone manners of her insurance company's staff that she treatened to cancel her policies with the company. In response, the insurance company asked her to come to the office to teach the company's employees how to speak on the telephone.

That was the beginning of the Telephone Doctor, a consulting firm which grosses nearly $1 million a year teaching corporate America how to be nice on the telephone. Ms. Friedman claims that "More business is lost to poor service and poor treatment than to a poor product. And yet it doesn't take any extra time to be nice." She also believes that *everyone* should be trained in telephone manners, not just the frontline receptionists and clerical staff.

Her "prescription" for curing telephone rudeness begins with five "forbidden phrases," words she says *nobody wants to hear*, least of all a customer. These are the phrases the Telephone Doctor advises her clients to eliminate from their vocabulary:

I don't know.

We can't do that.

You'll have to. . .

Just a second, I'll be right back.

"No" at the beginning of a sentence.

1. Examine each of these five forbidden phrases. Explain why you think they are so deadly to listeners, and tell what you would say instead.
2. Try out your substitutions through a mock telephone conversation with one other classmate. Let the rest of the class "listen in" to the conversation and, when ended, let them offer their suggestions and comments for improving your manners still more, or, conversely, their praise for your excellent manners.

*Deck, Cecelia, "Phone Doctor Says Common Sense Key," *Tulsa World* (January 19, 1989), G11.

Case Problem 3 Unit IV *Convenience Copiers or High-Volume "Stand-Alones"*

Manufacturers of sports equipment and clothing gear, Brandt, Inc. near Dallas, provided desktop copiers for each department of its company so that employees could photocopy documents readily without waiting for the services of the large-volume stand-alone copier in the company's centralized copy center.

At first, the employees cheered the decision of company officials in decentralizing the copying function. The inconvenience of using a centralized center for *all* their copying needs had been frustrating; many times the waiting period at the center had stretched to 30 minutes or more. Convenience copiers were to eliminate that problem.

However, problems with the photocopiers began a few months after installation. The desktop copiers which the company provided for the convenience of users were "down" about 50 percent of the time, unable to cope with the heavy usage demanded of them. After photocopying approximately 6,500 copies each month, the machines would go down, requiring the services of a technician before more copies could be made. At least one period of downtime was experienced every few weeks.

Something had to be done. The centralized system was reconsidered. Yet, departments were hesitant to surrender the convenience of the desktop units; when the units were working, they were handy for quick copying, and no one had to wait in line to use them.

1. What should the company do to remedy the situation? Should they retain the convenience copiers but limit their usage to the monthly volume recommended by the manufacturers?
2. Should they provide a large-volume stand-alone copier instead of or in addition to the desktop copiers?
3. What do you suggest?

Case Problem 4 Unit IV *On-Line Education, The New Wave*

American education is experiencing a quiet revolution. In place of chalkboards, lecture halls, formal classrooms filled with 30 to 40 students taking notes from the instructor, a TV monitor beams the instructor's message via satellite down to hundreds or thousands of viewers comfortably seated in their living rooms.

The electronic university is extending education beyond campus grounds to the remotest corners of a satellite's reach, downloading its instruction to masses of students formerly unable to share in the rich heritage of a college education.

Most people agree that the new wave of mass education will impact mightily on everyone touched by it, students and educators alike. Few agree, however, on the extent of the impact or how it will be manifested.

Consider the ramifications of a "TV degree" from your state university. Discuss these questions:

1. Persons formerly unable to pursue a higher education now have the opportunity to do so. How will the increased number of degreed persons affect the job market?
2. Will the quality of education suffer? Will the televised education compare favorably with the interpersonal relationship and dialog of teacher/student groups which takes place in the classroom?
3. Will the need for teachers diminish, since one teacher can now reach thousands via satellite?
4. Will all major areas of study adapt equally well to this form of educational delivery? Give examples.
5. Compare the advantages and disadvantages of electronic education. List as many pros and cons to this form of education as you can.

UNIT

V

ADMINISTRATIVE RESPONSIBILITIES

By assignment from company officials or working closely with them, the administrative assistant must often assume major personnel responsibilities.

Depending on the job description and the company structure, the administrative assistant's role may include many facets of human resource management—from the recruitment and selection of new support personnel to their training, supervision, and yearly evaluation.

The administrative assistant may also deal with the company's banking operations and track its investment portfolio. Both manual and electronic procedures enable him or her to deal with each of these activities swiftly and accurately.

15
Personnel Responsibilities

INTRODUCTION

Administrative assistants often work very closely with their principals in carrying out major personnel responsibilities. Their duties may include:

recruitment, selection, and orientation of new employees
development of training programs
development of job standards and evaluation of employees' job performance
supervision of administrative support personnel

The size of the company and the scope of this supervisory role determine how closely the administrative assistant is identified with these responsibilities. This chapter addresses each of them in some depth.

Some terms used herein include:

job rotation	EEOC
temps	CAI
structured interviews	in-house referrals

RECRUITMENT OF NEW PERSONNEL

As businesses diversify into new fields or expand their operations into new geographic regions, they create positions for additional personnel. Organizational shifts within the company and employee turnover add to the number of job vacancies.

At these times, the administrative assistant is often charged with the responsibility of recruiting new employees, particularly administrative support staff. First attempts at filling the positions may focus on those avenues which job seekers routinely check to contact potential employers: the classified ads of local newspapers, commercial employment agencies, and college and university placement centers.

If these resources fail to yield promising applicants, the administrative assistant may shift the recruitment search to other channels. Looking for part-time or full-time employees, the following sources may be considered.

"temps," or temporary workers, from temporary employment agencies
student interns
in-house referrals
recalled retirees

Classified Ads

Classified ads have several advantages as recruitment media. The cost is minimal; the lead time is short; and the responses are usually immediate. If, for example, a job vacancy occurs in midweek, an ad placed in the following Sunday edition can generate responses by Monday.

One disadvantage of classified advertising, however, is that it tends to draw many unqualified applicants. Hundreds of job seekers may have to be screened to find a few promising candidates. The screening process can be streamlined, however, if applicants are required to write a letter of application rather than applying in person.

Ad specialists at the newspaper office often help clients design appealing ads. They are familiar, too, with federal and state regulations regarding advertising for recruits in the classified ads.

Employment Agencies

Companies seeking secretarial and clerical personnel often use the services of commercial employment agencies. Agencies are usually effective in attracting job applicants, and they perform very helpful tasks for their employer clients.

For example, the agencies handle the initial testing and screening of job applicants, thus saving their clients the time and expense of doing so themselves. The employers, in turn, often pay the agency fee for the newly-hired employees after they have proven their worth to the company.

The goodwill generated over years of successful recruitment/employment endeavors builds a mutually beneficial relationship. The agencies come to understand the needs of the companies they serve, and the companies reward the agencies' recruiting efforts by regularly hiring their new recruits.

College and University Placement Centers

Colleges, universities, business schools, and most vocational centers accommodate their graduating students by providing them with job-placement services. For little or no fee, students get professional assistance in developing portfolios which include resumes, grade transcripts, and letters of reference.

When the placement center receives notice of job openings in the field of the student's choice, word is sent to the student so that he or she can follow up on the lead. By maintaining ties with employing firms in the area, the placement center is advised of openings as they occur. When students request it, the placement officers mail copies of student portfolios to prospective employers.

Temps

By definition, temps are persons registered with one of the many temporary agencies providing workers to company clients on a temporary basis. For example, temps are frequently used to replace vacationing workers and to help the office regulars during peak periods. Staffing with temps can effect substantial cost savings. For example, managers using temps rather than permanent staff can reduce overtime costs by using temps instead of regular staff members during peak periods; eliminate unemployment insurance claims which result from temporary staff cutbacks; and reduce costs of certain fringe benefits, such as sick leave, paid vacations, health insurance, and retirement funds.

The positive benefits of using office temporaries have prompted many companies to integrate them into their regular employment structure; temps have become regular staffers.

FIGURE 15-1 Students obtain valuable skills through employment as "temps" during summers and holiday vacations. *Courtesy of Manpower, Inc.*

Student Interns

Internship programs provide business firms with students who wish to gain work experience related to their classroom instruction. The teacher coordinators work closely with the students' job supervisors to insure that the students gain meaningful work experience and that they discharge their duties faithfully and well.

Internships are mutually beneficial: Students receive valuable work experience; companies receive the assistance of young, eager workers. The exchange of professional expertise is also beneficial. Schools are made aware of the training needs of business; businesses are updated on trends in technology, communication, and procedural techniques.

The primary benefit to businesses, however, is the ready source of trained personnel the internship programs provide. From the company-trained interns, the personnel office can select the best qualified candidates for permanent employment after the students graduate.

In-house Referrals

Current employees are often able to recommend good prospects for newly vacated positions. They understand the requirements for the positions and the qualifications applicants must have to fill them. Their recommendations can save the company valuable time. To encourage their employees to help recruit new workers, therefore, some companies offer a monetary reward to those whose recommendations result in the successful recruitment of a new employee.

Retiree Recalls

A growing number of businesses are looking to their recent retirees as a source of efficient labor. Recalled workers are accepting employment from their former employers with increasing regularity. On a part-time or full-time basis, retirees find fulfillment in sharing their expertise, and employers reap the benefits of experienced personnel who are familiar with company procedures.

PERSONNEL SELECTION

Selection of the best applicant from a group of promising candidates is the most difficult phase of the hiring process. However, the administrative assistant can minimize the risk of choosing the wrong candidate by utilizing the screening procedures recommended by personnel specialists. These include:

An occupational analysis of the job functions and skills required in the positions being filled

Tests designed to measure candidates' level of skill as identified in the occupational analysis

Careful scrutiny of candidates' application papers and a thorough check of references supplied

Interviews with top-ranking candidates

Adherence to legal constraints, particularly EEOC regulations

Occupational Analysis

The following occupational analysis for a clerk-receptionist illustrates the type of analysis used to describe administrative support positions. Working in conjunction with the staff, the administrative assistant can design similar analyses for each support position in the office. The analyses serve not only as screening devices but as job descriptors for newly hired employees.

OCCUPATIONAL ANALYSIS—CLERK RECEPTIONIST

Duties	*Important Tasks*
Clerical duties	Uses reference books or manuals Types basic forms, letters Types from rough draft Types and rules tabular materials Proofreads typed materials
Receptionist activities	Answers telephone; keeps records Greets callers or visitors Screens employer's callers
Filing activities	Sorts and files paper records Maintains cross-reference listings Handles confidential files
Stenographic and general duties	Operates transcribing machines Uses U.S. Postal manual and zip code directory Distributes incoming and outgoing mail Delivers messages Plans priorities for own workday Schedules appointments for employer
Computer-related activities	Keyboards documents into word processor Corrects, revises text Prints hard copy

Occupational Analysis—Clerk Receptionist

Relevant Tests

Standardized tests are available which purport to predict applicants' potential for success. However, individualized testing instruments developed by company supervisors are frequently better predictors of job success than are the standardized tests.

For example, skill in note taking and transcription can be measured through the use of cassette recordings, with the dictation given at varying speeds by the persons who will be utilizing the services of a new stenographer.

Simulated telephone conversations may be taped to test an applicant's skill in telephone usage. Stenographic skills may be evaluated through the use of short case studies. In-basket exercises may be designed from actual job samples to include tasks such as the following: the use of postal manuals and the zip code directory to complete an address or to determine postal rates; news releases to be proofread for errors; and an airline schedule to be read and interpreted, with the candidate listing flight options via that airline for a given date.

When a company designs its own tests, matching them to job requirements, it can be assured of relevant data on which to measure an applicant's success potential. In so doing, it is also conforming to the Equal Employment Opportunity Commission (EEOC) guidelines by giving all applicants an equal opportunity to succeed.

Test norms can be established by retaining scores and matching applicants' scores to their job performance over a number of years. The strengths and weaknesses of the tests can then be identified and improved.

Application Papers

Just as testing procedures must be related to the job, information requested on the application form must be relevant also. For example, unless the age of an applicant has a direct bearing on predicted job performance, the age of the applicant cannot be asked.

The information supplied on the application forms tells the administrative assistant how closely the applicant's education and experience match the knowledge and skills required on the job. It will be meaningful, too, as a basis for later interviews with applicants who are invited for interviews with company officials.

The references supplied, particularly those of current or former employers, provide very important information also. They should be checked prior to inviting candidates in for interviews.

Letters of application and personal resume sheets complete the application portfolios, providing special insights into the candidates' qualifications. Careful scrutiny of these papers, together with the application forms, the test scores, and the references supplied help narrow the search for the most promising job candidates. If the information gathered appears favorable, the candidates are issued an invitation to come in for an interview.

EMPLOYMENT APPLICATION
EISOR CORPORATION

PERSONAL INFORMATION

Name of Applicant ____________ Soc. Sec. No. ________________

Present Address ______________ Phone ______________________

City ________________________ State __________ Zip _________

TYPE OF EMPLOYMENT DESIRED

Position ______ Date you can start ______ Salary desired ______

Are you employed now? ______

May we inquire of your present employer? ______

EDUCATIONAL INFORMATION

School/College	Name and Address	Years Attended	Date Graduated	Course/Major

FORMER EMPLOYERS
(List four employers, starting with most recent.)

Date Month and Year	Name and Address of Employer	Salary	Position	Reason for Leaving
From ______ To ______				
From ______ To ______				
From ______ To ______				
From ______ To				

REFERENCES
(Give names of persons not related to you.)

Name	Address	Business	Years Acquainted

Interview Guidelines

Unless formally structured, interviews tend to yield subjective results. For example, one interviewer may recommend that an applicant be hired immediately; another, that the applicant be dismissed as unsuitable. Hence, the value of structured interviews; they increase objectivity, yielding a more accurate appraisal of a candidate's qualifications.

The Structured Interview Characterized by the following factors, the structured interview is:[1]

1. based primarily on job duties and requirements
2. objectively evaluated by more than one interviewer, preferably by a team of interviewers.
3. specific in types of questions asked. The questions must:
   a. assess the applicant's ability to perform job-related functions
   b. relate to personal commitments, such as willingness to travel, to relocate, to work overtime on occasion, and so on
   c. present problem situations in which the applicant must determine priority rankings and act in accordance with the priorities established

Interview Content From the occupational analysis drawn up earlier on each position, a list of job-related questions and discussion topics are easily selected for each interview.

Each interviewer is supplied with the same list of questions so that comparative evaluations can be made in follow-up sessions after all interviews have been completed. Interviewers are also given the latitude to pose further questions and topics at their own discretion.

Conducting Successful Interviews Candidates selected for interviews should be contacted by mail or telephone and offered a choice of interview dates. If multiple interviewers will be involved with each candidate, the candidates should be informed of this when the interview dates are set up.

Upon arrival, candidates are set at ease as quickly as possible. A friendly atmosphere in which the interviewer and the interviewee are equally at ease serves the best interests of both.

Federal Regulations The *Uniform Guidelines on Employee Selection Procedures* were adopted in 1978 by the Equal Employment Opportunity Commission (EEOC), the Civil Service Commission, and the Department of Labor.

The purpose of the guidelines is to provide a uniform set of principles for enforcing the equal employment opportunity laws. They apply to most employers with 15 or more employees.

The EEOC guidelines require that employers maintain strict objectivity

[1]Elliott D. Pursell, et al. "Structured Interviewing: Avoiding Selection Problems," *Personnel Journal* (November 1980), 907–912.

in designing application forms, entrance tests, and interview procedures. All information gathered from applicants must be strictly job related.

Job analyses enable the administrative assistant and other hiring officials to document for federal authorities the "job-relatedness" of their hiring policies.

ORIENTATION OF NEW EMPLOYEES

High turnover among newly hired stenographers and secretaries is frequently attributed to ineffective orientation programs. Newly hired employees, lacking direction and familiarity with company procedures, often terminate their employment within months of their initial hiring.

Effective orientation programs are one means of reducing this hazard. If planned and implemented well, orientation programs help new employees settle into their positions quickly and comfortably.

The objectives of an orientation program are threefold: to give employees a sense of security and acceptance among their fellow workers, to acquaint them with company procedures and their job responsibilities, and to reduce employee turnover.

Orientation Procedures

Each orientation program contains elements unique to the company for which it is designed. A typical program designed for a large insurance office supplies these directives to the person in charge of the orientation program:

1. Introduce new employees to coworkers.
2. Take the employee on a tour of the entire office complex, pointing out each departmental area.
3. Describe the services and clientele served by the company.
4. Explain the function of each department within the company.
5. Detail the duties and responsibilities of the new employee.
6. Supply written copies of job performance standards and review these with the employee.
7. Provide a copy of the office manual and review its contents with the new employee.
8. Review the daily schedule, including lunch and break periods.
9. Supply information on union membership, if an employee union exists.
10. Schedule an orientation review and question/answer period one week subsequent to the orientation.

Orientation Follow-up The most successful orientation programs are reevaluated periodically in order to maintain their relevancy and effectiveness. Follow-up interviews with new employees a few months after orientation often yield insights into the most (and least) effective components of the programs. Questionnaires completed anonymously by employees also help to evaluate the programs objectively.

Office Manual One of the most valuable tools for effecting a successful orientation is a well-written office manual or handbook. Distributed to new employees when they join the firm, office manuals prove a ready reference for answers to questions forgotten or ignored during orientation.

Typically included in an office manual are facts on holiday and vacation policies, salary reviews, sick-leave allowances, hospitalization insurance, and retirement programs. Excerpts from the office manual of the Eisor Corporation follow.

(i)

Eisor Corporation Office Manual Excerpts

PROBATIONARY

All employees will be considered probationary employees for their first sixty (60) calendar days of employment. Upon completion of sixty days of continuous service, employees shall then be placed upon the permanent list.

The probationary period may be extended for thirty (30) calendar days if needed by the supervisor for further appraisal of the new employee. Employees will not receive company benefits during the probationary period.

IDENTIFICATION CARDS

All employees will be issued an identification card upon employment. It is to be used as identification whenever the employee is dealing with the public. All ID cards will be returned to the company upon termination of employment.

UNION MEMBERSHIP

All employees are eligible to join the local union upon completion of their probationary period. Additional information will be given to each employee by the union representative.

EQUAL EMPLOYMENT OPPORTUNITY (EEO)

Employment of all individuals shall be determined on the basis of each individual's abilities and the company's overall staffing needs. The person's race, sex, age, creed, or national origin will have no bearing on the hiring decision.

(8)

Eisor Corporation Office Manual Excerpts, continued

TRAINING PROGRAMS

Administrative assistants sometimes assume full responsibility for a clerical/stenographic training program. They not only administer the program but design it and choose which employees are to take part in it. They may also instruct the trainees, evaluate their progress, and answer directly to company authorities for its success or failure.

Such a training program usually includes three phases: (1) assessment of employee training needs, (2) design of methods best suited to their needs, and (3) evaluation of results.

Phase 1: Assessment of Training Needs

A company's training needs can be assessed in several ways. For example, supervisors may examine the written job standards adopted for all stenographers, then tailor their training programs to fill the gaps between the skill levels called for and the skills demonstrated by their stenographers.

A survey of the personnel can be conducted to determine what training, if any, they would like to have to upgrade their knowledge or skill levels.

A review of the annual employee-performance appraisals can also provide insights into the training needs of employees. Some may need remedial training; others, some developmental training to prepare them for promotion to higher positions within the company.

Phase 2: Training Methods

Training methods vary widely, depending on the objectives pursued. For example, employees who need better skills to increase their accuracy, knowledge,

FIGURE 15-2 Manpower uses "Skillware," a computer-based training method, to train permanent operators at customer sites. *Courtesy of Manpower, Inc.*

or speed comprise one category; those who are striving for a promotion to a higher-level position comprise another. The training methods selected must fit the specified objectives.

Job-related Training Methods

For job-related skills, the following types of group instruction are particularly effective:

Job Rotation Each employee performs one job until a certain level of skill is achieved, then transfers to another job. Skilled operators provide the on-the-job training.

Job rotation is appropriate for some, but not all clerical tasks. For example, it is used frequently for training word processing operators.

Demonstrations Clerical and stenographic tasks lend themselves to this form of instruction. Operation of a dictation/transcription machine, a FAX transceiver, and a computer terminal require demonstration and hands-on experience to be meaningful.

Demos combined with job rotation reinforce the training. A videotape may be used for the demonstration in combination with a personal trainer.

Computer-assisted Instruction (CAI) CAI is a form of programmed instruction in which the trainees access information through instructions shown on the computer monitor. Designed primarily for one-on-one instruction, CAI can also be adapted to groups.

Lectures Lectures are especially appropriate when a great amount of information is to be imparted within a limited amount of time, when the information is complex or technical in nature, and when a large number of people must be accommodated. Films, slides, videotapes, and similar visual aids add interest and clarity to a lecture. Combined with discussion and visuals, the lecture method can be extremely effective.

In-basket Exercises Trainees are presented with a "basket" of communications and directives which are typical of a normal day's activities, such as a request to make hotel reservations, to compose a letter, to complete a form, or to proofread a news release. The trainee must decide in which order the tasks are to be done; then complete as many as possible within the time frame allowed.

Developmental Training Programs Developmental training programs prepare employees for promotions within the company. Only potentially successful candidates are chosen to take part in these programs. One or more of the following training methods is utilized in typical developmental programs.

Discussion groups focus on meaningful topics chosen by the leader. The

FIGURE 15-3 Computer-assisted instruction (CAI) shortens the training period and enables students to learn at their own pace. *Courtesy of Manpower, Inc.*

topics chosen may be deliberately controversial so as to provoke lively discussion by all the participants. Persons who can articulate well and can tolerate opposing views without rancour stand out in discussion groups as potential candidates for promotion.

In *role playing,* the instructor sets the scene for a hypothetical problem which is to be solved by the trainees. Assuming the roles of the principal participants, the trainees role play their parts, striving to find a satisfactory solution. The purpose of role playing is to involve participants in situations similar to those they may experience on the job, and to help them deal with them as they occur.

Seminars are similar to discussions in that the participants are required to interact with each other and the leader. One or more of the trainees is responsible for presenting concepts on a given topic which he or she has researched in some depth. The trainee leads the discussion on that topic, drawing as much meaningful discussion as possible from each person in the group. They are most successful when the group is small and the topics chosen are relevant to the group.

Case studies are hypothetical situations involving complex problems. After a case problem is presented, the leader solicits solutions from the participants, making clear that in "real life" each case may be solved differently, depending on ramifications unique to each situation. Eventually, one solution is agreed on by the group and offered to the team leader as the most practical one.

Training through case studies develops decision-making ability; it is a valuable tool for teaching young employees the importance of seeking counsel before making important decisions.

Phase 3: Evaluation of Training Programs

Evaluation of a training program must be based primarily on each employee's on-the-job effectiveness. The supervisor can usually gauge how effective the training program is in terms of improved office productivity and employee morale.

Evaluative comments may also be sought from employees who have taken part in the programs. Interviews with each participant, conducted immediately at the conclusion of training, and again six months later, may provide valuable insights into the program's merits. All programs must be updated periodically to fit changing circumstances and to remain meaningful.

Benefits of Training

Many benefits accrue to the company having an effective training program. Trained employees are more self-reliant and self-confident; they require less supervision; they usually have better attendance records than their coworkers; they take fewer sick-leave days; and they develop a stronger sense of loyalty to the company.

The time and money invested in training programs returns to the company many-fold, particularly through higher productivity and employee morale.

SETTING STANDARDS: APPRAISING JOB PERFORMANCE

Periodically, a company must appraise its employees' job performance, evaluating both the quality and the quantity of their work.

An administrative assistant who supervises clerical and stenographic personnel will participate not only in the appraisals, but in the development of job standards, one of the major components of the appraisal process and the criterion by which the employees' performance is evaluated.

Performance standards stem directly from the written description of duties involved in a specific position. That is, a job description sets forth in writing the specifics of a job before performance standards can be set.

Job Descriptions and Job Standards

Job descriptions explain in detail the duties and responsibilities of a given position. Typically, they include the following components: the job title, description of basic job functions, employee relationships and accountability channels, responsibilities, and standards of performance.

Job Title

Titles are standardized throughout the company. Insofar as possible, they also conform to those adopted by the Department of Labor's Dictionary of Occupational Titles (DOT).

For example, executive secretary, stenographer, and file clerk, as defined by the DOT, should match the titles and job descriptions adopted by the company.

Basic Job Function

The job function may be stated clearly in one or two sentences. For example:

> *Executive secretary.* As secretary to the corporate vice president, is closely allied to the vice president's responsibilities, assisting in administrative and secretarial duties at a high level of confidentiality and responsibility.

Relationships and Accountability Channels

The employees' relationships to fellow workers, superiors, and subordinates, plus the channels of authority to whom or through whom they report are defined in this component of the job description. For example, the administrative assistant:

> Reports to the corporate vice president. Supervises file clerks, stenographers, and the department secretary. Is accountable for operating the corporate office at a high level of efficiency; for maintaining a smooth-functioning and highly-productive office staff; and for preserving a favorable public-relations image of the corporate office.

Responsibilities of Administrative Assistant

Handles business correspondence addressed to the vice president

Screens calls and callers for the vice president

Arranges travel itineraries, transportation, and hotel accommodations for vice president's business trips

Composes correspondence for the vice president's signature

Takes dictation of letters, memos, and other business correspondence; transcribes the dictated material

Supervises clerical and stenographic aides

Maintains confidentiality of corporate records, meetings, and correspondence

Standards of Performance

Job standards set specific norms for each job, usually classified as average, above average, or superior job performance. Substandard performance levels may also be classed in terms of their variance from accepted norms. For example, a clerk stenographer position may include standards for the number of documents indexed and filed in an hour; or the number of envelopes addressed per day.

Only those duties which can be readily timed or counted lend themselves to predetermined performance levels. Administrative duties, such as dealing with callers, taking part in committee hearings, or editing news releases cannot be validly measured in terms of time and productivity levels.

Job descriptions and job standards do not remain static; they are updated and rewritten as jobs shift, or as working conditions change. They serve a twofold objective: teaching new employees what is expected of them; and providing supervisors with specific guidelines for directing and evaluating their subordinates' performance.

Performance Appraisals

The standards of performance outlined in the job description form the basis for the periodic appraisals of each employee. If the standards are met or exceeded, employees are recognized and commended for their good work. If performance levels fall below standard, employees are targeted for further training, or, in certain instances, termination.

Appraisal forms should be designed to match each job group. For instance, clerical and stenographic positions can be evaluated with one form of appraisal; secretarial workers, with another.

The following form is designed for a first-level management position at Eisor Corporation. Designed by a committee of supervisors and employees, the form represents the democratic approach to appraisals—one in which the employees themselves have some input in their own appraisals.

The Eisor appraisal form invites comments from both the employee and his or her supervisor relative to the performance and skill levels of the employee. The overall performance level, however, is described by the supervisor, who shares the completed form with the employee for his or her signature, along with that of his or her own.

Employees have a right to expect their appraisals to be done fairly and impartially. Although subjectivity may always be a factor, a fair appraisal procedure minimizes its effects. In a quality appraisal procedure:

1. Data on employee performance are kept on a continual basis by supervisors.
2. Appraisals are made at a regularly scheduled time; for instance, on the annual anniversary date of the worker's initial employment.
3. Supervisors share the ratings with the employees and consider input from them.
4. Each person is rated objectively.

Purpose of Appraisals

The purpose of appraisals is basically twofold: (1) to let employees know where they stand and how they can improve their job performance, and (2) to encourage and motivate good workers.

Appraisals, however, serve another very important function. They help management to identify three classes of workers:

Average workers: those who perform adequately, in accord with set standards.

Superior workers: those with exceptional work records who have potential for advancement.

Poor performers: those who cannot or will not perform up to standard.

Employees Rated "Average" "Average" workers constitute the majority of the work force. They are dependable, hard-working persons who contribute to a smooth-functioning organization. With encouragement and/or additional training, average workers can become top performers. Good stenographers, for example, may become top-level secretaries; and executive secretaries may become management trainees or administrative assistants.

Employees Rated "Superior" "Superior" employees rate special recognition for their job performance. One of the simplest but most effective means of showing appreciation to employees who rank "superior" is a letter of commendation, addressed to the employee, with copies sent to higher company officials. If the commendation is reinforced by assignments of greater responsibility, the praise becomes even more meaningful.

The company's developmental training programs, designed to prepare employees for advancement, may be opened to selected "superior" employees also. An invitation to enroll in the company's developmental programs is a special mark of distinction.

Status symbols, such as a new title, a larger office, or additional clerical support are marks of appreciation for deserving employees. Financial rewards and promotions are, of course, the most tangible evidence of employer appreciation. A salary increase, a bonus, or a promotion *and* a pay increase—these are the rewards most appreciated by deserving employees.

Employees Rated "Poor" "Poor" performers probably fall into one of two categories: (1) Those who lack the capacity to do their jobs well, even after repeated instructions, and (2) those whose negative or indifferent attitude is reflected in careless and frequent errors, slowdowns, overlong break periods, or frequent absences without cause.

Obviously, each group must be handled differently. Those in the first group must be terminated. No company can afford to retain employees who fail to respond to the instruction and training needed to perform their jobs satisfactorily.

Termination seems the obvious action for the second group, too; however, basic causes for the employees' attitude should be explored in some depth before termination notice is served.

Guidelines for Disciplinary Action The purpose of corrective discipline is to salvage workers who have potential for improvement. Certain rules of conduct

Performance/Skills	Comments: Employee	Comments: Supervisor
Communication: with customers with peers with supervisors		
Knowledge/Skill: performance level error rate need for supervision		
Planning/Organization: sets, meets goals time, task management delegation to subordinates		
Other: develops new procedures accepts changes makes decisions well ____________________ ____________________		

Overall performance/potential (by supervisor)

____

____

Signed ____________________ Employee/Date

Signed ____________________ Supervisor/Date

Eisor Corporation Employee Appraisal Form

should be followed in applying disciplinary measures. For example, in deference to the employees' feelings, supervisors should deal with offending workers in this way:

Correct workers individually and in private.
Warn, rather than punish, the first infraction of the rules.
Focus initial attention on the misconduct itself, not on the worker.

Terminating Poor Performers Employees who cannot perform their jobs satisfactorily, or who refuse to cooperate with their supervisors must be terminated.

Although terminating an employee is an unpleasant task, the consequences of postponing a termination can be costly for the company and unfair for the employee. Accordingly, if an employee is to be terminated, he or she should be told of the decision promptly and quietly, with his or her self-respect spared the embarrassment of a public display or put-down.

SUPERVISION OF EMPLOYEES

Personnel specialists agree that two of the most important characteristics of a successful supervisor are the abilities *to motivate* workers to perform up to the level of their potential, and *to delegate* meaningful tasks to those who are qualified to perform them. Of course, other factors affect one's supervisory success, but without these two skills, the supervisor is severely limited in his or her capacity to lead.

Motivation

Each person responds to motivational incentives differently. Most businesses have found, however, that planned incentive programs are effective motivators in inspiring their employees to greater levels of productivity.

Formal incentive programs demonstrate a company's appreciation for its workers. A variety of monetary and special marks of distinction can be awarded to deserving employees in appreciation for their loyalty and as motivators to even higher levels of dedication. Some of the most effective are:

special-recognition honors in the form of plaques or other marks of distinction
challenging project assignments
monetary rewards
letters of commendation

Special-recognition Honors Special-recognition honors are designed to recognize employees whose contributions to the company have been exceptional. Often, employee committees work with company officials in establishing such awards and in setting up the criteria for achieving them. They may also nominate the recipients for the awards.

FIGURE 15-4 Supervision and motivation of support personnel is a major responsibility of many administrative assistants. *Courtesy of Apple Computer, Inc.*

Employees who suggest innovative ideas, display special leadership skills, or volunteer service on difficult projects or committees are likely candidates for special-recognition honors.

Challenging Project Assignments Better and more challenging job assignments are, on occasion, offered to workers who have shown special dedication and skill in performing their regular duties. The challenging projects serve a twofold purpose: (1) employers can observe and identify employees who may qualify for higher-level positions, and (2) employees are enabled to try their skills at tasks above and beyond their job-description duties.

The challenged employees appreciate the vote of confidence placed in them by their employers and if successful, the chance for promotions. The company gains, too, when the assignments are completed successfully and promotable employees are identified.

Monetary Rewards Of all the tangible rewards presented to deserving employees, monetary rewards appear to be the most compelling, even when the amounts awarded are modest.

Studies have shown that monetary rewards need not be large to be effective. Moderate amounts of cash, awarded as earned, appear to have more incentive value than large amounts given annually. For example, a $50 bonus given in January has more impact than $600 given in December for a year's accumulation of credits. Frequent reinforcement builds employee rapport and loyalty to the company.

Letters of Commendation Written words of commendation demonstrate the employer's genuine appreciation of an employee's good work. Verbal praise, while good in itself, does not have the same impact on the employee's morale as the written word, duly signed by a major official. This is especially true if a copy of the commendation is filed in the employee's personnel folder.

Delegation

Delegation is vital to good supervision. It develops the skills of subordinates while it frees supervisors to perform essential higher-level activities.

Proper delegation can enrich jobs, lift employee morale, reduce turnover, and encourage subordinates' initiative. Frequent and appropriate delegation pays big dividends to companies, too, by grooming promotable employees for advancement.

Effective delegation does not mean, however, simply assigning the work to a subordinate. It is a complex process which requires planning, organization, and control of diverse activities which may have both short- and long-term consequences.

The delegated employee must be given authority along with responsibility for the assigned task if he or she is to carry out the duties satisfactorily within the designated time frame. Supervisors, however, may find it difficult to surrender authority to subordinates. Many have lived by the adage, "If you want it done right, do it yourself."

Some fear too that their subordinates' success will pose a threat to their own positions. Such attitudes, however, preclude any meaningful delegation. To counter such fears, supervisors should prepare *themselves* for advancement to higher positions by continual study and observation. Then, when offered the promotion they desire, their vacated positions can be filled by their best-qualified subordinates, those who have demonstrated the greatest potential for advancement through effective completion of delegated tasks. Everyone wins in the ensuing job shift.

What to Delegate Not all tasks should be delegated. Some must remain the sole responsibility of the supervisor. Determining which tasks *can* be appropriately delegated and to whom are major responsibilities in themselves. To determine the answers to these two questions, supervisors may find it helpful to probe these key questions:

What is the goal of this project?
Are special skills needed? If so, what skills?
How much interaction with peers and/or management is required?
How important is the project to the company?

What margin for error can be tolerated?
What is the target date for completion?

Depending on the project under consideration, other questions may be appropriate also. The answers will help identify not only which tasks can be delegated safely, but which employees have the greatest potential for completing them successfully.

Techniques of Delegation Effective delegation depends on several factors, including the complexity of the task, its overall importance to company objectives, and the amount of direction needed by the delegated employee. All of these will affect the delegate's level of success. Utilizing the following set of guidelines, the supervisor can expect an above-average level of success in delegating tasks to subordinates.

1. Define in writing:
   a. the task being delegated
   b. the amount of authority given the delegate
   c. the target date for completion of the task
   d. the standards by which the job will be evaluated
2. Clarify the extent of support and direction the delegated employee may expect to receive, including
   a. where he or she can find additional information
   b. at what intervals the employee should report to the supervisor
3. Encourage as much initiative and creativity as the nature of the job permits, letting employees determine how to accomplish the tasks in their own way
4. Upon completion, assess the employee's performance. Include in the assessment an evaluation of employee's ability to:
   a. work with peers
   b. follow through on directives
   c. generate innovative/creative ideas
   d. meet target dates
   e. execute planned projects successfully
5. Write the *successful* employee/delegate a letter of commendation detailing the basis for the commendation. File a copy of the letter in the employee's personnel folder, with copies forwarded to company officials.

The supervisor/employee relationship is interdependent. Both parties share in the benefits of successful delegation. The employee demonstrates talents for assuming greater responsibilities; the supervisor gains a more knowledgeable employee who can step in to fill his or her shoes when a promotional opportunity comes along.

SUMMARY

Administrative assistants often carry out major personnel responsibilities in the office. Their duties may include supervision of clerical and stenographic workers as well as recruitment and orientation of new employees.

Training is an important component of the personnel function also. The administrative assistant may assist in setting up job training programs to upgrade employees' working skills and developmental training programs to prepare them for advancement to higher positions.

Setting job standards for each position, giving special recognition to outstanding workers, and handling problem workers who fail to perform up to standard—these are personnel responsibilities which the administrative assistant must understand and be ready to practice.

The evaluation of employees' job performance may fall to the administrative assistant also. Carrying out this responsibility is sometimes difficult. When a worker must be terminated, the administrative assistant must act with discretion and compassion, conscious of the bruised self-esteem of the terminated employee. Employees rated as superior need praise and commendations as well as tangible rewards.

Supervision involves the dual role of motivation and delegation. Doing both well is the mark of good leadership, a characteristic of skilled supervisors.

QUESTIONS FOR REVIEW

1. Describe three common sources for new office recruits.
2. How do employers benefit from hiring "temps" instead of full-time employees?
3. In what ways are in-house tests preferable to standardized tests in the screening of job applicants?
4. What is the EEOC and how does it impact on hiring procedures?
5. How can in-house referrals benefit the employer who is searching for new employees?
6. What guidelines should the supervisor follow in delegating tasks to subordinates?
7. Are *all* tasks appropriate for delegating to subordinates? Explain your answer.
8. What is the purpose of formal employee appraisals? How often are they done in most companies?
9. List four procedures followed in quality appraisal programs.

QUESTIONS FOR DISCUSSION

1. Describe the benefits secretarial students can derive through employment as "temps" during summers and holidays.
2. Companies are rehiring their retired workers at an increasing pace. Tell how this phenomenon can benefit both the retirees returning to work and the companies who hire them.
3. Which of the instructional methods described as developmental do you consider the most effective for readying employees for promotion to the managerial ranks? Explain your choice.
4. Discuss this statement: *Delegation of important tasks to subordinates is dangerous. Successful delegates are a threat to their delegators."*
   a. Does the statement have merit? Why or why not?
   b. If yes, why would anyone in authority ever delegate tasks to subordinates?

5. Some managers and the companies they represent believe in dismissing poor performers promptly upon their first infraction of a rule. Do you agree with their philosophy? Why or why not? Explain your position.

SUGGESTED ACTIVITIES

1. Conduct a mock interview of candidates for a secretarial position in the Eisor Corporation. Students can take turns role playing the interviewer and the interviewee.
2. Invite a personnel manager to visit the class. Ask that he or she speak on the recruitment and selection procedures followed by his or her company. Ask pertinent questions of the speaker, especially on issues discussed in this chapter. For example, Does the company reward good employees? Does the company invite in-house referrals when a position opens suddenly?
3. Interview an officer from your campus placement center. Discuss:
   a. job application procedures, making resume sheets
   b. the qualities employers look for in office workers
   c. EEOC guidelines and how they affect the screening of job candidates
   d. salaries being offered to current graduates
   e. fees charged (by commercial agencies) for job-finding services

REFERENCES

ARTHUR, DIANE, "Guidelines for Effective Delegation," *Supervisory Management* (October 1979), 9–13.

BAYTOS, LAWRENCE M., "Easing the Pain of Terminations," *Personnel* (July–August 1979), 64–69.

BIRCH, WM. J., "Performance Appraisals," *Personnel Journal* (June 1981), 457–459.

DAVID, HARRY, "Don't Make Applicants Feel like Supplicants," *Nation's Business* (January 1982), 50.

EVERED, JAMES, "How to Write a Good Job Description," *Supervisory Management* (April 1981), 14–19.

GATEWOOD, ROBERT D. and JAMES LEDVINKA, "Selection, Interviewing, and EEO: Mandate for Objectivity," *The Personnel Administrator* (December 1979), 41–54.

GOODALL, JAMES G., PH.D., "The Neglected Art of Interviewing," *Supervisory Management* (July 1981), 114–117.

IMUNDO, LOUIS V., *The Effective Supervisor's Handbook.* New York: Amacom, A Division of American Management Associations, 1980.

LYONS, MORGAN, "The Older Employee as a Resource Issue for Personnel," *Personnel Journal* (March 1981), 178–186.

PURSELL, ELLIOTT D., et al., "Structured Interviewing: Avoiding Selection Problems," *Personnel Journal* (November 1980), 907–912.

SCHWARTZ, STANLEY J., "How to Dehire: A Guide for the Manager," *Human Resource Management* (Winter 1980), 22–25.

STEVENSON, JANET H., "Secretarial Selection: Myths and Realities," *Personnel Journal* (February 1981), 114–117.

16
Banking and Investments

INTRODUCTION

As representatives of their employers, administrative assistants may deal regularly with banks and investment firms. Their level of involvement with each, of course, will depend largely upon the size of their company and its organizational structure. But the more clearly they understand the terminology and procedures of each, the better they can serve their employers' interests.

Banking responsibilities are probably enhanced by electronic fund transfers between the company's office and the banks with which it does business. Termed *electronic banking,* electronic fund transfers between banks and their customers and between members of bank networks have become a dominant force in the banking industry. This chapter presents a brief overview of electronic and manual procedures related to both banking and investments.

Terms and acronyms in this chapter include:

EFT	POS
Treasury bills	Treasury bonds
MICR	OTC
certified check	bank draft
mutual funds	municipal bonds

BANKING RESPONSIBILITIES

The handling of checks and bank deposits for the company is often the responsibility of the administrative assistant. To do the job well, he or she must have a working knowledge of the following procedures:

1. Handling checks
   a. Writing checks and maintaining account balances
   b. Understanding the MICR coding on checks
   c. Endorsing checks for cash or deposit
2. Making deposits
3. Reconciling a bank statement
4. Using other forms of funds transfers

The administrative assistant must also be aware of the procedures involved in handling the petty cash fund, maintaining payroll records, and transacting business with the Federal Reserve.

Check-handling Procedures

Over 135 million checks are written each business day, transferring billions of dollars among bank users' accounts. Handling checks for personal and/or business use has become so routine that users tend to make errors with surprising frequency.

Bankers tell of many bank customers whose check-writing errors cost them

FIGURE 16-1 The capabilities of President Preston were first demonstrated as administrative assistant to the president of the bank, whom she later succeeded upon his retirement.

FIGURE 16-2 The Application System/400(TM) family of computers provides banks with a variety of software applications designed especially for banks and other financial institutions. *Courtesy of IBM Corporation.*

substantial sums of money each year. To eliminate or reduce such errors, they recommend the following practices when writing checks.

1. Check the figures, the date, and the payee's name for accuracy before releasing the check.
2. Leave no spaces before or after the dollar amounts.
3. Do not predate or postdate a check.
4. Sign checks in the same way that the account is registered with the bank; that is, with no added initials or name abbreviations (Jim for James).
5. Fill out the stub *before* writing the check, or do it *immediately* afterwards.
6. Do *not* make corrections on a check after it is written. Instead, rewrite the check.

Reading and understanding the coded information which speeds the processing of checks is another safeguard against errors.

MICR Coding

Check processing is automated. High-speed electronic machines sort checks at a speed approaching 100,000 checks an hour. An MICR (magnetic ink character reader) reads from left to right the coded digits imprinted along the bottom of the checks, deciphering four pieces of information.

1. The first two digits at the left show the bank's Federal Reserve district; the third digit identifies the Federal Reserve office or a special collection point; the fourth digit identifies the bank's state or a special collection point. Digits 5 through 8 are the commercial bank's identifier. The last digit verifies the routing number accuracy.

2. The customer's account number occupies the next eight digits, about center position at the bottom of the check.
3. The check number is to the right of the account number.
4. The dollar amount of the check is printed by the first bank receiving the check.

Check Endorsements

Endorsing a check means signing one's name or the company's name on the reverse side of the check (at the extreme left end) in order to present it for payment. Three types are commonly used.

1. A *blank endorsement* contains the payee's signature alone. The blank endorsement transfers ownership or title of the check to the person holding it at the time (the bearer). If the check is lost after being so endorsed, anyone may cash it.
2. A *special endorsement* names the person who must endorse the check *next* in order to receive payment.
3. A *restrictive endorsement* specifies what is to be done with the check; it limits further endorsement and controls final payment.

(See the sample endorsements in Figure 16–3.)

Making Deposits

When depositing checks in person or by mail, the administrative assistant should endorse the checks "for deposit only," followed by the company's stamp, with or without a signature. A record should also be kept by date of all checks and cash deposited to the company's account.

In order to expedite service at the teller window when making deposits personally, the depositor should:

1. List the amount of each check separately on the deposit slip.
2. Add all items on the slip—coins, currency, and checks, checking the accuracy of the total.
3. Retain a copy of the deposit slip.

Figure 16-3 Three types of check endorsements—blank, special, restrictive.

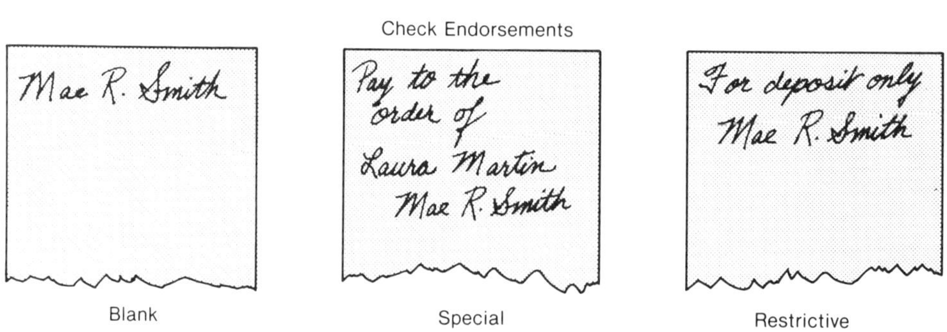

Reconciling a Bank Statement

In a small business without a full-time accountant, the administrative assistant may have to reconcile the company's bank statement each month. The following six-step procedure should simplify the task and reduce the risk of errors.

1. Sort checks numerically.
2. Add to the company's checkbook the interest earned, if any.
3. Subtract from the checkbook balance any charges imposed by the bank.
4. Check off in the checkbook each cancelled check returned with the bank statement.
5. List all outstanding (unpaid) checks by number and amount. Add these and subtract from the bank balance.
6. Add to the bank balance any deposits made but not yet credited by the bank to the company's account.

Upon completion of these procedures, the bank balance and the checkbook balance should agree. Software programs are designed to handle these chores electronically. (See Figure 16–4.)

FIGURE 16–4 The MONEYCOUNTS software program simplifies reconciliation of bank statements with checking account records. *Courtesy of Parsons Technology, Inc.*

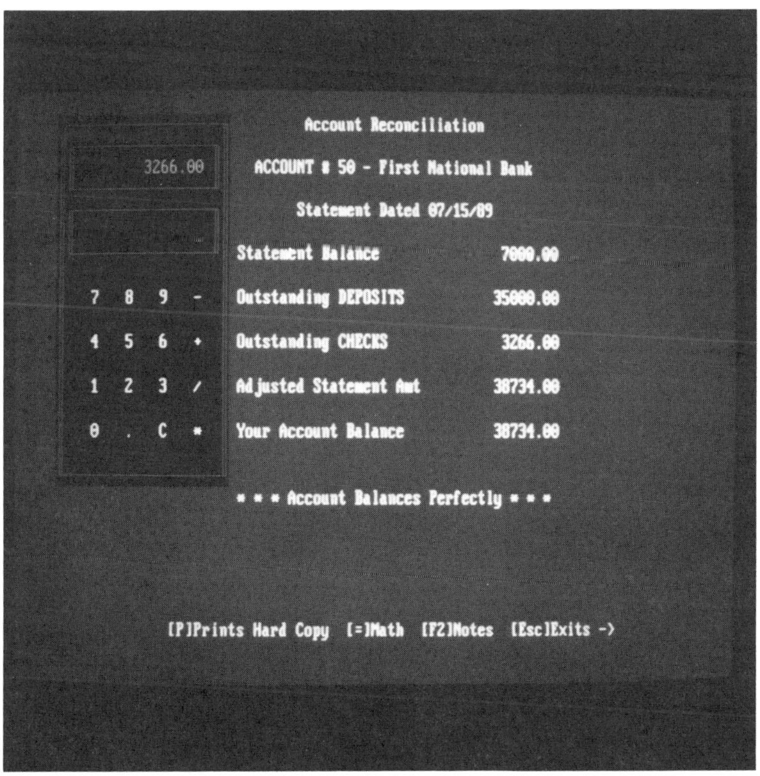

Other Forms of Fund Transfers

Certified Checks Certified checks are personal or business checks which are stamped "certified" by the bank to certify to the payee that sufficient funds are set aside to redeem the check. The amount is transferred from the drawer's account at the bank at the time of certification, and the check becomes the bank's obligation.

Cashier's Check (Official Check) A cashier's check is the bank's own order to make payment out of bank funds. It is usually used by companies or persons who do not have a checking account in that particular bank. The cashier's check is drawn up by the bank to a specified payee after the amount of the check plus a service fee are paid to the bank by the person requesting it.

Traveler's Checks Traveler's checks are purchased at banks or other financial agencies by travelers who, for security reasons, prefer traveler's checks to cash. Numbered in sequential order, the checks are purchased and signed by the buyer in the presence of the bank teller or other person handling the transaction.

When the check is cashed, the owner again signs his or her name on the face of the check in the presence of the person who is redeeming it. The two signatures can then be compared to verify the identity of the person cashing the check.

Sold in amounts of $20 to $500, traveler's checks are considered one of the safest ways of transporting money when traveling.

Bank Draft A bank draft is drawn up by a bank on its account in another bank. It differs from the cashier's check only in that it draws on funds it has on deposit in another bank, whereas the cashier's check draws on funds in the cashier's own bank.

Money Order Money orders may be purchased from the Postal Service or from banks. In either case, the amount of the money order plus a fee is paid to the Postal Service, or to a bank, for issuance of the amount specified. They are frequently used for sending money by mail, particularly by persons who do not have checking accounts. Like cashier's checks and bank drafts, they are the direct obligation of the issuer—that is, the Postal Service or the issuing bank.

Handling Petty Cash

A petty cash account is set up to pay for minor office expenses and supplies. Postage due or delivery costs, small supply items, and other incidental expenses are generally paid from the petty cash fund.

Initiated as an expense account for a set figure, the petty cash fund is replenished periodically as the funds are depleted. Each withdrawal is validated by a petty cash voucher on which the purpose, amount, and date of the withdrawal are recorded. An approval signature from the person responsible for the account and the name of the expense account to be charged are also included on the voucher.

If maintained accurately, the amount of recorded withdrawals plus the cash on hand equal the amount of the original fund. When the account needs replenishing, an entry is made in the petty cash account, distributing the payments to the proper expense accounts; then the petty cash box is refunded to its original amount.

Payroll and Tax Records

The company's financial responsibilities include the accurate maintenance of employee payroll records, including the withholding of social security and income tax from the employee's pay, and mailing the deducted taxes to the Internal Revenue Service.

For manually kept records, payroll registers are used. A separate page is reserved for each employee, with column headings designed for personal data, regular and overtime earnings, federal and state income tax withholding, FICA (social security) tax, miscellaneous deductions, and net pay. Summary pages for all employees are also maintained. Computerized payroll records are rapidly replacing the manual records, however. Many software programs are available for this purpose.

Federal Reserve Banks

As representatives of their employers, administrative assistants may have occasion to transact business directly with the Federal Reserve Bank in their area.

If their employers are not located in one of the twelve cities housing a Federal Reserve Bank, they can easily learn in which city the district's Federal Reserve Bank is located by calling a local bank. (See Figure 16-5.)

Useful information can be obtained directly from a Federal Reserve Bank. For example, the current discount rate (the rate charged member banks for loans from the Fed) is of primary concern to businesspersons who regularly borrow large sums from banks. The prime rate (interest rate the banks charge their best customers) is directly related to the discount rates the banks must pay for funds they receive from the Federal Reserve; the higher the discount rate, the higher the prime rate banks must charge their customers.

Treasury Securities

New-issue Treasury securities are also available through the Federal Reserve Banks. Treasury securities are loans issued to the public by the U.S. Treasury in the form of Treasury bills, notes, or bonds. They are the direct obligation of the United States government. New issues can be purchased, prior to issue, from any of the twelve Federal Reserve Banks.

District		Seal	District		Seal
1	Boston	A	7	Chicago	G
2	New York	B	8	St. Louis	H
3	Philadelphia	C	9	Minneapolis	I
4	Cleveland	D	10	Kansas City	J
5	Richmond	E	11	Dallas	K
6	Atlanta	F	12	San Francisco	L

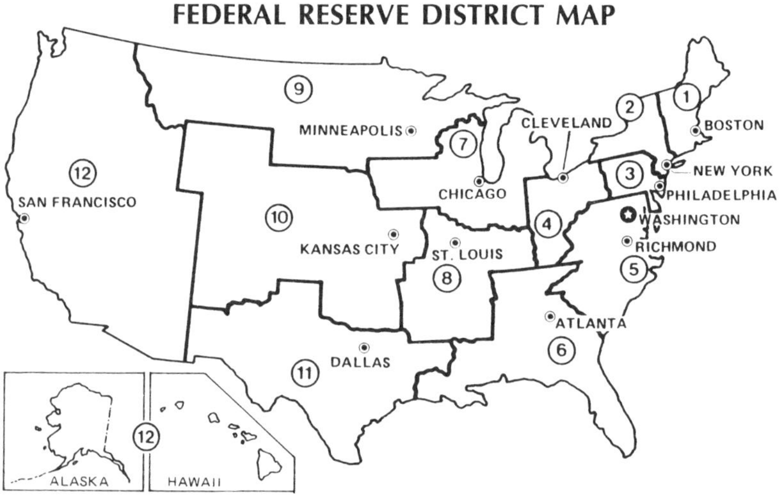

FIGURE 16-5 Map of the Federal Reserve Bank locations.

Treasury bills are short-term securities issued with 13-week, 26-week, and 52-week maturities. They are sold in minimum amounts of $10,000, and in multiples of $5,000 above the minimum. Subsequent to their original issue, Treasury bills may be purchased at prevailing market prices through investment security firms, as well as through banks.

Treasury notes and bonds have longer maturities than Treasury bills. Notes have a fixed maturity of two to ten years from date of issue. Bonds normally have a fixed maturity of more than ten years.

Periodically, Treasury notes and bonds are issued in minimum denominations of $1,000 and $5,000. Notes maturing in four years or longer, and all bonds, are usually available in minimum denomination of $1,000. Notes maturing in less than four years are usually offered in minimum amounts of $5,000, or multiples of $5,000.

Key information about the purchase of new offerings may be obtained by dialing a Federal Reserve Bank. Each bank has its own number which, when dialed, gives callers a recorded message telling the results of the most recent auction of Treasury bills.

The recorded message will also provide information on forthcoming issues of Treasury notes and bonds, such as the term of the securities, auction

FORM PD 5176-2
(January 1986)

OMB No. 1535-0069
Expires: 01-31-89

TREASURY DIRECT

TENDER FOR 26-WEEK TREASURY BILL

TENDER INFORMATION AMOUNT OF TENDER: $ ________

BID TYPE (Check One) ☐ NONCOMPETITIVE ☐ COMPETITIVE AT ___ . ___ %

ACCOUNT NUMBER ___ - ___ - ___

INVESTOR INFORMATION

ACCOUNT NAME

ADDRESS

CITY STATE ZIP CODE

TAXPAYER IDENTIFICATION NUMBER

1ST NAMED OWNER ___ - ___ - ___ (SOCIAL SECURITY NUMBER) OR ___ - ___ (EMPLOYER IDENTIFICATION NUMBER)

TELEPHONE NUMBERS

WORK ( ) - HOME ( ) -

PAYMENT ATTACHED TOTAL PAYMENT: $ ________

CASH (01): $ ________ CHECKS (02/03): $ ________

SECURITIES (05): $ ________ $ ________

OTHER (06): $ ________ $ ________

FOR DEPARTMENT USE

TENDER NUMBER 912794

CUSIP

ISSUE DATE

RECEIVED BY

DATE RECEIVED

EXT REG ☐

FOREIGN ☐

BACKUP ☐

REVIEW ☐

CLASS ☐

NUMBERS

DIRECT DEPOSIT INFORMATION

ROUTING NUMBER

FINANCIAL INSTITUTION NAME

ACCOUNT NUMBER

ACCOUNT NAME

ACCOUNT TYPE (Check One) ☐ CHECKING ☐ SAVINGS

AUTOMATIC REINVESTMENT

1 2 3 4 Circle the number of sequential 26-week reinvestments you want to schedule at this time

AUTHORIZATION

For the notice required under the Privacy and Paperwork Reduction Acts, see the accompanying instructions.

I submit this tender pursuant to the provisions of Department of the Treasury Circulars, Public Debt Series Nos. 1-86 and 2-86 and the public announcement issued by the Department of the Treasury.

Under penalties of perjury, I certify that the number shown on this form is my correct taxpayer identification number and that I am not subject to backup withholding because (1) I have not been notified that I am subject to backup withholding as a result of a failure to report all interest or dividends, or (2) the Internal Revenue Service has notified me that I am no longer subject to backup withholding. I further certify that all other information provided on this form is true, correct and complete.

SIGNATURE DATE

FIGURE 16-6 Application to purchase a 26-week Treasury bill.

and maturity dates, minimum purchase, closing time for the offering, and payment instructions. To put idle cash "to work," particularly while waiting to commit to a longer-term investment, Treasury bills are often purchased by company officials to yield a short-term return.

The addresses and telephone numbers of the twelve Federal Reserve Banks and their branches are listed at the end of this chapter. Personnel at the banks can answer questions on the purchase, exchange, or redemption of Treasury securities, but they are not permitted to offer investment advice.

ELECTRONIC BANKING

Electronic banking is the common term for many forms of computerized banking procedures. Most can be classified as electronic fund transfers (EFTs). The administrative assistant will be involved with most, if not all, of these procedures at some point.

Electronic Fund Transfers

Electronic banking procedures enable users to authorize transfers from their checking accounts to those of their creditors without ever leaving their homes; to have funds moved between a savings account and a checking account; and through automated teller machines to make deposits or withdrawals any day of the week.

Through the broad applications of electronic banking, corporate treasurers move funds freely and swiftly from one account to another, as needed; and companies initiate payment of goods and services at the time of purchase.

Merchants, hotel and airline clerks, and some hospital personnel use bank-owned EFT stations at their checkout points to verify users' checks, or to transfer money from the customers' or patients' accounts into their own accounts.

FIGURE 16-7 Chart of the growth of electronic banking since 1983, with growth anticipated to the year 2000.

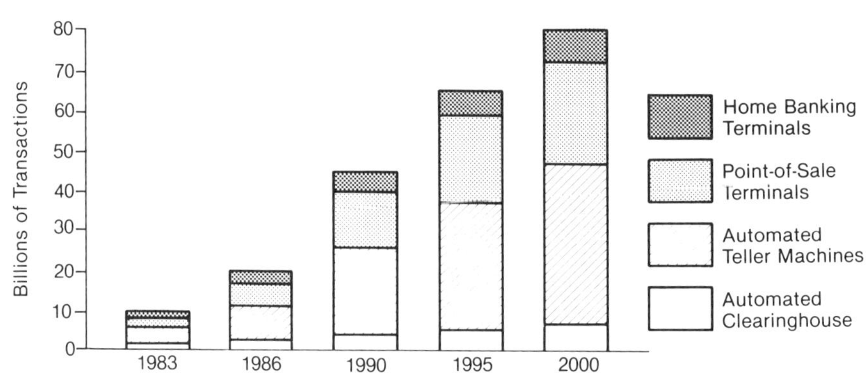

Electronic fund transfers (EFTs) can be defined as a set of electronic interrelationships. Commonly-used services under the EFT umbrella are:

Electronic banking networks, linking banks to banks
On-line communications links between banks and their customers
Automated teller machines (ATMs)
Smart cards
Point-of-sale transfers (POS)

Electronic Banking Networks

Banks in metropolitan areas communicate with one another and with member banks in rural areas via electronic telecommunication networks. One such network is the "Fed Wire," owned and operated by the Federal Reserve System, which links hundreds of member banks with the Federal Reserve Banks in a nationwide network. Millions of messages and dollars are transferred via this network, with hundreds of computer work stations handling the communications daily.

Another network, the "Bank Wire," is a cooperative funds-transfer network serving several hundred banks in the United States. "Swift" (Society for Worldwide Interbank Financial Telecommunications) is a cooperative international network which links banks in over 50 countries.

To speed up transfers, a growing number of automated clearinghouses and banking networks are added each year. As the public and rural banking areas come to appreciate the speed and convenience of banking networks, the volume of electronic transactions grows.

Banks' On-Line Links to Customers

Electronically linked to their banks, companies can transact business such as the following without ever leaving their own offices.

Check current balances in the company checking and savings accounts
Request balances owed on outstanding loans, mortgages, or credit card accounts
Command transfers of the proper amounts from their checking accounts, to be placed in the accounts of their creditors
Transfer funds from one account to another checking or savings account

The electronic systems speed up customer service, allow for instant verification of account balances and signatures, reduce the avalanche of paper work associated with manual systems, and reduce the bank's cost of each transaction by as much as two thirds. Customers also enjoy the convenience of immediate banking service from their own place of business.

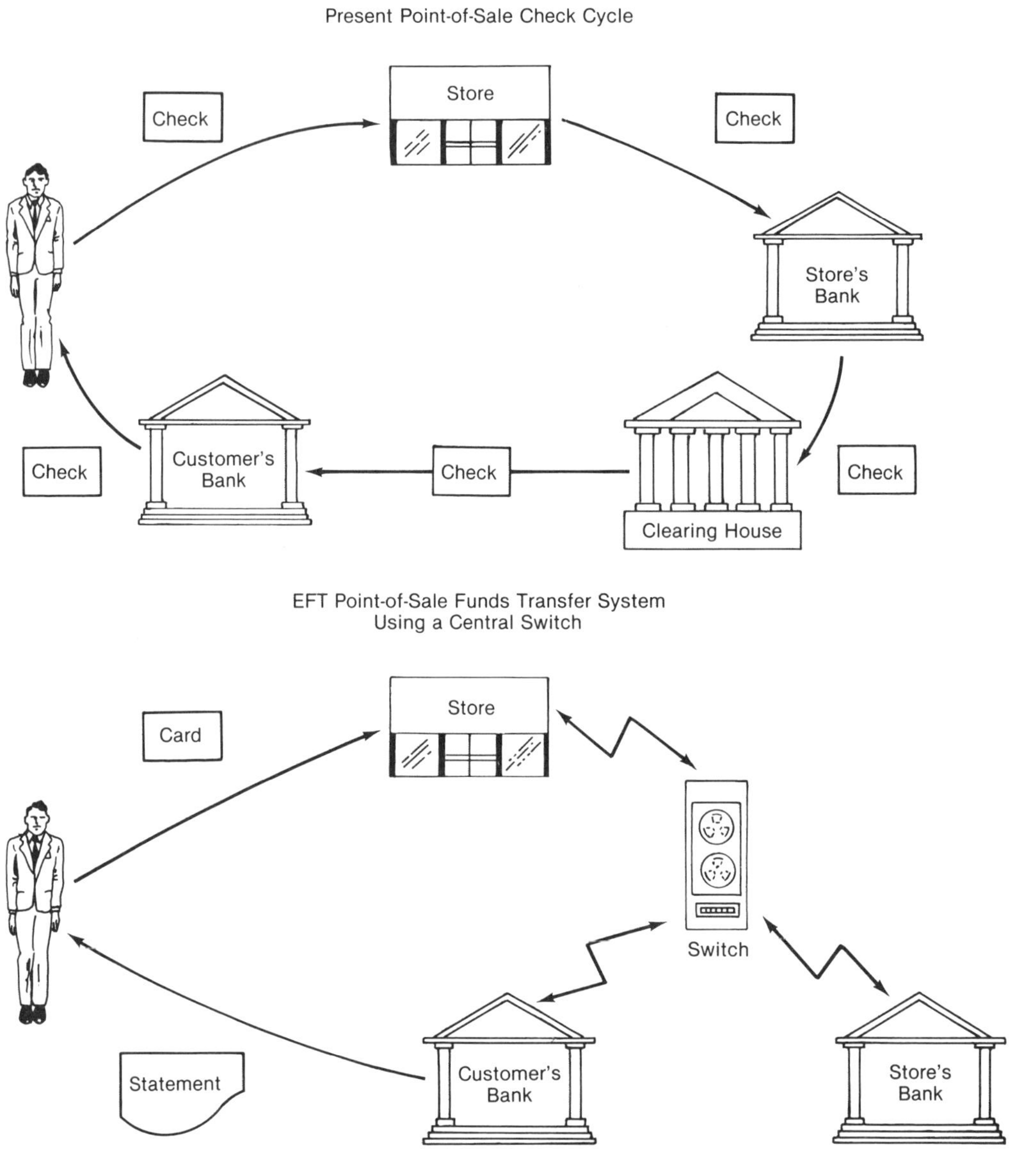

FIGURE 16-8 Point-of-sale check cycle compared with a funds transfer through an electronic-funds-transfer sale.

Automated Teller Machines (ATMs)

Another electronic convenience banks provide their customers is the automated teller machine. ATMs are electronic terminals that permit customer banking at almost anytime of the day or night. They are placed at stations on or off the bank premises.

FIGURE 16-9 The widespread use of ATMs (automated teller machines) has made banking convenience a priority item among bank customers. *Courtesy of IBM Corporation.*

To access the ATM, the customer uses a special plastic card containing the account number and personal identification number (PIN) to withdraw or deposit funds. The account number and credit limit are magnetically encoded on a strip of tape on the back of the customer's card.

When the customer inserts the card into the ATM, the terminal reads and transmits the data to a computer which processes the transaction. Instructions for operating the ATMs are displayed prominently at each ATM installation.

Smart Cards

Smart cards are similar to bank cards used in ATMs in that they can be used to get cash, but their primary function is that of a charge card.

Users spend smart cards by presenting them for payment of purchases as they shop. They differ from bank cards in that they have embedded on them a microchip containing the user's name, personal ID number, and the amount he or she is allowed to charge on the card.

As the user spends the card, the amount of the purchase is deducted from the stored balance, until users have completely cashed in their microchips. Once the card is completely spent, it must be replenished by the user's bank before it can be used again.

Originating in Europe, smart cards are enjoying increased popularity in the United States as an alternative to the magnetic-strip bank cards. Since they offer better protection from fraudulent use and abuse, smart cards may become the dominant plastic card of the future, replacing traditional charge cards.

Point-of-sale (POS) Transfers

Retail stores with the proper POS transfer equipment allow their customers to pay for purchases at the cashier's station by using a debit card in an electronic terminal. The POS procedure directly accesses the buyer's checking or savings accounts at their banks and transfers money to the merchant's account.

The transaction is similar to that of credit card usage, with one important exception: The money for the purchase is immediately transferred from the card user's account to the store's account, as opposed to credit card usage which postpones transfer and payment to the merchant.

POS transactions usually work like this:

1. A cashier punches a customer's electronic bank card number into the specially equipped cash register.
2. The customer punches his or her personal ID number into a keypad similar to the ATM keypad.
3. The information travels over telephone lines to the customer's bank.
4. A bank computer debits the customer's account and indicates to the cashier that the transaction is complete.
5. The customer is issued a ticket showing the amount of the purchase for later entry into the equivalent of a checkbook.

For all POS transactions, a central office known as the "switch" moves the entries between and among the customers' banks and those of the merchants from whom they buy services or consumer goods.

EFT Regulations

In response to the growing use of electronic fund transfers, Congress passed the Electronic Funds Transfer Act in 1978, defining the rights and responsibilities of EFT consumers and providers.

In order to make the most of EFT, the administrative assistant must become acquainted with the major points of this legislation, a copy of which is available from any Federal Reserve Bank. For example, the law provides that when signing up for EFT, users are entitled to the following *written* information:

1. An explanation of the customer's liability for unauthorized transfers
2. The telephone number and address of the office to notify in case of an unauthorized transfer
3. The bank's business days

4. The dollar amount and frequency of transfers allowed
5. Any applicable charges
6. A summary of the customer's rights to receive:
   a. receipts
   b. periodic statements
   c. notice that preauthorized transfers have taken place
7. A statement of rights to stop payments
8. A summary of the bank's liability for failure to stop a transfer
9. Circumstances under which information can be disclosed to a third party
10. Instructions to follow in event of errors

Growth in electronic banking is a certainty for the future. Measured in transactions processed, analysts predict that electronic payments will grow to 80 billion by the year 2000. Although the administrative assistant may not be frequently involved in EFT transfers, it is important that he or she understand its basics.

INVESTMENTS

Profitable investments may be critical to the company's financial success. The more profitable the company's investments, the greater its latitude for reducing the price of its goods and gaining an edge on its competitors.

Therefore, in addition to bank-related activities, the administrative assistant may assist his or her employer in keeping track of the company's investments. For this purpose, a registry will probably be maintained listing the company-owned shares of stock and bonds by name, dates of purchase, percent of gain or loss on shares sold, and the maturity dates and face values of bonds.

Tracking responsibilities may be handled manually or through computer software designed for this purpose. In either case, it is imperative that the administrative assistant understand basic investment concepts. By way of introduction, a brief explanation of investment terminology is appropriate.

Common and Preferred Stocks

Common and preferred stocks are securities which represent ownership shares in a corporation. When dividends on earnings are declared by the Board of Directors for distribution to shareholders, however, the preferred stockholders are normally limited to a fixed dividend while the common stockholders' dividends rise or fall in accord with the company's profits or losses.

In case of the company's liquidation due to poor earnings, however, preferred stockholders have a higher claim on remaining assets.

Claims of both common and preferred stockholders are junior to claims of bondholders or other creditors of the company. The terms *common stock* and *capital stock* are often used interchangeably when the company has no preferred stock.

New York Stock Exchange Composite Transactions

1. Stock—abbreviated name.
2. Dividend (if any).
3. Yield (%)—the current dividend of the company's stock divided by the current market price.
4. Price/Earnings (P/E) ratio—the market price of the stock divided by its per-share earnings.
5. Sales in hundreds—sold that day.
6. High—the highest price paid for the stock that day.
7. Low—the lowest price paid for the stock that day.
8. Close—last price paid that day.
9. Net change—the difference between the close and the previous day's close.

	52 Weeks Hi	52 Weeks Lo	Stock	Sym	Div	Yld %	PE	Vol 100s	Hi	Lo	Close	Net Chg
	47¾	34	Diebold	DBD	1.40	3.2	18	84	44⅝	44⅜	44⅜	+ ⅛
	36⅛	16½	DigitalComm	DCA		...	18	2152	21¼	20½	21	+ ¼
	122⅜	86⅜	DigitalEqp	DEC		...	11	5494	97¼	96	96⅜	+ ½
	63¼	39⅛	DillardStrs	DDS	.16	.3	16	75	58½	58	58½	...
	16½	12	DimeSvgNY	DME	.60	4.1	9	534	14½	14¼	14½	...
↑	98¾	60	Disney	DIS	.48	.5	23	2017	98⅞	98	98⅞	+ ¼
	28¼	23½	DivrsEngies	DEI	1.56	5.7	11	913	27⅜	27⅛	27¼	...
	6¼	3½	DivrsInd	DMC		...	14	8	5⅜	5⅜	5⅜	– ⅛
n	**9**	**6¾**	**DixonGp**	**DXN**	**.24e**	**3.1**	**8**	**40**	**7⅝**	**7⅝**	**7⅝**	**+ ⅝**
↑	45¼	40⅜	DominRes	D	3.20	7.0	11	981	45¾	45	45¾	+ ¾
	15⅜	9¾	Domtar	DTC	.50	...	...	74	12⅝	12⅜	12⅜	– ⅛
	25¾	16½	Donaldson	DCI	.38	2.2	11	141	17½	17⅜	17½	...
	46⅜	32	Donelley	DNY	.88	2.0	17	616	45	44¼	45	+ ½
s	35⅜	26⅝	Dover	DOV	.68	2.1	15	497	32⅞	32⅜	32⅞	+ ½
	100½	81	DowChem	DOW	3.20	3.6	6	6077	88¼	86⅝	88	+ ⅞
	38½	29¼	DowJones	DJ	.72	2.0	11	357	36⅜	35⅝	36	+ ⅛
	28⅝	14⅝	DowneySL	DSL	.40	1.5	7	119	27⅜	26¾	26¾	– ⅜
	22¾	14⅝	Dravo	DRV		...	25	157	19½	19	19	– ½
↑	42⅜	25⅜	DresserInd	DI	1.00	2.4	19	3571	42½	41¾	42¼	+ ¼
	7¼	3⅝	Dresher	DSR	.16	3.6	14	12	4½	4⅜	4½	...
	32⅛	24¼	Dreyfus	DRY	.52	1.8	13	1379	29⅛	28⅝	29	+ ¼
	10⅞	9⅞	DreyfusMuni	LEO	.78a	7.2	...	466	10⅞	10¾	10⅞	+ ¼
n	12	10¼	DreyfStrGvFd	DSI	1.08	9.9	...	258	11	10¾	10⅞	...
	113¼	78½	DuPont	DD	4.20	3.8	11	3234	112⅜	110⅝	111¾	+ ¾
	44½	38⅞	DuPont pf		3.50	8.2	...	4	42½	42½	42½	...
	55½	49⅝	DuPont pf		4.50	8.2	...	13	55	54½	55	+ ½
	9⅛	7⅝	DuffPhelps	DNP	.72a	8.5	...	2244	8⅝	8½	8½	...
	51⅛	42⅝	DukePwr	DUK	2.96	5.8	13	792	51	50⅜	51	+ ½
	93½	82	DukePwr pf		8.20	8.8	...	z300	93	93	93	...
n	6½	4⅞	DukeRltyInv	DRE	.68e	12.4	...	38	5½	5⅜	5½	...
	59⅜	46	DunBradst	DNB	2.00	3.5	21	2822	57⅝	57¼	57⅝	...
	23¼	20⅛	DuqLght pfA		2.10	9.6	...	z400	21⅞	21⅞	21⅞	...
	21½	18¼	DuqLght pf		2.00	9.9	...	z70	20¼	20¼	20¼	...
	21	18¾	DuqLght pf		2.05	9.9	...	z200	20¾	20¾	20¾	– ¼
	22⅝	19¼	DuqLght pfK		2.10	9.4	...	2	22¼	22¼	22¼	+ ⅛
	24	21½	DuqLght pr		2.31	9.7	...	z1000	23⅞	23¾	23⅞	– ⅛
↑	74¾	68	DuqLght pf		7.20	9.6	...	z130	75¼	75	75¼	+ ¾
	25⅜	22	DynaAmer	DYA	.20	.9	292	18	23⅜	23⅜	23⅜	– ⅛

-E-E-E-

FIGURE 16-10 Excerpt from NYSE daily stock reports.

Dividends

Dividends represent a portion of the profits earned by the company over a given period, and, when declared by company officials, are shared by the owners (shareholders). Although similar to interest earned in a savings account, dividends are not guaranteed to shareholders. During periods of low or negative profits, dividends are not declared.

Stock Dividends Stock dividends are dividends paid to company shareholders in the form of additional shares of stock rather than in cash.

Treasury Stock Treasury stock is stock issued by a company for purchase by the public, but later reacquired. It may be held in the company's treasury indefinitely, reissued to the public, or retired. It receives no dividends and has no vote while held.

Book Value The book value of a share of stock is computed by adding the company's assets, subtracting liabilities, and dividing by the number of common shares outstanding.

Mutual Funds A mutual fund invests in the stock of multiple corporations, then sells its shares to the public, usually through a national stock exchange.

Mutual funds are a means of participating in the stock market without undue risk. Buyers "spread" their risk over many corporations, hoping that any weakness demonstrated in one sector of the stocks will be offset by other stocks in the group which have above-average yield and growth potential.

Mutual funds are usually open ended; that is, fund managers buy into the market as they perceive opportunities for growth in certain corporations, and sell securities when they perform poorly. Some funds include bonds as well as stock shares.

Current values are published daily in *The Wall Street Journal* and other financial newspapers. No-load funds are those which charge no sales commission to customers at the time of purchase.

Stock Exchanges Stock exchanges are trading markets for publicly held shares of stock. Individual investors, as well as large investment groups, use the exchange to trade shares among themselves.

The American Stock Exchange, the New York Stock Exchange (sometimes referred to as the "Big Board"), and other exchanges list only companies that meet certain criteria; their requirements relate to company size, current earnings, market value of securities, and other criteria which vary from one exchange to another.

Due to technological advances in communication, investors can buy or sell shares of stocks in a matter of minutes. Brokers who are registered with the designated exchange can forward a buy or sell order to the exchange floor via computer, executing a transaction almost instantly.

Financial publications publish current values of all securities listed on the American Stock Exchange (AMSE) and the New York Stock Exchange (NYSE).

Over-the-counter Market (OTC) The OTC market is made up of securities not listed on a major securities exchange. Thousands of companies have insufficient earnings, shareholders, or shares outstanding to warrant membership in one of the major exchanges.

Their securities are traded over the counter between dealers who act as representatives for their customers. Referred to as a secondary market for bonds and stock exchange, the OTC is the principal market for U.S. government and municipal bonds.

NASDAQ NASDAQ is an automated information network which provides brokers and dealers with price quotations on OTC securities. It is an acronym for National Association of Securities Dealers Automated Quotations.

Dow-Jones Index The Dow-Jones composite index covers price movements of a group of stocks listed on the New York Stock Exchange. The Dow-Jones averages of these stocks are regarded as an important indicator of stock market activity.

Bonds Bonds are debt obligations of an issuer payable to the bondholder at maturity for the face value of the bond.

Bearer bonds do not have the owner's name registered on the books of the issuing company; therefore, they are payable to any holder (bearer) of the bonds.

Coupon bonds have interest coupons attached to the bond certificates. The coupons are clipped as they come due and are presented to a bank for payment.

Registered bonds are registered on the books of the issuing company in the name of the owner. Interest payments are sent to owners when due, as is the face value of the bond when it matures.

Municipal bonds are issued by a state or political subdivision, such as a county, city, town, or village. In general, interest earned is exempt from federal income taxes.

Government bonds are the direct obligation of the U.S. government; they are considered the highest-grade issues in existence.

Software for Investment Analysis

Spreadsheets are convenient general-purpose tools for analyzing investments. When data are revised, the built-in formulas and automatic recalculation of relative values make spreadsheets ideal tools for analyzing the impact of price changes.

Many analysts use general-purpose spreadsheet software to track the performance of their investments; others utilize one of many special-purpose templates designed specifically for this purpose. A template is a spreadsheet which includes the labels and formulas needed to construct an investment analysis program. The user inserts the data—stock name, date, purchase price, and number of shares bought—and at the user's command, the program performs the calculations needed.

Portfolio management packages generate reports on the current status of a company's investments. In a portfolio management program, the user stores key facts in the program as shares of stock or bonds are bought or sold. When an updated report on the value of the portfolio is needed, current values of the stock are entered, and the program generates a current status report on the portfolio holdings.

Portfolio management programs generate the figures necessary to calculate tax returns. On command, investment income, expenses, gains and losses for the year are calculated promptly and accurately.

Reading a Stock Table

The administrative assistant who is responsible for recording current entries in the company's stock register must understand how to read the stock listings in financial journals.

Figure 16–10 from *The Wall Street Journal* illustrates the abbreviated terms used in published listings.[1] The first two columns show the high and the low prices

[1]*The Wall Street Journal*, July 13, 1989, C4.

of shares over the past 52 weeks. Then, reading from left to right, each stock is listed by name, abbreviated symbol, yield (in percent), price/earnings ratio, volume of sales (that day), highest price that day, lowest price that day, closing price, and net change over previous day.

SUMMARY

The responsibilities of the administrative assistant often extend to financial matters beyond what he or she had envisioned as a student preparing for a business career.

In addition to routine banking activities, the administrative assistant may be called upon to track the performance of the company's investment portfolio. Software programs designed to speed and clarify investment portfolio management will be a part of the activities in these areas. It is imperative, therefore, that the administrative assistant acquire an understanding of the basic concepts and terminology of investments.

An understanding of the principal applications of electronic banking is also important. Within the last decade, electronic banking has come into its own as a force in simplifying and speeding the transfer of funds between banks and customers. It is predicted that by the year 2000, manual procedures will no longer be the dominant form of banking, as the number of banking transactions done electronically is projected to reach 80 billion annually.

The administrative assistant has little choice but to be ready for the shift to electronics in both banking and investment portfolio management.

QUESTIONS FOR REVIEW

1. To reduce errors and assure correct payment to the proper parties, one should use special care in writing checks. List six rules to observe when writing checks.
2. Explain the difference between a blank endorsement and a special endorsement. Which is preferable in terms of security? Explain your answer.
3. What are POS transfers? Are they available in every retail store?
4. List some of the rights of EFT users, as spelled out in the Electronic Funds Transfer Act of 1978.
5. Briefly define the following terms:
   a. mutual funds
   b. The New York Stock Exchange
   c. common stock
   d. bonds
6. What is the purpose of portfolio management software? Explain how such packages serve the user.
7. In what cities are the Federal Reserve Banks located?

QUESTIONS FOR DISCUSSION

1. Discuss ways that the "personal touch" may be maintained in the banking industry without losing the efficiency of electronic banking.
2. What services do the stock exchanges perform for investors? In your opinion, how does the economic health of the stock market impact on the American economy?
3. Someone questions the wisdom of your company's investing heavily in bonds rather than common stocks. Explain to the person why you believe there is less risk in bonds than in stocks. (Or set up a debate on the issue, with two classmates on each side taking opposing positions.)
4. The New York Stock Exchange has set up many regulations designed to protect investors who utilize its services. One of them is that corporations listing stocks on the exchange must publish earnings statements periodically, usually quarterly. In your opinion, how do these regulations help to protect investors?

SUGGESTED ACTIVITIES

1. The New York Stock Exchange recommends these five basic rules to anyone considering buying stock:
   a. Remember the risks as well as the rewards.
   b. Get the facts about the stock.
   c. Seek advice from a reliable broker.
   d. Always keep a cash reserve on hand.
   e. Tailor investments, whether in stocks or bonds, to your goals.

   Invite a local stockbroker to the class to discuss these rules. Ask the broker:
   f. How or where can one find factual information on a given stock?
   g. How much of a cash reserve should one keep on hand?
   h. Should cash reserves be kept in a savings account, in certificates of deposit, or in interest-bearing checking accounts?
   i. What kind of service should a stockholder expect from a broker?
2. Write to a public corporation to ask for their latest annual report. Share the report with classmates who have done the same. On the basis of the information contained in the reports, choose the stocks which you would most like to own. Explain your choice.

   If you were to attend an annual meeting of the corporation in which you own stock, what questions would you ask the president or the board of directors?
3. Collect recent issues of *The Wall Street Journal.* Read the stock prices reported from shares traded on the American Stock Exchange. Explain the figures quoted. Choose a stock or a mutual fund and keep track of its performance over a two- or three-week period.

GLOSSARY OF BANKING TERMS

Amortization: The gradual lowering of debt via payments of principal and interest; generally refers to real estate mortgages

Bank draft: A check written by a bank against its own funds on deposit in another bank

Bank money order: A check that is sold by a bank to a customer in any amount the customer specifies; fees charged depend on the dollar amount of the money order

Cancelled check: A check which has been paid and debited against the depositor's account

Cashier's check: The bank's own check, usually signed by the bank's cashier, and "purchased" for cash or a note payable

Certificates of deposit (CDs): Sometimes referred to as savings bonds or savings certificates, these deposits are payable on a specified future date. Usually, the longer the term of the deposit, the higher the rate of interest that can be earned on these loans.

Check: A written order instructing a bank to withdraw funds from the customer's demand-deposit account to pay a payee

Collateral: Anything of value that a bank accepts as security against the repayment of a loan

Debit and credit: Debit—a charge against a bank deposit account. Credit—funds added to the customer's account

Demand deposits: More familiarly known as checking accounts, demand deposits may be withdrawn by the customer without advance notice. Demand-deposit accounts are a convenience service for users. They provide proof of payment, should a dispute arise about any item which has been paid by check.

Installment loan: To be paid back in fixed amounts, including both principal and interest, over a predetermined period of time

Legal tender: Any money that must be accepted in payment of debts. Checkbook funds are not legal tender

Money market certificates: These certificates usually have a maturity of 26 weeks and can be purchased for $10,000 or more. Maximum interest is tied to the yield on 26-week U.S. Treasury bills, and the rate ceiling on new certificates is set every Thursday. Interest is not compounded.

Mortgage: A legal written transfer of ownership of property (but not of possession) from a debtor to a creditor in return for the loan of a specified amount of money. When the debt is repaid, the mortgage is no longer in effect.

NOW accounts: A checking account that pays interest. NOW stands for "negotiated order of withdrawal."

Overdraft: A check drawn for more than the balance on deposit

Payee: The person to whom a check is made payable

Promissory note: A written promise of one person to pay a specified amount to another person on demand or by a specified date

Regular savings accounts: Regular savings accounts earn interest usually at a lower rate than other savings options because although technically subject to a 30-day withdrawal notice, money can be withdrawn at any time without penalty.

Traveler's checks: Special checks supplied by the bank for a small fee; usually accepted in lieu of cash when traveling

U.S. savings bonds: Series EE bonds range in face value from $50 to $10,000. The purchase price per bond ranges from $25 to $5,000, one half the face value of each bond. Annual limitation on purchases is $30,000 face amount ($15,000 issue price) for any one person.

Interest rates on the ten-year maturity EE bonds are determined by the Department of the Treasury and are payable to bondholders at maturity or redemption. Interest is subject to federal income tax, but not to state or local income tax.

Series HH bonds are available only in exchange for outstanding E and EE bonds with a total redemption value of $500 or more. HH bonds reach maturity ten years after purchase. Interest is paid semiannually by the U.S. Treasury at a rate set by the Treasury.

REFERENCES

Federal Reserve Bank of New York, *The Story of Checks and Electronic Payments*. New York, 1984.

__________, *A Day's Work at the Federal Reserve Bank of New York*. New York, 1984.

Federal Reserve Bank of Philadelphia, *Options for Savers*. Philadelphia, PA, September 1984.

Federal Reserve Bank of Richmond, *Buying Treasury Securities at Federal Reserve Banks*. Richmond, VA., January 1982.

Federal Reserve System, *Public Information Materials, No. 8*, New York, October 1986–87.

Federal Trade Commission, *Electronic Banking*, Washington, DC, November 1982.

INGRAM, RON. "Goodbye Teller, Hello Card," *The Decatur Herald*, March 29, 1984, 22.

KERR, SUSAN. "Is the Computer Fostering a More Just Justice System?" *Datamation*, January 15, 1988, 45–55.

"Words of Wall Street," *The Wall Street Journal*, 1987/88 Educational Edition, Dow-Jones & Company.

Federal Reserve Bank Addresses

Board of Governors of the Federal Reserve System
Publications Services
Washington, DC 20551
(202) 452-3244

FRB Atlanta
Research Department, Publications Unit
104 Marietta Street
Atlanta, GA 30303-2713
(404) 521-8788

FRB Boston
Bank and Public Services Department
600 Atlantic Avenue
Boston, MA 02106
(617) 973-3459

FRB Chicago
Public Information Center
230 South LaSalle Street
Chicago, IL 60690
(312) 322-5112

FRB Cleveland
Public Information Center
P.O. Box 6387
Cleveland, OH 44101
(216) 579-2048

FRB Dallas
Public Affairs Department
Station K
Dallas, TX 75222
(214) 651-6289 or -6266

FRB Kansas City
Public Affairs Department
925 Grand Avenue
Kansas City, MO 64198
(816) 881-2402

FRB Richmond
Public Services Department
P.O. Box 27622
Richmond, VA 23261
(804) 643-1250

FRB St. Louis
Bank Relations and
Public Information Department
P.O. Box 442
St. Louis, MO 63166
(314) 444-8421

FRB San Francisco
Public Information Department
P.O. Box 7702
San Francisco, CA 94120
(415) 974-3234

FRB Minneapolis
Office of Public Information
250 Marquette Avenue
Minneapolis, MN 55480
(612) 340-2446

FRB New York
Public Information Department
33 Liberty Street
New York, NY 10045
(212) 791-6134

FRB Philadelphia
Public Information Department
P.O. Box 66
Philadelphia, PA 19105
(215) 574-6115

Case Problem 1 Unit V *Delegating Tasks Effectively*

The office supervisor has delegated an important job assignment to Dorothee, a very proficient secretary who joined the company one year ago. The supervisor has asked Dorothee to do analyses of all the clerk-steno positions in the company—four in all.

The analyses will be used in drawing up job descriptions and setting job standards for each position. Dorothee is honored to have this assignment, but she has some misgivings about it. She wonders:

> How can she gather this information without annoying the clerk stenos? How will they receive her questions if she quizzes them about their jobs?
>
> Should she just observe them at their work and ask no questions? If so, won't the clerk-stenos resent her watching and note taking?
>
> Who will handle her own regular duties while she does the job analyses?

1. How has the supervisor failed in delegation of this task to Dorothee? What should she have done that she did not do?
2. What can be done now to allay Dorothee's fears and restore Dorothee's confidence in herself?

Case Problem 2 Unit V *IRS Seeks a "Returnless" System*

The Internal Revenue Service is making rapid strides toward an income tax "returnless" system in which all tax returns will be filed electronically, eliminating the need for any paper filing. Tax preparers still have to file the W2s and 1099s to document the filed figures, but IRS employees will no longer have to open the returns and key the figures into the computer.

Some people, whose income is based solely on salary and who file on the short form, already have the option of filing electronically. Persons with home computers may even file directly with the IRS.

Not only does the IRS hope to gain efficiency and speed through the changeover to electronic files, but they also hope to improve their surveillance of tax "cheats" who attempt to hide undisclosed income. Taxpayers will benefit from the changeover in at least one respect; those eligible for refunds are promised them in half the usual time of six to eight weeks.

1. Discuss the impact the electronic filing of tax returns may have on the general economy. Is it more likely to unearth tax cheats and thus bring in more money to the national treasury?
2. Do you see any similarity between the anticipated "returnless" tax system and the much-touted "paperless" office of the 1970s? Explain your views.

Case Problem 3 Unit V *ATMs Boost Convenience-Store Business*

Automated teller machines (ATMs) offer convenience store shoppers quick cash for those last-minute purchases. In Oklahoma, more than 1 million customers now carry their bank debit cards to retrieve cash at the corner convenience store, grocery stores, and shopping malls. Because the ATMs are less expensive for banks to maintain than drive-in facilities, the ATM market is ripe for expansion.

According to Paul Confer, a director of EFTs in Oklahoma City, Oklahoma is leading the fifty states in the number of convenience-store ATMs. "We pioneered the concept with Quik-Trip in 1982," says Confer. Recently the money machines were put into more than 100 Seven-Eleven Stores, and in 1989, more than 100 Git-n-Go convenience stores in Missouri. According to Robert Snyder, director of sales and marketing at TransFund, a subsidiary of the Bank of Oklahoma, "The ATM/convenience store link is a natural. ATMs have helped boost convenience-store business."[3]

ATMs may be found too in Oklahoma hospitals, universities, and business sites; in Oklahoma City, even braille ATM machines have been installed for blind customers. In Tulsa, Phillips Petroleum Company is experimenting with the use of ATM cards at the point of sale. Customers can buy gasoline and other Phillips products with the ATM card at the Phillips gas station at 31st Street and Yale Avenue. The project is being expanded to two other locations in Tulsa and four in Bartlesville, Oklahoma.

1. How might the ATM card affect branch banking in the future?
2. Does the ATM card encourage
   a. cash withdrawals for trivial purposes?
   b. irresponsible money management?
   c. more cash purchases and less check writing?
3. How is the ATM/convenience-store link a "natural"?

[3]Teresa McUsic, "Oklahomans Don't Leave Home Without ATM Card," *Tulsa World,* January 29, 1989, G1.

UNIT

VI

CAREER PLANNING AND PROFESSIONAL GROWTH

As graduating students approach the end of their formal education, they must formalize their career objectives. Many opportunities for career development will be presented to them.

Continued formal education, workshop and seminar participation, and in-house training programs are a few of the many paths they may explore to prepare themselves for progression to higher-level positions.

Certification programs sponsored by professional associations offer unique opportunities for validating careerists' special competencies. Although such programs offer no college credits, many of them are validated by educational institutions who award credits for equivalent courses when the individuals are enrolled in formal degree programs.

17
Certification Programs

INTRODUCTION

Professional certification programs are one means of motivating career professionals to a level of excellence. As awards of merit, certificates give tangible evidence of the recipients' professional competence.

Growth in the programs in recent years is due in part to the vigor of the professional associations which sponsor them, and in part to the demands of employers for better qualified employees. Some companies require that administrative support personnel be professionally certified in order to quality for positions at the executive level. Others encourage their employees to become certified by offering to pay their application fees.

The following acronyms identify the certification programs described in this chapter:

CPS®	PLS
CAM	CMA
CRM	CDP
CSP	COAP

PROFESSIONAL CERTIFICATES: AWARDS OF MERIT

The formal component of the administrative assistant's education is usually earned prior to his or her income years. Basic foundation and skills courses are provided through associate's and bachelor's degree programs and through business and vocational schools. In terms of formal education, the administrative assistant is well prepared for entry into the business world.

Because it is necessary to continually upgrade one's knowledge and skills, however, the career-minded administrative assistant looks for an avenue of growth which will not only provide that knowledge and skill but will give tangible evidence of a higher level of achievement. Certification programs may be the answer.

Sponsored by professional associations as a mark of excellence, the certificates are awarded to qualified candidates who successfully complete a series of rigorous examinations, usually over a two-day period. Eight programs are described in this chapter in the following sequence:

1. Certified Administrative Manager
2. Certified Records Manager
3. Certified Office Automation Professional
4. Professional Legal Secretary
5. Certified Medical Assistant
6. Certified Data Processor
7. Certified Systems Professional
8. Certified Professional Secretary

CERTIFIED ADMINISTRATIVE MANAGER

The Administrative Management Society sponsors a certification program for the management generalist which fits the job description and responsibilities of many administrative assistants. CAM is the professional designation conferred upon those who successfully meet the standards set forth by the AMS in this program.

Candidates are required to meet five program standards. One of the most important is administrative management experience. Work experience must be validated as managerial before candidates can qualify for the examination. Candidates must provide character references, must demonstrate the ability to communicate and lead, and must pass a comprehensive four-part series of examinations within ten years of the date of enrollment in the CAM program.

Program standard 1 consists of a five-part examination. The first four parts of the CAM examination consist of short answer, multiple choice, and situation analysis questions, each requiring a brief one- or two-paragraph answer. A maximum of four hours is allotted for each of the first four parts of the examination.

Part I	Personnel Management
Part II	Financial Management, Control and Economics
Part III	Administrative Services
Part IV	Systems and Information Management

Part V of the CAM examination can only be taken after the candidate has successfully completed Parts I through IV. Consisting of an in-depth case prob-

The Board of Regents of the Academy of Certified Administrative Managers

and the Administrative Management Society

hereby awards to

the professional designation

CERTIFIED ADMINISTRATIVE MANAGER

in recognition of the successful completion of the Academy's requirements

through written examination and other means which demonstrate

possession of the knowledge, experience, leadership and character

essential to

effective administrative management.

Date

Certificate Number

C.A.M.

Certified Administrative Manager

Chairperson-Academy Board of Regents

President-Administrative Management Society

FIGURE 17-1 The Certified Administrative Manager certificate is a feasible goal for administrative assistants who are career oriented and positioned for promotion to the managerial ranks. *Courtesy of the Administrative Management Society.*

lem incorporating various management skills, it is to be completed by the candidate within 30 days of initial assignment.

Program standards 2, 3, 4, and 5 are equally important.

Management Experience (Program Standard No. 2) Candidates must have at least three years of experience at the administrative management level. Specifically, the candidate must exercise managerial authority and responsibility for at least one of the following organizational functions: personnel, finance, administrative services, or systems and information management.

Character (Program Standard No. 3) Candidates must have "high standards of personal and professional conduct." Each candidate is to sign the CAM Code of Ethics, and to furnish two reference letters—one personal and one professional.

Leadership (Program Standard No. 4) Candidates must provide "satisfactory evidence of significant leadership in voluntary organizations"—civic, fraternal, management, professional, religious, political, or social. They must list at least two organizations which can attest to their leadership ability.

Contributions to Effective Administrative Management (Program Standard No. 5) Candidates must show evidence of having made contributions to effective administrative management ideas and principles through oral and/or written communications; e.g., through speeches given, seminars moderated, or articles or books published.

Each candidate must determine his or her own preparation needs. For some, this may mean college, university, or home study courses; for others, joining a CAM preparatory course. In the areas where AMS chapters sponsor CAM courses, candidates are encouraged to enroll. A detailed syllabus, containing an outline of the subject matter covered by each part of the examination, as well as a list of suggested reference books, is supplied to each registrant by the AMS home office.

A one-time nonrefundable registration fee is payable at the time of application. Examination fees for each of the five parts of the examination are payable when the candidate notifies the Director of Professionalization he or she is ready to take the selected parts. Examinations are given twice each year at local test centers established with the cooperation of AMS chapters.

As with all certification programs, earning the CAM title does not guarantee salary increases or promotions. However, Certified Administrative Managers are gaining increased prestige among supervisors, peers, and subordinates within their own firms, and are widely recognized as experts in administrative management.

An application form and further information may be obtained by writing to the Director of Professionalization, Administrative Management Society, Willow Grove, PA 19090.

CERTIFIED RECORDS MANAGER

Candidates for Certified Records Manager must pass a six-part examination, including a comprehensive case study problem (Part VI) which applies the principles covered in Parts I through V. Recent revisions of the examination shift emphasis from multiple choice to essay questions for more in-depth coverage of the content. The six parts are titled:

I. Management Principles and Program Organization
II. Records Creation and Use
III. Records Systems, Storage, and Retrieval
IV. Records Appraisal, Retention, Protection, and Disposition
V. Equipment Supplies and Technology
VI. Case Studies

The case studies involve problems that interrelate all elements of the other five parts. Although candidates may take the first five parts in any sequence, Part VI can only be taken after the candidate has passed the first five parts. Retakes are allowed on any part of the examination as often as necessary, as long as all parts are successfully completed within a consecutive 5-year period.

FIGURE 17-2 The Certified Records Manager stores records on various types of media, including paper, magnetic disks, microforms and optical disks. *Courtesy of Fellowes Mfg. Co.*

In order to qualify for certification, candidates must have a minimum of 3 years full-time or equivalent professional experience in records management in three or more of the following categories:

1. Management of records management program
2. Records creation and use
3. Active records systems
4. Inactive records systems
5. Records appraisal, retention, and disposition
6. Records protection
7. Records and information management technology

The candidate must also have a baccalaureate degree from an accredited institution, although the ICRM Board of Regents may authorize substitution of additional qualifying professional experience for some of the required education.

Records managers in increasing numbers are coming to recognize the importance of CRM certification and are requesting information on CRM requirements.

Application forms and further information can be obtained from the ICRM Secretary, P.O. Box 8188, Prairie Village, KS 66208.

CERTIFIED OFFICE AUTOMATION PROFESSIONAL

One of the latest certification programs for personnel in the electronic office is the Certified Office Automation Professional (COAP) sponsored by the Office Automation Society International (OASI).

OASI, an associate member of the Institute for Certification of Computer Professionals (ICCP), was organized primarily for the purpose of certifying as office automation professionals those who deserve special recognition for their work with computers.

The ICCP also sponsors the Certified Data Processor (CDP) and the Certified Systems Professional (CSP) programs described later in this chapter. Through their collective programs, the ICCP has certified over 40,000 computer professionals.

Candidates for the COAP do not need to be computer experts to qualify, but they do need to have work experience with computers on a regular basis. Requirements to qualify for certification are:

1. At least four years of full-time employment using office systems, equipment, or software. Formal education, training, and continuing education can be substituted for two years' experience.
2. Compliance with the COAP Code of Professional Conduct.

Benefits of certification include a personalized plaque and official letter of certification from the Office Automation Society International (OASI). COAP

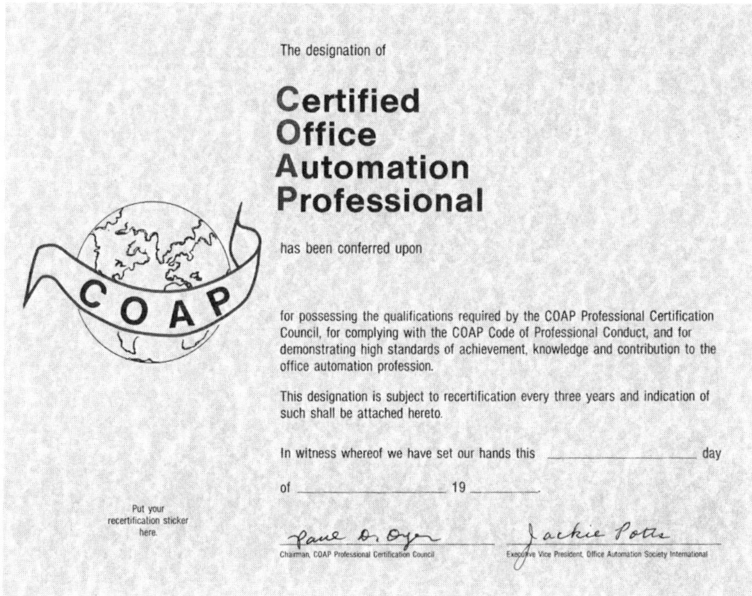

The designation of

Certified Office Automation Professional

has been conferred upon

for possessing the qualifications required by the COAP Professional Certification Council, for complying with the COAP Code of Professional Conduct, and for demonstrating high standards of achievement, knowledge and contribution to the office automation profession.

This designation is subject to recertification every three years and indication of such shall be attached hereto.

In witness whereof we have set our hands this ________ day

of ________ 19 ______.

Put your recertification sticker here.

Chairman, COAP Professional Certification Council

Executive Vice President, Office Automation Society International

FIGURE 17-3 The Certified Office Automation Professional certificate recognizes high standards of achievement in office automation. *Courtesy of the Office Automation Society International.*

certification validates one's professional competence with computers and gives COAPs a decided edge over competitors in the job-search phase of their careers.

Application forms and more information may be obtained from: Office Automation Society International, 15269 Mimosa, Dumfries, VA 22026.

PROFESSIONAL LEGAL SECRETARY

The National Association of Legal Secretaries (International) sponsors the PLS examination. Twice yearly it is given to candidates who possess: (1) a mastery of office skills and people skills; and (2) the ability to interact on a professional level with attorneys, clients, secretaries, legal assistants, office administrators, judges, and other court officials.

The examination includes seven parts:

Part I	Written Communication Skills and Knowledge
Part II	Ethics
Part III	Legal Secretarial Procedures
Part IV	Legal Secretarial Accounting
Part V	Legal Terminology, Techniques, and Procedures
Part VI	Exercise of Judgment
Part VII	Legal Secretarial Skills

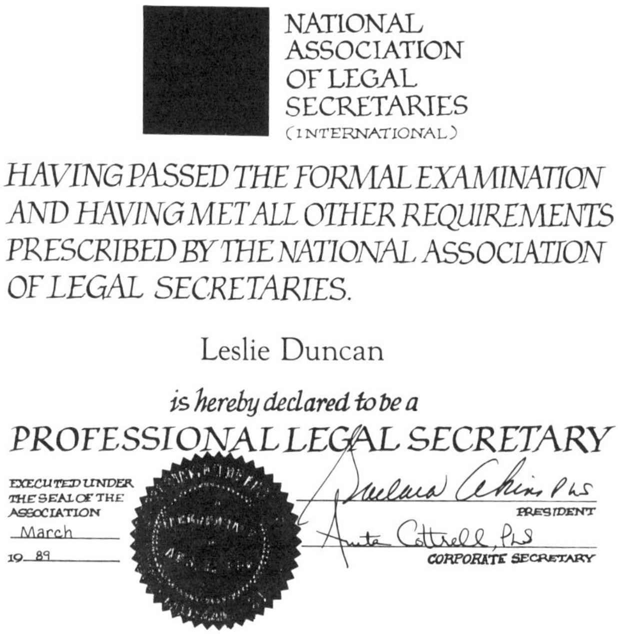

FIGURE 17-4 The National Association of Legal Secretaries awards the PLS certificate to qualifying candidates who pass the stringent seven-part examination administered twice annually. *Courtesy of the National Association of Legal Secretaries.*

Any person who has had three years' experience as a legal secretary under the direct supervision of a practicing lawyer may take the examination.

It is administered on the first Friday and Saturday in March and the last Friday and Saturday in September at testing centers approved by the NALS board. A list of centers is supplied to applicants with the application form.

Examination fees for NALS members are $85 for the full examination, and $15 to $20 for each part retaken. Non-NALS members pay twice these amounts. Some colleges grant academic credit for PLS certification; a list may be obtained from the NALS headquarters. A study guide to help candidates prepare for the examination is also available on request.

To obtain these materials and further information, write to: NALS Headquarters, 2250 East 73 Street, Suite 550, Tulsa, OK 74136.

CERTIFIED MEDICAL ASSISTANT

The American Association of Medical Assistants offers certification credentials for qualified medical assistants. The Certified Medical Assistant (CMA) examination is offered twice annually at approximately 100 test centers throughout the United States.

Purpose of the certifying examination is to identify medical assistants who have the knowledge and skills necessary to perform competently the routine clinical and administrative duties in the office of a primary care physician. An individual who is able to successfully demonstrate competence by passing the examination is designated a Certified Medical Assistant.

The certification examination is divided into three parts.

I. General
   a. medical terminology
   b. anatomy
   c. behavioral science
   d. medicolegal issues and ethics
II. Basic administrative procedures
   a. oral communication
   b. written communication
   c. bookkeeping, credits, and collections
   d. records management
   e. office facilities
   f. patient insurance
   g. nonpatient insurance
III. Clinical duties
   a. examination room techniques
   b. laboratory procedures
   c. administer specified medications
   d. emergencies

To be eligible for certification, candidates must verify their status in one of three categories:

1. Student or recent graduate in CAHEA-accredited program
2. Practicing medical assistant or practicing allied health professional
3. Medical assisting instructor

To assist potential candidates in assessing the program or prepare for the examination, the certifying board of the American Association of Medical Assistants (AAMA) provides a sample 120-question examination upon receipt of an application and the examination fee.

All correspondence should be addressed to the AAMA Certifying Board, 20 North Wacker Drive, Suite 1575, Chicago, IL 60606. The telephone number is (312) 899-1500.

CERTIFIED DATA PROCESSOR AND CERTIFIED SYSTEMS PROFESSIONALS

Two certificate programs offered by the Institute for Certification of Computer Professionals (ICCP) may interest administrative assistants whose educational backgrounds orient them toward electronic systems and computer applications.

The ICCP awards the Certified Data Processor and the Certified Systems Professional Certificate to qualified applicants who pass comprehensive examinations.

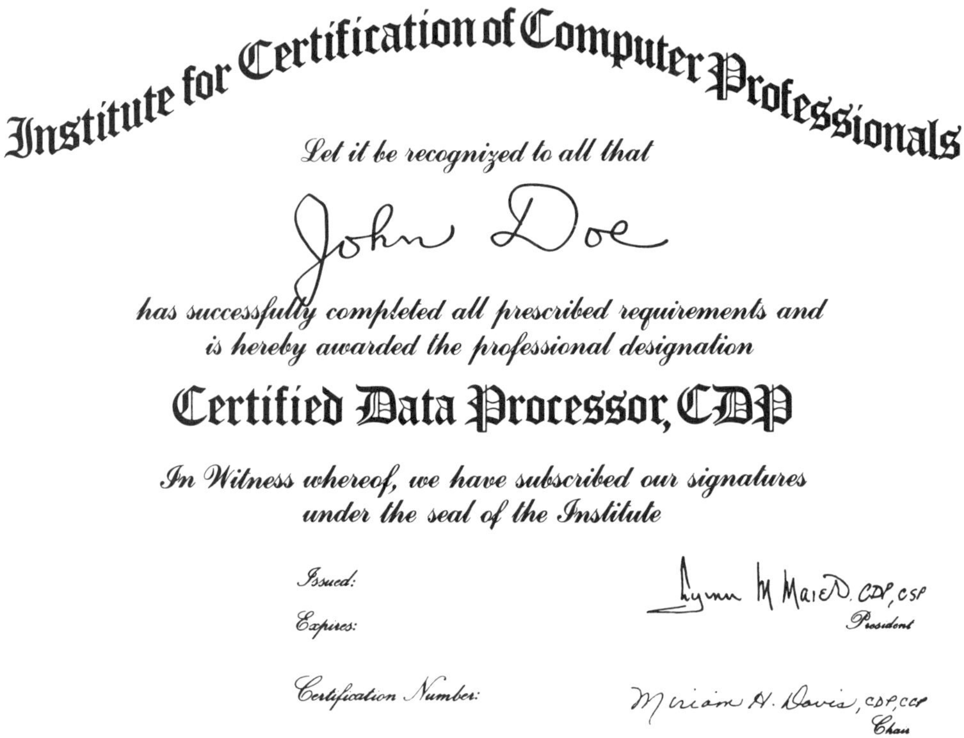
Institute for Certification of Computer Professionals

Let it be recognized to all that

John Doe

has successfully completed all prescribed requirements and is hereby awarded the professional designation

Certified Data Processor, CDP

In Witness whereof, we have subscribed our signatures under the seal of the Institute

Issued:

Expires:

President

Certification Number:

Chair

Institute for Certification of Computer Professionals

Let it be recognized to all that

John Doe

has successfully completed all prescribed requirements and is hereby awarded the professional designation

Certified Systems Professional, CSP

In Witness whereof, we have subscribed our signatures under the seal of the Institute

Issued:

Expires:

President

Certification Number:

Chair

FIGURE 17-5 Two certificates sponsored by the ICCP recognize computer expertise: Certified Data Processor, CDP; and the Certified Systems of Professional, CSP. *Courtesy of the Institute for Certification of Computer Professionals.*

The *Certified Data Processor (CDP)* examination is composed of five sections, each containing 60 questions. The five sections are titled:

1. Computer Hardware
2. Computer Programming and Software
3. Principles of Management
4. Methods and Applications
5. Systems

The *Certified Systems Professional (CSP)* examination is also composed of five sections, each containing 50 questions. The sections are titled:

1. Environment of Systems
2. Project Management
3. Systems Analysis
4. Systems Design and Implementation
5. Tools and Technologies

For both the CDP and the CSP examinations, all five sections must be passed within four test attempts or within four years, whichever comes first.

Once a section is passed, all remaining sections must be completed during the next three consecutive years or three test attempts, whichever comes first. Otherwise, credit will be lost for the passed section. Passing score is 70 percent for each of the five sections.[1]

The examinations are administered twice yearly—in May and November; application deadlines for each examination are April 1 and October 1 preceding the testing dates.

Correspondence and requests for information may be directed to: Institute for Certification of Computer Professionals, Suite 268, 2200 E. Devon Avenue, Des Plaines, IL 60018. Telephone (312) 299-4227. The ICCP also sponsors the Certified Office Automation Professional program described on page 394 of this chapter, through its associate member, the Office Automation Society.

THE CERTIFIED PROFESSIONAL SECRETARY

One of the most widely known certification programs is that of the Certified Professional Secretary, sponsored by Professional Secretaries International.

In order to earn the CPS® award, qualified applicants must pass a rigorous six-part, two-day examination given semi-annually by PSI. The examination in-

[1] "Certified Data Processor" and "Certified Systems Professional," *Institute for Certification of Computer Professionals,* Des Plaines, IL, 1987, 2.

FIGURE 17-6 The CPS_r Key is a mark of distinction for those who have achieved the Certified Professional Secretary certificate.

corporates basic business, communications, behavioral science, and technological information into six parts, titled:

I. Behavioral Science in Business
II. Business Law
III. Economics and Management
IV. Accounting
V. Office Administration and Communication
VI. Office Technology

The 1989 *Capstone* published by PSI describes the six parts of the examination as follows.[2]

Behavioral Science in Business tests the principles of human relations and organizational dynamics in the workplace. It focuses on needs, motivation, nature of conflict, problem-solving techniques, essentials of supervision and communication.

Business Law measures the secretary's knowledge of the principles of business law and knowledge of the effect of governmental controls on business. Understanding of the historical setting in which these controls developed is emphasized in preference to names and dates.

Economics and Management includes 35 percent economics and 65 per-

[2]*Capstone of the Secretarial Profession,* Professional Secretaries International, 10502 Northwest Ambassador Drive, Kansas City, MO 64195-0404, 1989.

cent management. Emphasis is placed on understanding of basic concepts underlying business operations. Key economic and management principles as well as the latest governmental regulations are included.

Accounting measures knowledge of the elements of the accounting cycle, ability to analyze financial statement accounts, ability to perform arithmetical operations associated with accounting, computing interest and discounts, and ability to summarize and interpret financial data.

Office Administration and Communication measures proficiency in subject matters unique to the secretary's position, including executive travel, office management, records management, and reprographics; and written business communication, including editing, abstracting, and preparing communications in final format.

Office Technology covers the secretary's responsibilities created by data processing, communications media, advances in office management, technological applications, records-management technology, and office systems.

Candidate Qualifications

In order to qualify as a candidate, applicants must meet certain work experience requirements. Those with a bachelor's degree need only 2 years' secretarial experience; those with an associate's degree need 3 years' secretarial experience. With no degree, the requirement is 4 years' secretarial experience.

FIGURE 17-7 Administrative assistants and executive secretaries with CPS status enjoy their annual conference, held in Laguna Beach in 1989. Courtesy of Professional Secretaries International.

Effective with the May 1990 examination, membership in Professional Secretaries International is required while the candidate is pursuing certification.

Currently employed business educators can qualify by submitting verification of a minimum of 12 months' cumulative secretarial experience within the past 25 years, or by meeting the requirement within six years of the approval date. Students may apply and be approved as candidates prior to their achieving work experience, but experience requirements must be met within six years of approval date.

Dates and Location of Examination Centers

Dates The examination is given twice yearly—the first Friday and Saturday in May, and the first Thursday and Friday in November.

Location CPS examination centers number about 250 throughout the United States, Canada, the Virgin Islands, Puerto Rico, Malaysia, the West Indies, and China.

Updating CPS Credentials Through Recertification

Recertification is mandated for all individuals who applied for CPS candidacy after January 1, 1988. A dated certificate, valid for five years, is issued each time recertification requirements are fulfilled. For recertification, 120 points must be obtained within the five years prior to recertification. Points are earned through a variety of activities, such as attending a CPS review course, taking CEU home-study courses, or attending seminars, workshops, or training sessions.

Value of CPS Certification

Increased compensation and more responsible job assignments often follow upon reception of the CPS "Mark of Excellence." Even where such tangible recognition is not forthcoming, the CPS values the award as a personal and professional triumph. The following quotations from newly certified CPSs are typical:

> "CPS was the best thing that ever happened to me!"
>
> "Because of my CPS rating, my boss gives me more responsibility and is receptive to my ideas and suggestions."
>
> "Overshadowing all else is the self-assurance the CPS certificate has given me. I feel that my CPS rating is the same as an open door for any future employment I might desire."

College Credits for CPS Rating

Many colleges and universities grant academic credits for the CPS rating, equating the credits with related academic courses. For example, Part II, Business Law, and Part IV, Accounting, are equated with equivalent courses and credits

professional Secretaries international®

through its department

institute for certifying Secretaries

certifies that

Pat Masters

has met the requirements of and satisfactorily completed
an established program of examinations and
has been awarded the rating of

certified professional Secretary®

Ronald D. Johnson DBA
Dean
Institute for Certifying Secretaries

1988

Frances R. Barr
International President
Professional Secretaries International

FIGURE 17-8 Professional Secretaries International® through its Institute for Certifying Secretaries sponsors the semi-annual two-day examination for CPS® applicants.

in these two subjects. A list of the colleges offering credit may be obtained from Professional Secretaries International.

Application and Preparation for the CPS Examination

An outline pertinent to the current examination is issued annually by PSI and is available for a nominal charge. For further information, write to Professional Secretaries International, 10502 Northwest Ambassador Drive, Kansas City, MO 64195-0404.

SUMMARY

A number of professional associations sponsor certification programs to recognize the professional excellence of their members or others working in their field of interest.

Several of the programs are designed for generalists; that is, secretaries and administrative assistants working in any industry. Others exist for those working in specialized fields.

Eight programs are described in this chapter. Listed in the order of presentation, they are Certified Administrative Manager, Certified Records Manager, Certified Office Automation Professional, Professional Legal Secretary, Certified Medical Assistant, Certified Data Processor, Certified Systems Professional, and Certified Professional Secretary.

QUESTIONS FOR REVIEW

Certified Administrative Manager

1. What organization sponsors the CAM certification?
2. How many program standards must be met by CAM candidates?
3. What constitutes Part V of the CAM examination?

Certified Records Manager

1. What constitutes Part VI of the CRM examination?
2. What types of work experience qualify one for certification?
3. Is a baccalaureate degree required?

Certified Office Automation Professional

1. Name two benefits of certification as a COAP.
2. What is the purpose of the COAP program?

Professional Legal Secretary

1. When is the examination administered?
2. How much experience as a legal secretary is required to qualify as a PLS candidate?
3. Name the seven parts of the examination.

Certified Medical Assistant

1. What group sponsors the CMA certification program?
2. Name and explain the three parts of the examination.

Certified Data Processor and Certified Systems Professional

1. When are the examinations for both administered?
2. Which organization sponsors both?
3. Name the five sections comprising each of the two examinations.

Certified Professional Secretary

1. Name the six parts of the CPS examination.
2. How often is the examination given?
3. Where are the examination centers?

QUESTIONS FOR DISCUSSION

1. Discuss the merits of professional certification programs for career-minded administrative assistants.
2. In your opinion, which of the programs discussed in this chapter are likely to benefit administrative assistants most directly and substantially? Give reasons for your choice.
3. Discuss the pros and cons of this statement: *Professional certification programs are more practical and valuable than an academic degree.*

SUGGESTED ACTIVITIES

1. Invite a Certified Professional Secretary to speak to the class to give students insight into the actual examination experience and the impact of the CPS certification on one's career success.
2. Plan a panel discussion, inviting as panelists the holders of certificates discussed in this chapter. Have panelists tell of their experiences in taking the qualifying examinations, the difference that achieving certification has made in their careers, and what advice, if any, they wish to pass on to students following in their footsteps.
3. Scrutinize the Sunday editions of large metropolitan newspapers; note the ads which specify "Certified ___________" wanted. List the job openings requiring professional certificates, including *all* types listed, not just those listed in this chapter.

REFERENCES

GOLEN, STEVEN, and SHIRLEY WHITE, "Professional Certification in Data Processing," *On Line* 2, no. 2 (Spring 1984), 11–13.

HENRY, DAVID C., "Preparing the Legal Information Processing Secretary," *Century 21 Reporter* (Fall 1984), 10–11.

STANKIEWICZ, JOYCE, CPS, "Rate Your Future; Become a CPS," *The Secretary* (April 1985), 12–13.

18 Career Planning and the Job Search

INTRODUCTION

Having acquired the professional skills and education necessary to launch a business career, the graduating student is ready to search for the position that will best suit his or her talents and ambitions. Although the immediate objective is to obtain the best position possible in terms of job satisfaction and salary, the administrative assistant must keep in mind the broader scope of total career objectives.

Professional growth is best assured by a serious commitment to further education and the aid of mentors. Personal networking systems may also be used, especially when a change in career paths is indicated. In short, the administrative assistant utilizes all possible resources to reach his or her career goals.

Terminology and acronyms introduced herein include:

networking	sponsors
PACE	PSI
USTES	CLEP
mentors	assessment centers

ESTABLISHING CAREER GOALS

At the point of entering the job market, the graduating student has formulated at least one major goal—that of pursuing a career as an administrative assistant. Having made that decision, it must now be decided where to put his or her knowledge and skills to work. As an administrative assistant, career opportunities are broad and varied. Offices within many industries are anxious for the services of an able assistant; finding the most appealing one is the next objective.

Two factors must be considered: the industry which has the most appeal and the type of work environment within the industry which he or she finds most suitable. For example, a position in one of the following industries may fulfill his or her career interests.

Publishing: dealing with well-known authors, or helping unknown writers get their manuscripts published

Travel: working out travel itineraries for clients, and traveling to all parts of the world to check out vacation spots

Entertainment: using one's administrative and secretarial skills to assist entertainers with their correspondence and record keeping

One's own entrepreneurial venture: contracting for administrative and secretarial services with business executives in large metropolitan areas

Assuming that the educational preparation has covered basic business courses, career aspirations need not be limited solely to that of administrative assistant, either. Having attained enough on-the-job experience to qualify, the career-minded individual may rightfully aspire to the ranks of management.

Personal and Professional Preferences

Preferences as to size and type of office within an industry are as important as the choice of an appealing industry. Job satisfaction itself is determined in large part by the extent to which one's talents are utilized in a "user-friendly" workplace. To clarify personal preferences, the job-seeker may want to consider these questions:

How important is money to me? Is it more important than job satisfaction or the chance for advancement?

Do I prefer the companionship of a large office staff? Or is the quiet of a small office and staff more appealing?

Do I enjoy meeting and dealing with the public?

Do I enjoy new challenges?

Is job security important? Would I hesitate to leave my job if it showed no potential for growth or promotion?

Do I like to work independently or do I prefer supervision and guidance?

How important is job status? Do I have a strong need to achieve at a high level?

One way to clarify one's professional preferences and needs is to rank them in order of priority. The priority rankings then serve as guides for seeking one's first position and in making a career shift later.

To "fine tune" these rankings, a person may wish to divide goals into two categories: immediate and distant, with distant defined as five years, ten years, or longer.

The following chart is formatted as a "fill-in" exercise for the graduating administrative assistant. In Part II of the chart, the lettered items listed in Part I are ranked by the user.

PRIORITY RANKINGS OF PROFESSIONAL NEEDS

PART I
PROFESSIONAL NEEDS AND PREFERENCES

A SALARY ($)	B LOCATION ( )
C ECONOMIC SECURITY	D SOCIAL LIFE
E JOB STATUS	F TRAVEL OPPORTUNITIES
G WORKING INDEPENDENTLY	H FRINGE BENEFITS
I EDUCATIONAL OPPORTUNITIES	J PROMOTIONAL OPPORTUNITIES
K ______	L ______
M ______	N ______

PART II
PRIORITY RANKINGS

IMMEDIATE	*DISTANT* ( )
1 ______	1 ______
2 ______	2 ______
3 ______	3 ______
4 ______	4 ______

Rank the preference items by inserting the letter identifying the lettered item in Part I in the user's order of preference in Part II. Blank lines in Part I are for the user's insertion of items not included in the list.

Chart: Professional Needs and Preferences

Goals: Long Term and Intermediate

Career goals are usually divided into two phases: long term and intermediate. Long-term goals are set as far down the road as one can visualize with any degree of certainty; intermediate goals involve critical points along the way which help one reach the ultimate goals. For instance, if one's long-term goal is to become president of a company within 15 years, intermediate goals might include the following job-related and educational objectives.

1. Five-year objective
   a. Education: Bachelor's degree at state university
   b. On the job: Office manager, local branch of firm
2. Ten-year objective
   a. Education: MBA degree
   b. On the job: Manager, office operations, corporate headquarters
3. Twelve-year objective
   a. Education: Company-sponsored management development programs
   b. On the job: Corporate officer's position
4. Fifteen-year objective
   a. President of the company

Flexibility is a key element in a well-defined set of objectives or goals. Since unforeseen factors may disrupt the most carefully laid plans, the goal seeker must be ready to alter his or her timetable accordingly. Rigidity may hinder rather than help a budding career. If goals are designed to accommodate unforeseen changes as they develop, they can contribute substantially toward reaching one's professional objectives at or near the time originally envisioned.

CONTINUING EDUCATION—KEY TO GROWTH

Settled into a comfortable position which fully utilizes his or her business skills, the newly employed administrative assistant may be prematurely lulled into a sense of complacency, believing that all formal education is now complete, with career and job tenure assured for life.

A more realistic approach, however, is to recognize the need for *continual* updating of one's knowledge and skills. Education is the key to professional growth and job security.

The opportunities for growth through education are numerous. Workshops, conferences, and seminars invite careerists to upgrade their skills; night courses scheduled by community colleges and universities entice participants to "learn as you earn;" and weekend college courses leading to higher degrees have become common in large metropolitan areas.

The smorgasbord of educational offerings may be broadly classified as *academic* and *nonacademic* programs. *Academic programs* emanate from institutions of higher education, including community and junior colleges, senior colleges, and universities. *Nonacademic ones* originate from a variety of other sources, such as management consultant groups, industry-related educational programs, organization-sponsored certificate programs, and such like.

During the course of his or her career, the administrative assistant is likely to draw substantial benefits from both academic and nonacademic sources.

ACADEMIC PROGRAMS

Formal academic programs are probably the most practical means of meeting one's educational goals. The courses offered cover every facet of business from basic skills designed for entry-level positions to graduate MBA courses.

An administrative assistant with an eye to the future may want to enroll in those courses which focus primarily on managerial skills. It is important also to strive for the highest academic degree and the broadest curriculum that one's time and budget will allow.

Academic Curricula: Nontraditional

Recent changes in traditional academic programs have made education increasingly attractive to adults. A wider selection of courses and degree programs have been developed, and areas of specialization have been expanded. For example, programs for administrative support personnel now include personnel management, electronic information systems, and computer software classes. These courses prepare students for both support roles and supervisory positions.

Many departments combine faculty and courses into interdisciplinary programs which give students a "taste" of many fields of study and a broad general education.

The CLEP program (college-level examination program) provides a nationwide network of test centers which administer tests for fifty or more college courses. Students who earn acceptable CLEP scores earn college credits for equivalent courses in the college curriculum. In metropolitan areas, courses are offered via television, with students viewing the instruction on TV, then completing written assignments and examinations proctored by a college coordinator.

Some universities give college credits for work experience in fields related to certain courses, equating the experience with the content matter of the courses. For example, a published author may be given credit for creative writing; or a political activist, credit in political science. Each such experience must be satisfactorily documented and its relevance carefully weighed against the content of the related course.

Flexible class schedules have been introduced to accommodate working people. One-day-a-week classes, weekend classes, one- or two-week short courses, and other nontraditional schedules have become an integral part of adult education programs.

Special Courses and Programs

Academic institutions also serve the needs of persons looking for special courses or nondegree programs. Nondegree students may enroll in *some* of the regular courses or in special workshops and seminars designed especially for them. College faculty conduct the special courses as well as the regular college offerings. Credits for the special courses may or may not be granted, depending on the program in which the student is enrolled and the academic level of the course.

Some colleges offer certification programs, as well as degree programs, to students. Similar in structure to degree programs, certification courses focus on specialized areas, such as secretarial science, computer science, or paraprofessional programs for aides. Community colleges and vocational schools are especially strong proponents of such programs.

NONACADEMIC PROGRAMS

Educational opportunities are not limited solely to educational institutions. A variety of other educational channels are ready to be explored. For example:

1. In-house training programs for company employees. Large organizations offer ongoing programs in fully equipped classrooms in company facilities.
2. Consulting agencies which offer workshops on a wide range of topics. Registration fees, ranging from under $100 up to $700 or $800, are paid by the employer.
3. Workshops offered by professional associations to prepare applicants for the annual examinations which they sponsor. For example, local chapters of the Professional Secretaries International (PSI) offer occasional workshops to prepare candidates for the CPS (Certified Professional Secretary) examination. (See Chapter 17 for details of the CPS and other certification programs sponsored by professional associations.)

In-house Training Programs

The size and scope of in-house training programs vary from one company to another; their objectives, however, are similar—to upgrade employees' productivity, or to prepare them for promotion.

Typically, company training centers are equipped with state-of-the-art audio-visual aids, including television monitors, screens, overhead projectors, VCR equipment, tapes, and computers or terminal screens. Teaching materials may include college texts and other materials tailored to specific company applications, plus computer software and training manuals.

Usually, a full-time training director coordinates the in-house educational programs, employing professors from local colleges and universities, or utilizing in-house personnel as instructors.

Although the majority of courses are geared to managerial personnel, many courses are designed specifically for the administrative support staff.

FIGURE 18-1 Nonacademic educational educational opportunities may consist of in-house training programs, replete with instructional materials, audio-visual aids, and instructors from within the company. *Courtesy of 3-M Corporation.*

Stenographers, clerks, and other clerical workers are urged to enroll in courses relevant to their positions. Typical course offerings for these workers include: computer keyboarding, word processing, business-letter writing, and machine dictation/transcription.

Courses for administrative assistants and managerial personnel focus on supervisory techniques, management styles, decision-making techniques, and personnel problems.

The administrative assistant who has the good fortune to work for a company having its own in-house program should enroll in courses which will update his or her knowledge and enhance promotional opportunities.

Assessment Centers

A relatively new evaluative technique, the assessment center, has company employees *role play* a series of simulated situations resembling real-life business problems. The purpose is to assess the employees' abilities to cope with the situations presented.

Typically, the participants play a business game, complete an in-basket exercise, or take part in leaderless group discussions as a part of the exercise. A group of assessors observe the participants' behavior during sessions, making note of their skills in responding to difficult situations.

After two to three days, the participants go back to their jobs, and the assessors compare their observations and complete a final evaluation. Their summary report evaluates each person's potential for advancement and prescribes a group of activities designed to build on their strengths.

A popular application for assessment centers is the selection of potential first-level supervisors. Interest in the center's success rate has led many companies to utilize them to identify potential high-level management personnel as well.

Large corporations which have utilized assessment centers include AT&T, IBM, Blue Cross and Blue Shield, General Electric, Ford, J. C. Penney, and Sears. Smaller companies have adopted modified versions of the assessment center concept.

Professional Associations

Another means of informal education often overlooked by business personnel is active participation in local clubs and chapters of national professional associations. Assuming active roles in such organizations can yield handsome dividends. For example, involvement in club activities can provide these benefits:

1. The opportunity to develop one's communication skills through interrelating with many types of personalities. Effective communication skills are, of course, basic to good human relations, and human relations skills are basic to career growth.
2. Leadership skills, including delegation of tasks, handling interpersonal problems among members, and dealing with job pressures, build one's potential for a position of authority.
3. Visibility—positions of authority bring public attention and acclaim, via news media, to one's leadership talents. The recognition is not lost on company officials when promotional opportunities occur.

Mentoring

A mentor is a person who takes a personal interest in another's career, helping that person to understand and succeed in it. The mentor is knowledgeable, usually through personal experience, of most facets of the position the person aspires to hold in the company. The term *mentor* is often used interchangeably with sponsor. However, the two terms are not synonymous.

Sponsors are influential persons within the company who take newcomers under their "wing," keeping an eye open to potential career paths for them to explore within the firm. Sponsors school their proteges on the "ins and outs" of company policy and politics in order to help them clear obstacles which might otherwise block their avenues to success.

Mentors, on the other hand, may or may not be employed by the same company as their proteges. Drawing on a wealth of personal insights and wisdom, mentors base their advice upon experience acquired in situations similar to that of their proteges. The mentors' support and encouragement have the same objective as that of company sponsors, however; namely, a high success level for their proteges.

Studies have shown that people who have the support of mentors or sponsors progress at a much faster pace in their careers than those who do not. One study of women executives revealed that all of them had one or more mentors during their career ascent.

A newly employed administrative assistant may within the first year of employment ponder these questions: "Should I choose a mentor or sponsor to help me advance in my career? If choosing a mentor, should it be one from inside the company?"

The answer depends on the situation. If after a reasonable length of time, no promising person surfaces within the company who might qualify, the administrative assistant should not risk making the wrong choice. It is wiser in this case to seek a support person outside the company.

In either case, the seeker must exercise extreme caution in approaching a potential sponsor or mentor. Otherwise, an unqualified advisor may damage, rather than help, the individual's career.

FIGURE 18-2 Students may find that their first permanent position after graduation provides promotional opportunities very quickly; they must be ready to respond.

FIRST CAREER EMPLOYMENT OF THE GRADUATE

Having acquired an education and established career goals, the graduating student is ready to review the job market and weigh employment opportunities.

The following Job Analysis Questionnaire, designed to help workers assess the career potential of their *current* positions, can be useful to job seekers as well.

Job Analysis Questionnaire

1. Do I like this job?
   a. The surroundings: the atmosphere? the setting?
   b. The office size: too large? too small?
   c. Coworkers: compatible?
   d. Job pressures: too much? too little challenge?
   e. Income: sufficient? salary increases likely?
2. Am I satisfied with the job level? Is it in keeping with my targeted goals?
3. Can my ultimate career goals be met here?
   a. Opportunity for advancement?
   b. Higher positions likely to be vacated?
   c. Promotions likely within *this* department? If not, can a lateral move be made to another department?
4. Does this job enhance my opportunities for better employment later, with another firm? Is it good training for future employment?
5. Overall, do the positive factors offset the negative factors?

As a *job applicant,* one uses the questionnaire as if currently employed. The responses reflect what the person *observes* to be true about the work setting and the chances for advancement. Its worth as a predictor depends upon how accurately the job applicant has gauged the work situation from outside the company.

After six months or more of employment, the questionnaire will demonstrate its special value as an instrument for evaluating one's current position in the light of career goals. A majority of "yes" responses indicates that a job has considerable promise for the current employee seeking opportunities to advance to a higher position.

First Career Position

After accepting the position that best meets the requisites for career success, the newly hired administrative assistant now assumes two major responsibilities. The first is to learn everything possible about the employing firm and its products or services. Research into the company's history and progress over the years may strengthen one's commitment to its continued progress. The new employee's position within the company's organizational structure will be clarified as well.

The second responsibility of the new administrative assistant is to perform all assigned duties with the dedication of a true professional. Nothing substitutes for quality work. The dedicated professional builds a career on the basic fundamentals, continually attentive to both productivity and quality workmanship.

Company executives will undoubtedly take note of the administrative assistant who manifests these qualities. When salary increases or promotions are being considered, these two factors may make the difference in whether or not a promotion is offered.

Up the Promotional Ladder

Seldom does a promotion come to deserving personnel as a complete surprise. The administrative assistant who begins employment with a career plan in hand has anticipated the desired promotion prior to its being offered, and is ready for it.

Preparedness is the primary key to promotion success. Certain guidelines to promotional readiness have been suggested by successful executives. The first is to prepare an understudy to replace you in your current position. Making yourself indispensable is self-destructive, especially when a promotion hangs in the balance. The good of the company supercedes the personal welfare of one employee, and an irreplaceable one will be locked into his or her present position indefinitely. Company officials will not promote you unless they can replace you. Have an understudy ready and waiting, able to take over your job when the time comes for you to move on.

Look into the qualifications required for the position you want; then become qualified for that position. If you lack the necessary education to qualify, plan to enroll in the courses needed or the academic program called for. If certain professional training is needed, take the appropriate steps to acquire the training.

If you lack the needed work experience, be prepared to wait patiently; or plan to offer something in its stead, such as your recent college education, or some closely related job experience.

Become qualified by taking these additional on-the-job steps:

1. Familiarize yourself with every aspect of the job; explore every avenue of information available to you for this purpose.
2. Learn the terminology used if you are not already conversant with the terms.
3. Observe the general procedures followed.
4. Be prepared to discuss the job and its responsibilities with company officials if they wish to test your familiarity with it.

Make yourself visible to company decision makers by making your presence known. Attract attention to yourself in a positive way; visibility is an important facet of one's promotional strategies.

When you have something worthwhile to share, let yourself be seen and heard. For example, one secretary's idea for weekly rap sessions to hear employees' complaints and to keep them informed of company activities alerted grateful supervisors to the leadership talents of the secretary. She was promoted to a supervisory position.

Visibility is also gained through acceptance of committee assignments, especially through chairing such committees. Presenting well-articulated reports at committee meetings draws favorable attention. Speaking engagements are another visibility tool, especially if publicized in the local press.

In the office, gaining visibility can be as simple as learning the names of everyone in the building, from the maintenance staff to the corporate officers, and addressing them by name when you meet them in the hall, on the elevator, or in the lunch room.

Speak up! Ask for promotion. Let the principals of your company know that you are interested in a promotion when the opportunity presents itself. Most companies prefer to promote from within but may be unaware which of their own employees are able and ready to be considered.

Speaking up for your own interests is no guarantee that you will gain the promotion you desire—at least not right away. But it *will* alert company officials to your interest. When the time comes, your name is likely to be high on the list of potential candidates for a promotion.

FIGURE 18-3 Holding an office in a civic organization provides visibility for an otherwise "invisible" worker; company officials notice and remember the "visible" persons when job promotions are being considered.

CAREER SHIFTS

Professional growth occurs at an uneven pace. As the administrative assistant proceeds with day-to-day responsibilities, his or her career progresses, usually without a conscious awareness of the growth phenomenon taking place.

The rate of growth may be at the proverbial snail's pace, or sometimes at the exhilarating rate of a speeding train. Not uncommonly, however, a career shows little sign of movement in any direction. Unhappily, the administrative assistant may discover the painful truth that the job does not offer any growth potential.

In order to advance, he or she must leave the current position, re-enter the job market, and start anew. Although the specter of re-entering the marketplace is more than a little unsettling, a number of agencies are ready to help individuals regain the initiative in their career-building plans.

Resources to utilize in getting back on track are these: personal networks, college placement centers, commercial placement agencies, governmental resources, and advertising media.

Personal Networks

In recent years, the concept of personal networks has become a familiar one among career-minded business people. Personal networks may be defined as a means of establishing contact with potential employers, clients, customers, or persons of influence via a network of friends, relatives, or acquaintances.

The objective is to "sell" one's product, services, or job talents through persons in the network who *know* the potential contact people, or have some influence on their decisions.

Networks serve many useful purposes, especially in expanding one's search for job leads. A logical place to start a personal network is in one's own family. The job-seeking careerist begins the root structure of a communications network by asking relatives for names of people to contact in the job search, or for names of companies with current job openings.

Close friends, social and business associates, fellow churchgoers, and former classmates expand the network further. Contacts made at conventions, trade fairs, and conferences featuring persons with mutual professional interests, may broaden the network into a wealth of resource persons. Ultimately, many more job leads are discovered by the job seeker than could possibly have been generated without a personal network.

Establishing a Personal Network Four simple steps define the sequence to follow in establishing a personal job-seeking network:

1. Make the first contacts with relatives or close friends; later, with friends, acquaintances, and other associates.
2. Make clear to them your purpose in asking their assistance; then *request* their assistance.

3. Leave your telephone number with them; retain their telephone numbers and addresses so that you can write or call them to keep them informed of your job status.
4. When a position is obtained, write a note of appreciation to the persons who helped you make the successful contact.

Formal networking organizations exist nationwide. Some are sponsored by professional associations and are geared to specific fields of interest. Others are diverse in nature and are open to general membership.

Placement Agencies

Commercial placement agencies endeavor to match the qualifications of their job applicants with those of their employer-clients. For a contracted fee, the agencies offer one or more of the following services to applicants: testing services to determine job qualifications, career counseling, composition of resumes and application letters, and interview techniques.

Before registering with an agency, the applicant should check the agency's success rate in placing applicants in good positions and its integrity in dealing with clients.

Fee structures vary from one agency to another. Some charge a fixed fee when their referral results in a hire. Others charge a percentage of the monthly or annual salary of the newly placed applicant. The employing firm frequently absorbs the agency fee if the new employee stays with the company a stated length of time, usually six months to a year.

Whatever the fee arrangement, the applicant will be asked to sign a contract agreeing to the terms. As with any legally binding contract, the signer should scrutinize it carefully before affixing his or her signature to it.

College Placement Centers

One of the most valuable resources available to college students or alumni is the college placement service. For a nominal fee, the placement office puts the student or alumnus on its mailing list to receive notices of new job openings. It also maintains a file of the applicant's letters of reference, a transcript of college credits and grades, and personal resumes. Duplicated copies of the entire set of credentials are mailed to potential employers upon request of the student.

The placement center personnel also assist students in drawing up their resumes and writing letters of application. Many hold seminars for graduating students to teach them successful interview techniques and to acquaint them with all facets of the job search. They also arrange for on-campus interviews with representatives of employing firms.

Advertising Media

One of the most widely used tools for publicizing job openings is that of newspapers and periodicals. For job seekers, the Sunday editions of metropolitan newspapers are especially accurate indicators of the job market in the geographic areas represented. A scan of the listings reveals the current market for various positions and the range of salaries being offered.

If job seekers are interested in working in a distant city, a subscription to the major newspaper of that city will give them insights into the employment picture there. The *Ayer Directory of Publications,* available at college libraries, lists thousands of newspapers and magazines by geographic area.

The Federal Government

The largest employer in the country is the U.S. government. The Office of Personnel Management (formerly the Civil Service Commission) maintains a central office in Washington, D.C., plus ten regional offices throughout the country.

Thousands of secretaries and other office workers are placed through this agency every year. Information brochures, job announcements, and application forms are available through the regional offices. A toll-free 800 number is listed in the telephone directory under United States Government.

PACE Higher-level positions in the government are placed through PACE, the Professional and Administrative Career Examination (formerly the Federal Service Entrance Examination). PACE evaluates applicants for jobs in management, technical, and professional areas. Applicants must be college graduates, or within nine months of receiving their baccalaureate degrees.

Administered by the Office of Personnel Management, the PACE examination is given monthly, except in August, at central locations nationwide. All scores are tabulated and reported within four to six weeks. Ratings of the examinees are distributed to government offices so that the names of qualified applicants are available for consideration whenever a vacancy occurs.

USTES The United States Training and Employment Service has 2,400 offices nationwide. Thousands of positions are filled every year through this government-sponsored placement agency. The service is free to job applicants and employers alike.

Although the majority of job referrals are into entry-level positions, USTES does offer services for professionals, too. It should not be overlooked as a potential resource.

Career Options

The administrative assistant making a career shift may find many options from which to choose. If the move is a shift from a disappointing first or second career venture, the options must be weighed with extreme care.

Career objectives may need to be revised in the light of new insights gained from the first work experiences. Possibly, interest in a particular industry will have clarified, narrowing the job search to that industry solely.

For example, one executive secretary discovered an interest in the travel industry, and set her sights on the hotel industry, particularly the booking of large conventions for hotel resorts. Another aspired to a career as a paralegal assistant to a local attorney, and another became interested in the publishing field, leading to a position as an editorial assistant.

Whatever industry the administrative assistant chooses to enter, the company targeted within that industry is the most important component of the choice. Not all companies within an industry are equally inviting.

The company's history of internal promotions is very important, as is their policy on promoting women. The number and average age of current employees also indicate the likelihood of early promotional opportunities. If 90 percent of the staff is 30 to 40 years of age, the chances for promotion are slim. If, on the other hand, the promotional climate is healthy, and the average age of upper-level personnel is 50 to 60, one has an excellent chance of ascending the career ladder within a reasonable length of time.

Four-part Strategy Whatever the new or redefined career goals are, the administrative assistant can be assured of professional success if he or she follows this four-part strategy:

1. Define career goals in writing, with target dates specified.
2. Pursue the achievement of the goals within the time frame set.
3. Choose the correct industry and company in which to work.
4. Build a positive self-image.

Professional Resume and Letter of Application

Two written documents summarize the job applicant's qualifications for the position of his or her choice. These are the professional resume and the letter of application.

The resume should include one's professional objectives, educational background, employment record, and personal data. It lists employer references, if any, and character references.

The covering letter, or letter of application, accompanies the resume, highlighting its outstanding features. Usually, it requests an interview and informs the reader when and where the applicant can be located.

Both of these documents should be checked carefully by someone with experience in writing professional resumes and letters of application.

SUMMARY

Goal setting is one of the most important components of a career plan. Both long-term and short-term objectives must be identified and target dates set for the achievement of each stated goal.

Enrollment in educational programs, both formal and informal, is basic to achieving recognition and advancement in business. One means of informal education is membership in professional associations which help members develop their leadership skills. Another is the use of mentors and/or sponsors to gain career insights and assistance.

Upon entering the job market, several resources are at the student's disposal. Commercial placement agencies, college placement centers, personal networks, and classified advertisements put the job seeker in touch with potential employers.

If the first position fails to fulfill career expectations, the administrative assistant may want to leave the current position and reenter the job market. Although difficult to do, a renewed sense of purpose can be found if the resulting job change puts his or her career back "on track."

QUESTIONS FOR REVIEW

1. How does the CLEP program serve the needs of adult learners and save tuition fees in the process?
2. Describe one means of clarifying and organizing your career path.
3. Are the terms *mentors* and *sponsors* synonymous? If not, explain the difference. Can a mentor be a sponsor also?
4. How does an assessment center identify potential leaders?
5. Name some of the leading corporations who use the assessment center process.
6. The primary key to promotions is preparedness. Name four guidelines to follow in preparing oneself for promotions.
7. What services are offered to students by college placement centers?
8. Define PACE and USTES. Explain the functions of each of these agencies.
9. How does a commercial placement agency differ from USTES?
10. Explain the four-part strategy for achieving career goals.

QUESTIONS FOR DISCUSSION

1. Discuss the following statement as it relates to newly employed graduates of your school. *Mentors are the easy way to get ahead. Persons with drive and determination do not need them; in fact, the use of mentors can be considered a form of weakness.* Do you agree with the statement? Explain your position.
2. Explain how work experience can be related to college courses and be accepted for credit in place of them. Which groups of people are best served by programs recognizing work experience as a valid substitute for actual course work?
3. How are leadership skills developed through membership in professional associations? Are such skills important when one is forging a career in business? If so, in what way might these skills be utilized in one's career?
4. Why is visibility so important in establishing one's credits and capabilities with company officials? How does the ambitious employee become "visible"?

5. Should employees who are seeking a promotion actually ask to be considered for promotions when they occur? That is, are they being too forward with management when they do so?

SUGGESTED ACTIVITIES

1. Ask to attend a meeting of one of the professional associations in your area. Discover as much as you can about the association: its objectives, date of formation, size of membership, frequency of meetings, etc. List the personal and professional benefits you might gain by membership in this organization.
2. Prepare a personal resume for use in applying for a position as administrative assistant in a local business. Include your career objectives, personal data, educational background, work experience, and references.
3. Write a letter of application to accompany your personal resume. Highlight the strengths described in the resume. Ask for an interview. Tell when and where you may be reached by phone or letter. Have the letter and the resume reviewed by your classmates.

REFERENCES

DEAL, TERENCE, and ALLAN A. KENNEDY, "Communications: Working the Cultural Network," *Modern Office Procedures* (February 1983), 12–14.

FIGGINS, ROSS, *The Job Game.* Englewood Cliffs, NJ: Prentice Hall, 1980.

HIGGINSON, MARGARET V., and THOMAS L. QUICK, *The Ambitious Woman's Guide to a Successful Career,* rev. ed. New York: Amacom, 1980.

JAFFEE, CABOT L., and JOSEPH T. SEFCIK, JR., "What Is an Assessment Center?" *The Personnel Administrator* (February 1980), 40–43.

NEMEC, MARGARET M., "Networking: Here's How at Equitable," *The Personnel Administrator* (April 1980), 63–64.

"Professional Connections," *Savvy* (December 1980), 21.

SHEERAN, LISA R., and DONNA FENN, "The Mentor System," *Inc.* (June 1987), 138–142.

WELCH, MARY-SCOTT, "Networking; How to Make It Work for You," *Glamour* (June 1981), 142, 145–146.

Case Problem 1 Unit VI *Personal Networks and Career Advancement*

Jane Ramirez joined a local chapter of a national network for women immediately after she moved to a large city on the East Coast. Her purpose was to make contacts with persons who could help her find a job in the strange city.

At the meeting, Jane met and talked with many of the members and explained her job-hunting situation. Although she appeared to enjoy making new acquaintances, Jane remained with her new-found friends only briefly after the business meeting was over. After collecting information from several members about their positions and places of employment and leaving her telephone number with them, Jane excused herself from the group. She said she was "too busy" to stay any longer. She left the group early in the evening to return to her apartment.

The next day, however, she telephoned three of the ladies she had just met, asking them to set up a job interview for her at their places of employment and to "please put in a good word" for her with the personnel department at their firms.

Her new "friends" were stunned at Jane's boldness. Having met her only briefly, they did not feel comfortable in recommending her to their employers. They were not sure how to respond to Jane's request.

1. Was Jane within her rights to use the network system as she did? Or was she presumptuous in asking for immediate help from her new acquaintances?
2. Describe how, in your opinion, Jane should utilize the network in helping her find the right position.

Case Problem 2 Unit VI *Career Opportunities for Administrative Assistants*

Although most people view the position of administrative assistant as an important and responsible one, many fail to see its potential for advancement to higher-level positions in management. In fact, some think of it as the terminal or highest-level position in its own career track.

Others see it differently, however. The vice president of a renowned business school calls it the "career of the decade." And experience has shown that capable administrative aides can and do advance to upper-management levels in those companies which promote "from within."

1. What accounts for the wide variance in views on this career? Can both sides be right? Explain. What factors might make the difference in getting on the promotional track or not?
2. Would you recommend that students choose a career as administrative assistant? Explain your position.

Case Problem 3 Unit VI *The "Late" Mr. Williams*

Bob Williams and Lucy Stotts have been assigned to write a proposal requesting federal funds for minority-group job training. Having been successful in getting funds for similar programs in the past, Lucy is confident that they can succeed again.

However, a problem which Lucy experienced previously in working with Bob may rear its ugly head again; that is, Bob's tendency to procrastinate. Bob fails to do his part of an assignment on schedule, waiting instead until the last minute to do so. Then he works overtime trying frantically to meet the scheduled deadline. On occasion, he has failed to make the deadline at all, depending finally on Lucy to complete his as well as her own tasks on the project. Up to now, Lucy has complied rather than lose the funding.

Lucy fears the same thing will happen again, and she does not know how to prevent it. Asking for another partner may force her to share her doubts with Bob's supervisor, perhaps causing him to be "called on the carpet." Yet, if she does *nothing*, she will probably have to finish *both* of their tasks for no additional compensation.

1. What would *you* do in this situation?
2. Would you talk to Bob's supervisor? If so, what would you say?
3. Would you talk to Bob himself? If yes, would you do so *before* you talked to the supervisor or *instead* of talking to the supervisor? In either case, what would you say to him?
4. Would you accept Bob "as is" and not try to change his attitude toward working faster and more efficiently?

Case Problem 4 Unit VI *An Unfavorable Appraisal*

Rita is completing her first year as supervisor of outside sales personnel for a mid-size publisher of children's books. She has just received from her department chairperson a copy of the appraisal on her first year's performance as supervisor. The appraisal is negative in tone, although no specific complaints are lodged against her to substantiate this unfavorable evaluation of her work.

Rita believes that her negative appraisal is discriminatory, based on sexual bias. The chairperson has on several occasions commended her for doing "OK" on a "man's job." She suspects that the chairperson resents her success and would like an excuse to have her demoted or moved to another department, despite her good performance record.

Statistics bear out her claim to a good performance record. Since she took over the supervisory position, sales have grown substantially, and company profits have reflected the increase in sales. She has had no personality conflicts with any of the staff or with company officials, including the chairperson. Therefore, she feels frustrated at receiving what she considers an "unfair" appraisal and wonders what her options are for improving her job situation.

1. Do you believe that Rita is justified in suspecting discrimination on the part of the chairperson? If so, what course of action do you recommend she follow in righting the situation?
2. Assuming that she remains in her present position, with the same chairperson, what advice would you give Rita to build a better relationship with her supervisor and improve his attitude toward her as a professional?

Index

A

B

C

D

N

O

P

Q

R

S

T

U

V

W

Z